Communications
in Computer and Information Science   349

Tanja Woronowicz Terry Rout
Rory V. O'Connor Alec Dorling (Eds.)

Software Process Improvement and Capability Determination

13th International Conference, SPICE 2013
Bremen, Germany, June 4-6, 2013
Proceedings

 Springer

Volume Editors

Tanja Woronowicz
University of Bremen, Germany
E-mail: worono@tzi.de

Terry Rout
Griffith University, Brisbane, QLD, Australia
E-mail: t.rout@griffith.edu.au

Rory V. O'Connor
Dublin City University, Ireland
E-mail: roconnor@computing.dcu.ie

Alec Dorling
InterSPICE Ltd, Cambridge, UK
E-mail: alec.dorling@interspice.uk.com

ISSN 1865-0929   e-ISSN 1865-0937
ISBN 978-3-642-38832-3   e-ISBN 978-3-642-38833-0
DOI 10.1007/978-3-642-38833-0
Springer Heidelberg Dordrecht London New York

Library of Congress Control Number: Applied for

CR Subject Classification (1998): K.6, D.2, J.1, J.3, C.2, K.4

Typesetting: Camera-ready by author, data conversion by Scientific Publishing Services, Chennai, India

Printed on acid-free paper

Springer is part of Springer Science+Business Media (www.springer.com)

Preface

On behalf of the SPICE Organizing Committee we are proud to present the proceedings of the 13th International Conference on Software Process Improvement and Capability dEtermination (SPICE 2013), held in Bremen, Germany, during June 4–6, 2013.

The SPICE Project was formed in 1993 to support the development of an international standard for software process assessment. The work of the project has eventually led to the finalization of ISO/IEC 15504 – Process Assessment, and its complete publication represented a climax for the work of the project. As part of its charter to provide ongoing publicity and transition support for the emerging standard, the project organized a number of SPICE Workshops and Seminars, with invited speakers drawn from project participants.

These have now evolved to a sustaining set of international conferences with broad participation from academia and industry with a common interest in model-based process improvement. This was the 13th in the series of conferences organized by the SPICE User Group to increase knowledge and understanding of the International Standard and of the technique of process assessment.

The conference program featured invited keynote talks, research papers, and industry experience reports on the most relevant topics related to software process assessment and improvement. The technical research papers were selected for presentation following peer review by members of the Program Committee. In addition, a number of tutorials were hosted.

SPICE conferences have a long history of attracting attendees from industry and academia. This confirms that the conference covers topics that are upto date, important, and interesting. SPICE 2013 offered a unique forum for industry and academic professionals to discuss their needs and ideas in the area of process assessment and improvement, and related aspects of quality management.

On behalf of the SPICE 2013 conference Organizing Committee, we would like to thank all participants. Firstly all the authors, whose quality work is the essence of the conference, and the members of the Program Committee, who helped us with their expertise and diligence in reviewing all of the submissions. As we all know, organizing a conference requires the effort of many individuals. We wish to thank also all the members of our Organizing Committee, whose work and commitment were invaluable.

June 2013

Tanja Woronowicz
Terry Rout
Rory V. O'Connor
Alec Dorling

Organization

General Chair

Alec Dorling   InterSPICE, UK

Program Chair

Terry Rout   Griffith University, Australia

Local Organizing Chair

Tanja Woronowicz   University of Bremen, Germany

Industry Chair

Matthias Brucke   Clustermanager Automotive Nordwest e.V., Germany
Michael Hoffmann   Aviabelt Bremen e.V., Germany

Proceedings Chair

Rory V. O'Connor   Lero, Dublin City University, Ireland

Tutorial Chair

Timo Varkoi   Spinet Oy, Finland

Social Networking Chair

Ravindra Joshi   Morphius Consulting, India

Publicity Chair

Carol Dekkers   Quality Plus Technologies, USA

Program Committee

Beatrix Barafort, Luxembourg
Matthias Brucke, Germany
Luigi Buglione, Italy
Aileen Cater-Steel, Australia
Melanie Cheong, Australia
Gerhard Chroust, Austria
Paul Clarke, Ireland
Francois Coallier, Canada
Antonio Coletta, Italy
Fabrizzio Fabbrini, Italy
Mario Fusani, Italy
Dennis Goldenson, USA
Christiane Gresse von
    Wangenheim, Brazil
Victoria Hailey, Canada
John Horch, USA
Linda Ibrahim, USA
Ravindra Joshi, India
Ho-Won Jung, South Korea
Rainer Koschke, Germany

Giuseppe Lami, Italy
Marion Lepmets, Luxembourg
Catriona Mackie, UK
Antonia Mas, Spain
Tom McBride, Australia
Fergal McCaffery, Ireland
Takeshige Miyoshi, Japan
Martin Möhrle, Germany
Risto Nevalainen, Finland
Rory O'Connor, Ireland
Hanna Oktaba, Mexico
Mark Paulk, USA
Patricia Rodriguez Dapena, Spain
Clenio Salviano, Brazil
Jean-Martin Simon, France
Fritz Stallinger, Austria
Robert Treffny, Germany
Timo Varkoi, Finland

Local Organizing Committee

Michael Boronowsky	University of Bremen, Germany
Matthias Brucke	Clustermanager Automotive Nordwest e.V., Germany
Martin Möhrle	University of Bremen, Germany
David Wewetzer	University of Bremen, Germany
Tanja Woronowicz	University of Bremen, Germany
Marta Michael-Zamorano	University of Bremen, Germany

Acknowledgments

The local organizers acknowledge the support of the Chair for TZI at the University of Bremen, Prof. Dr. Rainer Malaka; the Senator for Economic Affairs and Ports of the Free Hanseatic City of Bremen, Mr. Martin Günthner; and the Senator for Education and Science of the Free Hanseatic City of Bremen, Prof. Dr. Eva Quante-Brandt.

The conference organizers wish to acknowledge the assistance and support of the SPICE User Group, SPICE 2013 Program Committee, and reviewers in contributing to a successful conference.

Table of Contents

Process Quality

Safety as a Process Quality Characteristic 1
Timo Varkoi

Derivation of Green Metrics for Software 13
Giuseppe Lami, Luigi Buglione, and Fabrizio Fabbrini

Medical Device Software Processes

A Process Assessment Model for Security Assurance of Networked
Medical Devices 25
Anita Finnegan, Fergal McCaffery, and Gerry Coleman

The Approach to the Development of an Assessment Method for IEC
80001-1 37
Silvana Togneri MacMahon, Fergal McCaffery, and Frank Keenan

The Development and Current Status of Medi SPICE 49
Valentine Casey and Fergal McCaffery

Design and Use of Process Models

An Approach to Development of an Application Dependent SPICE
Conformant Process Capability Model 61
*Michael Boronowsky, Antanas Mitasiunas, Jonas Ragaisis, and
Tanja Woronowicz*

An Improvement of Process Reference Model Design and Validation
Using Business Process Management 73
*Olivier Mangin, Nicolas Mayer, Béatrix Barafort,
Patrick Heymans, and Eric Dubois*

Comparing SPiCE for Space (S4S) and CMMI-DEV: Identifying
Sources of Risk from Improvement Models 84
Ricardo Eito-Brun

Studies of Software Development

Assessing Software Product Management Capability: An Industry
Validation Case Study 95
Fritz Stallinger, Robert Neumann, and Robert Schossleitner

Using ISO/IEC 12207 to Analyze Open Source Software Development
Processes: An E-Learning Case Study 107
   Aarthy Krishnamurthy and Rory V. O'Connor

A Case Study on the Need to Consider Personality Types for Software
Team Formation 120
   Çağrı Murat Karapıçak and Onur Demirörs

Agile Development

Assessment of Agile Maturity Models: A Multiple Case Study 130
   Ozden Ozcan-Top and Onur Demirörs

Agile Software Development in System Engineering Conditions 142
   Ernest Wallmüller and Fred Kaminski

TestSPICE and Agile Testing – Synergy or Confusion 154
   Tomas Schweigert, Detlef Vohwinkel, Monique Blaschke, and
   Mohsen Ekssir-Monfared

IT Service Management

Can 'Soft' Organisational Problems Be Solved by 'Hard' Process
Reference Models? 165
   David Tuffley

Exploring the Impact of IT Service Management Process Improvement
Initiatives: A Case Study Approach 176
   Marko Jäntti, Terry Rout, Lian Wen, Sanna Heikkinen, and
   Aileen Cater-Steel

Software-Mediated Process Assessment in IT Service Management 188
   Aileen Cater-Steel, Wui-Gee Tan, Mark Toleman, Terry Rout, and
   Anup Shrestha

Assessment for Diagnosis

Balancing Agility and Discipline in a Medical Device Software
Organisation 199
   Martin McHugh, Fergal McCaffery, Brian Fitzgerald,
   Klaas-Jan Stol, Valentine Casey, and Garret Coady

Investigation of Traceability within a Medical Device Organization 211
   Gilbert Regan, Fergal McCaffery, Kevin McDaid, and Derek Flood

Usage of Multiple Process Assessment Models 223
   Stasys Peldzius and Saulius Ragaisis

Short Papers

Implementing innoSPICE in Support of Political European Innovation
Strategies 235
    Tanja Woronowicz, Michael Boronowsky, and David Wewetzer

Industrial Experience Report: BiSL as Driver for Innovating Business
Information Management in the Dutch Police Organization(s) 239
    Frank van Outvorst and Lex Scholten

Lessons from a Pilot Implementation of ISO/IEC 29110 in a Group
of Very Small Irish Companies 243
    Rory V. O'Connor and Marty Sanders

Critical Design Decisions in the Development of the Standard
for Process Assessment 247
    Terence P. Rout

Developing the Enterprise SPICE Strategy Using Enterprise SPICE 252
    Linda Ibrahim

Scorecard Based Project Performance Management 256
    Bharathi V. and Udaya Shastry

Parameterized Generation of Process Variants and Project-Specific
Operating Procedures from Business Process Models 261
    Jennifer Schöffler, Anne Kramer, and Norbert Kastner

Author Index 267

Safety as a Process Quality Characteristic

Timo Varkoi

Spinet Oy, Tampere, Finland
timo.varkoi@spinet.fi

Abstract. Software is increasingly been used to provide system functionality that is related to safety. From systems point-of-view safety is often considered to be a probabilistic property and development process has less significance. For software this approach is not necessarily valid. This article studies the applicable process scope in relation to safety requirements for software. Based on a new concept of process quality characteristics, process quality attributes for safety are tentatively defined. The aim of the presented process quality characteristic for safety is that risks related to achievement of safety goals in software development can be evaluated with process assessment. Key results would be increased trust in safety of software-intensive systems and established safety culture in development organizations.

Keywords: software process, safety, process quality, process assessment.

1 Introduction

Importance of safety in software development is increasing. Growing part of functionality is being developed using software. Industries that earlier have relied on electronic and electrical systems are turning into using software. Software based solutions have also helped in providing new functionality. Examples of these domains include automotive, medical, and energy industries.

Present day safety standards concentrate on the system aspect and their origins are mainly of hardware development. Reliability is a key concept when system or hardware safety is considered. Software products have their own product quality oriented standards, like ISO/IEC 25000 series [1], but there the role of safety is nominal. Safety-related activities in software development processes are to some extent presented e.g. in IEC 61508 standard [2], but the expected process attributes are missing.

In literature, many approaches to safety and reliability rely on probabilistic models. These models are difficult to apply to software due to the nature of software – there is no wear and tear in software and its reliability is difficult to evaluate without the system that runs it. Nevertheless, the studies of software reliability infer that the development process is an interesting factor of software reliability and safety.

This study defines an applicable process scope in relation to safety requirements for software. Based on a new concept of process quality characteristics, process attributes for safety are tentatively defined. The aim of this article is to test the idea of

T. Woronowicz et al. (Eds.): SPICE 2013, CCIS 349, pp. 1–12, 2013.

presenting safety, a highly important property in modern software development, as a process quality characteristic.

This article is structured as follows: Next, in Section 2, the concept of Process Quality is explained. Section 3 presents the existing process assessment models for safety domain. Section 4 discusses safety related processes based on literature review. Section 5 defines safety as a process quality characteristic. To conclude, section 6 summarizes the findings of this article.

2   Process Quality

For the time being, ISO/IEC JTC1/SC 7 Working Group 10 develops the ISO/IEC 15504 set of process assessment standards into a new set of ISO/IEC 33000 standards. In this development, a new concept of process quality has been introduced. Process quality concept harmonizes the terminology with product quality (Fig. 1). Process capability is seen as an important, but not the only, characteristic of a process. The basis of this thinking is that a process shall demonstrate successful implementation, trustworthiness, manageability and adaptability, which reaches beyond the capability approach that has guided process improvement and assessment from the 1990's.

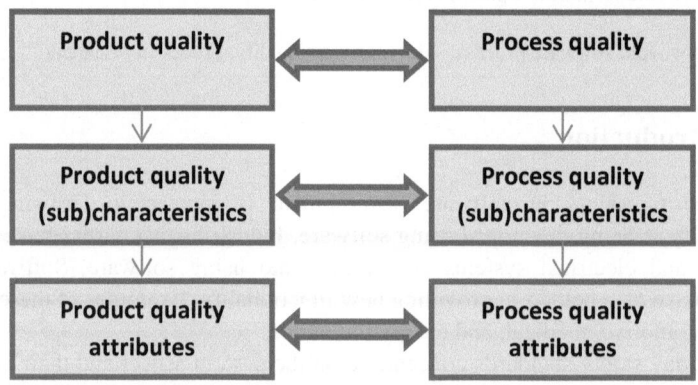

Fig. 1. Harmonized view of process and product quality concepts

Process quality is composed of quality characteristics, where the required set of characteristics depends on the applicable stakeholder needs and organization's business goals. In addition, process quality shall be measurable. The key terms can be defined as follows [3]:

- Process quality
  - o   ability of a process to satisfy stated and implied stakeholder needs when used in a specified context
- Process quality characteristic
  - o   a measurable aspect of process quality; category of process attributes that are significant to process quality

Earlier process assessment models have addressed capability as a process quality characteristic. In the future, several new characteristics of process quality are expected to arise, e.g. controllability, agility, and efficiency.

The concepts of process quality characteristics and attributes are used in this article to define safety as a new process quality dimension.

3　Existing Models for Safety Process Assessment

Safety, by definition, means the expectation that a system does not, under defined conditions, lead to a state in which human life, health, property, or the environment is endangered [4]. Safety is considered in at least two present process assessment models: CMMI +SAFE from Software Engineering Institute [5], and ISO/IEC 15504 Part 10 [6]. These models apply capability as the relevant process quality characteristic.

A Safety Extension to CMMI-DEV, +SAFE, defines two additional process areas to CMMI-DEV to be used for assessment and improvement of an organization's capabilities for providing safety-critical products. This extension can be used standalone i.e. only the two named processes can be assessed. There is no direct link to any safety standards. The processes and their specific goals are listed below [5]:

- Safety Management (Project Management process category)
    - o　SG1　Develop Safety Plans
    - o　SG2　Monitor Safety Incidents
    - o　SG3　Manage Safety-Related Suppliers
- Safety Engineering (Engineering process category)
    - o　SG1　Identify Hazards, Accidents, and Sources of Hazards
    - o　SG2　Analyze Hazards and Perform Risk Assessments
    - o　SG3　Define and Maintain Safety Requirements
    - o　SG4　Design for Safety
    - o　SG5　Support Safety Acceptance

+SAFE is intended to be used for capability assessment of a supplier or potential supplier of safety-critical products and to improve an organization's capability in developing, sustaining, maintaining, and managing safety-critical products. The model recognizes safety function, safety case and safety lifecycle in the same meaning as IEC 61508.

ISO/IEC TS 15504-10 defines three processes for safety management, safety engineering and safety qualification to extend the ISO/IEC 15504 process assessment models for system and software lifecycle processes. The three processes and their purposes and expected outcomes are [6]:

- Safety Management process
    - o　The purpose of the Safety Management Process is to ensure that products, services and life cycle processes meet safety objectives.

   o As a result of the successful implementation of the Safety Management process:

    1) Safety principles and safety criteria are established.

    2) The scope of the safety activities for the project is defined.

    3) Safety activities are planned and implemented.

    4) Tasks and resources necessary to complete the safety activities are sized and estimated.

    5) Safety organization structure (responsibilities, roles, reporting channels, interfaces with other projects or OUs …) is established.

    6) Safety activities are monitored, safety-related incidents are reported, analysed, and resolved.

    7) Agreement on safety policy and requirements for supplied products or services is achieved.

    8) Supplier's safety activities are monitored.

- Safety Engineering process
  - o The purpose of the Safety Engineering process is to ensure that safety is adequately addressed throughout all stages of the engineering processes.
  - o As a result of the successful implementation of the Safety Engineering process:

    1) Hazards related to product are identified and analysed.

    2) Hazard log is established and maintained.

    3) Safety demonstration for the product lifecycle is established and maintained.

    4) Safety requirements are defined.

    5) Safety integrity requirements are defined and allocated.

    6) Safety principles are applied to development processes.

    7) Impacts on safety of change requests are analysed.

    8) Product is validated against safety requirements.

    9) Independent evaluations are performed.

- Safety Qualification process
  - o The purpose of the Safety Qualification process is to assess the suitability of external resources when developing a safety-related software or system.
  - o As a result of the successful implementation of the Safety Qualification process:

    1) Safety qualification strategy for external resources is developed.

    2) Safety qualification plan is developed and executed.

    3) Safety qualification documentation is written.

    4) Safety qualification report is produced.

ISO/IEC TS 15504-10 provides a basis for performing a process capability assessment of processes with respect to the development of complex safety-related systems. It can be used standalone, too. There are links to IEC 61508 and ISO 26262 safety standards. The terminology used is similar to IEC 61508, including safety lifecycle, safety demonstration and safety case.

As we can see, the process scopes of both ISO/IEC 15504-10 and CMMI-DEV +SAFE cover roughly the same application areas: management, engineering and supply. Both models also consider that process capability defines the goodness of these processes and that capability levels are applicable. Anyhow, these models provide guidance when considering the important aspects of systems and software development in safety-related domains.

4   Safety from Process Perspective

Safety of a system is always considered as a characteristic of a product. There is no direct causality from the development process to the safety of a product. Despite of this, characteristics of the development process certainly can affect the safety of the product. The practice is that part of system functionality is considered to be safety-critical or safety-related and requirements for safety are set. Safety demonstration provides evidence that system or its components are considered safe within an acceptable risk.

Lots of of the studied literature relies on probabilistic models for safety. It seems that the same approach that has worked with electro-mechanical systems is believed to be applicable to software. The nature of software as a design rather than a product is largely ignored. Software reliability is a difficult concept and its quantification appears to be close to ineligible. On the other hand, most of the publications refer in some way to the development process as a factor of software reliability.

Lawrence [7] emphasizes software life cycle to improve safety and reliability. Smidts et al. [8] bases their work on heavy measurement of the development process to predict operational reliability. Chu et al. [9] apply quantitative methods to model software failures for probabilistic risk assessment (PRA).

The work of Leveson [10] sets reliability in totally new light when pursuing safety. Safety is seen in a wider perspective and the role of PRA is questioned. The relationship between reliability and safety is rejected. In her book, Leveson challenges the traditional models of causality that are based on the assumption that accidents are caused by component failure and making components reliable prevents accidents. The ideas are established on system theory. The book presents a new causality model and how it can be applied to safety engineering. Factors that affect in achieving safety goals can be divided into engineering, operations, and management. Leveson presents a new foundation for safety engineering. Two software reliability related postulations are presented in Table 1.

Table 1. Leveson's assumptions for new safety engineering principles [10]

Old Assumption	New Assumption
Safety is increased by increasing system or component reliability; if components do not fail, then accidents will not occur.	High reliability is neither necessary nor sufficient for safety.
Highly reliable software is safe.	Highly reliable software is not necessarily safe. Increasing software reliability will have only minimal impact on safety.

Fenton [11] uses probabilistic approaches to predict software defects and reliability. His work is focused on using Bayesian networks, but with a combination of both qualitative and quantitative measures.

The concepts of safety and reliability are used inconsistently in literature. The key findings are that there hardly is a direct connection between software reliability and safety, and that safety should not be considered as a characteristic of software. Nevertheless, all approaches take into account the development process as a source of safety risks. Therefore, safety analysis could benefit of process modeling and evaluation as a means to reduce software-related risks. Furthermore, process assessment models can be further developed to consider safety requirements and to address dependability including reliability issues. In summary, the safety related software development processes that emerge from the literature are:

- System requirements analysis (Chu)
  - o   system safety engineering (Leveson)
  - o   system architecture specification (Lawrence)
  - o   specification review and analysis (Leveson)
  - o   reuse (Leveson)
- Software requirements specification (Lawrence, Leveson, Smidts)
  - o   requirements safety analysis (Lawrence)
- Software design specification (Lawrence, Leveson, Smidts)
  - o   design safety analysis (Lawrence)
- Software implementation (Lawrence, Smidts, Lyu)
- System integration (Lawrence)
- Assurance (Leveson)
  - o   testing (Chu, Smidts, Leveson, Fenton, Lyu)
  - o   validation (Lawrence)
- Software installation (Lawrence)
- Software project management (Lawrence)
  - o   software safety planning (Lawrence)
- Software configuration management (Lawrence)
- Risk management (Fenton
- Measurement (Smidts, Fenton)

The processes are clustered to enable association to ISO/IEC 12207 Software Life Cycle Processes and ISO/IEC 15504-5 Process Assessment Model. The named processes can be found from the related authors' work.

The list of processes serves as a reference in selecting applicable process scope for assessment in Section 5.1. Findings of the literature review set additional emphasis on requirements specification, analysis and tracing. The next section discusses the concept of Process Quality Characteristic as a means to develop process assessments to support safety goals.

5   Safety as a Process Quality Characteristic

Safety could be presented as a process quality characteristic to enable process assessment. Process-related safety means definition of relevant process attributes that contribute in achievement of safer products. Here we use the wider concept of safety, freedom from unacceptable risk, instead of a more closed definition as a property of a state or system. It is important to distinct safety as process characteristic from product safety.

This section presents a preliminary model to address safety by process assessment. First, an applicable process set is considered, and then a tentative set of process quality attributes is defined. The description of the safety process quality attributes is the first application of process quality characteristic since the process capability framework.

The process set is defined based on the relevant literature findings combined with lifecycle processes found in one of the key functional safety standards. Then corresponding processes are collected from ISO/IEC 15504-5 Process Assessment Model.

Two sets of process attributes are constructed based on author's expertise in process assessments in safety-critical domain. The selection of attributes reflects the experiences gained with process capability assessment in safety domain. Capability levels tend to be of low interest when the aim is to ensure that risks related to achievement of safety goals are mitigated. Different sources of information were used to define the contents of the attributes. These include standards ISO/IEC 15504; ISO/IEC 25010; and IEC 61508.

5.1   Applicable Process Set

ISO/IEC 15504 Part 5 [12] defines a process assessment model for life cycle processes. There are altogether 60 processes divided into seven categories. In the beginning, for safety considerations we can limit the relevant processes into the software development related processes and categories as listed in Table 2.

Table 2. Relevant processes for safety domain assessment

Category	Process in ISO/IEC 15504-5
System Lifecycle Processes (ENG)	
	ENG.1 Stakeholder requirements definition
	ENG.2 System requirements analysis
	ENG.3 System architectural design
	ENG.4 Software implementation
	ENG.5 System integration
	ENG.6 Systems qualification testing
Software Implementation Processes (DEV)	
	DEV.1 Software requirements analysis
	DEV.2 Software architectural design

Table 2. (*continued*)

DEV.3 Software detailed design
DEV.4 Software construction
DEV.5 Software integration
DEV.6 Software qualification testing
Software Support Processes (SUP)
SUP.1 Software documentation management
SUP.2 Software configuration management
SUP.3 Software quality assurance
SUP.4 Software verification
SUP.5 Software validation
SUP.6 Software review

The rationale for selecting the processes is the combination of the literature findings and the relevant safety standards. The literature study brought up a list of processes (in Section 4) with a relation to software reliability and safety. Processes in Table 2 correspond to those processes except for the management processes (project management, risk management and measurement). Management processes do exist in ISO/IEC 15504-5 and may be considered in the later phase, if needed. In this model the management aspect will be covered by the extended process quality attribute set (in chapter 5.2). Documentation management is included to meet the documentation requirements of safety standards.

The second reference for the process scope is the IEC 61508 standard Part 3. The software development life cycle is depicted as a V-model (Fig. 3):

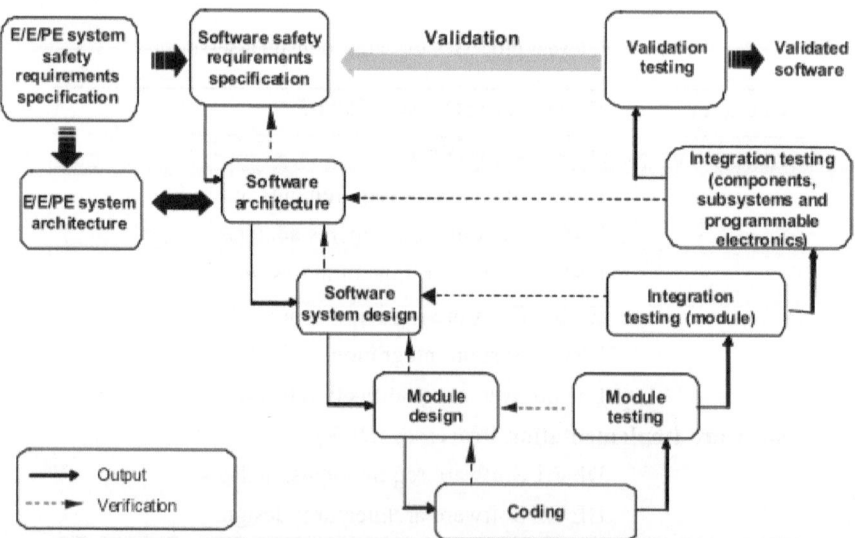

Fig. 2. Software systematic capability and the development lifecycle (the V-model) [2]

Also the IEC 61508 V-model processes are covered by the selected process set of Table 2.

5.2   Process Quality Attributes for Safety

Next, we specify tentative sets of process quality attributes (PA) for process assessment in safety domain. The basic set is intended to include attributes that meet the elementary requirements for trustworthy software development. The extended set adds process attributes that support management of processes that support safety activities. Especially the extended set requires further elaboration.

In a process assessment, each process is evaluated using a set of process quality attributes. As a result, when achievement of attributes is evaluated, better understanding of process related risk is gained. Each process attribute shall be described with corresponding Generic Practices, Generic Resources and Generic Work Products to enable collection of adequate assessment evidence.

Basic Set of Process Quality Attributes for Safety

The basic set is intended to define the process quality attributes that are essential to deliver safe software and to demonstrate trustworthiness of the processes. All of the attributes should be applicable to the ENG and DEV processes in Table 2, and for the SUP processes at least PA 1 and PA 2 are applicable.

First concern is to check that the process exists; process performance is the standard attribute for this. Process dependability ensures that the process is robust enough for continuous software development with high quality requirements. The literature emphasizes requirements specification and management; this is covered by requirements control attribute. Safety engineering adopts practices from safety process assessment models. Descriptions for the basic set attributes are:

- **PA 1 Process performance**
    - o   PA 1.1 process achieves its defined process outcomes
        - ▪   activities are performed and work products produced

- **PA 2 Process dependability**
    - o   PA 2.1 reliability
        - ▪   process performs as required in normal conditions
    - o   PA 2.2 availability
        - ▪   process can be performed when needed
    - o   PA 2.3 maintainability
        - ▪   process can be modified easily to add capabilities
        - ▪   performance can be improved
        - ▪   faults and errors can be corrected

- **PA 3 Requirements control**
    - o   PA 3.1 traceability
        - ▪   process supports traceability

- o PA 3.2 specifications coverage
  - functional, non-functional and safety requirements are included
- o PA 3.3 constraints
  - unwanted functionality is excluded
- o PA 3.4 safety analysis
  - requirements relationship to safety is understood
- o PA 3.5 reuse
  - requirements are analyzed for reuse opportunities
  - safety requirements of the reusable components are analyzed

- **PA 4 Safety engineering**
  - o PA 4.1 safety demonstration
    - safety cases and other argumentation are evaluated
  - o PA 4.2 reviews
    - reviews are performed and documented
  - o PA 4.3 verification and validation
    - testing that work products meet their requirements and are applicable for their intended use
  - o PA 4.4 quality assurance
    - processes and work products comply with standards, requirements and plans

Extended Set of Process Quality Attributes for Safety

The extended set intends to evaluate the implementation of safety culture. Safety management is the first step to organization-wide safety policy. Process compliance looks at both external and internal process definitions. Risk management aims at reducing and controlling process related risks including information security. Quantitative management attribute aligns safety process quality to ISO/IEC 15504 process capability level 4. Descriptions for the extended set attributes are:

- **PA 5 Safety management**
  - PA 5.1 safety strategy alignment
  - PA 5.2 safety life cycle
    - defined activities involved in the implementation of safety-related systems
  - PA 5.3 responsibilities and resourcing
  - PA 5.4 monitoring
  - PA 5.5 test and simulation environments

- **PA 6 Process compliance**
  - PA 6.1 standards
  - PA 6.2 defined process
  - PA 6.3 process tailoring

- **PA 7 Risk management**
    - PA 7.1 management of events that effect achievement of business goals
    - PA 7.2 qualitative and quantitative risk analysis for a process
        - probabilistic risk analysis
    - PA 7.3 information security
        - preservation of confidentiality, integrity and accessibility of information during the execution of a process

- **PA 8 Quantitative management**
    - PA 8.1 quantitative analysis
        - measurement objectives
        - measures
    - PA 8.2 quantitative control
        - techniques
        - causes of variation

6   Conclusions

This report studies software safety from process point of view. The idea is that risks related to achievement of safety goals can be evaluated with process assessment using specifically defined process quality attributes.

Process quality is composed of quality characteristics, where the required set of characteristics depends on the applicable stakeholder needs and organization's business goals. In addition, process quality shall be measurable.

Probabilistic models for safety are difficult to apply to software. Assessment of the software development processes may provide additional information to evaluate safety risks of software intensive systems. It requires that process assessment models are further developed to take into account safety requirements and to address e.g. dependability issues.

A new concept of Process Quality Characteristics is presented in this article and two tentative sets of process quality attributes for process assessment in safety domain were developed to support achievement of safety goals in software development. A set of applicable development related processes is also defined.

The basic set of process quality attributes for safety is intended to include attributes that meet the elementary requirements for trustworthy software development. The extended set adds process attributes that support implementation of safety culture in an organization.

The aim of the presented process quality characteristic for safety is that risks related to achievement of safety goals can be evaluated with process assessment using specifically defined process quality attributes.

The presented process safety approach and the defined process quality characteristic for safety are tentative. Hopefully this article opens discussion of how software processes can support the increasing safety requirements for software.

Acknowledgements. This work has been partially funded by Finnish national nuclear safety program SAFIR2014. In project CORSICA, new approaches and V&V methods have been developed for software-intensive system safety. A method called Nuclear SPICE implements an assessment approach for safety-critical domain.

References

1. ISO/IEC 25010:2011 Systems and software engineering–Systems and software Quality Requirements and Evaluation (SQuaRE)–System and software quality models (2011)
2. IEC 61508-3 Ed. 2.0, Functional safety of electrical/electronic/programmable electronic safety-related systems – Part 3: Software requirements (2009)
3. ISO/IEC 33001 DIS, Information technology – Process assessment – Concepts and terminology (2013)
4. ISO/IEC/IEEE 24765:2010, Systems and Software Engineering Vocabulary, http://pascal.computer.org/sev_display/index.action
5. +SAFE, V1.2, A Safety Extension to CMMI-DEV, V1.2, CMU/SEI-2007-TN-006 (March 2007)
6. ISO/IEC TS 15504-10.4:2011, Information technology — Process assessment — Part 10: Safety extension (2011)
7. Lawrence, J.D.: Software Reliability and Safety in Nuclear Reactor Protection Systems. NRC, CR6101 (1993)
8. Smidts, C.S., et al.: A Large Scale Validation of a Methodology for Assessing Software Reliability. NRC (2011)
9. Chu, T.-L., et al.: Development of Quantitative Software Reliability Models for Digital Protection Systems of Nuclear Power Plants. NRC (2011)
10. Leveson, N.G.: Engineering a Safer World: Systems Thinking Applied to Safety. MIT (2011)
11. Fenton, N., Neil, M., Marquez, D.: Using Bayesian Networks to Predict Software Defects and Reliability. In: Proceedings of IMECHE 2008 (2008)
12. ISO/IEC 15504-5:2012, Information technology – Process assessment – Part 5: An exemplar Process Assessment Model (2012)

Derivation of Green Metrics for Software

Giuseppe Lami[1], Luigi Buglione[2,3], and Fabrizio Fabbrini[1]

[1] Consiglio Nazionale delle Ricerche - Istituto di Scienza e Tecnologie della Informazione
Via Moruzzi, 1 – I-56124 Pisa, Italy
{giuseppe.lami,fabrizio.fabbrini,mario.fusani}@isti.cnr.it
[2] Engineering.IT Spa
Via Riccardo Morandi 32 – I-00148 - Rome, Italy
luigi.buglione@eng.it
[3] Ecole de Technologie Supérieure (ETS)
1100, Notre-Dame Street West - Montréal, Québec - Canada H3C 1K3

Abstract. Sustainability of software depends on several factors including the processes deployed to develop, operate, maintain and dispose software systems. To make such sustainability-related processes actually deployable and controllable, specific green metrics and indicators are necessary. In this paper we propose a sound methodological approach to derive green metrics and we provide also a significant set of metrics, derived according to such an approach, able to address different aspects of software sustainability.

Keywords: software sustainability, software process, metrics, ISO/IEC 25010, Environmental factors.

1 Introduction

The environment preservation and the CO2 emissions reduction are among the most important challenges human beings are facing today. Since 1987 the Organization of United Nations has identified the sustainable development (i.e. the responsible use of the earth resources in order to "*meet the needs of the present without compromising the ability of future generations to meet their own needs*") as a priority [14].

All the human activities shall be involved in the effort for preserving the environment, including those related to the production and use of ICT systems.

While many efforts have been done in carbon emissions reduction related to ICT systems both from the point of view of the hardware power consumption and software optimization, a deep and widespread green culture in the ICT domain is still to be achieved [19].

In this paper we address the point from the sustainability of software process perspective. Software process determines and drives the organizational *modus operandi* in all the activities directly and indirectly related to the software development and use. The availability of models and methods for assessing and improving software process in terms of sustainability contributes, not only to producing greener products, but also to spreading sustainability culture at company level.

T. Woronowicz et al. (Eds.): SPICE 2013, CCIS 349, pp. 13–24, 2013.

In order to give practitioners the possibility to deploy and control the sustainability-related processes, the availability of metrics is necessary. In this paper, we address such a point by providing a methodological approach to deriving sustainability metrics (called green metrics) to be used in setting up sustainability objectives, controlling the development of software and evaluating the final products.

The paper is structured as follows: Section 2 provides the background works on software sustainability (from the viewpoint of the software process) this paper is based on. In Section 3 a refined set of basic software-related assets responsible for environmental negative effects is provided. Section 4 focuses on a methodological approach to derive sustainability factors (i.e. technical and managerial solutions adopted during the development and operation of a software product that determine the actual environmental impact of sustainability assets), and provides an exemplar set of them. Section 5 provides a set of sustainability (green) metrics able to address a wide range of aspects related to software. In Section 6 conclusions are finally provided as well as the indication of the future research directions.

2   Background

This paper is based on some preliminary achievements described in previous papers. In particular, [1] provides a process model composed of the definition of a core set of processes able to address the basic activities to be performed in order to introduce and integrate the greenness culture in organizations developing software. Sustainability Engineering and Sustainability Management are among those processes. The definition of such processes follows the rules stated in the ISO/IEC 15504 standard [13], that is moving towards the new 33xxx series[1]. The aim of the Sustainability Engineering process is to define sustainability objectives and to apply methods and techniques able to match them; the aim of the Sustainability Management process is to ensure the achievement of established sustainability objectives in software development. In order to make these two processes deployable in practice, it is necessary to define a set of effective and meaningful sustainability indicators to set up sustainability objectives as well as a set of related metrics to verify and control their achievement in software development and operation.

A step forward towards the actual deployment of sustainability-related processes is provided in [2]. In fact it addresses the need of establishing sustainability objectives and measuring them by a few, common-sense measures using a goal-oriented approach. The starting point is the observation that sustainability should be managed (and therefore measured) from different viewpoints and considering different entities. According to this observation the overall sustainability concept has been decomposed into a set of assets (i.e. Infrastructures, People, Processes, and Product) able to include the necessary viewpoints to manage software sustainability in a complete manner. As discussed in [2], the measurement of sustainability must be done considering it as part of different views and entities. One possibility is to consider the *product* view, adding a further product characteristic in the ISO/IEC 25010:2011 [7] taxonomy, as shown in Figure 1.

---

[1] See http://www.spiceusergroup.org/ for most recent updates for the 33xxx series project.

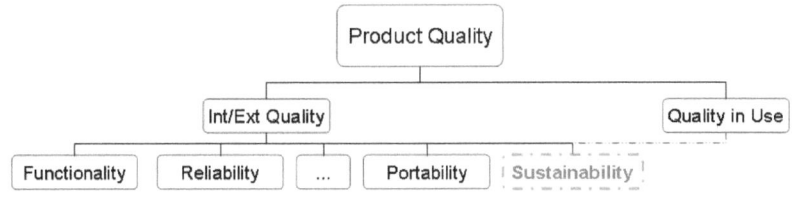

Fig. 1. A revised view for ISO 25010:2011

Sustainability would be more comprehensive than the sole 'maintainability', because it can be seen in the middle between the two typical views expressed right now in the ISO standard (Internal-External vs. Quality in Use). In this context, tailoring the initial definition, product sustainability could be defined as *"the capability of the software product to meet current needs of required functionalities without compromising the ability to meet future needs"*. Of course, this is only a first level positioning to be further developed.

The further step we intend to make with this paper is to provide, in a coherent way with respect to [1] and [2], a method to define actual and meaningful sustainability metrics for software to make possible the deployment of sustainability-related processes.

3   Derivation of Software Sustainability Assets

In [2], starting from the overall concept of software, the principal assets responsible for carbon emissions at software development and operation time has been derived.

In order to corroborate and refine such a decomposition we take into account a recent extended survey based on theoretical and empirical studies from the literature [3] that is focused on the most relevant success factors for software projects. The success factors in [3] are generic and they have been derived without taking into account specifically sustainability purposes, nevertheless they are general enough to be considered valid for a wide range of purposes, including sustainability. For this reason we will address them with the aim of integrating and refining the sustainability asset derivation for software.

According to [3] the most relevant success factors for software projects can be grouped into the following classes:

- People & Actions
- Development process
- Project Content
- Institutional Context

These classes are consistent with the sustainability assets derived in [2] and they can be mapped onto each other as Figure 2 shows.

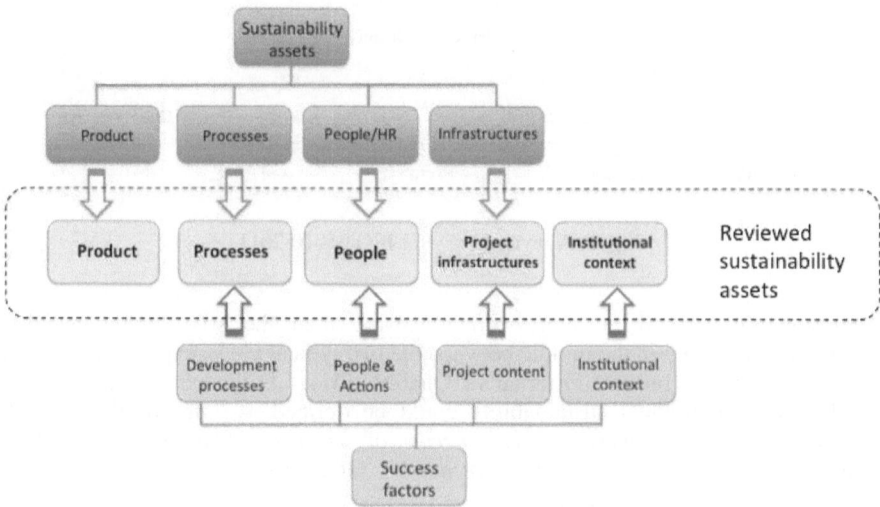

Fig. 2. Derivation of the reviewed set of Sustainability Assets

A new set of assets (shown in Figure 2 as 'Reviewed Sustainability Assets'), that takes into account both the original assets derived in [2] and the success factors taken from [3], is provided and discussed in the following:

- *Product*: the intrinsic characteristics of the software product (i.e. the way it is built) and of its components as well as the characteristics of the hardware needed to execute the software, represent important factors affecting sustainability.
- *Processes*: according to the process adopted to develop, operate, maintain and dispose a software product the environmental impact may vary.
- *People*: knowledge, experience and culture of people involved in development and use of a software product as well as their management are key factors in any context, sustainability included.
- *Project Infrastructure*: the specific infrastructures as well as the way they are used in the software life cycle may influence the environmental impact.
- *Institutional context*: the organizational environment in which software projects are deployed, along with its rules and opportunities, impacts on all the activities made in software development and use, then it cannot be ignored as a sustainability asset.

4   Software Sustainability Factors

The actual environmental impact (in terms of carbon emissions) of each sustainability asset depends on different sustainability factors, i.e. technical and managerial solutions adopted during the development and operation of a software product.

In this section we address the derivation of sustainability factors that can contribute to reducing CO_2 emissions.

Many sustainability factors can be found out on the basis of everyday experience and deductions. Anyway, in order to make such a derivation process more systematic and sound, we take into account the classification of sustainability effects provided in a recent report issued in the framework of the "Saving the Climate @ the Speed of Light", an ETNO (European Telecommunications Network Operators' Association) and WWF (World Wildlife Fund) joint project for the sustainable use of ICT that addresses the importance of ICT for the global sustainability [4]. That report presents a roadmap for the production and use of ICT, aiming at reducing the gap between the academic studies on ICT and the actions of policymaking organizations devoted to put into practice initiatives for CO_2 emissions reduction. In particular, in order to clarify the different ways ICT can contribute to the reduction of CO_2 emissions and sustainable development, it identifies three levels of Effects of ICT in terms of environmental impact: Direct, Indirect and Systemic Effects. The level of interest in this paper is the one related to Direct Effects. Direct Effects refer to those caused by ICT infrastructure and equipment, e.g. the resource consumption (including materials and energy) when producing ICT equipment, the energy consumption when using ICT, and the effects of the resulting electronic waste.

Many environmentally negative effects can be identified as belonging to the category of Direct Effects. The most relevant are:

- Greenhouse Gas Emissions
  - Power waste
  - Effort/Time waste
  - Fuel waste
- Material waste production
- Paper waste

The availability of classes of environmental impact types may improve the sustainability factors derivation. In fact, the approach we propose is based on deriving sustainability factors by considering every singular effect for each sustainability asset. Such a bi-dimensional approach can be represented as Figure 3 shows.

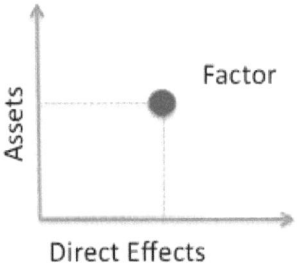

Fig. 3. Bi-dimensional approach for Factors derivation

Table 1 represents an initial set of sustainability factors. It doesn't aim at being exhaustive but it can be used as a starting point for further developments.

Table 1. Sample of Factors

Software Direct Effects	Sustainability Assets				
	People	Project infrastructure	Processes	Institutional context	Product
Power waste	---	Tool efficiency Tool suitability	Process Efficiency Process Predictability Process Capability	Team location	Algorithmic/ code efficiency
Effort/time waste	Team compositi on	Tool efficiency Tool suitability	Process Efficiency Process Predictability Process Capability	Team location	Maintainability
Material waste production	---	Avoidance of environmentally hazardous materials	---	---	Avoidance of environmentally hazardous materials
Paper waste	---	---	Dematerialization	---	---
Fuel waste	---	Teleconferences	---	Flexi-work Team location	---

5   A Sample of Sustainability Metrics for Software

Moving from the above-presented analysis, now it's time to provide some samples with some sustainability metrics for software projects. A well-known technique applied for deriving a set of measures is GQM (Goal-Question-Metric) [5] formalized quite 30 years ago by Victor Basili and then refined during time by several variants (e.g. the GQ(I)M by SEI [11]) and also with an associated process [6]. The technique takes into account a decomposition of main *goals* to be achieved into a series of *questions* to be answered for achieving those goals and that can find answers by a measurement activity, thus by one or more associated *metrics.*

One of the improvements to this approach in terms of details to be described from the beginning, at the design phase for each measure kept/derived from the list of goals comes from ISO, that's the MIM (Measurement Information Model), proposed as an appendix of the 15939:2007 standard on the Measurement process [8][2]. An application of such MIM fields has been recently elaborated by the MASP working group of Automotive SPIN Italia [10]. Figure 4 shows a high-level view about the fields that could be considered and the desired information accuracy.

As in the figure, one of the customized fields from the original ISO template is about the 'measurable entity', based on the EAM (Entity-Attribute-Measure) taxonomy [9].

---

[2] Such ISO standard – as well as the CMMI MA (Measurement and Analysis) process are both derived from the PSM (Practical Software & Systems Measurement) project (see www.psmsc.com and [20]).

At the beginning it could seem a trivial information but it can be really valuable in the selection of the final set of measures to include into a small, manageable set of measures, because it can reveal whether or not an organization is properly balancing those measures by entity and its related attributes. Just a short example for software projects: Function Points (FP) or Lines of Codes (LOC) are product-based measures, respectively measuring the size of functional user requirement for a software solution and the length of the source code for a software solution. Thus, both share the same entity but with different attributes. But from a contractual viewpoint they are typically used and applied for managing 'projects', where a project is an entity comprehending a product, not the opposite. Thus, in a measurement plan it would be expected to have few measures taking into account – as measurable entities – the <u>project</u> (e.g. earned value), the <u>resources</u> (e.g. percentage of resources usage) as well as the <u>product</u> (e.g. using FP or LOC) or the <u>process</u> (defectiveness rates, etc.).

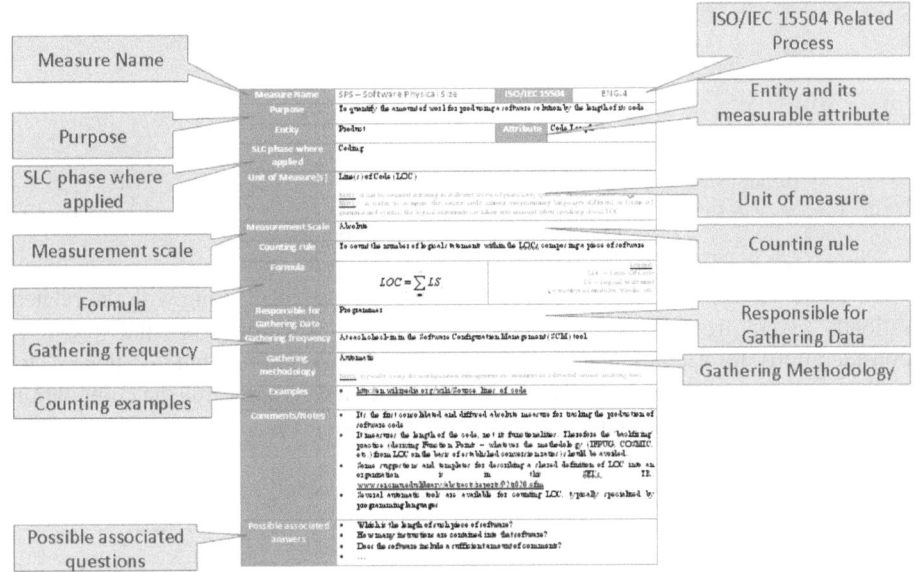

Fig. 4. Metric Card: structure and fields

The need to refine such basic GQM information is simple and common-sense based: as Tom Demarco said 'you cannot control what you cannot measure'. But coming back in the logical flow, 'you cannot measure what you cannot define' and still 'you cannot define what you don't know'. Thus, often a reason why people are resistant to measure can come from bad, incomplete or inaccurate definitions of what should be measured for a real comparison for benchmarking activities. Just a short example: what is a LOC? Does it include also commented lines or not? Should we count physical or logical lines? About Function Points did we refer to 'FP' as 'unadjusted' or 'adjusted' values including the so-called 'Value Adjustment Factor' (VAF)? Any answer can lead to different numbers, representing for managers the supporting information for the decision-making process. Thus, a wrong or not sufficiently detailed (and communicated) definition for a measure could lead to business errors, but the 'corrective action' from the beginning – as also the ITIL CSI (Continual Service Improvement) guide strongly suggests.

Applying the same 'balancing criteria' and having a reduced space for presenting here the full and detailed content for our proposal, in the rest of this section a list of possible 'green metrics' will be presented. The purpose is to present at least the core information from the EAM taxonomy mapped onto the bi-dimensional scheme presented in Section 4, in order to provide – possibly – such balanced view on the measurable entities for a measurement plan. In Figure 5 such a mapping is shown.

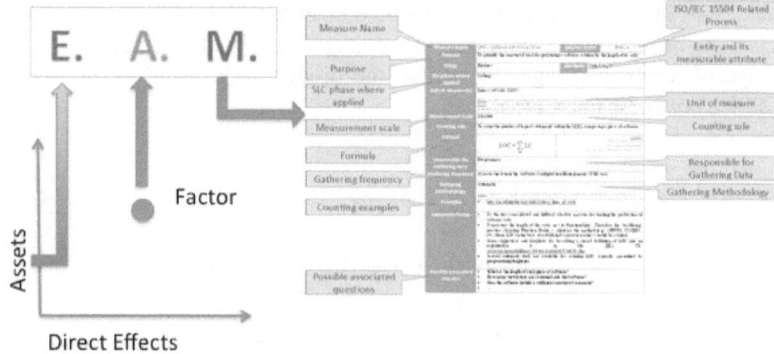

Fig. 5. E.A.M. taxonomy mapping

In Table 2 some sustainability (green) metrics are presented along with the related rational given from a sustainability perspective. According to the previous considerations, for each of them the corresponding Entity and Attribute is shown. The metrics included in Table 2 can be considered as the first step towards the compilation of full Metric Cards, compliant with the scheme used in [10].

Table 2. A sample set of 'green metrics'

Entity People			
Attribute	Team Composition	**Measure Id.**	Fitness for Role (FfR)
		Measure Formula	RP= number of competences and skills required by the project role; AP=number of actual competencies and skills of the person allocated to the project role. FfR=AP/RP
		Measure Rational	The higher FfR the better. Note: The fitness-for-role of the people involved in a project allows a saving in terms of effort spent.
Entity: Project Infrastructure			
Attribute	Teleconferences	**Measure Id.**	% teleconference meetings (PTM)
		Measure Formula	NT=Number of teleconferences; NF=Number of face-to-face meetings. PTM= NT / (NT+NF)
		Rational	The higher PTM, the more fuel saved. Note: PTM allows the monitoring and control of the number of travels due to meetings related to project's activities.

Table 2. (*continued*)

	Tool efficiency	**Measure Id.**	Earned Value (EV)
		Measure Formula	ET=Actual effort spent using the tool; PE= planned effort using the tool; EV=PT/ET
		Rational	The smaller EV, the higher the effort saved. Note: The typical EV concept could be applied also to a part of the management of a project, monitoring the efficiency of the suggested tools at least in terms of reduction of the effort/time waste. In some cases – referring to Table 1 – it could also refer to the reduction of power waste, finding new 'green ways' to accomplish to the same operational goals.
	Tool suitability	**Measure Id.**	Tool functionalities usage rate (TUR)
		Measure Formula	NF= number of functionality allowed by the tool; UF: used functionalities of the tool; TUR=UF/NF
		Measure Rational	The higher TUR, the more resource savings. Note: TUR can be used to evaluate if the tool is over-dimensioned for the actual needs.
	Dematerializ ation	**Measure Id.**	% of hardcopies of project's documents (PHP)
		Measure Formula	Z=amount of project's documents; ND_i=number of released versions of the document i; SDV= $ND_1+ND_2+ ... + ND_Z$ NH=number of hardcopies of project documents; PHP= NH/SDV
		Measure Rational	The smaller PHP, the more paper saved. Note: PHP intends to monitor and control the consumption of paper printed, noting when its usage would be over an acceptable threshold, going more 'virtual' than 'physical' in the distribution of information across the project stakeholders. It can help also help in determining better document communication and distribution strategies over the media applied by a project.
Entity: Institutional Context			
Attribute	Flexi-work	**Measure Id.**	% of work time spent at home (WAH)
		Measure Formula	MHO=amount of Man Hours spent at Office by project team; MHH=amount of MAN Hours spent at home by project team; WAH=MHH/(MHH+MHO)
		Measure Rational	The most appropriate value depends on the specific local conditions. Note: WAH can be used to properly balance the quality of produced work with the available 'quality time' for doing it, avoiding time wastes for travelling and being concentrated on a task. It is useful also to let people with temporary mobility inabilities stay involved. On the contrary, it is to be avoided too much time at home in order to do not reduce the right 'social time'.

Table 2. (*continued*)

		Measure Id.	Team Entropy (TLE)
	Team Location	Measure Formula	$\sum_{k=1}^{m}\sum_{i=1}^{n}(l_i\,team_k)/(size\,(team_k))$ where: m=number of project teams; n=number of spatial condition; li=spatial conditions where team_k operates.
		Measure Rational	There is not an optimal, absolute TLE value, because depending on the l_i spatial conditions (square meters, logistics, etc.). Note: TLE describes if team members' movement results in spatial clusters of workers or not, determining the probability of all members being co-located. More details in [15]
Entity: Product			
	Avoidance of environmentally hazardous materials	Measure Id.	Percentage hazardous waste per total waste generated (PHW)
		Measure Formula	NHW=Not-treated hazardous waste; THW=Total hazardous waste; PHW=NHW/THW
		Measure Rational	The lower the PHW, the better. Note: It can be applied to any resource that if not properly treated when wasted could generate any kind of environmental danger (i.e. toners, plastic, etc.). It can have more relevance for ISO 14001 certified companies, but in general could be related to any ISO 9001 certified entity. More details in [16]
Attribute	Algorithmic/ code efficiency	Measure Id.	Computational cost of software (CCS)
		Measure Formula	NF=number of functionalities implemented by software; NPC_i=average CPU cycles required by the functionality i^{th} implemented by software; CCS=NPC_1+NPC_2+ … + NPC_NF
		Measure Rational	The lower CCS, the more power saved. Note: CCS allows the control of the computational cost of software independently of the target hardware environment.
	Maintainability	Measure Id.	Information Flow Complexity (IFC)
		Measure Formula	LOC_A= lines of Code of A; FANIN_A=number of calling subprograms + global variable read in A; FANOUT_A=number of called subprograms + global variable set in A; IFC_A=LOC_A * $(FANIN_A * FANOUT_A)^2$
		Measure Rational	The lower IFC the better. Note: A is a generic software component. IFC it can be applied at different levels of granularity: individual functions, modules, methods, classes of a program. More details in [17]
Entity: Process			
Attribute	Process Efficiency	Measure Id.	Peaks and Lows (PAL)
		Measure Formula	UCL= Upper Control Level; LCL = Lower Control Level; PAL = amount of work days the effort spent is out of the range [UCL, LCL]

Table 2. (*continued*)

		Measure Rational	The lower PAL the better. Note: PAL allows controlling over-busy and idle phases of the software project. PAL comes from the observation of typical statistical control cards from TQM studies. [18]
Process Predictability		**Measure Id.**	Schedule Variance
		Measure Formula	BCWP: Budgeted Cost of Work Performed; BCWS: Budgeted Cost of Work Scheduled → SV=BCWP – BCWS
		Measure Rational	The closer SV to 0, the better. Note: SV is a typical project-based measure for determining if the activities run are (or not) aligned with plans, for any eventual re-planning.
Process Capability		**Measure Id.**	ISO/IEC 15504 Process Attributes Ratings (PAR)
		Measure Formula	Details on the determination and interpretation of PAR are provided in [13]
		Measure Rational	The higher PAR, the better. Note: Higher capability processes give higher confidence in achieving process objectives and then in reducing risks of waste of resources (effort, power, paper, …)

6   Conclusions and Future Works

The approach we proposed in this paper can be considered as a particular version of the well-known GQM paradigm [5]. In this case the Goals correspond to the sustainability Assets, the way Factors are derived can be associated with the derivation of Questions from which finally Metrics are derived. The EAM (Entity-Attribute-Measure) analysis is a simple but effective way to validate an initial set of measures selected for being included into a measurement plan and determines if the distribution by entity and related attribute(s) is properly balanced and valid for a certain project/organization or needs to be re-modeled, inserting/deleting some measures, also taking into account the cost for their management across the project/activity lifetime. Whether 'information is the power' is a valuable affirmation, also the nature and number of data and related information to manage is a critical success factor (CSF) to carefully take into account. In particular, a set of sustainability, green metrics as the ones presented above could represent an opportunity to properly shape projects starting to be more and more 'agile' not only about the way to produce a software, but mostly from the beginning in the way to act and think strategically.

The set of metrics provided in this paper doesn't aim at being exhaustive, but it represents a sound starting point towards the actual deployment and control of those sustainability-related processes for software defined in previous works.

Next steps to accomplish moving from the outcomes of this work shall be focused on enlarging and completing the set of metrics presented by creating a MIM-based document with plenty of details for their actual use. Moreover, these green metrics should be validated by means of empirical experiments.

References

[1] Lami, G., Fabbrini, F., Fusani, M.: Software Sustainability from a Process-Centric Perspective. In: Winkler, D., O'Connor, R.V., Messnarz, R. (eds.) EuroSPI 2012. CCIS, vol. 301, pp. 97–108. Springer, Heidelberg (2012)

[2] Lami, G., Buglione, L.: Measuring Software Sustainability from a Process-Centric Perspective. In: Proceedings of IWSM/MENSURA 2012, Assisi, October 17-19. CPS Publisher (2012)

[3] McLeod, L., MacDonell, S.G.: Factors that Affect Software Systems Development Project Outcomes: A Survey of Research. ACM Computing Surveys 43(4), Article 24 (October 2011)

[4] Pamlin, D., Szomolànyi, K.: First Report for Reduced CO2 emissions in the EU and Beyond. Saving the Climate @ the Speed of Light joint ETNO and WWF initiative (2008), doi:http://goo.gl/A5IaY

[5] Basili, V., Caldiera, G., Rombach, D.: Goal/Question/Metric paradigm. In: Marciniak, J.C. (ed.) Encyclopedia of Software Engineering, vol. 1, pp. 528–532. John Wiley and Sons, New York (1994)

[6] Van Solingen, R., Berghout, E.: The Goal/Question/Metric Method. A practical guide for Quality Improvement of Software Development. Mc-Graw Hill (1999) ISBN 0-07-709553-7

[7] ISO/IEC 25010:2011 - Systems and software engineering – Systems and software Quality Requirements and Evaluation (SQuaRE) – System and software quality models (March 2011)

[8] ISO/IEC 15939:2007 - Systems and software engineering – Measurement process (2007)

[9] Buglione, L., Ebert, C.: Estimation. In: Encyclopedia of Software Engineering. Taylor & Francis Publisher (June 2012), http://goo.gl/Tl7ta, ISBN: 978-1-4200-5977-9

[10] MASP, Metric Cards for Automotive Software Projects, version 1.0, TR-2012-01, Metrics for Automotive Software Projects (MASP) working group, Automotive SPIN Italy, Technical Report (October 2012), http://goo.gl/ZbvhC

[11] Park, R.: Goal-Driven Software Measurement: A Guidebook (Technical Report CMU/SEI-96-HB-002). Software Engineering Institute, Carnegie Mellon University, Pittsburgh (1996)

[12] Cabinet Office, ITIL v3 Continual Service Improvement – 2011 Edition (August 2011)

[13] ISO/IEC IS 15504-x – Information Technology – Process Assessment. Parts 1 to 10 (2003-2010)

[14] United Nations General Assembly. Report of the World Commission on Environment and Development: Our Common Future. Transmitted to the General Assembly as an Annex to document A/42/427 - Development and International Co-operation: Environment (1987)

[15] Dorn, C., Truong, H.-L., Dustdar, S.: Measuring and Analyzing Emerging Properties for Autonomic Collaboration Service Adaptation. In: Rong, C., Jaatun, M.G., Sandnes, F.E., Yang, L.T., Ma, J. (eds.) ATC 2008. LNCS, vol. 5060, pp. 162–176. Springer, Heidelberg (2008)

[16] IMCA, Guidelines for the Use of Environmental Performance Indicators, IMCA-SEL-010, International Marine Contractors Association (January 2004), http://www.imca-int.com/media/73138/imcasel010.pdf

[17] Henry, S., Kafura, D.: Software Structure Metrics Based on Information Flow. IEEE Transactions on Software Engineering SE-7(5), 510–518 (1981)

[18] Juran, J.M., Godfrey, A.B.: Juran's Quality Handbook, 5th edn. Mc Graw – Hill (1998)

[19] Murugesan, S., Gangadharan, G.R., Harmon, R.R., Godbole, N.: Fostering Green IT. IEEE IT Professional 15(1), 16–18 (2013)

[20] McGarry, J., Card, D., Jones, C., Layman, B., Clark, E., Dean, J., Hall, F.: Practical Software Measurement: Objective Information for Decision Makers. Addison-Wesley (2001)

A Process Assessment Model for Security Assurance of Networked Medical Devices

Anita Finnegan, Fergal McCaffery, and Gerry Coleman

Regulated Software Research Group, Dundalk Institute of Technology & Lero,
Dundalk, Co Louth, Ireland
{anita.finnegan,fergal.mccaffery,gerry.coleman}@dkit.ie

Abstract. The recent introduction of networked medical devices has posed many benefits for both the healthcare industry and improved patient care. However, because of the complexity of these devices, in particular the advanced communication ability of these devices, security is becoming an increasing concern. This paper presents work to develop a framework to assure the security of medical devices being incorporated into an IT network. It begins by looking at the development processes and the assurance of these through the use of a Process Assessment Model with a major focus on the security risk management processes. With the inclusion of a set of specific security controls, both the Healthcare Delivery Organisations and the Medical Device Manufacturers work together to establish fundamental security requirements. The Medical Device Manufacturer reports the achieved security assurance level of their device through the development of a security assurance case. The purpose of this approach is to increase awareness of security vulnerabilities, risks and controls among Medical Device Manufacturers and Healthcare Delivery Organisations with the aim of increasing the overall security capability of medical devices.

Keywords: Process Assessment Model, Security Assurance, and Security Assurance Cases, Networked Medical Devices.

1   Introduction

In terms of medical devices, design innovations over the last number of years have led to many outstanding benefits for patient care and healthcare providers. Such innovations include the increased use of software that has allowed Medical Device Manufacturers (MDMs) to add sophisticated functionality to devices such as insulin pumps that automatically detect dangerous glucose levels and administer the required insulin dosage to a diabetic patient. In the last few years we see an increase of interoperable and networked medical devices. Such medical devices have functionality to communicate via healthcare IT networks, wirelessly, across the Internet and from device to device. With this rise in the use and availability of networked medical devices, patients can now receive around-the-clock care even in the comfort of their own home outside the healthcare environment. This also benefits

T. Woronowicz et al. (Eds.): SPICE 2013, CCIS 349, pp. 25–36, 2013.

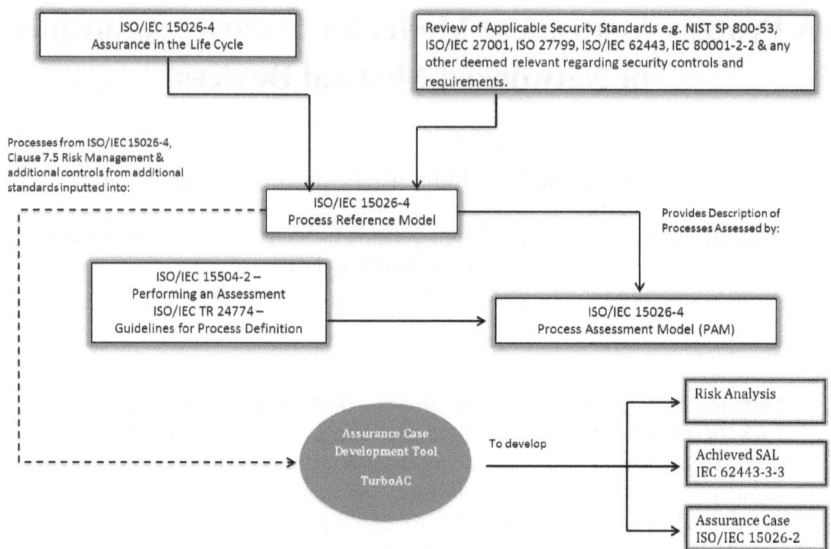

Fig. 1. Approach Overview

Healthcare Delivery Organizations (HDOs) greatly as the resource demand to administer this care is significantly reduced. HDOs utilize a wide range of networked devices from hard-wired monitoring devices such as diagnostic equipment (CT scanners) to implanted medical devices such as defibrillators. Clearly the benefits of networking these devices are significant but in using such technology, a new set of risks arise which are associated with their use. These are security risks, threats and vulnerabilities. In a report issued by the Department of Homeland Security [1], typical threats associated with each type of device (implantable, external and portable medical devices) are highlighted. As this technology is relatively new, the fear among the medical device industry is that the security for these devices is insufficient and has not been thoroughly addressed in terms of research and design. What is probably most concerning is that malicious attackers have not yet fully exploited these devices but do have potential to do so. This became evident through a number of controlled hacking demonstrations where security researchers proved the vulnerability of medical devices. One such incident was at the 2011 Black Hat Security Conference in Las Vegas where, a diabetic security researcher hacked his own insulin pump during his presentation. This raised a lot of concern among the medical device domain and led to the interjection of the US government, which prompted the US Government Accountability Office (GAO) inquiry into the FDA's assessment of medical devices in terms of security. The outcome of this was a report published in August 2012 [2] detailing the lack of consideration for both intentional and non-intentional security vulnerabilities during the FDA's PMA and 510k approval processes.

This paper outlines work being carried out to address security issues for medical devices to be incorporated into an IT network. Subsection 1.1 introduces our approach to address the problem background. Following on from this the paper divides the framework looking at process assurance and product assurance. Section two describes process assurance and discusses key standards. Section three details how the final product assurance in terms of security is addressed. Finally section four concludes the paper detailing next steps and the expected impact this work will have to the medical device industry including the HDOs, MDMs and also in terms of regulatory compliance assessment.

1.1   Overview

This work aims to address security in networked medical devices and build awareness of the types of security vulnerabilities and threats that can negatively impact the safety of patients. A key objective is to strengthen the relationship between MDMs and HDOs and also increase the HDO IT administrations' awareness of the security capability of the medical devices incorporated into their IT network.

This is achieved through the development and use of a Process Reference Model (PRM), a Process Assessment Model (PAM) and a Process Measurement Framework in compliance with IEC/ISO 15504-2 [3] for the assurance of MDMs development processes and establishment of a process capability level. In addition to this, this work will also develop a separate framework to establish security assurance levels of the final product in relation to a series of security controls. This will involve the use of a tool for the risk management process which also incorporates Security Assurance Case development. This will assist HDOs to better understand the suitability of the medical device for installation into their IT network. It will also impact MDMs in their design decisions during development of the medical devices. Figure 1 shows a high-level overview of the research objectives and framework, which is discussed in detail in the following two sections.

2   Security Process Assurance

2.1   The Process Assessment Model in Compliance with ISO/IEC 15504

As previously mentioned, ISO/IEC 15504 will be utilized to establish the development process capability level. Compliance with IEC/ISO 15504 results in the following outputs; a Process Reference Model (PRM), a Process Assessment Model (PAM) and a process capability level.

For the purpose of this research, the most suitable Process Reference Model (PRM) is defined in ISO/IEC 15288 – Systems Engineering – System Life Cycle Processes [4] will form the foundation for the PAM. ISO/IEC 15288 provides a process framework that covers the entire life cycle of systems from cradle to grave. A system is defined in this standard as having one of more of the following:

- *Software, hardware, humans, processes (e.g. review processes), procedures (e.g. operator instructions), facilities and natural occurring entities (e.g. water, organisms, minerals).*

As ISO/IEC 15504-6 [5] uses ISO/IEC 15288 as the external PRM, this has been selected as a suitable foundation for the PAM. ISO/IEC 15504-6 details an exemplar PAM that also includes the process attributes that are compliant with ISO/IEC 15504-2. The PAM contains two dimensions; the Process Dimension and the Capability Dimension. The Process Dimension utilizes the processes as defined in ISO/IEC 15288 and describes these in terms of their 'Process' and 'Outcome' dividing these into four groups. These are Agreement, Enterprise, Project and Technical processes. The PAM expands the PRM with the use of Performance Indicators called Base Practices (BP) and Work Products (WP). Base Practices are the basic required activities that specifically address the process purpose. They describe 'what' should be done in order to address the process but do not detail 'how' it should be done. Work Product performance indicators are the result of performing the process and are used to review the effectiveness of each process. Combined evidence of Work Practice characteristics and the performance of Base Practices provide the objective evidence of achievement of the 'Process Purpose'.

Table 1. ISO/IEC 15504-2, Rating Scale

Indicator	Meaning	Value
N	Not Achieved	0 to 15% achievement
P	Partially Achieved	>15% to 50% achievement
L	Largely Achieved	>50% to 85% achievement
F	Fully Achieved	>85% to 100% achievement

The Capability Dimension, as set out in ISO/IEC 15504-2, utilizes six Capability Levels from Level 0, 'Non Performing' to Level 5, 'Optimizing'. As defined in ISO/IEC 15504-2, the measurement framework is based upon a set of Process Attributes of which there are a total of nine associated with Levels 1 through to 5. These Process Attributes represent measurable characteristics required to manage and improve each process. The extent of achievement of each attribute is defined on a rating scale indicated in ISO/IEC 15504-2 and represented in Table 1. In ISO/IEC 15504-6, these Process Attributes include Generic Work Practices, which belong to a set of Process Capability Indicators. These indicators are the means of achievement of the capability addressed by each of the Process Attributes within each of the associated Capability Levels.

The PAM is being developed in compliance with ISO/IEC 15504-2. ISO/IEC 15504-6 will form the foundation of the model as it contains the processes necessary for compliance with ISO/IEC 15288. To further extend the PRM and the PAM, additional processes from ISO/IEC 15026-4 [6] will also be included in order to address security assurance. ISO/IEC 15026-4 is mainly utilized where additional assurance for a critical property, such as dependability, safety or security, is required for a system or software. The standard is used as an add-on to an already existing life cycle process standard such as ISO/IEC 15288.

2.2   Building Additional Assurance into the PAM

Due to the criticality of medical device security, additional assurance during the development life cycle is achieved through the inclusion of ISO/IEC 15026-4 – Systems and Software Engineering – Systems and Software assurance – Assurance in the life cycle - processes in the PRM.

ISO/IEC 15026-4 is a relatively new standard providing a process framework (Systems Assurance Process View) for software or systems that require an assurance claim for particular systems aspects that require additional attention, otherwise known as critical properties. Critical properties are usually in areas where substantial risk is involved such as safety, dependability, reliability and in this case, security. The standard presents a set of add-on processes, activities and tasks with guidance and recommendations. These processes, activities and tasks are intended to build upon the Agreement, Project and Technical processes as set out in ISO/IEC 15288. Therefore conformance to this standard is achieved through the demonstration of these additional processes as well as conformance with the Agreement, Project and Technical processes of ISO/IEC 15288. For this reason, demonstration of additional assurance specifically addressing security, through the use of this standard relates and integrates well with the Process Assessment Model as set out in ISO/IEC 15026-4. Table 2 presents the relationship between ISO/IEC 15288, ISO/IEC 15504-6 and ISO/IEC 15026-4. The black cells represent the family of processes addressed in ISO/IEC 15288. The grey shaded cells indicate processes that include additional recommendations for the assurance of the final product in terms of security being the critical property. With the successful implementation of ISO/IEC 15026-4, the following expected outcomes are:

a) A subset of requirements for the achievement of critical properties is defined.
b) Assurance claims, their justification, and the body of information showing the achievement of the assurance claims for the critical properties are established as an element of the system.[1]
c) A strategy for achieving these assurance claims and showing their achievement is defined.
d) The extent of achievement of the assurance claims is communicated to affected stakeholder.

---

[1] Assurance claims, the framework and reasoning for use is detailed in section 3.2 of this paper.

Table 2. Standards Process Relationship

Agreement Processes		
ISO/IEC 15288	**ISO/IEC 15504-6**	**ISO/IEC 15026-4**
Acquisition Processes	AGR.1	7.1
Supply Processes	AGR.2	
Enterprise Resources		
ISO/IEC 15288	**ISO/IEC 15504-6**	**ISO/IEC 15026-4**
Enterprise Environment Management Process	ENT.1	
Investment Management Process	ENT.2	
System Life Cycle Processes Management Process	ENT.3	
Resource Management Process	ENT.4	
Quality Management Process	ENT.5	
Project Resources		
ISO/IEC 15288	**ISO/IEC 15504-6**	**ISO/IEC 15026-4**
Project Planning Process	PRJ.1	7.3
Project Assessment Process	PRJ.2	
Project Control Process	PRJ.3	
Decision-Making Process	PRJ.4	7.4
Risk Management Process	PRJ.5	7.5
Configuration Management Process	PRJ.6	7.6
Information Management Process	PRJ.7	7.7
Technical Resources		
ISO/IEC 15288	**ISO/IEC 15504-6**	**ISO/IEC 15026-4**
Stakeholder Requirements Definition Process	TEC.1	7.8
Requirements Analysis Process	TEC.2	7.9
Architectural Design Process	TEC.3	
Implementation Process	TEC.4	
Integration Process	TEC.5	
Verification Process	TEC.6	7.10
Transition Process	TEC.7	
Validation Process	TEC.8	
Operation Process	TEC.9	7.11
Maintenance Process	TEC.10	7.12

3   Security Product Assurance

To specifically address security as the system critical property, the PAM again, will be further extended. In this section we focus on the Security Risk Management Processes and introduce new considerations and tools to be utilized during security risk management activities (Process Reference PRJ.5 from ISO/IEC 15504-6). Section 3.1 discusses security standards, security controls and the development of a validated expert reviewed set of security controls to be adopted by this framework in assuring the security of medical devices. Section 3.2 then discusses security assurance cases, the benefits of developing security assurance cases and how security assurance cases are employed in this framework. Finally, section 3.3 introduces a schema for generating a security assurance value for the final product and discusses the benefits of generating such a value to the medical device industry.

3.1   Security Controls for the Risk Management Process

IEC/TR 80001-2-2 - *Application of risk management for IT-networks incorporating medical devices - Guidance for the communication of medical device security needs, risks and controls* [7] is a technical report which sets out to promote the communication of security controls, needs and risks of medical devices to be incorporated into IT networks between MDMs, IT vendors and HDOs. This technical report presents 20 security capabilities that both the HDOs use to communicate their security requirements prior to acquisition of a medical device and the MDMs use to communicate the final status of the product in relation to those security capabilities. This technical report will form the foundation for the security risk management process in that; the 20 capabilities here will be included in the risk management process. Reasons for exclusion of capabilities or those deemed unnecessary for a particular product must still be justified and documented. For example, in ISO/IEC 15504-6, Process PRJ.5 - Risk Management Process, the process purpose is to identify and assess threats and monitor the risks throughout the life cycle. The PAM further extends this with the inclusion of Base Practice *'PRJ.4.BP.2: Identify Risks'* as a performance indicator. These processes are further adapted to address security risks in addition to project or product risks. The outcome of this work will be the inclusion of a list of security risks here, which a MDM must address during the security risk management process in order to ensure the desired security capability of the medical device is achieved. For each of these security risks, evidence must be provided to prove that the Base Practices were carried out with the full list of controls considered. For example, consider the security capability from IEC/TR 80001-2-2, *Automatic Log Off*, the MDM must consider this control and establish whether there is a risk associated with the elimination of the control. If no risk is associated, evidence will be provided and documented to prove this. If, however, a risk is identified due to the elimination of this control then the MDM must follow through the rest of the Base Practices for the Security Risk Management Process. These are:

PRJ.4.BP.3	*Determine the Risk Occurrence Probability*
PRJ.4.BP.4	*Evaluate the Risk Consequence*
PRJ.4.BP.5	*Prioritize Risks*
PRJ.4.BP.6	*Select Risk Treatment Strategies*

Base Practice PRJ.4.BP.6, Select Risk Treatment Strategy will be the security control, *Automatic Log Off* functionality.

One of the first steps in this work was to determine the security controls that should be included in the security risk management process. This was done by carrying out a cross-standard review of all security controls to establish if there are gaps in the 20 capabilities of IEC 80001-2-2. The standards reviewed were ISO/IEC 27001 [8], ISO/IEC 27799 [9], ISO 15408 [10], IEC 62443-3-3 [11] and NIST SP 800-53 [12]. Each of these standards and guidance documents similarly highlight security classes and controls and, as a result many controls are presented in numerous standards. For this reason a security control matrix has been developed to map the controls from each standard and identify those similar to compile a complete set of controls addressed in all standards. Those controls that relate will be rated in terms of their similarity. Following on from this, a gap analysis will be conducted in order to identify further capabilities that should be included in IEC 80001-2-2. This will be achieved through the use of expert opinion. The expert users from industry plus the FDA will validate the controls. The validated security controls will form the foundation for the security risk management process. A Technical Report will be published in the coming months detailing this security matrix gap analysis with the anticipation that IEC/TR 80001-2-2 will be revised based on this. The architecture of this framework will then be somewhat consolidated to use only the capabilities outlined in IEC 80001-2-2 as opposed to a multitude of standards. This will provide benefits for MDMs and HDOs in that they only need update their security risk management processes in line with one source standard.

3.2   Security Assurance Cases – Building-In Assurance

In support of IEC/TR 80001-2-2, development of security assurance cases are a key element of this framework for the interchange of security assurance information between MDMs and HDOs. Traditionally, assurance cases in the medical device domain have been used to address safety concerns. Since April 2010, Infusion Pump manufacturers have been operating under the Infusion Pump Improvement Initiative where a draft guidance document [13] recommends the use of assurance cases for use during the approval process for new Infusion Pumps entering the market. The FDA recommends the use of assurance cases to communicate information about the safety of the device and how risks have been identified and mitigated [13].

"In making this demonstration of substantial equivalence for your infusion pump, FDA recommends that you submit your information through a framework known as an assurance case or assurance case report."

Assurance cases can be defined as "a reasoned and compelling argument, supported by a body of evidence, that a system, service or organization will operate as intended for a defined application in a defined environment [14]. They are most often used when the requirement to demonstrate that a system or software exhibit a critical property that is usually risk-related and requires additional assurance such as safety, dependability or, in this case, security. Assurance cases are quite often compared to legal cases where a claim is supported by a comprehensive argument showing how evidence supports the overall claim. Therefore, the three main components of an assurance case as defined in the GSN standard [14] are:

1. **Claim**   A proposition being asserted by the author that is a true or false statement i.e. the system is adequately secure.
2. **Argument**   A body of information presented with the intention to establish one or more claims through the presentation of related supporting claims, evidence and contextual information.
3. **Evidence**   Information or objective artifacts being offered in support of one or more claims. Evidence may include component test results, policies, code reviews, training records, good processes among others.

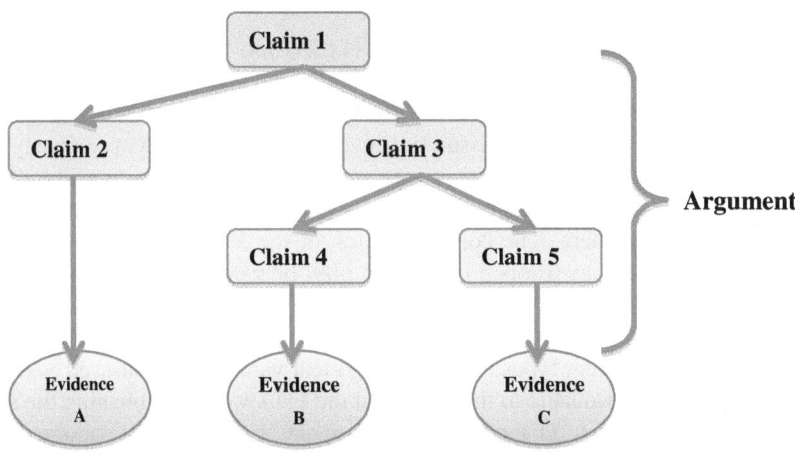

Fig. 2. Assurance Claim Structure

Looking at Figure 2 (a simplistic layout of an assurance case) we can now say:

If Evidence A **then** Claim 2
If Evidence B **then** Claim 4
If Evidence C **then** Claim 5
If Claim 4 **&** Claim 5 **then** Claim 3
If Claim 2 **&** Claim 3 **then** Claim 1

For this work, the proposed method for development of the security assurance cases focuses fundamentally on the security capability requirements as agreed between the HDO and the MDM (section 3.3). During the security risk management process, the manufacturer will utilize a software tool for the development of the risk analysis and the FMEA. This tool has been specifically developed for manufacturers of safety critical products to assist in the development, management and maintenance of the risk management processes. This particular tool works quite well with the artifacts of this framework as it automatically generates an assurance case through the progression of the FMEA process. The security assurance case arguments and evidence will relate directly to the achievement of each of the security capabilities and so for example, if 'Authentication' is defined as a requirement by the HDO then the evidence could detail login and password controls as implemented by the MDM. The assurance case will clearly identify the relationships between the claims to assist manufacturers in developing a meaningful and thorough argument resulting in adequate evidence to support a higher level claim stating that the system is acceptably.

To further ensure the strength of the argument, guidelines will also be published to assist the MDMs in establishing the security assurance level of their product based on the evidence gathered. This is discussed in more detail in the following subsection.

3.3   Establishment of the Final Product Security Assurance Level

Communication of a Security Assurance Level (SAL) to HDOs will provide a simple and meaningful method for establishing suitability of the device for the users need and its environment. To do this, IEC 62443-3-3 is being used as a guide for establishing the system security assurance level by the MDMs. As previously stated, the HDO will determine the appropriate security capabilities from within IEC/TR 80001-2-2 along with any other validated capabilities from other standards should they not be included here. The communication of the security capabilities from the HDO is used as a means to open discussion only between the HDO and the MDM. The purpose of this is to build awareness of security risks, threats and vulnerabilities among HDOs. MDMs carry out the security risk management processes thereafter. With regards the different types of SAL, the critical value is the achieved SAL (SAL-A) since this is most valuable to the HDO and the FDA when establishing the security capability of the product. Post product development, the MDM will communicate the SAL-A to the HDO which will be based on the agreed target SAL (SAL-T) level (0-4) as determined by both the MDM and HDO at the start of the acquisition process. The SAL vector detailing the assurance level and security capabilities is presented here:

$$SAL\text{-}A = (FR, domain) = \{AC \; UC \; DI \; DC \; RDF \; TRE \; RA\}$$
$$SAL\text{-}A = (FR, domain) = \{3 \; 3 \; 3 \; 3 \; 2 \; 1 \; 0\}$$

Table 3. IEC 62443-3-3 Foundational Requirements

Foundational Requirement	Code
Identification and Authentication Control	IAC
Use Control	UC
Data Integrity	DI
Data Confidentiality	DC
Restricted Data Flow	RDF
Timely Response to Events	TRE
Resource Availability	RA

For each of the parameters within the vector (refer to table 3 for Foundational Requirements (FR) descriptions), a value of zero to four will be used to represent the SAL level for that particular requirement. A SAL Level 4 represents medical devices that have undergone most rigour in terms of security assurance. Following on from this, the MDM will then verify the selected SAL level through the use of the SAL Mapping Matrix as shown in Annex B of IEC 62443-3-3, which will also be included in the PRM. This information, prior to a HDO installing the medical device into their IT network will be communicated to them by the MDM.

4   Conclusion

This paper presents a two-step framework for the assurance of networked and interoperable medical devices in terms of security. The framework combines an array of standards, guidance documents and processes to create a step by step process for

MDMs to use during development. The objective is to decrease the risk of potential security vulnerabilities associated with the use of networked medical devices. As one component of the framework is a process assessment model with an associated measurement framework it provides great benefits to the FDA and for external assessors in establishing process quality. The framework presented in this paper is twofold, addressing process assurance and also final product security assurance separately.

The output for the process assurance component is:
1. The development of an extended PAM and PRM.
2. A validated set of applicable and meaningful security controls to be adopted and included in the Risk Management process of the PAM.
3. The publication of a technical report detailing the security controls required for consideration in using this framework.

The expected output for the product assurance component is:
1. A technical report detailing the strategy and framework for carrying out the Risk Management process with the use of a software tool.
2. A framework for addressing the security controls and building a security assurance case around these controls.
3. A framework for the assignment of achieved security assurance levels for a networked medical device.

It is expected that this framework will be trialled with MDMs and HDOs in both Europe and the US. In applying this, MDMs will have three major outputs upon application.

These outputs are:
1. A process maturity level for the development of the product.
2. An achieved security assurance level (SAL-A) for the final product.
3. A security assurance case detailing in depth, the arguments and evidence supporting the security claim for the medical device. This assurance case will be used to communicate the security assurance of the product to the HDO where the medical device will be installed.

Currently no such framework exists to address both the development processes and the security product capabilities of networked medical devices. This is the primary focus of this work, hence, it is envisaged that the output of this work will positively impact the medical device domain by building awareness of security vulnerabilities, threats and related risks for HDOs and MDMs [15].

Acknowledgements. This research is supported by the Science Foundation Ireland (SFI) Stokes Lectureship Programme, grant number 07/SK/I1299, the SFI Principal Investigator Programme, grant number 08/IN.1/I2030 (the funding of this project was awarded by Science Foundation Ireland under a co-funding initiative by the Irish Government and European Regional Development Fund), and supported in part by Lero - the Irish Software Engineering Research Centre (http://www.lero.ie) grant 10/CE/I1855.

References

1. DHS, Attack Surface: Healthcare and Public Heath Sector (2012)
2. Government Accountability Office, Medical Devices, FDA Should Expland Its Consideration of Information Security for Certain Types of Devices, GAO (2012)
3. ISO/IEC, 15504-2: 2003 Software Engineering - Process Assessment - Performing an Assessment (2003)
4. ISO/IEC, 15288 - Systems engineering — System life cycle processes (2008)
5. ISO/IEC, 15504-6:2008 Information technology — Process assessment — An exemplar system life cycle process assessment model (2008)
6. ISO/IEC, 15026-4: Systems and Software Engineering - Systems and Software Assurance - Assurance in the Life Cycle (2012)
7. IEC, TR 80001-2-2 - Application of risk management for IT-networks incorporating medical devices - Guidance for the disclosure and communication of medical device security needs, risks and controls, International Electrotechnical Committee, p. 30 (2011)
8. ISO/IEC, 27001 Information Technology - Security Techniques - Information Security Management Systems - Requirements (2005)
9. ISO, EN ISO 27799:2008 Health informatics. Information security management in health using ISO/IEC 27002 (2008)
10. ISO/IEC, 15408-1 Information Technology - Security Techniques - Evaluation Criteria for IT Security, Introduction and General Model 2009 (2009)
11. IEC, 62443-3-3 – Security for industrial automation and control systems - Network and system security – System security requirements and security assurance levels Introductory Note 2011 (2011)
12. NIST, 800-53 Recommended Security Controls for Federal Information Systems and Organisations, U.S.D.o. Commerce (2009)
13. FDA, Total Product Life Cycle: Infusion Pump - Premarket Notification [510(k)] Submissions - Draft Guidance (2010)
14. Consulting (York) Ltd., GSN Community Standard Version 1 (2011)
15. Finnegan, A., McCaffery, F., Coleman, G.: Development of a process assessment model for assessing security of IT networks incorporating medical devices against ISO/IEC 15026-4. In: Healthinf 2013, Barcelona, Spain (2013)

The Approach to the Development of an Assessment Method for IEC 80001-1

Silvana Togneri MacMahon, Fergal McCaffery, and Frank Keenan

Regulated Software Research Group, Department of Computing & Mathematics, Dundalk Institute of Technology & Lero, Dundalk, Co. Louth, Ireland
{silvana.macmahon,fergal.mccaffery,frank.keenan}@dkit.ie

Abstract. IEC 80001-1 is a risk management standard that addresses the risks associated with the incorporation of a medical device into an IT network. Our research in the area of IEC 80001-1 has to date been focused on the development of a Process Reference Model (PRM) and Process Assessment Model (PAM) for assessment against IEC 80001-1. In this paper we present the approach to the next phase of our research which focuses on the development of an assessment method which will be used to perform an assessment using the IEC 80001-1 PAM. The assessment method will ensure a standardized approach to performing an assessment while identifying key success and will contain a list of questions which will allow assessors to determine the capability level of processes within the PAM. The results of the assessment can be used as a basis for process improvement.

Keywords: IEC 80001-1, ISO/IEC 15504 – Process Assessment, Risk Management, Medical IT Networks, Assessment Method.

1 Introduction

When using a medical device, the safety of the patient must be the primary concern. In order to ensure that the use of medical devices do not compromise the safety of the patient, medical devices are stringently regulated by the authorities within the region in which they are to be marketed. However, other factors may influence the safety of a device which has achieved regulatory compliance, such as the incorporation of that device into an IT network.

Traditionally, if a medical device was to be added to a network, the medical device manufacturer who provided the device would also provide the network. This method of networking devices led to a situation where a hospital may have a plethora of private networks. This can become unmanageable and has led to medical devices being designed to be incorporated into the hospitals general IT network which allows for true interoperability. Hospital networks can carry traffic which can range from life critical patient data to emails. The incorporation of a device into a network can introduce risks that may not have been considered during the design and manufacture of the medical device.

T. Woronowicz et al. (Eds.): SPICE 2013, CCIS 349, pp. 37–48, 2013.

These risks were identified when, in 2003 and 2004, the FDA received a cluster of attacks on hospitals which led to the FDA producing guidance on cyber security for networked medical devices incorporating off the shelf software [1]. During the preparation of this guidance it was recognized that the whole area of networking of medical devices would need to be reviewed. To be effective, a standard would need to be addressed not only to medical device manufacturers but also to the HealthCare Delivery Organizations (HDO) who were responsible for the establishment and maintenance of these networks and to providers of other IT technology who may be the providers of the hospitals general IT network. This was to be the origin of IEC 80001-1: Application of risk management for IT-networks incorporating medical devices - Part 1: Roles, responsibilities and activities [2].

IEC 80001-1 is a risk management standard which addresses the risks specifically associated with the incorporation of a medical device into an IT network. IEC 80001-1 advocates a life cycle approach to risk management and emphasizes the need for a new level of cooperation and communication among all parties involved in the performance of risk management activities [3]. Risk management activities are performed in order to preserve the 3 key properties of the network – Safety, Effectiveness and Data and System Security. Safety ensures that harm is not caused to the patient or to the user of the medical device. Effectiveness is the ability of the device to produce the intended result from the usage of the medical device for the patient and the HDO. Data and System Security is concerned with ensuring that information assets are protected from degradation in terms of availability, confidentiality and integrity. The standard is addressed to Responsible Organisations (ROs), Medical Device Manufacturers (MDMs) and Providers of Other IT Technology (POs). An RO is defined as an entity, usually a HDO, responsible for the establishment and maintenance of a medical IT network. Currently, there is no method by which HDOs can assess the capability of their risk management processes against the requirements of IEC 80001-1.

Section 2, of this paper presents the PRM and PAM which has been developed to facilitate assessment against the requirements of IEC 80001-1. An assessment cannot be completed using the using a PRM and PAM alone but requires in addition the use of an assessment method. Section 3, details the approach to the development of an assessment method which (in conjunction with the PAM) may be used to assess against IEC 80001-1. Section 4, presents the conclusions of this paper and also presents future work in this area.

2   IEC 80001-1 PRM and PAM

2.1   Approach to the Development of the PRM and PAM for IEC 80001-1

Research to date has focused on the development of a PRM and PAM for IEC 80001-1. In order to develop the PRM and PAM, a review of the requirements of IEC 80001-1 was undertaken. Once these requirements were understood, it was necessary to determine the approach of how these requirements were to be organised to form the PRM and PAM. ISO/IEC 15504 -2 [4], sets out the requirements for the development of PRMs and PAMs. ISO/IEC 15504-5 [5] provides an exemplar PAM for the processes which are contained in ISO/IEC 12207 [6]. These standards were reviewed to ensure that the PRM and PAM which were developed for IEC 80001-1 would be compliant with the requirements of SPICE.

IEC 80001-1 takes a life cycle approach to risk management. IEC 80001-1 is similar to ISO/IEC 20000-1 Information technology - Service management - Part 1: Service management system requirements [7] and ISO/IEC 20000-2 Information technology - Service management - Part 2: Guidance on the application of service management systems [8] which also take a life cycle approach but do so in the context of Service Management. In order to develop the PRM and PAM, a review of the development of assessment models and methods for these Service Management standards was undertaken. The research focused on models which are compliant with the requirements of ISO/IEC 15504-2 and particularly focused on the method of development of the Tudor IT Service Management Process Assessment (TIPA) [9]. TIPA can be used for assessment against ISO/IEC 20000 or another Service Management standard – the Information Technology Infrastructure Library (ITIL) [10, 11]. The TIPA model no longer updates the PAM for assessment against ISO/IEC 20000 but was used as an input for the development of ISO/IEC TS 15504-8 [12] which is the international standard for assessment against ISO/IEC 20000. This model was reviewed for its applicability to the requirements of IEC 80001-1 and was also reviewed from the perspective of the approach that was taken to the development of the model.

While ISO/IEC 15504-2 is detailed in terms of the requirements for PRMs and PAMs it does not provide guidance on how to organise domain requirements in a way that can produce an ISO/IEC 15504-2 compliant PRM or PAM. This was recognised during the development of TIPA and the TIPA transformation process was developed to address this need [13, 14]. The TIPA transformation process is a goal oriented requirements engineering technique which can be used to produce PRMs and PAMs. The transformation process also takes into account the requirements of ISO/IEC TR 24774 Systems and software engineering - Life cycle management - Guidelines for process description [15] which provides guidance on how the most common elements of processes should be described. Based on the successful use of the TIPA transformation process in the development of an assessment model for ISO/IEC 20000, the TIPA transformation process was used in the development of the PRM and PAM for IEC 80001-1 which are described in the following sections of this paper.

2.2   IEC 80001-1 PRM

This section of the paper describes the IEC 80001-1 PRM. Using the approach detailed in the section above, the IEC 80001-1 was developed to describe the risk management processes which are contained within IEC 80001-1. The IEC 80001-1 PRM contains 14 processes. These processes are divided into 2 process categories. The Primary Process Category contains processes which are implemented in the performance of risk management activities while the Organisational Process category is concerned with the planning of the performance of the risk management activities contained within the Primary Process Category. The representation of standards in the PRM for IEC 80001-1, follows the same "Plan, Do, Check, Act" approach that is used in the PRM for ISO/IEC TR 20000-4 Information technology - Service management - Part 4: Process reference model [16]. This approach is maintained due to the lifecycle approach which is used in both standards. The processes within the PRM are shown in the figure 1.

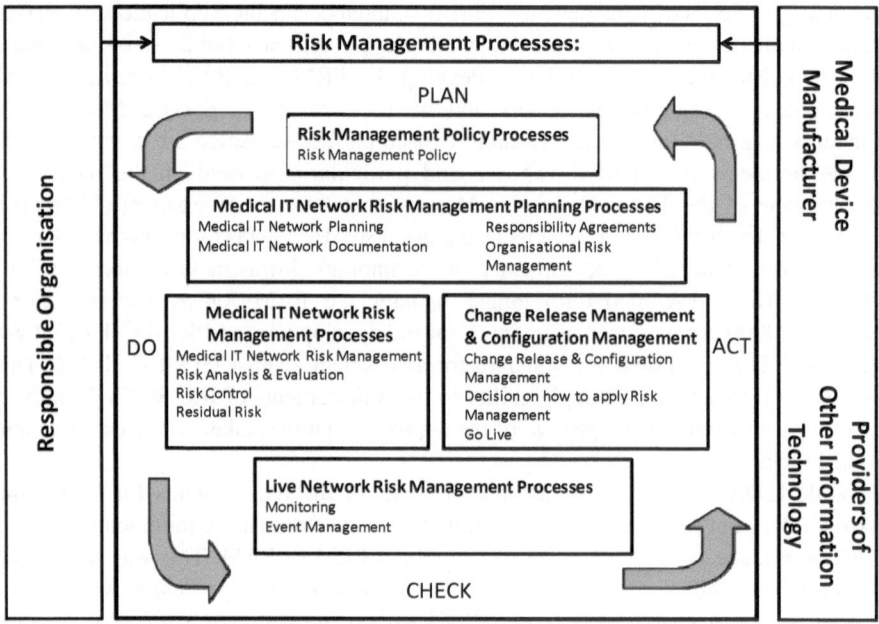

Fig. 1. Processes within the IEC 80001-1 PRM showing process categories, process groups and "Plan, Do, Check, Act" Approach

Organisational processes are contained within 2 process groups within the "Plan" section of the lifecycle while the remaining 3 process groups contain the Primary processes. As illustrated within figure 1, the RO, MDM and OP are involved in risk management activities throughout the lifecycle. Each of the 14 processes is described in terms of the process purpose and the process outcomes. The descriptions of the processes are compliant with the requirements of ISO/IEC 15504-2 and ISO/IEC TR 24774. The PRM provides a description of the processes that will be assessed by the PAM.

2.3   IEC 80001-1 PAM

The PAM extends the PRM with the addition of a measurement framework. The addition of the measurement framework, as described in ISO/IEC 15504-2, can be used as the basis for an assessment through which the capability level of the process can determined. The results of the assessment can identify strengths and weaknesses within the performance of the process which can then be used as the basis for process improvement. To allow the capability level of the process to be determined, the descriptions of processes within the PRM are extended to include base practices and work products. A base practice is an activity that is performed in order to achieve the process purpose. A work product is used or produced during the performance of the process.

The IEC 80001-1 PAM can be used for assessment of all 14 processes within the IEC 80001-1 PRM. In accordance with the requirements of ISO/IEC 15504-2, Table A.1 in Annex A shows the mapping of the processes within the PRM to the PAM. The IEC 80001-1 PAM maintains traceability from the requirements of IEC 80001-1 to the outcomes of the process, the base practices to achieve the outcomes and the work products used or produced during the implementation of the process. This traceability is shown in Annex C of the IEC 80001-1 PAM.

The IEC 80001-1 PAM described in this paper was presented at the September 2012 meeting of IEC SC 62A JWG7 standards meeting in Vienna and as a result the PAM has been raised as a New Work Item Proposal in January of 2013 and will be circulated to member states for comment. The final PAM is scheduled for inclusion as part of the IEC 80001-1 family of standards.

3   Approach to the Development of the Assessment Method for IEC 80001-1

In order to perform an assessment against the requirements of IEC 80001-1, a PRM and PAM are not sufficient. An assessment method is also required. An assessment method provides details on the organizations performance through using a set of questions (related to each process) to enable the assessor to determine the capability level at which the process is being performed. In order to develop the assessment method to accompany the IEC 80001-1 PRM and PAM, a number of factors will need to be considered which are discussed in section 3.1.

3.1   IEC 80001-1 Assessment Method – Goals and Concerns

The goal of the PAM is to allow ROs to assess the capability of risk assessment processes which have been used to manage the risks associated with the incorporation of a medical device into an IT network. However risk management activities are not performed by the medical IT network risk manager in isolation. In order to perform risk management activities effectively, requires input from all risk management stakeholders. This not only requires communication between the RO and MDMs and POs but also requires a high level of communication within the RO among risk management stakeholders. These stakeholders can include clinicians, IT department staff and bio medical departments. The development of an assessment method for the IEC 80001-1 PAM will need to address all risk management activities from the perspective of these groups.

An RO is defined within IEC 80001-1 as an entity responsible for the establishment and maintenance of a medical IT network but this can vary from a General Practitioner who has established a small network incorporating a medical device to a large hospital that has a large number of medical devices which have been incorporated into the IT network. The development of an assessment method will need to take into account this variation in scale among ROs and ensure that the capability level of processes can be successfully assessed regardless of the size of the RO in which the process is taking place.

During the development of the assessment method, consideration must also be given to the fact that the standard requires that an appropriately qualified medical IT network risk manager is appointed. In practice due to resource constraints and due to the variations in scale in the RO, the medical IT network risk manager may not be fully versed in the performance of risk management activities. The assessment method will need to ensure that capability levels can be accurately measured through self-assessment and that where opportunities for improvement are identified, that recommendations can provided for process improvement and commonly understood capability levels can be communicated to risk management stakeholders regardless of the experience level of medical IT network risk manager. In addition given these resource constraints, the assessment method will need to be a light weight method, not in terms of reduced number of processes from the PRM but in terms of resource usage, in order not to place additional burden on staff during the performance of the assessment.

In order to inform the development of the assessment method and to address these concerns, sections 3.2, 3.3 and 3.4 present the development of the assessment method which centers on a review of both standards for assessment methods of related assessment methods in the area of medical device development, Service Management and Risk Management.

3.2   Process Assessment Standards

In order to inform the development of the assessment method, a review of the standards related to the performance of an assessment has been conducted. These standards provide a standardized approach to the performance of an assessment and will ensure that capability levels can be understood and communicated. This standardized approach will also help to inform how the assessment method can be scaled to accommodate assessment of HDOs of varying sizes. The standards which have been reviewed are ISO/IEC 15504-2 [4] and ISO/IEC 15504-3 [17]. A review of the requirements of the Appraisal Requirements for CMMI® Version 1.3 (ARC) [18] and the Standard CMMI Appraisal Method for Process Improvement (SCAMPI), Version 1.3 [19] was also undertaken and is discussed in this section.

Clause 4 of ISO/IEC 15504-2 sets out the requirements for performing an assessment and ensures that the output of the assessment is self-consistent and also ensures that evidence is given to substantiate any ratings that are given during the assessment. This standard requires that assessments are documented and that the documentation process is sufficient to meet the scope of the assessment. This standard requires that the documented process contains as a minimum the following activities – the assessment should be planned, the required data should be collected and validated and on the basis of the validated data, a process attribute rating should be assigned for each process which should then be reported to the assessment sponsor. ISO/IEC 15504-2 also defines the roles and responsibilities of the assessment sponsor, the competent assessor and the assessor. The requirements for defining the initial assessment input and the requirements for recording the assessment output are also discussed within this standard.

ISO/IEC 15504-3 provides guidance on performing an assessment. This standard builds on the requirements expressed in ISO/IEC 15504-2 in terms of assessments and provides additional guidance on the use of tools in performing an assessment, competency of the assessment team and assessment approaches. This standard also outlines success factors for process assessment. In developing the assessment method for IEC 80001-1 these success factors will need to be taken into account and be incorporated into the assessment method. The planning, data collection and validation, the process attribute rating and reporting are discussed in detail as are the roles and responsibilities of those involved in the assessment.

Appraisal Requirements for CMMI (ARC) defines the requirements for appraisal or assessment methods and is intended for use not only with CMMI but also can be used for assessment of other reference models. ARC defines 3 separate classes of appraisal which are based on the degree of rigor of the assessment with the appraisal classes being Class A, B and C with Class A being the most rigorous. ARC provides high level guidance for developers of appraisal methods and discusses the benefits and features of CMMI Appraisal Methods. Requirements for CMMI Appraisal Method Class Structure are also discussed with classes being differentiated on the basis of the types of objective evidence gathered, the ratings generated, the organisational unit coverage required and the requirements of the appraisal team leader. The requirements for CMMI appraisal methods are also discussed and it is these requirements which will be reviewed for applicability to IEC 80001-1.These requirements include documentation requirements, planning and preparation requirements prior to the appraisal, the rating generated during the appraisal and requirements for the communication of this rating. Our research focuses on requirements for a Class C appraisal as this is the most lightweight appraisal approach.

As with ARC, our review of SCAMPI will focus on Class C [20]. Requirements for SCAMPI appraisal, as with ARC, focus on the planning and preparation of an appraisal, the conducting of the appraisal and the reporting of the results. These requirements will also be considered for their applicability in the development of the assessment method for IEC 80001-1.

The review of process assessment standards in combination with a review of available assessment methods as detailed in section 3.3 forms the basis of the development of the assessment method. Using these standards as a foundation for the development of the assessment method will address a number of the concerns which were highlighted in section 3.1. Basing the assessment method on these standards will facilitate a common understanding of capability levels as expressed in these standards. This common understanding can be used as the basis for fostering communication among various risk management stakeholders. The issue of scaling the method for assessment of HDOs of various sizes is not addressed in these standards but will be addressed during the validation of the assessment method and will form part of the future work of this research. The following section of this paper will discuss other assessment methods that will be reviewed to inform the development of the IEC 80001-1 assessment method and review both general assessment methods and those which are used in the medical device domain.

3.3   Review of Assessment Methods

To further inform the development of the assessment method, a review of other available assessment methods will be undertaken. This review will focus on assessment methods which have been developed for the assessment of the capability of processes for developing medical device software. A review of assessment methods for standards similar to IEC 80001-1 will focus on the TIPA assessment method. As a lightweight assessment method is required for IEC 80001-1, our research will focus on lightweight assessment methods. The review will focus on a lightweight assessment method based on ISO/IEC 15504, Rapid Assessment for Process Improvement in software Development (RAPID) [21], and a similar lightweight method based on CMMI, Express Process Appraisal method (EPA) [22]. Two additional assessment methods will also be reviewed in depth – TIPA: an ISO/IEC 15504 compliant assessment method to assess against ITIL and ISO/IEC 20000. These are standards which have been identified as being similar to IEC 80001-1. The review will also study the Med-Adept [23] method for assessment of medical device software development processes. As development of the assessment method progresses, other assessment methods may also be reviewed in addition to those mentioned in this paper. Figure 2 shows the standards discussed in section 3.2 and the assessment methods which will inform the development of the IEC 80001-1 assessment method.

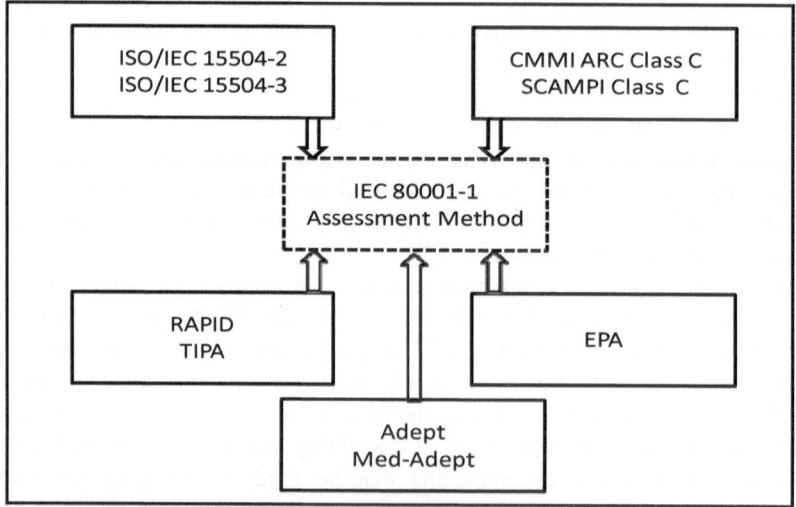

Fig. 2. Approach to the Development of IEC 80001-1 Assessment Method

This section provides a brief description of each assessment method and the reason for the review of each method in terms of its applicability to IEC 80001-1 and its ability to inform the development of the assessment method for IEC 80001-1.

Rapid Assessment for Process Improvement in Software Development (RAPID)

RAPID is a lightweight ISO/IEC 15504 compliant assessment method with a limited scope of 8 processes. This assessment method has been chosen for review due to its compliance with ISO/IEC 15504 (the PRM and PAM which have been developed for assessment of IEC 80001-1 are also compliant with ISO/IEC 15504) and due to the inclusion of the risk management process within the 8 processes which have been selected for assessment.

The RAPID assessment instrument contains a comprehensive set of 210 questions which will be reviewed focusing on the questions related to the risk management process. As a lightweight assessment method, the RAPID method requires two assessors in order to perform the assessment. The key focus of the RAPID assessment is to identify the strengths of the organisation and also to identify risks and improvement opportunities.

Express Process Appraisal (EPA)

The EPA method was developed in 2003. EPA is aimed at small to medium enterprises and focuses on foundational processes that will bring the most benefit to these organisations and reduce the scope of CMMI. EPA is based on 6 processes of the continuous representation of CMMI.

EPA does not provide a rating. EPA is aimed at organisations that have little or no experience of software process improvement programs. EPA has been chosen for review due to the fact that it is aimed at organisations lacking in experience of process improvement programs. This is a concern in the development of the assessment method. As IEC 80001-1 is aimed at ROs, these organisations will generally not have had experience of process improvement programs so the assessment method will need to address this issue. EPA has also been chosen for review as it forms the basis of the Adept [24] and Med Adept assessment methods which are discussed in the following section.

Adept and Med Adept

Adept which was developed on 2007, is based on EPA, however, Adept extends the processes contained in EPA to include 11 processes, with 4 processes being mandatory and the remaining 8 being optional. Adept is based on ISO/IEC 15504 and CMMI processes.

Med-Adept is based on the Adept assessment method. The Med-Adept method provides a method for assessment of processes which are deemed applicable for medical device software development both for those currently producing medical device software and those who wish to become medical device software developers. Med-Adept method provides coverage of 11 CMMI process areas, 12 ISO/IEC 15504-5 and 11 AAMI/IEC 62304 processes. The Med-Adept process also includes the Risk Management process. Med-Adept will be reviewed due to its inclusion of the risk management process which is based on the risk management processes contained in IEC 62304:2006 Medical device software - Software life cycle processes [25] combined with the risk management process areas from CMMI and ISO/IEC 15504. Risk management processes within IEC 62304 are based on ISO 14971 [26] which is closely aligned with IEC 80001-1.

Tudor IT Service Management Process Assessment (TIPA)

The TIPA assessment method allows for assessment against two standards which are similar to IEC 80001-1 – ISO/IEC 20000 and ITIL. These standards take a life cycle approach to Service Management. Due to the lifecycle nature of ISO/IEC 20000, it is reviewed in Annex D of IEC 80001-1 for its ability to meet the requirements of IEC 80001-1. While TIPA is not a lightweight assessment method, its assessment of standards which are similar to IEC 80001-1 and the involvement of multiple stakeholders in the Service Management process makes it relevant for inclusion as part of this review of assessment methods. The TIPA assessment method approaches the assessment through 6 main phases – Definition, Preparation, Assessment, Analysis, Results Presentation and Closure. Each of these phases will be reviewed in detail to assess if the outlined approach is suitable for assessment of IEC 80001-1. The results from the review of each of the models will inform the development of the assessment method for IEC 80001-1.

3.4   Validation of the IEC 80001-1 Assessment Method

The assessment method is being developed based on the approach outlined in the previous sections of this paper. The assessment method will be validated in a hospital context. The assessment method will be used to assess the capabilities of risk management processes. For validation, we will use a previously implemented medical device network project which took place in the Intensive Care Unit of the hospital as a case study against which the assessment method will be applied. This was a large scale project incorporating a large number of medical devices and will simulate a large scale project in a HDO. The assessment method will also be validated using data from a smaller scale implementation project which took place in a clinic within the hospital. This will simulate a small scale implementation and will allow validation to take place to ensure that the assessment method can be scaled for use in smaller scale HDOs.

4   Conclusion and Future Work

In order to allow HDOs to be assessed against IEC 80001-1, a PRM, PAM and assessment method is required. Research to date has focused on the development of the PRM and PAM for IEC 80001-1. The PAM for IEC 80001-1 has been raised as a New Work Item Proposal in January 2013 and will be subject to comments from member states. The PAM will be updated and validated on the basis of these comments. A trial of the final PAM will take place in a large hospital environments in both the US and Ireland. Future work will focus on the development and validation of the IEC 80001-1 assessment method. The assessment method will be developed in accordance with the approach described in this paper and will allow for an assessment against IEC 80001-1 to take place. This assessment method will accompany the IEC 80001-1 PAM which is scheduled for inclusion in the IEC 80001-1 family of standards.

Having an assessment method for IEC 80001-1 will allow HDOs regardless of size to assess the capability of risk management process for the incorporation of medical devices onto an IT network. These capability levels can then be used as a basis for process improvement which will allow risk management activities to be performed more efficiently and will allow the benefits of networked medical devices to be realized while ensuring that the intended outcome for the patient is achieved while ensuring the safety of the patient and the security of the network.

Acknowledgments. This research is supported by the Science Foundation Ireland (SFI) Stokes Lectureship Programme, grant number 07/SK/I1299, the SFI Principal Investigator Programme, grant number 08/IN.1/I2030, and supported in part by Lero - the Irish Software Engineering Research Centre grant 10/CE/I1855.

References

[1] Guidance for Industry - Cybersecurity for Networked Medical Devices Containing Off-the-Shelf (OTS) Software, Food and Drug Administration (2005)

[2] IEC, IEC 80001-1 - Application of Risk Management for IT-Networks incorporating Medical Devices - Part 1: Roles, responsibilities and activities. International Electrotechnical Commission, Geneva (2010)

[3] Cooper, T., et al.: Getting Started with IEC 80001: Essential Information for Healthcare Providers Managing Medical IT-Networks. AAMI (2011)

[4] ISO/IEC, ISO/IEC 15504-2:2003 - Software engineering — Process assessment — Part 2: Performing an assessment, Geneva, Switzerland (2003)

[5] ISO/IEC, ISO/IEC 15504-5:2012 Information technology – Process assessment – Part 5: An exemplar software life cycle process assessment model, Geneva, Switzerland (2012)

[6] ISO/IEC, ISO/IEC 12207:2008 - System and Software Engineering - Software Life Cycle Processes, Geneva, Switzerland (2008)

[7] ISO/IEC, ISO/IEC 20000-1:2011 - Information technology —Service management Part 1: Service management system requirements, Geneva, Switzerland (2011)

[8] ISO/IEC, ISO/IEC 20000-2:2005 - Information technology – Service management – Part 2: Code of Practice, Geneva, Switzerland (2005)

[9] Barafort, B., et al.: ITSM Process Assessment Supporting ITIL: Using TIPA to Assess and Improve your Processes with ISO 15504 and Prepare for ISO 20000 Certification, vol. 217. Van Haren, Zaltbommel (2009)

[10] Cartlidge, A., et al.: An introductory Overview of ITILv3 (2007)

[11] The Cabinet Office, ITIL 2011 - Summary of Updates. Crown Copyright, Norfolk (2011)

[12] ISO/IEC, ISO/IEC TS 15504-8 - Information technology – Process assessment – Part 8: An exemplar process assessment model for IT service management, Geneva, Switzerland (2012)

[13] Picard, M., Renault, A., Cortina, S.: How to improve process models for better ISO/IEC 15504 process assessment. In: Riel, A., O'Connor, R., Tichkiewitch, S., Messnarz, R. (eds.) EuroSPI 2010. CCIS, vol. 99, pp. 130–141. Springer, Heidelberg (2010)

[14] Barafort, B., et al.: A transformation process for building PRMs and PAMs based on a collection of requirements – Example with ISO/IEC 20000. Presented at the SPICE, Nuremberg, Germany (2008)

[15] ISO/IEC, ISO/IEC TR 24774:2010 - Systems and software engineering — Life cycle management — Guidelines for process description, Geneva, Switzerland (2010)

[16] ISO/IEC, ISO/IEC TR 20000-4:2010 - Information technology — Service management - Part 4: Process reference model, Geneva, Switzerland (2010)

[17] ISO/IEC, ISO/IEC 15504-3:2004 Information technology – Process assessment – Part 3: Guidance on performing an assessment, Geneva, Switzerland (2004)

[18] Busby, M., et al.: Appraisal Requirements for CMMI (Registered Trademark) Version 1.3 (ARC, V1. 3), DTIC Document 2011 (2011)

[19] SCAMPI Upgrade Team, Standard CMMI Appraisal Method for Process Improvement (SCAMPI) A, Version 1.3: Method Definition Document (2011)

[20] Hayes, W., et al.: Handbook for Conducting Standard CMMI Appraisal Method for Process Improvement (SCAMPI) B and C Appraisals, Version 1.1 (2005)

[21] Rout, T.P., et al.: The rapid assessment of software process capability. In: First International Conference on Software Process Improvement and Capability Determination, pp. 47–56 (2000)

[22] Wilkie, F., et al.: The Express Process Appraisal Method (2005)

[23] McCaffery, F., Casey, V.: Med-Adept: A Lightweight Assessment Method for the Irish Medical Device Software Industry. Presented at the EuroSPI, Grenoble, France (2010)

[24] McCaffery, F., et al.: Adept: A unified assessment method for small software companies. IEEE Software 24, 24–31 (2007)

[25] IEC, IEC 62304:2006 Medical device software – Software life cycle processes, Geneva, Switzerland (2006)

[26] ISO, ISO 14971:2007 - Medical Devices - Application of Risk to Medical Devices. International Organisation for Standardization, Geneva (2007)

The Development and Current Status of Medi SPICE

Valentine Casey and Fergal McCaffery

Regulated Software Research Group,
Dundalk Institute of Technology & Lero, Dundalk, Co. Louth, Ireland
{Val.Casey,Fergal.McCaffery}@dkit.ie

Abstract. There is increasing demand for effective software process assessment and improvement in the medical device industry. This is due to the expanding and complex role that software now plays in the operation and functionality of medical devices. This paper outlines the development and current status of Medi SPICE a software process assessment and improvement model which is being developed to meet the specific requirements of this safety-critical domain. This includes the selection of the most appropriate software process improvement model on which to base Medi SPICE. Its initial development and restructuring to conform to ISO/IEC 15504-5:2012 and ISO/IEC 12207:2008. The structure and content of its process reference model is outlined and an industry based trial assessment of 11 of its processes is discussed. Current and future work is considered including the timeframe for the release of a full version of the Medi SPICE model.

Keywords: Medical Device Software, Software Process Improvement, SPI, ISO/IEC 15504-5:2012, SPICE, ISO/IEC12207:2008, IEC 62304:2006.

1 Introduction

Medical device development is a highly regulated industry and the level of rigor required is determined by the potential hazard/risk the device may pose to patients, healthcare professionals and third parties [1]. Initially medical devices were composed of hardware or had very limited software content. Over recent years this has changed and the role and importance that software plays has continued to increase [2]. In many situations this has necessitated the development and inclusion of increasingly large software components which facilitate the operation and increased functionality that medical devices now provide [3]. In these circumstances it is not surprising that the size, scope and complexity of medical device software has substantially increased [4]. It has also resulted in a number of injuries and fatalities which were directly attributable to medical device software related faults [5]. The important role that software now plays in medical devices has been recognized by the European Union (EU). This is reflected in the latest amendment to the Medical Device Directive (MDD) (2007/47/EC) [6] which states standalone software may now be classified as an active medical device in its own right. This is a significant development and in January 2012 the European Commission released a guidance

T. Woronowicz et al. (Eds.): SPICE 2013, CCIS 349, pp. 49–60, 2013.

document for the qualification and classification of standalone medical device software MEDDEV 2.1/ [7] to provide additional clarity on this important change.

The Food and Drug Administration (FDA) who are responsible for the regulation and approval of medical devices in the United Sates (US) have also recognized the increasingly important role that software plays in this domain. As a consequence they have published a number of software specific guidance documents for medical device software development over the last number of years. In this context to remain up to date with current trends in the mobile platform and software industry the FDA have recently published a document called *Draft Guidance for Industry and Food and Drug Administration Staff - Mobile Medical Applications* [8].

Given the potential safety-critical nature of medical device software it must be developed in compliance with the relevant regulations and recommended international standards of the geographical location where the medical device is to be marketed. This must be done in order to receive regulatory approval [9]. To market a medical device in the EU the receipt of the CE mark is essential and in the US FDA approval is required. In Australia, registration and approval is provided by the Therapeutic Goods Administration (TGA) and in Canada, by Health Canada. These and similar approval bodies in other countries recommend conformance to a number of international standards and technical reports to help achieve compliance with national regulatory requirements. These include IEC 62304:2006 [10], ISO 14971:2007 [11], ISO 13485:2003 [12], EN 60601-4:2000 [13], IEC/TR 80002-1:2009 [14], IEC 62366:2007 [15], IEC/TR 61508:2005 [16], and IEC 60812:2006 [17].

The level of regulatory compliance required is determined by the relevant regulatory body from a predefined classification scheme based on the potential risk/hazard posed by the medical device. This is typified by the FDA who have 3 levels of concern and the EU who have 4 classes based on perceived potential hazard, ranging from low risk to high risk. A Medical device is evaluated against the relevant scheme and a classification is determined. Based on this evaluation the organization developing the device is required to establish design controls in line with the medical device's classification level. The higher the classification of the device, the more stringent the design controls and constraints that must be complied with [18].

While regulatory bodies provide classification schemes, regulations, lists of approved or harmonized standards, technical reports and in some cases guidance documents the information is high-level and specific methods for performing the essential activities required have not been provided [19]. In these circumstances it is not surprising that medical device organizations producing software are compliance centric in their approach to its development. This has been compounded by the fact that a domain specific software process assessment and improvement model which addresses the specific requirements of the highly regulated medical device software industry has not been available. Given this situation there has been very limited adoption of software process improvement in the medical device industry [20].

When the level of software in medical devices was small and the role it played had a limited impact this was not such an important issue. As stated this has now substantially changed and there is a specific requirement for highly effective and efficient software development processes to be in place [21]. In addition these processes need to be defined and adopted to facilitate the production of the required deliverables in the correct manner in order to achieve regulatory approval [18].

To address this requirement the Regulated Software Research Group (RSRG) at Dundalk Institute of Technology (DkIT) is developing Medi SPICE [22] a medical device domain specific software process assessment and improvement model. The objective of Medi SPICE is to facilitate efficient medical device software process assessment and improvement by incorporating software engineering best practice coupled with the regulatory requirements of the medical device industry. This work is taking place in association with members of the SPICE User Group, members of relevant international standard bodies and representatives from the medical device software industry. This collaborative process is a key aspect of the development of Medi SPICE [23].

The remainder of this paper is structured as follows: Sections 2 outlines the initial development of what subsequently became Medi SPICE. Section 3 presents the development of Medi SPICE which includes the initial processes which were developed and the restructuring of the model which took place as a result of the release of ISO/IEC 12207:2008 [24] and ISO/IEC 15504-5:2012 [25]. The definition of the Medi SPICE Process Reference Model (PRM) and a trial assessment of 11 of its Process Assessment Model (PAM) processes are also discussed in this section. Section 4 concludes the paper with a brief overview of the current status of Medi SPICE and the schedule for the full release of the model.

2 The Initial Development of a Software Process Assessment and Improvement Model for the Medical Device Industry

Having identified the initial requirement for process improvement in the area of medical device software development a number of preliminary studies were undertaken [26]. This work culminated in an extensive literature review being carried out which focused on the development of a domain specific software process assessment and improvement model for the medical device industry [18]. This incorporated analysis of software process improvement models including the Capability Maturity Model Integrated for Development (CMMI-DEV) [27] and ISO/IEC I5504-5:2006 [28]. While CMMI-DEV and ISO/IEC I5504-5:2006 are effective and comprehensive models for general software development they do not address the specific requirements which are essential for regulated software development [29]. For other safety critical industries this has resulted in the development and deployment of domain specific software process assessment and improvement models which includes Automotive SPICE [30] for the automotive industry and SPICE for SPACE [31].

It was recognized a similar approach was required for the medical device domain. To initiate this key aspects of medical device software development were focused on and gap analysis undertaken. This included the areas of Configuration Management and Software Risk Management. This resulted in the development of a Configuration Management Capability Model (CMCM) [32] and a Risk Management Capability Model (RMCM) [33] both for use in the medical device software Industry. These models were based on CMMI-DEV and while they proved effective for the specific areas they addressed it was recognized that a more extensive approach was require. At this point a key question had to be considered which was should CMMI-DEV or ISO/IEC I5504-5:2006 be used at the basis for the development of a comprehensive medical device software process assessment and improvement model? The strengths of CMMI-DEV and ISO 15504-5:2006 were both identified and evaluated in the context of the requirements of medical device software development. A key factor to emerge at this stage was the importance of IEC 62304:2006 *Medical device software - Software life cycle processes*.

2.1   Development of IEC 62034:2006 and its Relationship with ISO/IEC 12207

As the medical device industry added software to their products consideration had to be given as to how that software could be developed. Having considered the alternatives ISO/IEC 12207:1995 [34] was selected as the most appropriate standard to implement for medical device software development. As with the use of other standards in this domain the goal was to minimized risk and the possibility of medical device failure. While ISO/IEC 12207:1995 was an effective standard it was developed for general software development and did not address the specific requirements of the medical device software industry [18]. This was highlighted by a review of the standard by the Association for the Advancement of Medical Instrumentation (AAMI) software committee.   This resulted in the decision to develop and implement a new domain specific standard for medical device software development ANSI/AAMI SW68:2001 [35]. When this work was undertaken ISO/IEC 12207:1995 was used as the foundation on which ANSI/AAMI SW68:2001 was based. ANSI/AAMI SW68:2001was revised and as a result a new standard IEC 62304:2006 was developed and released.   The major differences between the two standards are that in IEC 62304:2006 three software safety classes are identified and a safety class is required to be assigned to each software system. Based on the assigned safety class specific processes and tasks are required.   There is no longer a distinction made between primary and supporting processes and 2 processes were removed which had been part of ANSI/AAMI SW68:2001. Some of the requirements from these processes were moved to other processes where relevant in IEC 62304:2006 [36].

IEC 62304:2006 provides coverage of the medical device software development processes. As a result this standard plays a key role in the development and maintenance of medical device software. It is harmonized with the European Medical Device Directives and is approved by the FDA as a consensus standard. IEC 62304:2006 is solely focused on software development and maintenance and does not address Requirements Elicitation and Validation which are considered system level processes. For the development of medical device software based on IEC 62304:2006 it is required that a Quality Management System (QMS) is in place e.g.   ISO 13485:2003 and a risk management process conformant with ISO/IEC 14971:2007 is established.   As IEC 62304:2006 was developed based on ANSI/AAMI SW68:2001 the relationship with ISO/IEC 12207:1995 has been maintained.   This is highlighted in the standard as it states that its concepts and approach have been derived from ISO/IEC 12207:1995/ Amd 1:2002 [37] /Amd 2:2004 [38] and have been tailored to the requirements for medical device software development. The differences in IEC 62304:2006 are outlined in Annex C.6 of the standard and they include:

a) The standard excludes system level processes.
b) Processes seen as duplicating activities which are documented elsewhere for medical devices are omitted.
c) A safety risk management process and software release process have been added
d) Documentation and verification are incorporated into the development and maintenance processes

The key relationship between the IEC 62304:2006 and ISO/IEC 12207:1995/Amd 1:2002/Amd 2:2004 is also outlined at the process, task, and activity level in Table C.5 in Annex C.6.

2.2 The Selection of the Software Process Assessment and Improvement Model on Which to Base the Model for the Medical Device Industry

As a result of our preliminary studies and literature review the key relationship between IEC 62304:2006 and ISO/IEC12207:1995/Amd 1:2002/Amd 2:2004 was defined and the level of its importance recognized as outlined in Section 2.1. While this was the case it was still important to evaluate CMMI-DEV and its relationship to IEC 62304:2006. In 2009 the Software Engineering Institute published a white a paper *"CMMI and Medical Device Engineering"* [39] which presents a high-level description of how CMMI-DEV does not provide adequate coverage for medical device software developments with particular reference to IEC 62304:2006 [18]. The objective of the white paper was to help facilitate the extension of CMMI to address this, but it also highlighted the considerable level of restructuring that would be required and the paper only considered this at a high level.

In contrast ISO/IEC 15504-5:2006 had been developed based on the PRM outlined in ISO/IEC 12207:1995/Amd 1:2002/Amd 2:2004. As a result of our detailed analysis of both ISO/IEC 15504-5:2006 and IEC 62304:2006 it was clear there was direct relevance, and synergy between these standards. This was due to their common foundation, both being based on ISO/IEC 12207:1995/Amd 1:2002/Amd 2:2004. In addition Automotive SPICE had been successfully developed and implemented [40] and it addressed a mission critical domain not dissimilar to Medical device software development. Having evaluated and analyzed the alternatives the decision was taken to base the development of the medical device software process assessment and improvement model on ISO/IEC 15504-5:2006. The title Medi SPICE was selected for the model to reflect this decision [22]. While it was recognized that where relevant ISO/IEC 15504-5:2006 would have to be amended and extended to meet the specific requirements of the medical device domain.

3 The Development of Medi SPICE

Having identified the specific requirements which needed to be addressed and having selected an overall structure and strategy the development of Medi SPICE commenced [19].   An initial task was the formal identification of the overall objectives of undertaking a Medi SPICE assessment.   These were defined as to determine the state of a medical device organization's software processes and practices in relation to best practice and the regulatory requirements of the industry. The goal of such an assessment should be the identification of areas where process improvement can take place and to facilitate such improvement.   It was also recognized that Medi SPICE should be capable of being utilized as part of a process to select software suppliers when an organization wishes to distribute, offshore or outsource part or all of their medical device software development.   In this context Medi SPICE should be able to be used to evaluate the software process capability of third party organizations or/and remote divisions and thereby provide key input into the selection process [41].

Work then commenced on the development of a preliminary Medi SPICE PRM. The initial focus was on the software engineering processes and some supporting processes. This preliminary PRM contained 11 processes:

- Software Requirements Elicitation
- System Architectural design
- System Requirements Analysis
- Software Requirements Analysis
- Software Construction
- Software Integration
- Software Testing
- Configuration Management
- Change Request Management
- Software Verification
- Software Validation

These processes were based on the structure of ISO/IEC 15504-5:2006, ISO/IEC 12207:1995/Amd 1:2002/Amd 2:2004 and where relevant IEC 62034:2006.   The outcomes defined incorporated best software engineering practice and the regulatory requirements of the medical device software domain. On completion, these processes were released for review by members of the SPICE User Group, international standards experts and representatives from the medical device software industry. Based on their feedback the processes were further updated and amended.

A key aspect of the development of Medi SPICE is the desire to ensure the model conforms to the latest revisions and additions to the medical device regulations, relevant international standards, technical reports and guidance documents.   It soon became apparent that the release of ISO/IEC 12207:2008 would have a direct impact on the development of Medi SPICE.

3.1   The Impact of the Release of ISO/IEC 12207:2008 on Related Standards

The structure of ISO/IEC 12207:2008 is substantially different to that of ISO/IEC 12207:1995/Amd 1:2002/Amd 2:2004.   This is reflected in the name of ISO/IEC 12207:2008 *Systems and software engineering - Software life cycle processes* which highlights that the standard has been extensively revised. This took place in tandem with the revision of ISO/IEC 15288:2002 [42]. As a result it no longer just addresses the requirements of the software engineering life cycle processes. It now also addresses the system engineering processes as well. This development has impacted on the revision of standards which have been derived from ISO/IEC 12207:1995/Amd 1:2002/Amd 2:2004. In this context of particular relevance to Medi SPICE was the release of ISO/IEC 15504-5:2012 and the current revision of IEC 62034. ISO/IEC 15504-5:2012 now conforms to the structure of ISO/IEC 12207:2008. As part of the current revision of IEC 62034 to facilitate its next release a mapping was required to be undertaken between the processes of IEC 62034:2006 and ISO/IEC 12207:2008.

A member of the RSRG is also a member of the IEC SC62A JWG3 Standards Working Group (the IEC 62304 development team) and the RSRG were invited to contribute to this mapping. To facilitate this it was important to analyze in detail the relationship between IEC 62034:2006 and ISO/IEC 12207:1995/Amd 1:2002/Amd 2:2004 which is documented in Table C.5 of the current version of the standard. A member of the RSRG prepared an extended version of this table to include the complete details of the ISO/IEC 12207:1995/Amd 1:2002/Amd 2:2004 activities and tasks on which those of IEC 62304:2006 are based. As a result of analyzing this information and comparing it with ISO/IEC 12207:2008 a direct mapping was made.

Due to the restructuring that took place in ISO/IEC 12207:2008 the names and locations of a number of relevant processes, activities and tasks changed from the previous release of the standard. As a result of further analysis it became clear that at the task level very minor adjustments had been made i.e. the term "developer" had been changed to "implementer" and notes had been added to some tasks. The only exception was the ISO/IEC 12207:1995/Amd 1:2002/Amd 2:2004 task 6.4.2.2 Process Verification which had been removed from ISO/IEC 12207:2008. This is important as it is utilized in IEC 62304:2006 as the basis for the Verify Integration Tests Procedures task. Details of this analysis and mapping were documented and provided to the IEC SC62A JWG3 Standards Working Group to assist with the definition of the relationship between the next release of IEC 62304 and ISO/IEC 12207:2008.

3.2   The Development of the Structure of the Medi SPICE PRM

The selection of the appropriate processes for inclusion in the Medi SPICE PRM was a key activity. The objectives of this were twofold: one was the selection of effective life cycle processes which would facilitate medical device software development. The second was to facilitate conformance to the relevant medical device regulations, standards and guidance documents. To achieve this, a prepublication version of ISO/IEC 15504-5:2012, IEC 62304:2006 and ISO/IEC 12207:2008 were analyzed in detail. The analysis outlined in Section 3.1 on the mapping between IEC 62304:2006 and ISO/IEC 12207:2008 was of particular value in this context. This work was undertaken in tandem with an analysis of the relevant medical device regulations, standards, technical reports and guidance documents. In this context particular reference was made to ISO 13485:2003 and ISO 14971:2007. Based on this analysis the structure of the Medi SPICE PRM was defined as consisting of a system life cycle processes category with 4 process groups and a software life cycle processes category with 3 process groups. Initially 42 processes and 15 subprocesses were identified. This included a medical device specific Software Risk Management process which was not part of ISO/IEC 15504-5:2012 or ISO/IEC 12207:2008. The addition of this process was necessitated by the requirement for specific management of the technical risk associated with medical device software development as outlined by IEC 62304:2006, ISO 14971:2007 and IEC/TR 80002-1:2009. The proposed structure of the Medi SPICE PRM was sent for review by members of the SPICE User Group, international standards experts and representatives of the medical device software industry. Based on their feedback the number of processes was increased to 44 with the addition of the Software Development Planning and Software Release processes. As a result the Medi SPICE PRM was structured as follows:

System Life Cycle Processes Category
- 3 Agreement Processes and 7 Subprocesses;
- 6 Organizational Project - Enabling Processes and 6 Subprocesses;
- 7 Project Processes;
- 10 Technical Processes and 2 Subprocesses.

Software Life Cycle Processes Category
- 8 Software Implementation Processes;
- 9 Software Support Processes (including Software Risk Management);
- 1 Supplementary Process.

3.3   The Development of 13 Medi SPICE PRM & PAM Processes

Having defined the structure of the Medi SPICE PRM work began on the development of the PRM processes. It was decided to initially focus on the 13 processes which had a particular relevance to IEC 62034:2006. These processes are:

- Software Development Planning;
- Software Requirements Analysis;
- Software Architectural Design;
- Software Detailed Design;
- Software Construction;
- Software Integration;
- Software Qualification Testing;
- Software Release;
- Software Maintenance;
- Software Risk Management;
- Software Configuration Management;
- Software Change Request Management;
- Software Problem Resolution.

In line with ISO/IEC 15504-2:2003 [43] for each of these processes an ID, a process name and a process purpose was defined. Based on the process purpose outcomes were identified which incorporated best practice and the medical device software regulatory requirements. In this context the source of each outcome was recorded and where relevant each received an IEC 62304:2006 safety classification. The work carried out on the development of the preliminary PRM processes (outlined in Section 3) was of value when undertaking this work. On completion these PRM processes were sent for review by members of the SPICE User Group, international standards experts which included members of the IEC SC62A JWG3 Standards Working Group and representatives from the medical device software industry.

As a result of the positive feedback received from the reviewers it was decided to develop PAM processes for the 13 PRM processes in conformance with ISO/IEC 15504-2:2003. It was recognized that this could facilitate undertaking an industry based trial assessment of these processes. In this context the RSRG had been approached by a European based medical device company "Medical Incorporated" (a pseudonym) with the request that a trial assessment of some of their software development processes should be carried out. The 13 PAM processes were developed which involved the identification of the specific practices which facilitate the achievement of the relevant process outcomes. The sources of the specific practices were annotated with reference to best practice and the medical device software regulatory requirements. Where relevant an IEC 62304:2006 safety classification was recorded for specific practices. For each process relevant input and output work products were also identified and recorded. These PAM processes were then reviewed by members of the SPICE User Group, international standards experts and representatives from the medical device software industry.

3.4   The Industry Based Medi SPICE Trial Assessment

Having received favorable feedback from the reviewers of the PAM processes, plans for undertaking the industry based Medi SPICE trial assessment commenced. The need for a qualified ISO/IEC 15504 assessor to undertake the assessment was recognized. Given the imbedded nature of the majority of medical device software and specifically of the software being assessed for Medical Incorporated, the selection of an Automotive SPICE lead assessor was identified as appropriate. While this was the case it was also recognized that training would have to be provided to address the specific requirements of the medical device software domain. In consultation with the company 3 Automotive SPICE Assessors agreed to undertake the training and the assessment. They were a Lead Assessor, an Assessor and a Provisional Assessor. Having reviewed the PAM processes and based on the requirements of the company it was decided for the trial 12 of the 13 processes would be assessed and the Software Maintenance process was excluded.

A date for the assessment was agreed and the Assessors undertook the medical device domain specific training provided by the RSRG and reviewed the PAM processes in detail. It was also agreed that a member of the RSRG would participate in the assessment as a medical device software Technical Expert and provide support to the Assessors as and when required. The assessment took place over a 5 day period. Having commenced it was decided that 11 rather than 12 processes would be assessed as the project under review had not reached the Software Qualification Testing stage. The assessment was successfully undertaken and 8 processes were assessed as largely achieved at level 1 and 3 fully achieved. The results of the assessment were presented and discussed with the company. Based on the assessment results specific guidance was provided to Medical Incorporated to facilitate process improvement which was presented in the full findings report.

As this was a trial assessment it was important that the effectiveness of the Medi SPICE PAM processes were evaluated. To this end after the assessment the 3 Assessors were interviewed and they provided positive feedback on the content of the Medi SPICE PAM processes. With regard to the medical device domain training for the Assessors two issues were identified that required attention. These were the use of Software Of Unknown Provenance (SOUP) and the handling of residual risk. While these had been discussed as part of the training it emerged during the assessment that the Assessors were confused about them with respect to medical device software development. These issues were clarified by the RSRG medical device software Technical Expert when they arose. These were discussed with the Assessors and it was recognized that it was important to ensure both of these topics are comprehensively addressed as part of any future Assessor training program.

It was also important to evaluate the relevance and effectiveness of the Medi SPICE PRM processes and the assessment to the organization. To this end the Senior Technical Manager, Software Quality Manager, and a Senior Software Engineer who had all participated in the assessment were interviewed. Each highlighted the relevance of the focus placed on specific aspects of the processes being assessed. When required the assessment team's ability to explain what and why specific information was being requested was considered of value. Of particular importance was the final report which they considered presented a realistic assessment of their processes. The recommendations for improvement were recognized as relevant and of value and a process improvement program is planned based on the assessment findings. While it was clearly stated and recognized this was a trial assessment all aspects of the assessment and its outcomes were very positively received by Medical Incorporated.

4   Current Status and Future Plans

The development of the remaining Medi SPICE PRM processes is currently under way. The number of RSRG team members working on the development of Medi SPICE has recently been increased and it is now planned to release a draft version of the full Medi SPICE PRM by June 2013. It is also planned this will be followed by the release of the draft version of the full Medi SPICE PAM by October 2013. It is anticipated that a full release of the Medi SPICE model will take place in December 2013.

Acknowledgments. This research is supported by the Science Foundation Ireland (SFI) Stokes Lectureship Programme, grant number 07/SK/I1299, the SFI Principal Investigator Programme, grant number 08/IN.1/I2030 and supported in part by Lero - the Irish Software Engineering Research Centre grant 10/CE/I1855.

References

1. Maisel, W.H.: Medical device regulation: an introduction for the practicing physician. Annals of Internal Medicine 140(14), 296–302 (2004)
2. Lee, I., Pappas, G., Cleaveland, R., Hatcliff, J., Krogh, B., Lee, P., Rubin, H., Sha, L.: High-Confidence Medical Device Software and Systems. Computer 39(4), 33–38 (2006)
3. Abraham, C., Nishiharas, E., Akiyama, M.: Transforming healthcare with information technology in Japan: A review of policy, people, and progress. International Journal of Medical Informatics 80(3), 157–170 (2011)
4. Rakitin, R.: Coping with defective software in medical devices. Computer 39(4), 40–45 (2006)
5. McQuaid, P.A.: Software Disasters—Understanding the Past, to Improve the Future. Journal of Software: Evolution and Process 24(5), 459–470 (2012)
6. European Council, Council Directive 2007/47/EC (Amendment). Official Journal of the European Union, Luxembourg (2007)
7. European Commission, MEDICAL DEVICES: Guidance document- Qualification and Classification of stand alone software (MEDDEV 2.1/6), Brussels, Belgium (2012)
8. US FDA, Draft Guidance for Industry and Food and Drug Administration Staff - Mobile Medical Applications (2011), http://www.fda.gov/downloads/MedicalDevices/DeviceRegulationandGuidance/GuidanceDocuments/UCM263366.pdf (accessed March 12, 2013)
9. Vogel, D.A.: Medical Device Software Verification, Validation and Compliance. Artech House, Norwood (2010)
10. IEC 62304:2006, Medical device software—Software life cycle processes. IEC, Geneva (2006)
11. ISO 14971:2007, Medical Devices — Application of risk management to medical devices. ISO, Geneva (2007)
12. ISO 13485:2003, Medical devices — Quality management systems — Requirements for regulatory purposes. ISO, Geneva (2003)
13. BS EN 60601-1-4:2000, Medical Electrical Equipment, Part 1 - General requirements for safety. BSI, London (2000)
14. IEC/TR 80002-1:2009, Medical device software Part 1: Guidance on the application of ISO 14971 to medical device software. BSI, London (2009)
15. IEC 62366:2007, Medical devices - Application of usability engineering to medical devices. IEC, Geneva (2007)
16. IEC/TR 61508:2005, Functional safety of electrical/electronic/programmable electronic safety related systems. BSI, London (2005)
17. IEC 60812:2006, Analysis technique for system reliability - Procedure for failure modes and effects analysis (FMEA). IEC, Geneva (2006)
18. Mc Caffery, F., Burton, J., Casey, V., Dorling, A.: Software Process Improvement in the Medical Device Industry. In: Laplante, P. (ed.) Encyclopedia of Software Engineering, pp. 528–540. CRC Press Francis Taylor Group, New York (2010)
19. Mc Caffery, F., Dorling, A.: Medi SPICE: An Overview. In: International Conference on Software Process Improvement and Capability Determinations (SPICE), Turku, Finland (2009)
20. Denger, C., Feldmann, R., Host, M., Lindholm, C., Shull, F.: A Snapshot of the State of Practice in Software Development for Medical Devices. In: First International Symposium on Empirical Software Engineering and Measurement, Madrid, Spain (2007)
21. Mc Caffery, F., Coleman, G.: The Need for a Software Process Improvement Model for the Medical Device Industry. International Review on Computers and Software Journal 2(1), 10–15 (2007)

22. Mc Caffery, F., Dorling, A.: Medi SPICE Development. Software Process Maintenance and Evolution: Improvement and Practice Journal 22(4), 255–268 (2010)
23. Casey, V., Mc Caffery, F.: Medi SPICE and the Development of a Process Reference Model for Inclusion in IEC 62304. In: The 7th International Conference on Software Paradigm Trends (ICSOFT), Rome, Italy (2012)
24. ISO/IEC 12207:2008, Systems and software engineering - Software life cycle processes. ISO, Geneva (2008)
25. ISO/IEC 15504-5:2012, Information technology - Process Assessment - Part 5: An Exemplar Software Life Cycle Process Assessment Model. ISO, Geneva (2012)
26. Mc Caffery, F., Donnelly, P., Dorling, A., Wilkie, F.G.: A Software Process Development Assessment and Improvement Framework for the Medical Device Industry. In: The Fourth International SPICE Conference, Lisbon, Portugal (2004)
27. CMMI Product Team, Capability Maturity Model® Integration for Development Version 1.2. Software Engineering Institute, Pittsburgh, PA (2006)
28. ISO/IEC 15504-5:2006, Information technology - Process Assessment - Part 5: An Exemplar Process Assessment Model. ISO, Geneva (2006)
29. Casey, V., Mc Caffery, F.: Med-Trace: Traceability Assessment Method for Medical Device Software Development. In: European Systems and Software Process Improvement and Innovation Conference. Roskilde University, Denmark (2011)
30. Automotive SIG, Automotive SPICE Process Assessment V 2.2 (August 21, 2005)
31. Cass, A., Volcker, C., Winzer, L., Carranza, J.M., Dorling, A.: SPiCE for SPACE: A Process Assessment and Improvement Method for Space Software Development. ESA Bulletin 107, 112–119 (2001)
32. Mc Caffery, F., Coleman, G.: Developing a Configuration Management Capability Model (CMCM) for the Medical Device Industry. International Journal of Information Systems and Change Management 2(2), 139–154 (2007)
33. Mc Caffery, F., Burton, J., Richardson, I.: Development and Evaluation of a Risk Management Capability Model (RMCM) for the Medical Device Industry, Nuremberg, Germany (2008)
34. ISO/IEC 12207:1995, Information Technology — Software life Cycle Processes. ISO, Geneva (1995)
35. ANSI/AAMI SW68:2001, Medical device software - Software life cycle processes. AMMI, Arlington (2001)
36. ANSI/AAMI/IEC 62304:2006, Medical device software - Software life cycle processes. AAMI, Arlington (2006)
37. ISO/IEC 12207:1995/Amd.1, Information Technology — Software life Cycle Processes Amendment 1. ISO, Geneva (2002)
38. ISO/IEC 12207:1995/Amd.2, Information Technology — Software life Cycle Processes Amendment 2. ISO, Geneva (2004)
39. Walker, D.W.: CMMI and Medical Device Engineering. Software Engineering Institute (September 29, 2009)
40. Fabbrini, F., Fusani, M., Lami, G., Sivera, E.: Software Engineering in the European Automotive Industry: Achievements and Challenges. In: 32nd Annual IEEE International Computer Software and Applications, COMPSAC 2008 (2008)
41. Casey, V.: Developing Trust in Virtual Software Development Teams. Journal of Theoretical and Applied Electronic Commerce Research 5(2), 41–58 (2010)
42. ISO/IEC 15288:2002, Systems Engineering — System life cycle processes. ISO, Geneva (2002)
43. ISO/IEC 15504-2:2003, Software engineering - Process assessment - Part 2: Performing an assessment. ISO, Geneva (2003)

An Approach to Development of an Application Dependent SPICE Conformant Process Capability Model

Michael Boronowsky[1], Antanas Mitasiunas[2], Jonas Ragaisis[2],
and Tanja Woronowicz[1]

[1] Bremen University, TZI, Am Fallturm 1, Bremen, 28359, Germany
[2] Vilnius University, 3 Universiteto Street, Vilnius, LT-01315, Lithuania
mb@tzi.de, antanas.mitasiunas@maf.vu.lt,
jonas.ragaisis@gmail.com, worono@tzi.de

Abstract. The Process capability modeling elaborated by the world-wide software engineering community during the last 25 years became a tool for systematization and codifying knowledge and experience of process oriented activities. This tool is designed to improve the predictability of activity results, i.e. process capability. Namely, ISO/IEC 15504 defines a process capability dimension and the requirements for any external process definition to be applicable process capability dimension. Enterprise SPICE defines a domain-independent integrated model for enterprise-wide assessments and pertinent improvement. On the other hand, any application domain contains application specific knowledge and experience that is not covered in width and depth by domain independent process modeling. The purpose of this paper is to address the problem of application dependent SPICE conformant process modeling integrated with application independent components. It will be illustrated with the developer processes of the innovation, knowledge and technology transfer process model innoSPICE.

Keywords: innovation and knowledge transfer, process capability model, SPICE, Enterprise SPICE, innoSPICE.

1   Introduction

Some three decades ago, software developers started to seek for established and confirmed procedures and solutions to cope with the software crisis that was caused by recurrently exceeding project costs and schedules as well as the failure of functionality and quality. Inspired by traditional engineers, the software engineering community has developed standards and models such as ISO/IEC 15504 and CMMI that have been used by numerous software organizations around the world for guiding tremendous improvements in their ability to improve productivity and quality. The concept of software process capability, which expresses process predictability, became an efficient working tool for process and product quality management.

The results of software engineering in terms of software process are generalized to any process capability assessment and improvement. Based on these experiences

T. Woronowicz et al. (Eds.): SPICE 2013, CCIS 349, pp. 61–72, 2013.

other domains, such as education and innovation management, started a pioneering way following the software engineers: Software engineering as an extremely creative activity was expressed in process oriented terms. The validated innovation and technology transfer process capability maturity model and the education process capability model [1-3, 13] are further successful confirmations of the expression of creative activities in the sense of knowledge intense and little determinacy in process oriented terms.

The purpose of this paper is to provide a methodology for application dependent SPICE conformant process modeling integrated with application independent components. This concept will be discussed based on the example of the innovation, knowledge and technology transfer developer process capability model innoSPICE.

State of the art in process capability maturity modeling and innovation, knowledge and technology transfer process modeling is provided in sections 2. The sections 3, 4 and 5 contain the authors' contribution to process capability maturity modeling and its application to innovation, knowledge and technology transfer. Section 6 proposes a process capability improvement approach for innovation, knowledge and technology transfer based on a guided self-assessment for motivation of application domain dependent process capability modeling. The last section concludes the achieved results and provides future.

2   Motivation and Process Capability Modeling

How to keep software projects within planned scope, schedule and resources? Out of all the innovative disclosures only 1% to 2% result in really successful commercial enterprises [8]. How to achieve better results in knowledge and technology commercialization? How to improve education? How to improve learning? How to improve export? How to improve public sector institutions' services? How to improve enterprises' performance? There are many more of similar questions. Some of these tasks are already resolved, some are under development and some to be addressed in the future. These tasks are different. At the same time a need for improvement of process oriented activities is common for all these tasks, if learning is a process oriented activity, too.

Process capability modeling elaborated by the world-wide software engineering community during the last 25 years became a tool for systematization and codifying knowledge and experiences of process oriented activities. This is designed to improve the predictability of activities' results, i.e. the activities' process capability. As the result of the process capability modeling evolution, ISO/IEC 15504 defines a process capability dimension and the requirements for any external process definition to be applicable within process dimension. Enterprise SPICE defines a domain independent integrated model for enterprise-wide assessments and improvement.

The software engineering community has considerably contributed to the state of the art of process modeling: when numerous attempts to solve the software crisis applying technological and methodological approaches were not successful, software engineers consequently turned to organizational issues aiming to keep software projects within the planned scope, schedule and resources.

This approach is based on the assumption that product quality can be achieved by the means of process quality – process capability. High process capability cannot be established at once during the launch of an activity. It only can be improved applying an iterative procedure of process capability assessments and improvement. The research in this area is based on ideas which originated from capability maturity models (CMM) developed since 1987 by the Software Engineering Institute (SEI) of Carnegie Melon University. These models have evolved into CMMI version 1.3 [4-6] known as CMMI for Development, CMMI for Acquisition and CMMI for Services.

In parallel, the international community has developed an international standard for process assessment ISO/IEC 15504: Process assessment framework, also known as project SPICE (Software Process Improvement and Capability dEtermination) initiated by the Ministry of Defence of UK in 1991 [11, 12]. ISO/IEC 15504 represents the third generation of process capability maturity models that refer to an external process reference model. The process capability assessment framework is defined in the normative part of ISO/IEC 15504-2. In this context, an approach taken by ISO/IEC 15504 referring to the external process reference model is particularly important. It enables to extend a model's application area outside the software engineering. An external process reference model must satisfy the requirements of process definition in terms of process purpose and outcomes.

The third main source in the process capability maturity arena is iCMM v2.0 (integrated Capability Maturity Model), leading to the issues of model integration and architecture representation, developed by US Federal Aviation Administration in 2001. It had significant impact on the current state of CMMs area [10] and is along the same lines as ISO/IEC 15504 (SPICE) and CMMI models. Based on the external process reference model approach, the convergence of SPICE and iCMM models is possible and, in fact, it is completed as the Enterprise SPICE initiative. FAA iCMM was the baseline during the development of SPICE based Enterprise Process Reference Model (PRM) and a supplementing Process Assessment Model (PAM). Enterprise SPICE has been developed by a joint effort of more than one hundred experts representing 31 countries from all continents. The first stage of Enterprise SPICE [7] project is completed now and the draft of the future standard is publicly available.

Hundreds of various generic and specific organizational maturity models have been developed. Among them [16] is of particular importance in this context. These models mainly provide the characteristics of maturity levels. However, very few of them provide a decomposition of an activity modeled as a collection of processes defined in minimal terms, namely, a process name, a process purpose and the process outcomes.

3   An Adjusted Approach to Process Capability Modeling

The main idea of this work is to integrate an application dependent SPICE conformant process modeling with the application independent capability dimension and process dimension components. The goal of such integration is to keep the application dependent component as simple as possible and to maximize the reusable part of the solution for improvement results of process oriented activity.

ISO/IEC 15504 introduces the concepts of a capability measurement framework and of an external process model. This enables to limit the effort for the creation of a process capability model: only the creation of a SPICE conformant external process model is needed and the existing capability dimension can be reused. In addition, Enterprise SPICE as a generic SPICE conformant and domain independent external process model can be applied. It consists of Life cycle, Organizational and Support process categories. Enterprise SPICE is defined at a quite abstract and low granularity level. However any application domain contains application specific knowledge and experience that cannot be comprised in width and deep by domain independent process modeling. In order to express domain dependent issues, the processes of Application category should be defined to address the body of knowledge of a particular application area that is not represented at sufficient level by Life cycle, Organizational and Support process categories of the Enterprise SPICE process model. Therefore, the development of SPICE conformant process capability model for particular application domain can be restricted by the development of Application category processes description only. Enterprise SPICE model applies quite close however not identical concept of Application area introduced in [9] that consists of application practices. An application practice is implemented by the set of base practices that belong to one or more Enterprise SPICE processes. To assess the capability of an application area and application practices the associated base practices shall be assessed in the context of their performance for application practices. In this case the body of knowledge of application area should implicitly define performance context of base practice to be assessed.

The purpose of Application process category concept introduced here is to reflect directly the body of knowledge in terms of essential processes and base practices of application that are not represented by Enterprise SPICE model at the extent needed by the improvement task in width and depth. An example of such processes for innovation, knowledge and technology transfer area could be the 'Research and Development project proposal preparation process' provided in the section 5.

The application of provided methodology enables to develop application dependent process capability model which is an ISO/IEC 15504 conformant model that reuses the ISO/IEC 15504 capability framework. It also reuses the Life cycle, Organizational and Support process categories from the Enterprise SPICE process dimension and provides the Application category's processes which satisfy the requirements to process definition established by ISO/IEC 15504. The Application category can consist of processes that further extend or detail the Life cycle, Organizational and Support process categories. For instance, in the case of public administration institutions services improvement, the Application category should extend and detail the Organizational and Support process categories.

4   Innovation, Knowledge and Technology Transfer Process Capability Modeling

Innovation, knowledge and technology transfer improvement is a complex domain with many intangible benefits and obstacles. Conventionally/formally, the management of innovation, knowledge and technology transfer activities was a black box approach comparing its inputs and outputs or using statistical data. The approach taken by the development of innoSPICE was the "white box" approach, i.e. the innovation, knowledge and technology transfer activities were decomposed into a set of processes and their performance descriptions. An important concern about such approach is how they reflect on the creative aspects of any innovation and transfer activity. Of course, creativity can't be modeled by process-based notions but the question arises: "Is the transfer of knowledge and technologies towards innovation a completely creative activity?" If yes, then a process oriented approach would not be suitable to create an innovation, knowledge and technology transfer model.

The approach to codify process oriented knowledge for activity modeling is based on the successful experience of the software engineering community in software development process modeling. At first sight, software development can be seen as a completely creative activity. However, it was modeled by tens of processes, hundreds of practices and work products. Of course, there remain creative elements, but they do not eliminate the process oriented approach as a whole.

Process capability is related to process predictability. Organizational maturity expresses the way how an organization's activities are performed - the improvement path of these activities to achieve better results. The process capability concept enables measuring the state of performance of the organization's activities and to plan specific steps for processes capability improvement. A process high capability cannot be established at once during the launch of an activity. It only can be increased applying an iterative procedure of process capability assessments and improvement actions.

An innovation concept is close to the understanding of improvement, because an innovation contains inherent improvement. Per definition, an innovation is a new product, process, service or work environment implemented with value [14]. Thus, an innovative organization is improving organization. And thus knowledge transformation to value and/ or knowledge commercialization is an innovation process.

The full value chain of innovation can be modeled consisting of three pure roles: knowledge development, transfer of knowledge and its implementation. In the real world set up, organizations can perform one, two or all three of these pure roles. Fundamental research institutions, for example, perform mainly knowledge development while applied research institutions often develop knowledge and transfer it into practice. Industrial corporations can develop knowledge, transfer and implement it. The knowledge and best practice experiences related to these three roles compose body of modeling innovation, knowledge and technology transfer.

The process capability modeling approach can be applied to improve innovativeness of an organization. Modeling of organization's domain independent activities can reuse Enterprise SPICE Organizational, Life cycle and Support process categories. The innovation related activities can be modeled by the Application process category that respectively consists of three subcategories covering the pure roles of the entire innovation process: knowledge development, transfer and implementation.

Enterprise SPICE processes are ISO/IEC 15504 conformant. To be able to apply the ISO/IEC 15504 capability framework, the processes of the Application category also must satisfy the requirements of ISO/IEC 15504 to process descriptions. From there, an application dependent ISO/IEC 15504 conformant process capability model can be build by:

- development of an Application process category;
- reuse of Enterprise SPICE Organizational, Life cycle and Support process categories;
- reuse of ISO/IEC 15504 capability framework.

Following this approach to application domain dependent process capability model architecture in the case of innoSPICE model Application process category can be represented by innoSPICE Primary process category. As an example of application category processes of the innovation, knowledge and technology transfer process capability model innoSPICE, the knowledge development subcategory is provided in the next section.

5   innoSPICE Knowledge Development Process Subcategory

The research on knowledge development is addressed by many authors. Particularly [8, 17] provide a structured approach to knowledge development, its transfer and implementation in the context of research and industry collaboration. The description of research maturity levels is provided in [15]. At a high abstraction level, the knowledge development activity can be modeled by an application area concept introduced in [9] by referencing to Research and innovation process and Life cycle process category defined in [7].

According to ISO/IEC 15504-2, requirements for a PRM process description must comply in minimal terms of process purpose and outcomes that are achieved as a result of the successful process implementation. In addition to the PRM a Process Assessment Model contains a set of indicators – base practices that explicitly addresses the purpose and outcomes, as defined in the PRM, and that demonstrate the achievement of the process attributes within. The description of several innoSPICE processes [1-2] that can be attributed to Application process category knowledge is provided in Table 1.

Table 1. innoSPICE knowledge and technology development processes

APP.1. Research and Development Project Proposal Preparation	
Process Purpose	To develop and submit a competitive research and development project proposal for a target research and development program according to the program's objectives, priorities and requirements
Process Outcomes	1) Research and Development programs related to innovation and knowledge and technology transfer are identified; 2) R&D program's objectives, priorities and requirements are analysed; 3) Interest in project proposal submission is confirmed; 4) The feasibility of potentially winning the project proposal is analysed and the knowledge creation project proposal concept is generated; 5) Decision for the project proposal preparation is taken; 6) The consortium for submission and implementation of a competitive research and development project proposal is build; 7) A competitive knowledge creation project proposal is developed according to the target program's objectives, priorities and requirements, and submitted in the time established by the program.

Table 1. (*continued*)

Process Base Practices
BP1: Identify Research and Development Program. [Outcome 1]
BP2: Analyze Research and Development Program. [Outcome 2]
BP3: Confirm the Interest in Project Proposal Submission. [Outcome 3]
BP4: Analyze Feasibility of Competitive Project Proposal Preparation. [Outcome 4]
BP5: Take a Decision for Project Proposal Preparation and Submission. [Outcome 5]
BP6: Generate Research and Development Project Proposal Concept. [Outcome 4]
BP7: Build the Consortium. [Outcome 6]
BP8: Establish Research and Development Project Proposal Preparation Strategy. [Outcome 7]
BP9: Develop Research and Development Project Proposal. [Outcome 7]
BP10: Submit Research and Development Project Proposal. [Outcome 7]
BP11: Communicate with Program's Authorities. [Outcome 7]

APP.2. Applied Science Knowledge Creation	
Process Purpose	To create new applied science knowledge and/or technology having commercial potential by applying and adapting basic science knowledge for domain-specific applications
Process Outcomes	1) The domain specific problem to be solved related to knowledge / technology commercialization is identified; 2) The domain specific problem to be solved related to knowledge/ technology commercialization is analyzed; 3) An overview of potentially interesting basic scientific knowledge and successful applications is performed; 4) An overview of adaptations of basic scientific results to the domain specific application is performed; 5) New applied scientific knowledge is created, i.e., the basic scientific results are adapted and, tools and methods are developed accordingly to the domain-specific problem to be solved; 6) Experiments are performed to confirm adequacy of the new proposed applied scientific knowledge; 7) Results of the experiments are analyzed and interpreted.

Process Base Practices
BP1: Identify External Opportunities. [Outcome 1]
BP2: Identify Internal Opportunities. [Outcome 1]
BP3: Identify Internal Constraints. [Outcome 1]
BP4: Identify Benefits. [Outcome 1]
BP5: Identify Main Difficulties. [Outcome 2]
BP6: Analyze Feasibility. [Outcome 2]
BP7: Perform An Overview. [Outcomes 3, 4]
BP8: Collect Ideas. [Outcomes 2, 5]
BP9: Propose New Solution. [Outcome 5]
BP10: Evaluate the Solution. [Outcome 6]
BP11: Interpret the Solution. [Outcome 7]

Table 1. (*continued*)

APP.3. Experimental Science Knowledge Creation	
Process Purpose	To create new knowledge and/or technology-validating hypothesizes through experiments
Process Outcomes	1) The hypotheses to be validated are identified; 2) The hypotheses to be validated are analyzed; 3) An overview of related experimental validations is performed; 4) New models are proposed and/or validated; 5) The environment for experimentations is designed and set up; 6) Experiments are performed to test the hypotheses; 7) Results of the experiments are analyzed and interpreted.

Process Base Practices
BP1: Identify External Opportunities. [Outcome 1]
BP2: Identify Internal Opportunities. [Outcome 1]
BP3: Identify Benefits. [Outcome 1]
BP4: Identify Main Difficulties. [Outcome 2]
BP5: Analyze Feasibility. [Outcome 2]
BP6: Perform An Overview. [Outcome 3]
BP7: Collect Ideas. [Outcomes 2, 4]
BP8: Propose New Experimental Knowledge. [Outcome 4]
BP9: Identify Required Elements. [Outcome 5]
BP10: Plan the Experiments. [Outcome 5]
BP11: Install the Experimental Environment. [Outcome 5]
BP12: Perform Experiments. [Outcome 6]
BP13: Analyze and Interpret the Results of Experiments. [Outcome 7]

APP.4. Prototype Development	
Process Purpose	To develop a prototype that adapts applied or experimental science results for technological use and adapting technological knowledge for practical use
Process Outcomes	1) The prototype requirements are defined; 2) The prototype requirements are analyzed; 3) An overview of similar implementations is performed; 4) The prototype is designed and developed; 5) The prototype is tested and verified; 6) The prototype is validated and improved if necessary.

Process Base Practices
BP1: Define and Analyze Requirements for Prototype. [Outcomes 1, 2]
BP2: Identify Technological Difficulties. [Outcome 2]
BP3: Perform an Overview. [Outcome 3]
BP4: Identify and Acquire Required External Technology and Knowledge. [Outcome 4]
BP5: Design a Prototype. [Outcome 4]
BP6: Develop a Prototype. [Outcome 4]
BP7: Test and Verify a Prototype. [Outcome 5]
BP8: Evaluate a Prototype. [Outcomes 6]
BP9: Identify Problems. [Outcome 6]
BP10: Identify Improvements. [Outcome 6]

6   Guided Self-assessment Based Process Capability Improvement

An application domain independent process capability model by definition can't contain domain specific features. However, process capability improvement is always domain specific. Such gap can be addressed mainly by external consultants or by the process owner if the process capability model contains domain specific knowledge and enable tracing the model's wording to the organization's activity which should be improved. Application domain dependent process capability model enables a participative approach to process capability improvement introduced here. On the other hand, a participative approach to process capability improvement reinforces the importance of application domain dependent process capability modeling.

A process reference model should be more abstract than a process assessment model. However, a process assessment model always remains more abstract than a real organization's activity model. A unified assessment model must be suitable to assess and represent, in unified terms, the assessment results of various different organizations. On the other hand, the granularity of an assessment model should be sufficiently high to achieve comparable assessment results and to avoid too big assessment mistakes. So, three levels of abstraction of the process dimension can be distinguished:

- Process Reference Model – identification of processes defined in minimal terms, namely, a process name, a process purpose and the process outcomes;
- Process Assessment Model – in addition to process description within the Process Reference Model, it contains the description of several Base Practices and, possibly, work products. Successful performance of base practices ensures the achievement of the process purpose and the process outcomes. The PAM can be understood as a collection of best practices related to an organization's activity that is used as a reference standard for structuring, assessment, comparison and improvement of the organization's activity;
- Activity model – more detailed description of the real activity performed by a particular organization using a wording which is accepted by organization.

Hence, a capability maturity model can be understood as codifying process oriented knowledge. Process capability maturity modeling can be treated as a method, system of notions, "language", tool, best practice etc. It allows the equally the knowledge systematization of process oriented activities and the description of real activities performed by a particular institution. An application dependent capability model can be applied:

- for the assessment of an application area process capability performed by an institution;
- for the exchange of best practices contained within the application area activity model;

- for the definition of target process capability profiles based on assessment results and performance goals; and
- for the improvement of the application area activities to reach a target process capability profile using the available best practices.

The traditional approach to process capability assessment and improvement foresees a formal assessment performed by an external assessor or an assessment team and the preparation of an assessment report including recommendations for process capability improvement. Such an approach suits well for the process capability determination dedicated to external use. However, it is not sufficient for internal process improvement – people tend to agree more easy to perform institution- internally defined processes rather than those defined by third parties.

In this section a participative approach to process assessment and improvement is introduced. According to the participative approach, a process improvement program consists of 6 steps and preliminary to the formal assessment, it includes the development of an application area specific activity model for the assessed institution.

Step 1. *Development of the institution's application area process oriented activity model, by using terms and notions that are used in its daily work based on an participative approach:* While any institution/ enterprise performs specific activities, in many cases these activities are implicit, not documented, , and not expressed by a common vocabulary describing the content and transferring the knowledge and/or experiences on it. The process activity model therefore should be developed applying a participative approach with the personnel as the process owner, guided by a competent consultant using wording and vocabulary as it is used in daily activity.

Step 2. *Mapping of the institution's activity model developed in Step 1 with a standardized application area process capability maturity model:* Process activity models are different in different institutions whereas a process capability assessment should be performed using a unified process assessment model to ensure comparability of process capability assessment results. Therefore processes defined in the process activity model need to be mapped to the process assessment model defining the process assessment scope in standardized terms. The mapping result is a collection of assessable processes that overlap with the activity model's processes.

Step 3. *Guided self-assessment of an institution's application area process capability and conceiving of the actual capability profile:* External supervision is needed to receive comparable assessment results while a self-assessment approach is needed to make the institution's personnel true owner of the process definition. Evidence to establish the process capability will be found in the process activity model, in work products created by real activities and personnel interviews. The results of the institution's application area process capability assessment is produced as a process capability profile. The processes' capability is assessed at first only at capability level 1, i.e. to what extent the process is performed and process goals and process outcomes are achieved. The processes which are fully performed at capability level 1 can be assessed at higher capability levels.

Step 4. *Definition of an institutions' target process capability profile based on its performance goals:* Defining a target process capability profile is a creative work based on an institution's goals and its strategy. One institution might decide to improve those processes having the lowest capability. The decision of another institution might be stressing on core business processes and to further improve their best processes in order to reach a higher capability level. The main challenge that should be addressed is linking the institution's goals and strategy with its processes and their capability.

Step 5. *Update an institutions' application area activity model developed in Step 1 to achieve the target capability profile defined in Step 4:* While an institution will improve its process capability based on a target profile done in terms of standard process assessment model, it will continue the activities based on the internal wording and vocabulary, i.e. it will apply the same or an updated activity model. The application of a process capability maturity model therefore does not mean the rejection of the current activity model and the shift to the standard process assessment models. The PAM is the management tool for process capability improvement only. Using this tool, an institution acquires the knowledge indicating where the institution is and where it wants to go. Thereby the institution can define the appropriate path to achieve a desired goal, i.e., to define improved activity model based on the model developed in Step 1 achieving a target capability profile.

Step 6. *Act according to the updated application area activity model and go to Step 2 for continuous iterative improvement.*

If the process capability improvement is included in application area process, an institution's activities will definitely achieve the needed quality independently of the initial stage of the institution's process capability.

Conclusions and Future Work

The paper provides the following new results in process capability maturity modeling and application area dependent process capability assessment and improvement: A methodology is proposed for SPICE conformant application domain dependent process capability modeling based on the ISO/IEC 15504 capability framework and Enterprise SPICE domain independent external process model; Based on the proposed methodology, an updated architecture of a SPICE conformant Process Assessment Model of innovation, knowledge and technology transfer process capability model innoSPICE is proposed; A participative approach to application domain dependent process capability assessment and improvement is introduced. Following remaining future work should be done: validation of application dependent process capability modeling approach versus application area implementation by referencing to base practices of a domain independent process model. An experience gained in application of methodology proposed for development of application domain dependent process capability models by supplementing missing processes only revealed a weakness of methodology that result in fragmented at some extent body of knowledge developed as an application process category.

References

1. Arelis, S., Besson, J., Mitašiūnas, J., Mitašiūnas, A., Woronowicz, T.: Enhanced innovation and technology transfer model. innoSPICE®: Innovation, Knowledge- and Technology Transfer Capability Maturity Model. Version 1.0, pp. 1–132

2. Besson, J., Woronowicz, T., Mitasiunas, A., Boronowsky, M.: Innovation, Knowledge- and Technology Transfer Process Capability Model – innoSPICE™. In: Mas, A., Mesquida, A., Rout, T., O'Connor, R.V., Dorling, A. (eds.) SPICE 2012. CCIS, vol. 290, pp. 75–84. Springer, Heidelberg (2012)

3. Boronowsky, M., Woronowicz, T., Mitasiunas, A.: BONITA – Improve Transfer from Universities for Regional Development. In: The Proceedings of the 3rd ISPIM Innovation Symposium held in Quebec City, Canada, December 12-15 (2010) ISBN 978-952-265-004-7

4. CMMI-ACQ, CMMI for Acquisition, Version 1.3. Software Engineering Institute (2010)

5. CMMI-DEV, CMMI for Development, Version 1.3. Software Engineering Institute (2010)

6. CMMI-SVC, CMMI for Services, Version 1.3. Software Engineering Institute (2010)

7. Enterprise SPICE. An Integrated Model for Enterprise-wide Assessment and Improvement. Technical Report - Issue 1. The Enterprise SPICE Project Team, 184 psl. (September 2010), http://www.enterprisespice.com/page/publication-1

8. Gardner, P.L., Fong, A.Y., Graham, L.S.: From Innovation to Enterprise – the Role of Technology Commercialization in Sustaining Economic Growth. IEEE. Technology Transfer Division, TRIUMF, Canada (2004)

9. Ibrahim, L., Jarzombek, J., Ashford, M., Bate, R., Croll, P., Horn, M., LaBruyere, L., Wells, C.: Safety and Security Extensions for Integrated Capability Maturity Models. U.S. Federal Aviation Administration (2004)

10. Ibrahim, L., Bradford, B., Cole, D., LaBruyere, L., Leinneweber, H., Piszczek, D., Reed, N., Rymond, M., Smith, D., Virga, M., Wells, C.: FAA-iCMM. The Federal Aviation Administration Integrated Capability Maturity Model for Enterprise-wide Improvement. U.S. Federal Aviation Administration (2001)

11. ISO/IEC 15504-2, Information Technology – Process Assessment – Part 2: Performing an Assessment. International Standards Organization (2003)

12. ISO/IEC 15504-5, Information Technology – Process Assessment – Part 5: An Exemplar Process Assessment Model. International Standards Organization (2006)

13. Mitasiunas, A., Novickis, L.: Enterprise SPICE based education capability maturity model. In: Niedrite, L., Strazdina, R., Wangler, B. (eds.) BIR 2011 Workshops. LNBIP, vol. 106, pp. 102–116. Springer, Heidelberg (2012)

14. Oslo Manual. Guidelines for Collecting and Interpreting Innovation data. A Joint publication of OECD and Eurostat, 3rd edn. (2005)

15. Narasimhalu, A.D.: PA Research Capability Maturity Model for Managing Technological Innovations. In: PICMET 2006 Proceedings, Istambul, Turkey, July 9-13 (2006)

16. People Capability Maturity Model (P-CMM), Version 2.0, 2nd edn. Software Engineering Institute, Carnegie Mellon University. CMU/SEI-2009-TR-003, ESC-TR-2009-003 (2009)

17. Rombach, D.H., Achatz, R.: Research Collaborations between Academia and Industry. In: Future of Software Engineering (FOSE 2007). IEEE-CS Press, Washington, DC (2007) ISBN 0-7695-2829-5/07

An Improvement of Process Reference Model Design and Validation Using Business Process Management

Olivier Mangin[1], Nicolas Mayer[1], Béatrix Barafort[1], Patrick Heymans[2], and Eric Dubois[1]

[1] Public Research Center Henri Tudor,
29, av. J. F. Kennedy, L-1855 Luxembourg-Kirchberg, Luxembourg
{olivier.mangin,nicolas.mayer,beatrix.barafort,
eric.dubois}@tudor.lu
http://www.tudor.lu
[2] PReCISE, University of Namur, INRIA Lille-Nord Europe
Université Lille 1 – LIFL – CNRS, France
patrick.heymans@fundp.ac.be

Abstract. During the design of a Process Reference Model (PRM), the modeler needs to describe processes. According to ISO/IEC 15504-2, each process shall be described in terms of a process purpose and process outcomes. The process purpose is "*the high level measurable objectives of performing the process and the likely outcomes of effective implementation of the process*". A process outcome is "*an observable result of a process*". The set of process outcomes shall be necessary and sufficient to achieve the purpose of the process. However, no method exists as ISO proposes requirements and guidelines (respectively in ISO/IEC 15504-2 and ISO/IEC 24774 for process description) for developing process models. So there is a need to support the development of a process model and the verification of the completeness of the process outcomes in the context of process design. This article proposes a structured approach to answer this challenge based on business process management and requirements engineering principles. We especially consider the use of both the transformative view and coordination view of a process to support the design and the validation of PRM processes based on a collection of requirements.

Keywords: Process Reference Model, ISO/IEC 15504, process design, process validation, process verification.

1   Introduction

In 2003, the International Organization for Standardization (ISO) published the ISO/IEC 15504-2 standard [4] for performing process assessment. This standard is part of a series providing the requirements to conduct a process assessment and to design process models; guidelines for process improvement or capability determination; and exemplar process models. These assessment standards are not limited to a specific field of activity; there can be applied to various industry sectors. The most

T. Woronowicz et al. (Eds.): SPICE 2013, CCIS 349, pp. 73–83, 2013.

known applications of ISO/IEC 15504 are software development life cycle processes (ISO/IEC 15504-5), Automotive SPICE [2], and Enterprise SPICE [3].

Performing a process assessment requires two process models. The ISO/IEC 15504-2 [4] is the standard which gives the minimum requirements for process model design. The first process model is the Process Reference Model (PRM). It contains "*definitions of processes in a life cycle described in terms of process purpose and outcomes, together with an architecture describing the relationships between the processes*" [23]. The second one is the Process Assessment Model (PAM) which is a framework "*suitable for the purpose of assessing process capability, based on one or more Process Reference Models*" [23]. A main issue in the design of a PRM is that ISO/IEC 15504 gives requirements on what should contain a PRM but there are no guidelines or recommendations in order to ensure that the set of outcomes is necessary and sufficient to achieve the purpose of the process and then the completeness of the process.

In Business Process Management (BPM) literature, a process has multiple definitions. In one hand, the ISO [18] defines "*a process as a set of interrelated or interacting activities which transforms inputs into outputs*". This is the *transformative view* of a process. On the other hand, business process researchers emphasize the fact that the processes require communicative actions between interested parties in order to fulfill the process purpose [1]. This is the *coordination view* of a process. In this context, several studies consider the process as a transaction between two interested parties: a customer and a supplier. In this study, we consider the use of these two views to support the design of PRM. In particular, the coordination view, which does not appear at the ISO standard level, will guide the modeler to verify the completeness of the process outcomes.

According to Keen [1], the transformative view is too restrictive. This definition excludes the processes that have no clear flows between sub tasks. That is the reason why we also propose to introduce methods which highlight these flows inside a process. Multiple studies [13, 14] recommend a way to express these transactions. In this paper, we thus propose to enhance the elaboration of process descriptions, conforming with the requirements given in the ISO/IEC 15504-2 standard, with the existing practice using *Goal Oriented Requirements Engineering* (GORE) modeling techniques [21], and a lifecycle model: the Action Workflow Loop (AWL) [13], extracted from BPM literature. We will show how we use the combination of GORE and AWL to support and validate a design of ISO/IEC 15504 compliant processes when this activity is based on a collection of requirements such as depicted in Fig. 1. The use of AWL will ensure the completeness of a process.

To summarize, the purpose of this paper is to propose a structured approach to support design and validation of process descriptions in the context of the elaboration of a PRM based on a collection of requirements using GORE techniques to design the processes with their outcomes and AWL which highlights the coordination view of the processes to ensure its completeness. Please note this paper does not intend to provide a method at the standard level to design PRMs. This paper is organized as follows: Section 2 exposes the related works concerning process model design. Section 3 discusses the selected method to ensure the completeness of the process.

Section 4 explains the structured approach we propose to support process validation. Section 5 focuses on its application on the ISO/IEC 27001 PRM design, a standard giving the requirements for Information Security Management System [22]. Finally, Section 6 draws conclusions.

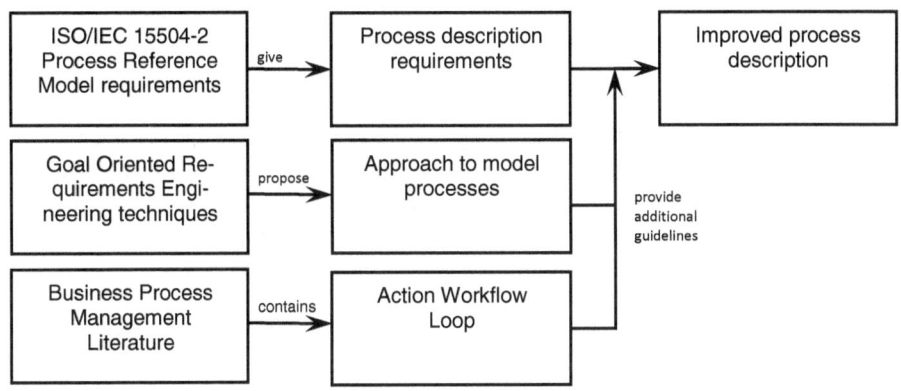

Fig. 1. Overview of the involved concepts

2   State of the Art

Process Reference Model design is subject of growing interest in the literature. Since ISO/IEC 15504 is not limited to software development processes, many initiatives proposed PRM and PAM for various domains such as automotive sector [2], enterprise processes [3], IT security [17], IT service management [5, 6], knowledge management [7], internal financial control [8], industrial processes [9], regulation compliance [10], public university research laboratories [11], and medical devices [20]. However, these papers presenting new process models do not focus on their design method. They present their new process model and its context of use and give very few details on how they were designed.

Regarding articles describing the design of a process model, we identified two different approaches. The first one [9] consists in extracting processes and their outcomes from subject matter experts in the corresponding community of practice, e.g., through interviews, workshops and surveys. But in very specific domains such as information security, this may be hard to achieve due to limited resources dedicated to this design and/or the difficulty to find the adequate experts to consult. Indeed it requires persons to be found with both expertise: in the ISO/IEC 15504 standard and in the application domain of the process model. Moreover, it may be difficult to reach a consensus on the processes and outcomes among the different experts through weakly structured interviews.

The second method uses a goal tree based methodology [6, 15]. From the experience of the authors, they noticed that experts of the community of practice do not like to read and analyze textual description of processes, and their comments tend to focus more on the form than on the core of the process model. The use of goal trees, thus, helps to refocus the experts on the core concepts of the model thanks to a graphical representation.

In a similar way, Rifaut and Dubois [10] defined a PRM from the Basel II regulation. They started by extracting a flat list of requirements from the regulation. They separated implementation practices (*How*) from business goals (*What*). Then, they used a GORE modeling technique to discover the purpose of the various requirements, and group them according to their high level goal. They used goal diagrams to structure outcomes and indicators. Rifaut and Dubois claim that the usage of GORE techniques demonstrates the full coverage of the regulation and allows keeping traceability between purposes and outcomes. Nevertheless, this method necessitates a formal collection of requirements including clear role definition and it does not ensure that the designed process is complete. We propose to use a light version of this method, explained in section 4, to design a first version of the processes.

3   The Action Workflow Loop

The ISO/IEC 15504-2 standard requires that the set of process outcomes constitutes the conditions necessary and sufficient to achieve the purpose of the process. But this standard does not explain how to verify the completeness of the process outcomes. As mentioned in the introduction, the ISO considers a process as the set of actions which transform the inputs into outputs [18]. But according to Keen [1], a process requires coordination. Based on this view, business processes follow multiples phases: requests, offers, agreements and commitments.

This theory is based on project lifecycle management. In 1988, Peter W. G. Morris [12] highlighted the existence of an invariant sequence in project management. At first, a demand exists. Then a study is made to answer this demand. This study, after an evaluation, receives the authorization to be implemented and developed. Once the project on action, it needs to be maintained and tested to find opportunities of new demands. In this section, we present how this concept has been transformed to fit the business process context.

In 1992, Medina-Mora et al. [13] applied this lifecycle concept to support work in organizations. He created the AWL which breaks down the business process as a loop constituted of four generic phases (see Fig. 2.). He describes the phases as follow:

— **Proposal:** the customer requests (or the performer offers) completion of a particular action according to some stated conditions of satisfaction
— **Agreement:** the two parties come to mutual agreement on the conditions of satisfaction [...]. This agreement is only partially explicit in the negotiations, resting on a shared background of assumptions and standard practices.
— **Performance:** the performer declares to the customer that the action is complete.
— **Satisfaction:** the customer declares to the performer that the completion is satisfactory.

Therefore, these generic communicative steps can be used to describe a process. The process is achieved thanks to agreements between the governance and the performer of the process. In the context of our article, to highlight the existence of these four steps in the process outcomes is a good way to verify if the process is complete. Indeed, if the process outcomes consider the four phases, then the achievement of the process will perform the loop.

In [14], van der Aalst introduces a BPM lifecycle which is an extension of the AWL. The BPM considers also a lifecycle composed of four phases. While the three first phases does not introduce new concepts, the fourth phase, namely the diagnosis phase, analyses the process to identify problems and find opportunities for improvement. In our context, this phase is not relevant. The ISO/IEC 15504 requires the process outcomes to be the minimum activities to achieve the process purpose. This requirement excludes improvement activities from the process outcome list. This is the reason why we do not consider this BPM lifecycle in our study.

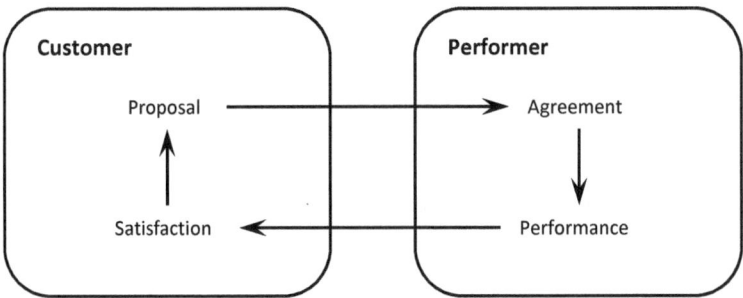

Fig. 2. The action workflow loop

4   A Structured Approach to Support Process Validation

In this article, we propose to combine the use of the GORE techniques based on the method given in [10] and the use of the AWL to design PRM and to ensure the completeness of the process descriptions in particular for process outcomes required by the ISO/IEC 15504-2. This approach is divided in four tasks described below. The next section will illustrate through examples this approach.

4.1   Reformulate Requirements in an Atomic Requirement List

At first, we broke down the collection of requirements into atomic requirements, which is a recognized best practice in *Requirements Engineering*. An atomic requirement is a requirement that cannot be further decomposed into multiple requirements. This can be done by splitting sentences containing multiple verbs and multiple objects. These requirements are collected in a list.

4.2   Elicit the Process Based on Requirement Purposes

In order to complete this task, the requirements from the list are considered as potential outcomes for the processes. A technical and semantic analysis is done to discover what the purpose of each requirement is. Once the purposes of all the requirements are identified, the requirements are gathered according to their purpose. These purposes constitute the processes of the PRM.

4.3   Organize the Requirements in Goal Trees

Once the processes identified, the requirements related to each process are organized in trees, i.e., each process is organized as a tree. The name of the process, based on the purpose of the requirements, is the root of the tree. The atomic requirements are the leaves of the trees. These requirements are clustered according to their implied observable result. The observable results are process outcome candidates. The intermediary nodes of the tree are these process outcome candidates. The outcome sentence is written according to the expected observable result of the clustered requirements. It considers also the recommendations from the ISO/IEC TR 24774 [19]. This technical report provides guidelines for process description such as *"An outcome shall be phrased as a declarative sentence using a verb in the present tense"*.

4.4   Verify the Completeness of the Process Outcomes

Once these process outcomes identified, we still need to verify if their completion allows the achievement of the process purpose. At this given time, we use the AWL introduced in the previous section. The purpose of this task is to verify if the set of process outcomes covers all the phases of the loop. This verification is done by checking if each outcome corresponds to a phase of the loop, i.e., proposal, agreement, performance, and satisfaction. Note that an outcome can correspond to multiple phases.

An outcome corresponding to the *proposal* phase considers an activity which is collecting the information for the execution of the process. This phase can be the identification or the definition of the objectives of the process. An outcome corresponding to the *agreement* phase consists of verifying if the collected information is adequate. This phase can be the management approval of the objectives previously identified. An outcome corresponding to the *performance* phase is made up of all the core activities of the process. This phase can be the performance of the activities or the supply of the resource to fulfill the objectives of the process. Finally, an outcome corresponding to the *satisfaction* phase includes all the actions undertaken to monitor the activities completed during the previous phases. This phase can be the communication, the review or the monitoring of the previous activities.

If this verification fails, at least one outcome must be added or transformed to consider all the phases of the loop. In this case, a new iteration of the third step can be done, or new requirements can be proposed for addition in the source document (i.e. an ISO standard) to create a new process outcome. A full example of this approach is given in the next section.

5   An Application to the ISO/IEC 27001 Standard

The ISO/IEC 27001 [22] is a standard in the field of information security. This document gives a list of requirements, structured in clauses, which are necessary in the establishment of an Information Security Management System (ISMS). In the case of the translation of the ISO/IEC 27001 standard in a PRM, the proposed approach has been applied to design information security management processes. The full study is presented in [16]. That study focuses on generic management system processes which are elaborated through the reuse of another PRM [24] covering the requirements of an IT service management system given in the ISO/IEC 20000-1 standard [25], and also presents specific Information Security processes.

5.1   Reformulate Requirements in an Atomic Requirement List

At first, we broke down the ISO/IEC 27001 normative sentences into atomic requirements. For example, the requirement from the clause 4.2.1 of the ISO/IEC 27001: *"Identify and evaluate options for the treatment of risks"* This requirement is split into 2 atomic requirements: *"Identify options for the treatment of risks by applying appropriate controls"* and *"Evaluate options for the treatment of risks by applying appropriate controls"*. At the end of this operation, the ISO/IEC 27001 standard yielded 273 atomic requirements. In the context of this paper, we limited the study to a subset of 55 atomic requirements. Indeed, most of the atomic requirements of the standard were already treated according to a methodology explained in [16] which reuses existing descriptions of management system processes.

5.2   Elicit the Process Based on Requirement Goals

To elicit processes from these requirements, we gathered the requirements according to their goal. In the previous sub section, the requirements *"Identify options for the treatment of risks by applying appropriate controls"* and *"Evaluate options for the treatment of risks by applying appropriate controls"* were identified. Their goal is to complete a risk treatment process. A "Risk Treatment" process is created. The purpose of risk treatment process is to select controls to reduce, retain, avoid, or transfer the identified risks. The other requirements are found by performing a key-word based search on the atomic requirement list. In this example, we used the key-word *"treatment"*. A set of 26 atomic requirements from the list are linked to this process.

5.3   Organize the Requirements in Goal Trees

Based on the previous example, the requirements are organized in trees. During this task, process outcomes are written. In our example, the requirements *"Identify options for the treatment of risks by applying appropriate controls"* and *"Evaluate options for the treatment of risks by applying appropriate controls"* are brought together to develop the outcome *"Options for the treatment of risks are identified and evaluated"*. As displayed on Fig. 3, the root node is the name of the process, the leaf nodes are the atomic requirements, and the intermediary nodes are the process outcomes.

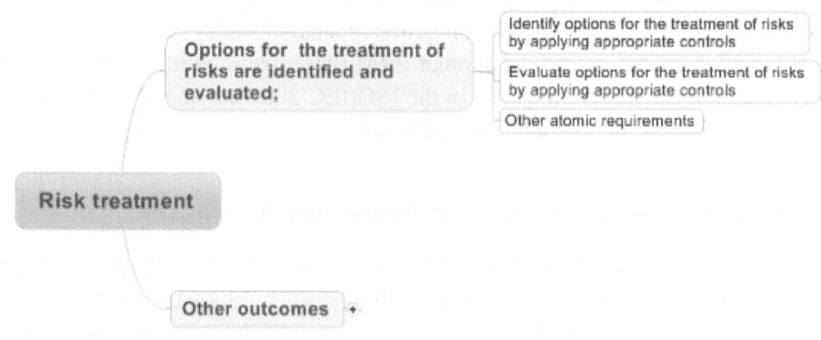

Fig. 3. Design of the risk treatment process goal tree

5.4   Verify the Completeness of the Process Outcomes

The next step consists to determine if the process outcomes cover the 4 phases of the AWL. This example explains the transformation of another process, the *"Risk Assessment"* process. This process is already modeled in a goal tree depicted in Fig. 4. The purpose of this process is to identify assets and the risks they face. The intermediary nodes of the tree depicted in Fig. 4 are the process outcomes. The first two outcomes of the tree sketched in Fig. 4 are: *"A suited risk assessment approach is selected according to the business context, and the legal and regulatory environment;"*, and *"criteria for accepting risks are developed;"*. These two outcomes make up the proposal phase of the process. Indeed, these outcomes are preparing the core activity of the process. The core activities of the process corresponding to the performance phase of the loop are the three next outcomes namely *"assets and their owners are identified;"*, *"risks are identified using the risk assessment approach;"*, and *"identified risks are analyzed and evaluated;"*. The last outcome *"risks are monitored according to reviews, audits and ISMS scope modifications."* makes up the satisfaction phase of the process.

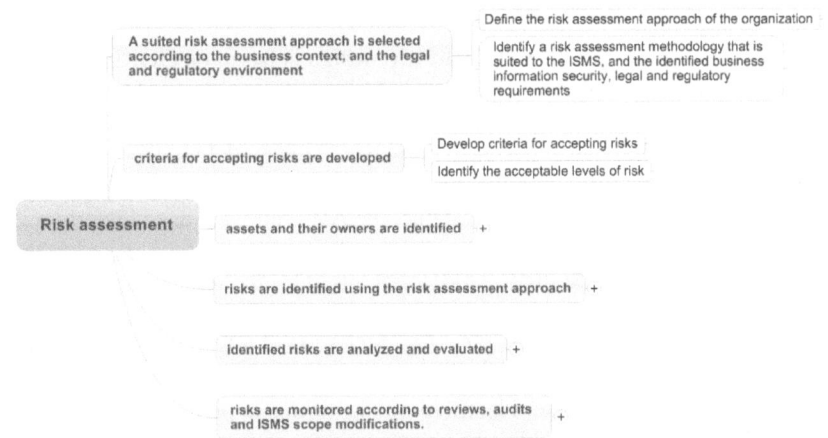

Fig. 4. First version of the risk assessment goal tree

At that moment, no process outcome was linked with the second phase of the AWL namely the agreement phase. We thus inspected the requirement list to find the requirements linked to the missing phase. The missing outcome was about an agreement on the criteria for accepting between the developer of this criteria and the management. We added the process outcome "*criteria for accepting risks are approved by the management;*". The new goal tree is depicted in Fig. 5, it shows the four phases of the AWL. In this case, AWL helped us to discover a missing outcome in our process.

Fig. 5. Risk assessment process goal tree after the AWL Study

6   Conclusion

The approach to support ISO/IEC 15504 PRM design is based on GORE methods and the AWL. The GORE methods helped us to design a first version of the process descriptions. The AWL, stemming from BPM literature, provided a support to verify the completeness of the previously designed processes. This modeling approach is used in the context of the elaboration of a PRM based on the ISO/IEC 27001 requirements.

Such as depicted during the prior example, the AWL allowed us to identify missing elements in process descriptions. These missing elements concerned most of the time the agreement phase. The ISO/IEC 27001 often provides the requirements in a different section of the standard in particular the "Management responsibility" section. This approach has been applied to the ISO/IEC 27001 standard, the elaborated process descriptions consider the four phases of the loop and are, thus, complete. Some missing process outcomes have been identified thanks to this approach such as explained in the previous section. Currently, the requirements concerning approval are in the "*Top management commitment*" section of the ISO/IEC 27001 standard. So the requirement needing management approval is sometimes disconnected from the approval requirement. We think that the standard would be modified to move the approval requirements immediately after their requirements needing approval.

The perspective of this work is to support ISO/IEC 15504 process model designers to enhance their process description with a structured way to create processes and to write the process description. But it does not aim at becoming a prescriptive PRM design approach at the ISO standard level. This structured approach will also be useful in process verification. The AWL part of our approach can be used to verify *a posteriori* the design of a PRM. The process outcomes can be analyzed thanks to the AWL to check the completeness of the process and the quality of the process descriptions.

Acknowledgement. This present project is supported by the National Research Fund, Luxembourg.

References

1. Keen, P.G.W., Inc NetLibrary: The Process Edge: Creating Value Where It Counts. Harvard Business School Press, Boston (1997)
2. http://www.automotivespice.com
3. http://www.enterprisespice.com
4. ISO/IEC 15504-2: Information technology – Process assessment – Part 2: Performing an assessment (2003)
5. Malzahn, D.: A service extension for spice? In: SPICE Conference, Seoul, South Korea (2007)
6. Barafort, B., Renault, A., Picard, M., Cortina, S.: A transformation process for building PRMs and PAMs based on a collection of requirements – example with ISO/IEC 20000. In: SPICE Conference, Nuremberg, Germany (2008)

7. Di Renzo, B., Valoggia, P.: Assessment and improvement of firm's knowledge management capabilities by using a KM process assessment compliant to ISO/IEC 15504. A case study. In: SPICE Conference, Seoul, South Korea (2007)

8. Ivanyos, J.: Implementing process assessment model of internal financial control. In: The International SPICE Days, Frankfurt/Main, Germany (2007)

9. Coletta, A.: An industrial experience in assessing the capability of non-software processes using ISO/IEC 15504. Software Process: Improvement and Practice 12(4), 315–319 (2007)

10. Rifaut, A., Dubois, E.: Using goal-oriented requirements engineering for improving the quality of ISO/IEC 15504 based compliance assessment frameworks. In: 16th IEEE International Requirements Engineering Conference, Barcelona, Spain, vol. 16, pp. 33–42. IEEE Computer Society (2008)

11. Silva, J.V.L., Nabuco, O.F., Salviano, C.F., Reis, M.C., Maciel Filho, R.: Towards an ISO/IEC 15504-based process capability model for public university's research laboratory. In: SPICE Conference, Seoul, South Korea, vol. 2007, pp. 12–21 (2007)

12. Morris, P.W.G.: Managing Project Interfaces—Key Points for Project Success. In: Project Management Handbook, pp. 16–55. John Wiley & Sons, Inc. (2008)

13. Medina-Mora, R., Winograd, T., Flores, R., Flores, F.: The action workflow approach to workflow management technology. In: Proceedings of the 1992 ACM Conference on Computer-Supported Cooperative Work, Toronto, Ontario, Canada, pp. 281–288. ACM (1992)

14. van der Aalst, W.M.P., ter Hofstede, A.H.M., Weske, M.: Business Process Management: A Survey. In: van der Aalst, W.M.P., ter Hofstede, A.H.M., Weske, M. (eds.) BPM 2003. LNCS, vol. 2678, pp. 1–12. Springer, Heidelberg (2003)

15. Picard, M., Renault, A., Cortina, S.: How to Improve Process Models for Better ISO/IEC 15504 Process Assessment. In: Riel, A., O'Connor, R., Tichkiewitch, S., Messnarz, R. (eds.) EuroSPI 2010. CCIS, vol. 99, pp. 130–141. Springer, Heidelberg (2010)

16. Mangin, O., Barafort, B., Heymans, P., Dubois, E.: Designing a Process Reference Model for Information Security Management Systems. In: Mas, A., Mesquida, A., Rout, T., O'Connor, R.V., Dorling, A. (eds.) SPICE 2012. CCIS, vol. 290, pp. 129–140. Springer, Heidelberg (2012)

17. Barafort, B., Humbert, J.P., Poggi, S.: Information security management and ISO/IEC 15504: the link opportunity between security and quality. In: SPICE Conference, Luxembourg (2006)

18. ISO 9000:2005: Quality management systems – Fundamentals and vocabulary (2005)

19. ISO/IEC TR 24774:2010 systems and software engineering – life cycle management – guidelines for process description

20. Mc Caffery, F., Dorling, A.: Medi SPICE: An Overview. In: SPICE 2009 Conference (2009)

21. Van Lamsweerde, A.: Goal-oriented requirements engineering: A guided tour. In: Fifth IEEE International Symposium on Requirements Engineering, Toronto, Canada, pp. 249–262. IEEE (2001)

22. ISO/IEC 27001: Information technology – security techniques – information security management systems – requirements (2005)

23. ISO/IEC 15504-1: Information technology – Process assessment – Part 1: Concepts and vocabulary (2004)

24. ISO/IEC TR 20000-4 Information technology – Service management – Part 4: Process reference model (2010)

25. ISO/IEC 20000-1: Information technology – Service management – Part 1: Service management system requirements (2011)

Comparing SPiCE for Space (S4S) and CMMI-DEV: Identifying Sources of Risk from Improvement Models

Ricardo Eito-Brun

Universidad Carlos III de Madrid
c/ Madrid, 124 – Getafe (Madrid), Spain
reito@bib.uc3m.es

Abstract. This paper analyses the differences between SPiCE for Space (S4S) snd CMMI-DEV v1.3. S4S (ECSS-Q-HB-80-02) is the software process assessment model used by the European Space Agency (ESA) based on ISO/IEC 15504-2 and the process reference model ISO/IEC 15504-5. CMMI-DEV, widely used in the United States and adopted by companies worldwide, is a requirement for subcontractors working for NASA projects. This means that companies in the aerospace sector need to demonstrate compliance with the requirements and practices described in both models. The objective of this paper is to identify the gap in the base practices proposed in S4S and CMMI-DEV. This analysis of differences is necessary, as long as the gaps between these models can translate into potential risks for those companies focused just on one of the models. European aerospace companies must deal with the need of working and being assessed from two different perspectives: S4S and CMMI-DEV. Getting a detailed picture of the differences between these models may help companies focus their improvement strategies and avoid potential pitfalls when being assessed.

Keywords: Assessment and improvement models, SPiCE for Space, S4S, CMMI-DEV, Model comparison, Risk identification.

1 Introduction

S4S is the software process assessment model used by the European Space Agency (ESA) to assess the capability of ESA contractors, although the ESA ECSS standards do not forbid the use the CMMI-DEV model. S4S is based on SPiCE (*Software Process Capability dEtermination*) and inherits the assessment requirements and measurement framework proposed in ISO/IEC 15504-2 and in the *exemplary process assessment model* described in the ISO/IEC 15504-5 (it can be said that S4S reuses the ISO/IEC 15504-5 with a few additions). S4S adds some specific aspects needed for the development of software in the aerospace industry.). S4S also considers the requirements from the ESA's ECSS standards, and adds processes, practices and work products whose origin are the requirements in the standards ECSS-E-ST-40C and ECSS-Q-ST-80C. The S4S model also identifies the capability level that should be

T. Woronowicz et al. (Eds.): SPICE 2013, CCIS 349, pp. 84–94, 2013.

requested to the software process depending on the software criticality (this is part of the S4S' informative annex *A. Examples of target profiles*). S4S is also the preferred assessment model to evaluate the level of compliance with the requirements in the ECSS standards.

ECSS-Q-HB-80-02 ([1] part 1, p. 9) mentions the following advantages of having a standardized approach for process assessment and improvement:

- *"lead to a common understanding of the use of process assessment for process improvement and capability determination;*
- *facilitate capability determination in procurement;*
- *contribute to increase the efficiency and competitiveness of an organization*
- *be controlled and regularly reviewed in the light of experience of use;*
- *be changed and improved only by international consensus;*
- *Encourage harmonization of existing schemes."*

For organizations involved in software development for the aerospace sector, S4S may be useful to understand their processes, identify to which extent their processes may fulfill requirements and to assess other organizations' processes when subcontracting software-related services. For customers of software development companies, the deployment of the S4S assessment model helps reduce the risks related to the selection of software suppliers by establishing controls.

Völcker et al. [2] and Devic [3] provide a detailed description of the origin of S4S, starting in 1999 with the first assessments based on this model and the *Software Process Improvement* (SPI) started by ESA that combined the continuous improvement cycle described in ISO/IEC 15504-7 with S4S principles. Völcker ([2], p. 119) also remarked the possibilities of adding to the S4S an additional third dimension (besides the Processes and Capability dimensions) to capture the level of risks related to processes and focus improvement initiatives on the most sensitive areas.

S4S was included in 2011 within the ECSS standards system as a *handbook* with code ECSS-Q-HB-80-02. This handbook has two parts:

- The first one, the *Framework*, defines the concepts, the assessment method and the way to focus improvement actions.
- The second one establishes the extensions to the Process Assessment Model (PAM PAM) ISO 15504-5. Its objective is to serve as an assessment tool for assessors providing them with different processes' indicators: base practices, work products, etc.

Regarding the differences between S4S and the exemplary process assessment model defined in ISO/IEC 15504-5, ECSS-Q-HB-80-02 (part 1 p. 25) indicates: *"The S4S assessment model expands the ISO/IEC 15504 exemplar assessment model by:*

- *Adding new processes in the process dimension, with are specified by the ECSS Standards and by*
- *Adding the definition and use of assessment indicators. Indicators for process performance are the base practices, the work products, and the work product characteristics."*

On the other hand, CMMI-DEV [4] is adopted by companies worldwide, and the compliance with different levels of this model – usually ML3 - is a requirement for subcontractors working for NASA projects. The existence of these two models means that European companies in the aerospace sector need to demonstrate compliance with the requirements and practices stated in both models and must identify the differences and gaps in their base practices, as these gaps may translate into potential risks for companies considering just on one of the models.

The differences between S4S and CMMI-DEV not only affect the proposed assessment schemas and rating framework, but the goals and practices that both models establish for the processes. The present work deals only with the analysis of the differences in the base practices (or specific practices, using CMMI terminology). The scope of this analysis excludes the mapping between the capability and/or maturity levels and the differences in the measurement frameworks. This decision is based on the fact that no previous comparison between base practices has been identified in the professional bibliography, although it is possible to find articles [5], [6], [7] and [8] that compare the measurement framework and the capability/maturity levels used by CMMI and ISO 15504 (we remark that S4S inherits the ISO 15504 measurement framework).   The analysis of the professional and academic bibliography has identified related studies focused on the comparison of CMMI-DEV specific practices with PMBOK [9].

2   Approach: Selection of Comparison Criteria

The conclusions exposed in this paper are the result of a detailed comparison made by the author between the base practices in the CMMI-DEV and S4S improvement models. Traceability between CMMI-DEV and S4S at the process, goals and specific practices level has been completed. Both CMMI and ISO/IEC 15504 establish a process model, and for each process a set of goals or expected results of the process implementation. Organizations being assessed according to these models have to demonstrate the achievement of these goals. In addition, CMMI and S4S establish a set of practices and work products that are used by assessors to verify the process implementation and the achievement of its objectives. Although there are minor differences in the terminology used by CMMI and ISO/IEC 15504, both models share a common approach based on processes, goals and results, practices and work products (CMMI uses the terms *process areas*, *specific goals*, *specific practices* and *work products*, and ISO/IEC 15504 *processes*, *outcomes*, *base practices* and *work products*).

Initially, the author of the study considered the possibility of comparing just the processes' goals. In S4S and CMMI-DEV assessments what is being assessed is the achievement of processes *outcomes, and the* practices and work products are just considered as indicators that may help the assessment team determine the achievement of the process goals. This means that an organization could achieve the process objectives implementing practices or generating work products different to those specified in the models.

The approach was reviewed to base the comparison on the base practices instead of the goals. The decision to base the comparison in the set of base practices was due to the fact that, in the practical terms, assessors and organizations implementing process improvement usually take as a reference the processes' practices and work products. In addition, in the case of S4S there is a high level of cohesion between the outcomes and the base practices (it is possible to say that in most of the cases there is one base practice per process outcome). In the case of CMMI, the specific practices and goals are more detailed than in S4S. Another factor to consider when justifying our decision is that S4S is focused on a continuous assessment model, and continuous assessment models have put the focus on the implementation of practices ([10], p. 75): *"In a continuous model such as EIA 731, goals are not specifically stated, which puts even more emphasis on practices"*

To record the traceability between the base practices in both models, for each base practices in S4S a record has been created containing the equivalent CMMI generic or specific practices, sub-practices or CMMI paragraphs that correspond – totally or partially – with the practice in S4S. In those cases in which it has not been possible to establish equivalence, the reason for this decision has been recorded in a separate field. These records - reviewed by other academic colleagues - are available upon request to other researchers and practitioners interested in this line of work (further, additional validation by other parties is considered valuable to improve and enhance the work conclusions).

3   Comparison between CMMI-DEV and S4S

This section summarizes the results of the comparison between the base practices in these models. As stated in the introduction of the paper, the study is just focused on the comparison of the base practices, and other aspects like the comparison of the capability dimension or indicators like work products are out of the scope of this analysis.

3.1   Comparison at the Processes Level

The main differences at this level can be summarized as follows:

- S4S includes processes focused at the "organizational level", as for example those processes within the process groups REU (Reuse), MAN (Management) or RIN (Resources and Infrastructure). This can be understood as an intention of the model for being deployed following a top-down approach, starting from a detailed planning of some activities to be executed at the organizational level. In CMMI-DEV – with the exception of the process areas linked to the high maturity levels – processes are usually instantiated at the project level. Sample S4S processes to be instantiated at the organizational level are those related to the management of information, knowledge or with the systematic reuse and domain engineering. For these processes, it has been difficult to find equivalent practices in CMMI-DEV.

- S4S makes a difference between the acquisition (ACQ) and supply (SPL) processes. Processes within the ACQ group are instantiated when the organization acquires products or services, and processes within the SPL group are instantiated when the organization acts as a supplier.

  CMMI includes a single process area, SAM (Supplier Agreement Management), which is instantiated when the organization acquires any product or service from third parties. Due to that, the equivalences between the practices in the S4S's SPL have to be identified in other CMMI process areas, like PP (Project Planning), RD (Requirements Development) o TS (Technical Solution).

- In the engineering group processes, S4S makes a distinction for the different levels (system and software) at which the processes are instantiated. There are separated processes for the analysis of requirements at the system (*ENG.2. System Requirements Analysis*) and software (*ENG.4. Software Requirements Analysis*) level and the same happen with the testing, design and integration processes.

  CMMI-DEV has a single process for these activities (RD for requirements elaboration, TS for the design of the technical solution, PI for integration or VER for verification), and the model remarks that these processes are instantiated at the product or component level as needed.

  The parallelism between processes at the system and software levels can also be observed at the level of base practices, concretely for those practices related to regression testing. S4S includes separate practices for the execution of regression tests at different levels, while CMMI-DEV just makes a short mention in one comment within the PMC process area.

- CMMI groups, within the TS process area, activities that are treated as separate processes in S4S, corresponding to high level design, detailed design and coding.

- S4S includes processes related to the system operation, maintenance and support that are not covered by CMMI-DEV. To identify equivalences to these processes it is necessary to use the CMMI for Service constellation.

3.2   Comparison at the Practices Level

S4S includes 364 base practices. There are 279 (76.65%) practices for which equivalent CMMI-DEV practices or sub-practices have been identified. There are 34 (9.34%) base practices for which a partial matching has been identified and 51 (14.01%) with no clear equivalence in CMMI-DEV (see figure 1). Partial matching refers to those cases in which the S4S practice is not clearly requested by CMMI-DEV in the same terms or with the same level of detail than in S4S.

A summary of the content of the missing practices (that is to say, practices in S4S for which no equivalent is found in CMMI-DEV) is presented in the paper conclusions. It is anticipated that the missing practices are mainly related to activities related to communication and with processes related to infrastructure management (technical infrastructure, resources, knowledge and information management and reuse organization).

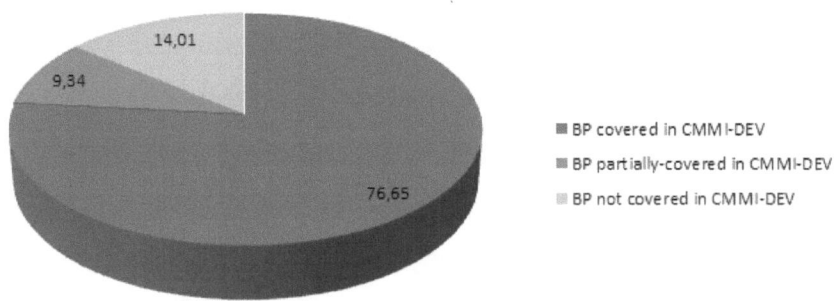

Fig. 1. Percentage of S4S BP covered by CMMI-DEV

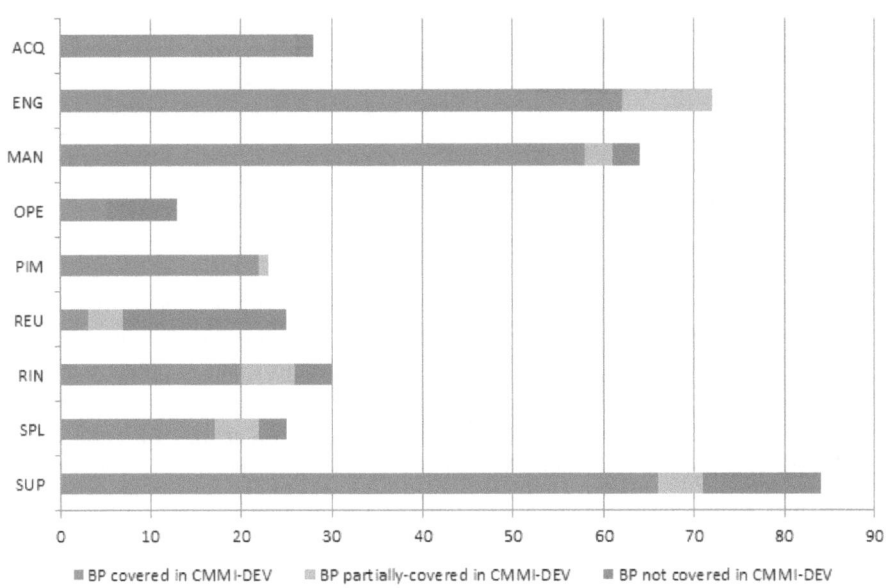

Fig. 2. Number of S4S BP covered by CMMI-DEV per Process Group

Taking this information as a basis, the degree of matching between S4S and CMMI-DEV practices per process group is shown in figure 3 (the X axis corresponds to the number of base practices in the S4S process groups):

A supplementary view of this degree of matching is shown in figure 4, where the X axis corresponds to the percentage of S4S practices within each process group covered by CMMI:

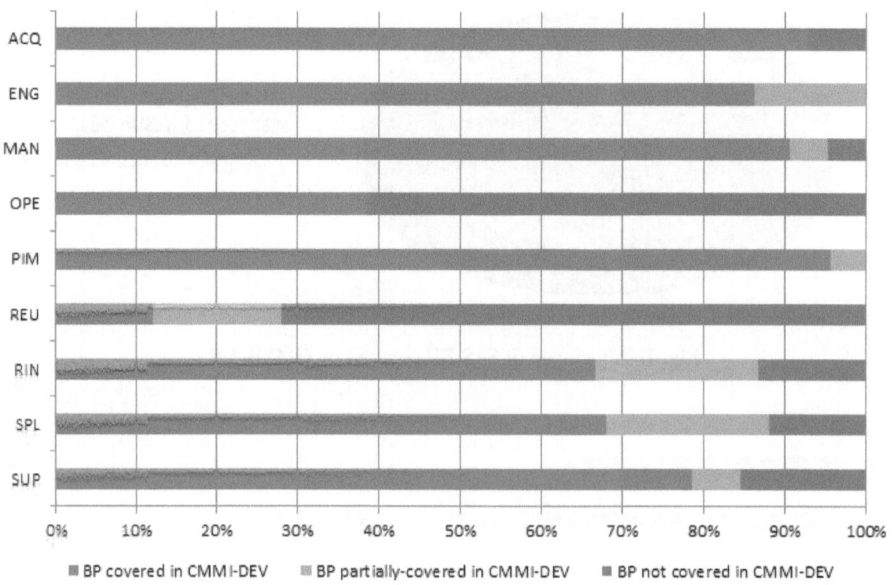

Fig. 3. Percentage of S4S BP covered by CMMI-DEV per Process group

This chart clearly shows which processes are covered with less detail in CMMI-DEV, as for example the software reuse (REU) and support to operations (OPE). Other processes, like those related to infrastructure (RIN) and supplier tendering (SPL) show a wider, although still partial, degree of coverage.

At the level of individual processes, the degree of matching or equivalence between the practices in S4S and CMMI-DEV is shown in the figures 4 and 5 (the first one in absolute terms and the second one as a percentage).

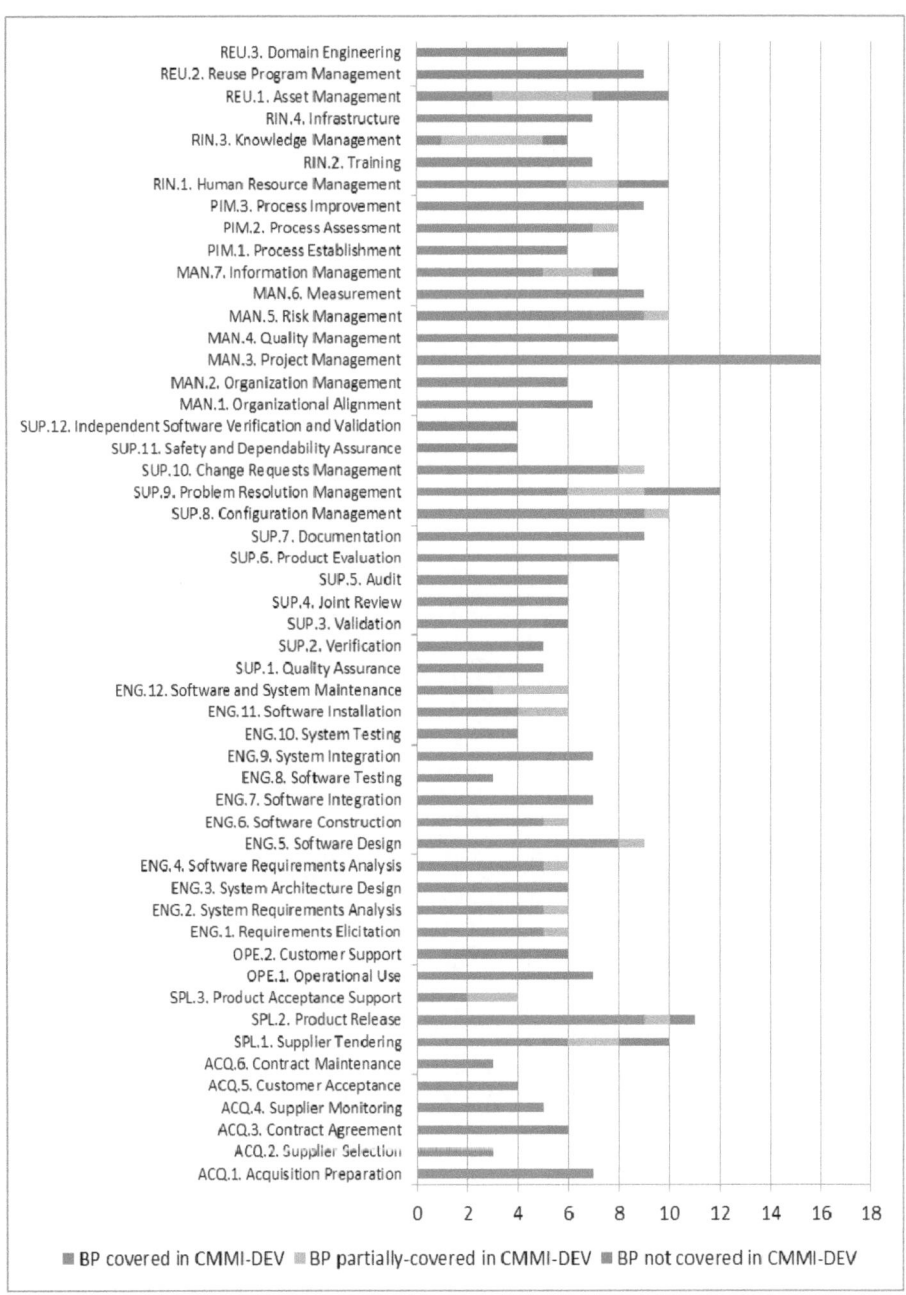

Fig. 4. S4S BP covered by CMMI-DEV per Process. X axis indicate the number of practices in each process

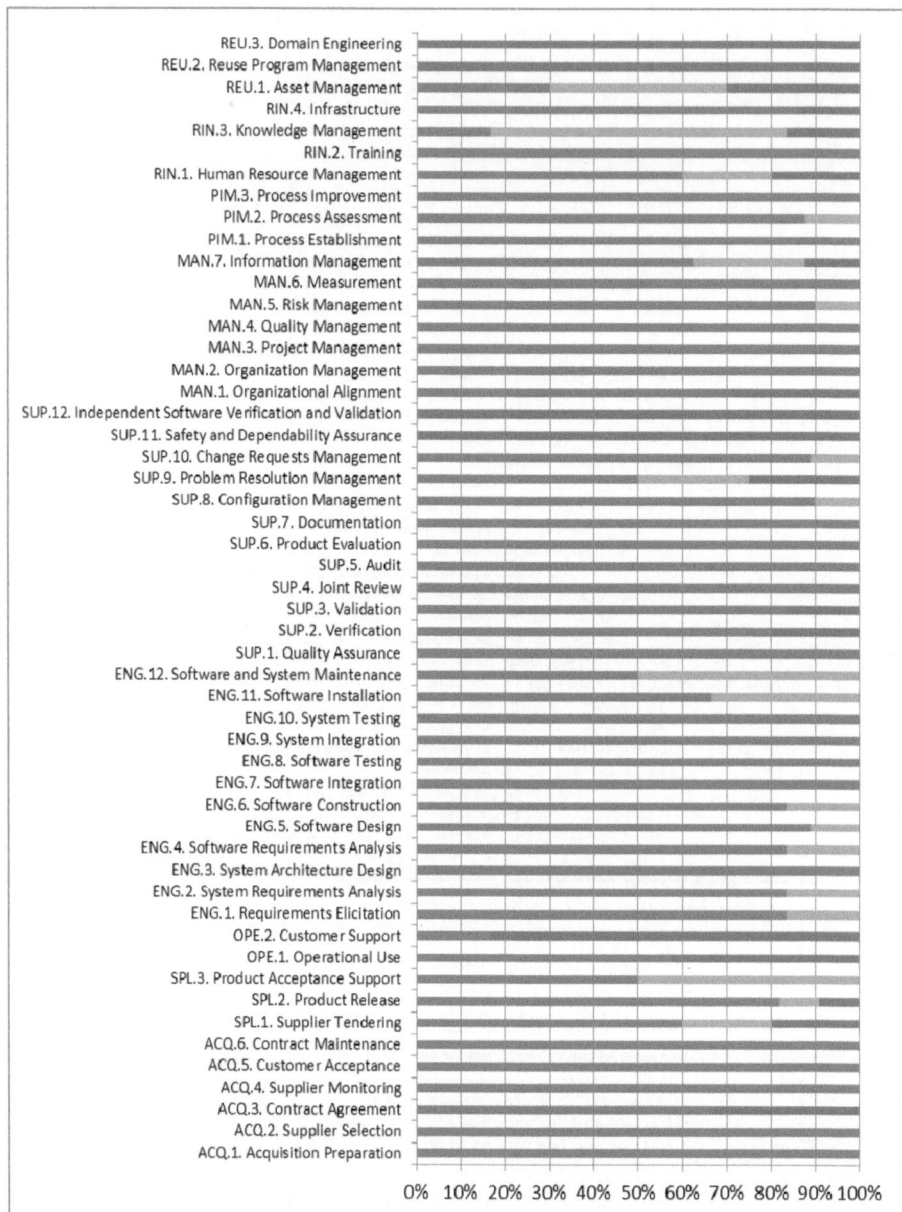

Fig. 5. Percentage of S4S BP covered by CMMI-DEV per process

4   Conclusions

The conclusions of this work may be helpful for S4S assessors to identify S4S areas that may not be totally covered by companies involved in improvement programs based on CMMI-DEV. In addition, companies working with the CMMI-DEV model can take these conclusions as a reference to identify additional areas of improvement. Main differences are identified in the S4S group processes related to software assets reuse strategies and infrastructure management (this includes knowledge, infrastructure, information and human resources management), as well as processes related to customer support.

It is remarked anyway that the lack of equivalences for some practices defined in S4S. This mainly affect to the practices in the above mentioned processes, and to those related to contract management (ACQ.3.BP5, ACQ.3.BP6), establishing communication interfaces during tendering (SPL.1.BP1), customer enquiry screening (SPL.1.BP2), establish customer proposal evaluation criteria (SPL.1.BP3), and more specific aspects related to product management like establishing a product release classification and numbering scheme (SPL.2.BP3), adapting the product to customer's environment (SPL3.BP2), organizing and managing product support (OPE.2.BP1), monitoring product performance (OPE.2.BP3) or assessing and benchmarking customer satisfaction (OPE.2.BP4, OPE.2.BP5 and OPE.2.BP6). The need of supporting the Customer in product evaluation during the tender process is also strongly remarked in S4S (SPL.3.BP3).

In general, aspects related to communication at different levels (starting at the tendering process, including the communication of verification and validation results to stakeholders and the management of alerts) and top-down management strategies are covered with a greater level of detail by S4S practices. Regarding technical practices, S4S remarks some relevant points like the definition of branching strategies, the analysis of dependencies between changes, the testability of the software design, regression testing strategies at different levels (unit, integration, system) and the analysis and implementation of software adaptations.

Companies involved in CMMI-DEV-based improvement programs should consider the differences between the two models to identify practices that require additional effort and closer monitoring. As there are some differences in the focus of the two models, some relevant business and engineering practices could be missed. These conclusions should not be understood as a statement of the completeness of one model over the other, but as additional requirements to consider when planning and implementing an improvement program.

Future, related lines of work include:

- The analysis and comparison of the terminology used in both models, to identify those aspects in which each model focuses. As an example, S4S makes a greater focus on concepts like regression testing; reuse and information needs, to name a few. This activity may be related with the work of Pardo [11], that analysis the elaboration of ontology to be used as a framework to compare different improvement models.

- Analyze to which extent organizations that take as a reference one model or another present weakness in those areas in which the selected model makes less emphasis. The research question is: to which extent the selection of one improvement method or another impose conditions or limits the performance of the organization when implementing specific technical or management activities?

References

1. ECSS-Q-HB-80-02, Space product assurance – Software process assessment and improvement. ESA-ESTEC Requirements and Standards Division (April 16, 2010)
2. Völcker, A., et al.: SPiCE for SPACE: A Process Assessment and Improvement Method for Space Software Development. ESA Bulletin 107, 112–119 (2001)
3. Devic, M.-O., Escorial Rico, D., Richter, S.: Reflecting on ten years of Software Process Assessment and Improvement initiatives by the European Space Agency. In: 18th European Systems and Software Process Improvement and Innovation Conference (EuroSPI 2011) (2011)
4. CMMI-DEV. CMMI® for Development, Version 1.3: Improving processes for developing better products and services. CMU/SEI-2010-TR-033. SEI (CMMI Product Team), 468 p. (November 2010), http://www.sei.cmu.edu/library/abstracts/reports/10tr033.cfm
5. Rout, T., et al.: SPICE in retrospect : Developing a standard for process assessment. The Journal of System and Software (80), 1483–1493 (2007)
6. Rout, T., Tuffley, A., Cahill, B.: CMMI Evaluation: Capability Maturity Model Integration Mapping to ISO/IEC 15504-2:1998. Version 1.0. Defence Material Organisation; SQI (2001), http://www.griffith.edu.au/__data/assets/pdf_file/0004/88501/CMMIMappingReport.pdf
7. Hwang, S.M.: Process Quality Levels of ISO/IEC 15504, CMMI and K-Model. International Journal of Software Engineering and its Applications 3(1), 33–42 (2009)
8. Peldzius, S., Ragaisis, S.: Comparison of maturity levels in CMMI-DEV and ISO/IEC 15504. In: AMERICAN-MATH 2011/CEA 2011 Proceedings of the 2011 American Conference on Applied Mathematics and the 5th WSEAS International Conference on Computer Engineering and Applications, pp. 117–122 (2011)
9. von Wangenheim, C.G., et al.: Best practice fusion of CMMI-DEV v1.2 (PP, PMC, SAM) and PMBOK 2008. Information and Software Technology (52), 749–757 (2010)
10. Ahern, D.M., Clouse, A., Turner, R.: CMMI Distilled: A Practical Introduction to Integrated Process Improvement, 2nd edn., 305 p. Addison-Wesley, Boston (2004)
11. Pardo, C., et al.: An ontology for the harmonization of multiple standards and models. Computer Standards & Interfaces (34), 48–59 (2012)

Assessing Software Product Management Capability: An Industry Validation Case Study

Fritz Stallinger[1], Robert Neumann[1], and Robert Schossleitner[2]

[1] Software Competence Center Hagenberg, Softwarepark 21, 4232 Hagenberg, Austria
{fritz.stallinger,robert.neumann}@scch.at
[2] STIWA Automation GmbH, Salzburger Straße 52, 4800 Attnang-Puchheim, Austria
robert.schossleitner@stiwa.com

Abstract. Software product management is expected to link and integrate business and product related goals with core software engineering and software life cycle activities. Nevertheless, traditional software process improvement approaches like ISO/IEC 12207 lack the provision of explicit and detailed software product management activities. – In this paper we share the results of a real-world industrial pilot validation of an emerging process reference model for software product management capable for integration with ISO/IEC 12207. The results are discussed with respect to a qualitative evaluation of the reference model and analyzed with respect to enhancements of the model.

Keywords: software product management, process reference model, process assessment, case study, ISO/IEC 12207, ISO/IEC 15504.

1 Introduction, Motivation, and Goals

Software development organizations are increasingly challenged with the need to develop and maintain software as a product. This challenge and the implied transition towards product-oriented development cause a change in the whole organization, require the consideration of the views and needs of further stakeholders, and generally stress the importance of business and market considerations. Nevertheless, to exploit the potential of product- and consequently reuse-focused development approaches, core software engineering activities like requirements engineering, architecture engineering, or quality assurance have to be closely linked and aligned with strategic and economic product aspects.

Software product management is generally expected to link and integrate such business and product related goals with core software engineering and software life cycle activities. It is thus considered a key element in the transition towards product-oriented software engineering and expected to contribute to closing the gap between business and product related goals and software life cycle activities. Nevertheless, traditional software process improvement approaches and respective underlying best practice-based process models like ISO/IEC 12207 on software life cycle processes [1] generally lack the provision of explicit or detailed software product management practices.

T. Woronowicz et al. (Eds.): SPICE 2013, CCIS 349, pp. 95–106, 2013.

Following our long-term vision to enable and support the transition of software developing organizations towards product-oriented development approaches by providing the necessary guidance for establishing software product management, a best practice reference model for product-oriented software engineering conformant to the requirements of ISO/IEC 15504 [2] for process reference models has been proposed (cf. [3], [4]).

The work presented in this paper reports on a case study intended to contribute to the validation of the emerging reference model. The goals of this initial pilot application are to validate the proposed process reference model for software product management (PM-PRM) with respect to its applicability, completeness, clarity, etc., and to identify respective enhancements and improvements to the PM-PRM.

The remainder of this paper is structured as follows: section 2 provides an overview on the applied process reference model for software product management; section 3 shortly characterizes the assessed organization; section 4 presents the assessment results together with a summary of the underlying rationales; section 5 presents the results of the validation in terms of a qualitative evaluation of the process reference model and derived directions for its further enhancement; section 6 concludes the paper.

2   Process Reference Model for Software Product Management

The underlying process reference model for software product management used in the case study is comprised of 13 processes grouped into three categories:

- The *Software Product Management Processes* category comprises the core product management and product planning processes, which are the *Product Portfolio Management Process, Product Life Cycle Management Process, Product Roadmapping Process, Release Planning Process, Product Planning Process*, and *Product Controlling Process*.
- The *Software Product Management Support Processes* category comprises the processes that support any of the other processes in the reference model. These are the *Market Monitoring Process, Customer Interface Management Process, Funding Process*, and the *Product Innovation Process*.
- The *Software Engineering Lifecycle Processes* category comprises the core engineering processes interfering with product management. These are the *Requirements Engineering and Management Process, Domain and Product Line Scoping Process*, and the *Asset Identification Process*.

The model is presented in detail in [4] including descriptions of the proposed process outcomes. Figure 1 illustrates the process structure of the model. All 13 processes were evaluated in the present case study. Their purpose descriptions are provided in section 4 as part of the of the assessment results discussion. The model resulted from the analysis of software product management and product-oriented development frameworks and models, which all showed some lack in covering product management practices comprehensively and completely.

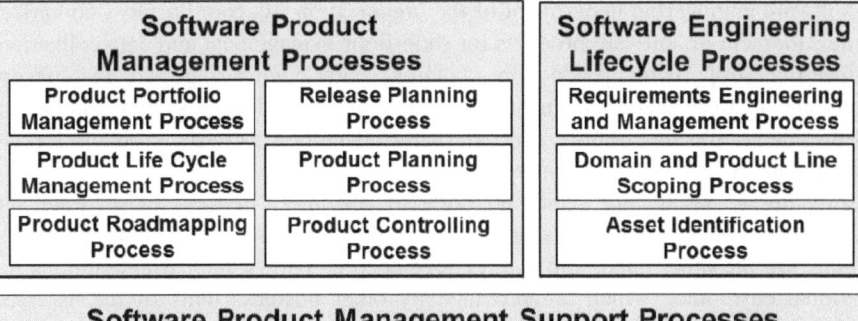

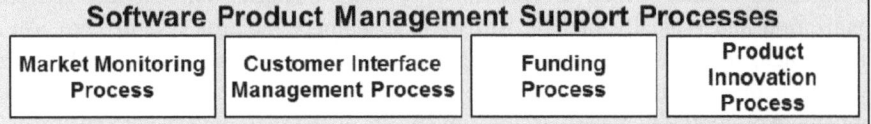

Fig. 1. Software Product Management Process Reference Model

The *reference framework for software product management* of van de Weerd et al. [5], for example, focuses on the core activities of product management. Although it provides high-level links to other involved stakeholders more detailed descriptions of these relationships and the required practices are missing. The *Framework for Software Product Line Practice* [6] as well as the *software product line engineering framework* [7] are both specifically linked to the software product line engineering development paradigm and focus on the specific concepts and activities involved therein. The *Microsoft Solutions Framework* [8] describes the product management role in terms of responsibilities and relationships with other roles, thus lacking the integration with core software engineering activities.

These analyzed frameworks each have specific foci and are often coupled to specific development paradigms. They further lack integration with core software engineering activities. On the other hand, analysis of ISO/IEC 12207 on software life cycle processes [1], which describes such core software engineering activities, shows a lack of coverage of major software product management activities. The upcoming international standard ISO/IEC 26550 on reference processes for product line engineering and management [9] seems to address some of these issues, but it remains to be seen if and how the focus on software and system product lines impacts the applicability of this reference model to product-oriented development contexts in general.

3   Characteristics of the Assessed Organization

The assessed organization provides products and services in the areas of high performance manufacturing automation, product design suitable for automation, linear feeding systems and entangling devices, manufacturing services, and technical software. It is a member company of a larger group, which operates locations in Austria but also in the U.S. and Germany. The assessed organizational unit (OU) is the software engineering department of the organization. Its core business comprises the development of software products for shop-floor management and data collection, engineering support for production planning, data engineering and IT concept development, stress analysis of manufacturing systems, production system simulation, and the integration of in-house and externally developed software products for the development of individual customer solutions.

Software is, on the one hand, provided to customers in form of separate and typically customized products with accompanying services like installation or user training. On the other hand, software is developed as part of industrial solutions for individual customers, which are provided by other business units of the assessed organization and typically include hardware, machinery, control systems, etc. As a consequence, software requirements originate not only from end customers but also from the involved engineering disciplines and the respective business units within the company, e.g. *application engineering*, which acts as the main interface to customers, *control system engineering*, or *mechanical engineering*.

Further details on the company and its development as well as its business context are available in [10].

4   Assessment and Results

For the assessment two high ranking managers and a product manager of the OU were interviewed with a focus on two of the OU's core products. The assessment was performed in a one-day workshop including an introductory presentation to software product management and the underlying reference model, the assessment itself, and an immediate feedback discussion. In a separate short workshop the results were presented and discussed in detail with the participants.

Figure 2 presents the evaluation results for each process. Each process attribute (PA) is evaluated using an NPLF-scale in accordance to ISO/IEC 15504, denoting the percentage of achievement of the specific process attribute (N: 0% - 15%, P: 16% - 50%, L: 51% - 85%, F: 86% - 100%). The assessment focused on evaluating capability level 1 (CL1), i.e. to which degree are the processes performed and the respective process outcomes achieved. Capability levels 2 and 3 were only roughly evaluated with the assessors' judgment based on information gathered during the interviews and their knowledge of workflows and practices from the long running business relationship with the OU. CL2 and CL3 therefore were not systematically evaluated.

The following sub-sections shortly present for each process the identified strengths and weaknesses mirrored against the process purpose, which reflect the justification for the evaluation of capability level 1 (CL1).

Product Portfolio Management Process
The purpose of the Product Portfolio Management Process is to ensure that the business strategy and goals of the organization are properly addressed and achieved by the totality of the organization's products.

Development of new products or product enhancements is highly driven by customers and therefore also very well aligned with customer needs. Strategy, on the other hand, and market analyses are no active drivers. Development and establishment of an explicit product strategy has been just recently started and the need for systematic market and trend analyses is recognized. Resource requirements and opportunity costs for specific product development efforts are analyzed, but their general necessity and costs – especially for product variants – are typically not considered. Single products are not managed individually. Instead the whole product portfolio is managed as a single unit. This mainly stems from the release strategy of providing a new release of all products jointly once a year (cf. Release Planning, below). Weaknesses of the portfolio and potential new products to overcome them are identified, but derived improvement strategies or plans are just partly considered.

Process Capability Dimension	CL1	CL2		CL3	
Process Dimension	PA1.1	PA2.1	PA2.2	PA3.1	PA3.2
SOFTWARE PRODUCT MANAGEMENT PROCESSES					
Product Portfolio Management Process	P	N	N	N	N
Product Life Cycle Management Process	L	N	N	N	N
Product Roadmapping Process	N	N	N	N	N
Product Planning Process	P	P	N	N	N
Release Planning Process	F			P	P
Product Controlling Process	P	P	P	N	N
SOFTWARE PRODUCT MANAGEMENT SUPPORT PROCESSES					
Market Monitoring Process	L	P	N	N	N
Customer Interface Management Process	L	P	P	P	P
Funding Process	L	P	N	N	N
Product Innovation Process	L	N	N	N	N
SOFTWARE ENGINEERING LIFE CYCLE PROCESSES					
Requirements Engineering and Management Process	L				P
Domain and Product Line Scoping Process	L	P	N	N	N
Asset Identification Process	P		P	N	N

Fig. 2. Assessment Results – Ratings for Capability Levels 1, 2, 3

Product Life Cycle Management Process

The purpose of the Product Life Cycle Management Process is to conserve and expand a product's potentials and attractiveness throughout its life cycle or – where necessary - to eliminate it from the product portfolio. Due to the strong customer focus, introduction of new and elimination of existing products is performed in tight coordination with customers, although typically features rather than entire products are introduced or eliminated. Elimination decisions regarding features are mostly triggered by highly increased maintenance costs properly considering dependencies to other features and products. The life cycle of the OU's products is rather long and its management is highly driven by customers while organizational goals have almost no influence. Changes to products are typically implemented as a reaction to changes in the general conditions which are not monitored and recognized early enough. Only for commercial third party software products and components a systematic monitoring of such changes is performed.

Product Roadmapping Process
The purpose of the Product Roadmapping Process is to outline the plans and expectations for the products in the product portfolio over a period of time with respect to features, schedules, and dependencies between products. Concerning the long-term planning of products, an overall strategy across all products has only just recently been developed. Therefore, themes and topics for the long-term development of products are not yet derived from this strategy. Since product development is mainly driven by customers, there are also no documented long-term plans for products or features exceeding one year in the sense of product roadmapping. Further, long-term changes to markets, technologies, or legal constraints are not considered. However, the need for such long-term plans and roadmaps has been realized.

Product Planning Process
The purpose of the Product Planning Process is to specify both the strategic and technical plans for a product. Strategic and technical plans and goals are defined and coordinated with the customers and aligned with customer problems (esp. core customers). But again, these plans address the entire portfolio and are discussed rather on the feature-level than product-level. Planning of resources and schedules is performed for all products for about one year ahead driven by the release cycle. The use of assets is coordinated internally with relevant stakeholders and third-party software or components are evaluated systematically using checklists. On the other hand, cost-benefit-analyses on product-level are not performed and existing plans are not systematically adapted to changed conditions.

Release Planning Process
The purpose of the Release Planning Process is to plan and define product releases and to ensure smooth deployment to the customer and on-going operation of the product. A release strategy is defined and the OU releases a new version of all products in the portfolio jointly once a year. Monthly maintenance releases are provided and customers can decide whether to patch their products or not. Therefore, the releases of individual products are well coordinated and synchronized with each other. Release activities are well planned, requirements are selected for implementation, and releases are approved. The launch of a new release is well coordinated with the customers, who also are supported and trained. On the other hand, there is no planning of releases for a longer term than one year.

Product Controlling Process
The purpose of the Product Controlling Process is to track the achievement of product goals and objectives and to guide product management decision making. The main success criterion which is systematically monitored is the fulfillment of product requirements. There are no further success criteria which are based on or derived from technical or strategic product goals. Sales numbers are analyzed on a quarterly basis against planned values and technical controlling is performed on product and component level while commercial controlling is not.

Market Monitoring Process

The purpose of the Market Monitoring Process is to observe and analyze the external factors of sales and procurement markets that determine or influence product success. The OU maintains a strong relationship via direct contacts not only with their current customers but also with non-customers (partly even with competitors), potential future customers, and suppliers to gain the necessary information about the needs and the trends in the different application domains. With current customers, especially core customers, regular meetings take place. Through these contacts the OU is aware of important market developments and trends, although no systematic market analysis or monitoring of long-term technological developments are performed. There is also no alignment of analyses or information gathered with product or portfolio planning activities.

Customer Interface Management Process

The purpose of the Customer Interface Management Process is to manage the relationships and commitments between an organization and its customers. The OU employs close relationships and direct and long-term oriented contacts to their customers, especially with their core customers. The roles and responsibilities that are involved at the customer interface are well defined. Customers are assigned to defined contact persons and a centralized customer support is operated. Customer expectations are controlled ad-hoc within customer meetings, but there is no internal coordination prior to such meetings. Further, international customers are insufficiently supported with regard to language skills of the involved personnel. Furthermore, customer support is performed by typically few and consequently overloaded employees, which could cause a decrease in customer service quality.

Funding Process

The purpose of the Funding Process is to plan and establish adequate financing of software development efforts in order to secure the evolution of products or the product line. Since the products mainly evolve within customer projects driven by customer requests, these customer projects are the main type of funding employed at the OU. New product developments are incorporated – in coordination with the customers – within customer projects where appropriate. Additional internal funding and respective budgets for customer-independent projects or developments are hard to obtain. However, if specific budgets are approved, there is a strong support by top management for such projects. Besides that no further funding sources are actively pursued.

Product Innovation Process

The purpose of the Product Innovation Process is to extend the product portfolio with new or enhanced products that satisfy customer needs. The OU employs an innovation-friendly environment with open discussions and high interactivity between employees. This innovation culture is actively fostered and supported by top management and involves different business functions (e.g. development, sales, key account) into the innovation process. Ideas are actively searched and evaluated, but exclusively in an informal way. One side effect is that mostly those ideas receive broad attention that are adopted by an employee and actively argued and supported. There is no organization-wide innovation strategy in place.

Requirements Engineering and Management Process

The purpose of the Requirements Engineering and Management Process is to identify, specify, and manage stakeholder and product requirements in a systematic and repeatable way. Through the close relationship to its customers, the OU's requirements engineering is consequently aligned with customers and their needs. The OU has a high capability to realize the actual problems of a customer and also to confront customers with potential problems they may not yet have recognized themselves. On the other hand, the requirements of internal stakeholders are insufficiently considered. Future product variants and the desired degrees of freedom are jointly coordinated between internal experts and customers. Decisions for or against the realization of specific requirements and respective trade-offs are neither systematically analyzed nor documented, partly because of missing evaluation criteria. The handling of changes to requirements highly depends on the employees and their experience and is not performed in a systematic way. Technical requirements are well documented, but there is no systematic and integrated requirements recording, for example using dedicated tools.

Domain and Product Line Scoping Process

The purpose of the Domain and Product Line Scoping Process is to determine the relevant entities within the domain and the domain boundaries, to establish product commonalities and variability, and to ensure that this information is captured, appropriately represented, and communicated to stakeholders. The OU exhibits a very good understanding of the domain, its boundaries, and especially of the customer problems in the domain. Gaps in domain knowledge are compensated through support by partners and their specific expertise. Commonalities and variability within the domain and domain features are identified, but domain information is not well documented. Dependencies between entities in the domain, e.g. between features, products, or stakeholders, are not captured and there is no documented assignment of features to products.

Asset Identification Process

The purpose of the Asset Identification Process is to identify and define particular assets that cover the commonalities of and are shared by multiple products in the product line and thus are developed for reuse. Cross-cutting concerns of the software products are addressed through a component-based approach. Components for reuse are identified and aligned with the strategy, and their potential for other existing products is estimated, but the impact on future or potential products is not considered. The resulting components are mainly implementation-level assets, while assets that are based on engineering artifacts (e.g. architecture, requirements specification) are insufficiently identified. Further, there are no criteria for asset selection within projects. Costs for asset development and use are only analyzed afterwards, but not estimated prior to asset definition and development.

Overall, the *Software Engineering Life Cycle Processes* and *Software Product Management Support Processes* are well performed. The core *Software Product Management Processes*, on the other hand, lack achievement of the respective outcomes and exhibit high improvement potential. Only the *Product Life Cycle Management Process* and the *Release Planning Process* are satisfactorily performed as a result of the employed release strategy of systematically releasing the whole product portfolio once a year.

5   Validation Results

The main goal of the assessment was to perform a pilot application of the proposed software product management process reference model and validate whether it achieves its purpose. A further goal was to identify respective improvement directions and enhancements for the model.

5.1   Qualitative Evaluation of the Underlying Process Reference Model

In the feedback session the participants of the organization confirmed a satisfactory clarity and understandability of the process and process purpose descriptions, which also contributed to revealing misunderstandings early in the assessment discussion. Participants often could directly identify the respective areas, activities, roles, etc. in the OU which relate to the specific process or process outcome discussed. They also found the processes to be complete and could not identify any missing topics they deemed important with respect to the organizations practices and needs and that were not covered by the model.

Further, the general concept of process assessment based improvement and evaluation of achievement of process outcomes and capability levels was well understood and considered helpful to focus on specific topics while still having the overview on all relevant topics. Therefore, also from the assessors' perspective, the model is considered well applicable and supporting the understanding and evaluation of software product management practices.

During the results presentation there was a high level of agreement by the participants of the assessed organization with the assessment results of the assessors. Between the assessors there were only few discrepancies in their individual evaluations and agreement could be quickly reached. The model can therefore be considered satisfactorily accurate and capable to provide reasonable evaluations. Some potential improvements of the reference model that were revealed in the interviews are described in the following subsection.

5.2   Directions for Enhancement of the Process Reference Model

Glossary: A glossary with the definitions and descriptions of the terms used in the reference model would help to achieve a common understanding between participants even more quickly. Although within the discussions the meaning of specific terms could be clarified, a glossary would provide a sound basis for understanding and allow elaborating the company-specific view or understanding (e.g. the mapping of artifacts used in the model to company-specific artifacts) more systematically.

Product- vs. Portfolio-Level Processes: The reference model should state more clearly whether a specific process is intended to be instantiated on the product level (and therefore multiple times) or on the portfolio level, i.e. whether it addresses one specific product or all products in the portfolio. Therefore, the process descriptions should state more clearly and consistently throughout the outcomes, whether the product or the portfolio is addressed by the process. If no clear statement can be made (e.g. *product roadmapping process*), a notes section should elaborate this issue.

Clarifications: During the discussion of the *Product Roadmapping Process* it was not clear whether the process description demands one roadmap covering all products or if it allows for maintaining multiple roadmaps (e.g. for specific products, or product groups). There should be at least a notes section clarifying the issue. Further, the use of the terms "asset" and "core asset" resulted in some confusion. It should be checked whether the original definitions in the source frameworks are still suitable for the reference model and whether the distinction is still valid and needed. Depending on the results, the term(s) should be defined in a glossary and used consistently in the model.

Product vs. Product Line: Throughout the model, the terms product and product line are often used interchangeably ("product or product line"). Nevertheless, product lines are only one approach to product-oriented software engineering. Since we aim to address product management in general, the model should only address 'products' in its descriptions and not any specific engineering approaches. If there are product line specific issues, or specific outcomes have to be adapted in a software product line context, this should be addressed using notes in order to keep outcome descriptions short and clear.

Strategy Process: Strategic issues of product management are currently addressed in both the *Product Portfolio Management Process* and the *Product Planning Process*. A separate *Product Strategy Process* that captures the relevant strategic issues in a single process would support focused discussions within the interviews.

Work Products and Roles: In order to make the interaction between processes more clear, it would be helpful to have defined work products that are produced within specific processes and used by other processes. Also, the use of defined roles would help during assessment. The core work products and roles could be used in the process model descriptions, but mainly they should be captured in more detail in an appropriate assessment model.

Consistent Wording: Words like "established", "defined", "identified", "documented", etc. should be used more consistently throughout the model.

Distributed Asset Identification: Activities concerning the identification of assets overlap the *Product Planning Process, Domain and Product Line Scoping Process*, and *Asset Identification Process*. It should be made clearer in the process outcome descriptions, which activities are specifically meant and in which context they take place, e.g. the identification which of the existing assets can be used in a product (*Product Planning Process*) vs. the identification of potential assets or asset proposals (*Domain and Product Line Scoping*) vs. specification of assets for reuse (*Asset Identification Process*).

Customer Interface Management Process: Outcome 3 addresses the evaluation of customer requests regarding feasibility and desirability to integrate them into the products. This outcome would better fit into the *Requirements Engineering and Management Process*.

Product Innovation Process: The *Product Innovation Process* currently exclusively focuses on innovation strategy and idea generation. During the interviews other topics concerning innovation briefly came up. It might be suitable to integrate them into the model, e.g. innovation goals and types, organizational issues (central innovation management, roles, etc.), establishing innovation culture, measurement of innovation success, incentives. The appropriate level of detail, by which the broad topic of innovation should be addressed in the context of software product management, still needs to be determined.

6   Summary and Conclusions

The paper presented an assessment case study carried out as part of the validation of an emerging process reference model for software product management. The underlying process reference model is described in detail in [3], [4]. The goals of the presented pilot application were to initially validate the process reference model with respect to its applicability, completeness, clarity, etc., and to identify respective enhancements and improvements to the model.

Overall, the feedback from the assessed organization's participants confirmed a satisfactory level of clarity and understandability of the descriptions of the elements of the process reference model and a high completeness of the model. From the assessors' point of view, the model is considered well applicable and supports the understanding and evaluation of software product management practices. Nevertheless, more case studies within different organizations have to be performed to further examine the validity of the proposed process reference model.

In an accompanying analysis, some potential improvements of the process reference model could be revealed from the pilot assessment. An analysis of these issues and the derivation of suggested enhancements addressing them have been performed post-assessment (cf. section 5.2).

As software is increasingly developed as part of an overall, often multidisciplinary system, it is also worth investigating best practices for the application of the concepts of reuse and product-orientation at the system-level of software-intensive systems. Initial work in this direction addresses the integration of the process reference model for software product management as presented here with one for enhancing system life cycle processes with reuse and product-orientation. The resulting model that can be used as add-on to ISO/IEC 12207 is presented and discussed in [11] and can serve as a framework for process assessment and improvement in contexts where software is developed and evolved as a product and at the same time is part of an overall software-intensive system product.

Acknowledgements. This work is supported by the *COMET*-Programme of the *Austrian Research Promotion Agency (FFG - Österreichische Forschungsförderungsgesellschaft)* within the project *INSPiRE* (INtegrated and Sustainable PRoduct Engineering, 2012-2014).

References

1. ISO/IEC 12207:2008: Systems and software engineering — Software life cycle processes. International Standards Organization (2008)
2. ISO/IEC 15504-2: Information Technology – Process Assessment. International Standards Organization (2003)
3. Stallinger, F., Neumann, R., Schossleitner, R., Zeilinger, R.: Linking Software Life Cycle Activities with Product Strategy and Economics: Extending ISO/IEC 12207 with Product Management Best Practices. In: O'Connor, R.V., Rout, T., McCaffery, F., Dorling, A. (eds.) SPICE 2011. CCIS, vol. 155, pp. 157–168. Springer, Heidelberg (2011)
4. Stallinger, F., Neumann, R.: Extending ISO/IEC 12207 with Software Product Management: A Process Reference Model Proposal. In: Mas, A., Mesquida, A., Rout, T., O'Connor, R.V., Dorling, A. (eds.) SPICE 2012. CCIS, vol. 290, pp. 93–106. Springer, Heidelberg (2012)
5. van de Weerd, I., Brinkkemper, S., Nieuwenhuis, R., Versendaal, J., Bijlsma, L.: Towards a Reference Framework for Software Product Management. In: 14th IEEE International Requirements Engineering Conference, pp. 319–322. IEEE Computer Society, Minneapolis (2006)
6. A Framework for Software Product Line Practice, Version 5.0, http://www.sei.cmu.edu/productlines/frame_report/index.html
7. Pohl, K., Böckle, G., van der Linden, F.: Software Product Line Engineering – Foundations, Principles, and Techniques. Springer, Berlin (2005)
8. Microsoft Solutions Framework, http://msdn.microsoft.com/de-de/library/bb979125.aspx
9. ISO/IEC FDIS 26550:2013: Software and Systems Engineering - Reference model for product line engineering and management. International Standards Organization (2013)
10. Stallinger, F., Neumann, R., Schossleitner, R., Kriener, S.: Migrating Towards Evolving Software Product Lines: Challenges of an SME in a Core Customer-driven Industrial Systems Engineering Context. In: Second International Workshop on Product Line Approaches in Software Engineering (PLEASE 2011), pp. 15–19. ACM, New York (2011)
11. Stallinger, F., Neumann, R.: From software to software system products: An add-on process reference model for enhancing ISO/IEC 12207 with product management and system-level reuse. In: Cortellessa, V., Muccini, H., Demirors, O. (eds.) 38th Euromicro Conference on Software Engineering and Advanced Applications (SEAA 2012), pp. 307–314. IEEE Computer Society (2012)

Using ISO/IEC 12207 to Analyze Open Source Software Development Processes: An E-Learning Case Study

Aarthy Krishnamurthy[1] and Rory V. O'Connor[2]

[1] School of Electronic Engineering, Dublin City University, Ireland
[2] School of Computing, Dublin City University, Ireland
aarthy.krishnamurthy2@mail.dcu.ie, roconnor@computing.dcu.ie

Abstract. To date, there is no comprehensive study of open source software development process (OSSDP) carried out for open source (OS) e-learning systems. This paper presents the work which objectively analyzes the open source software development (OSSD) practices carried out by e-learning systems development communities and their results are represented using DEMO models. These results are compared using ISO/IEC 12207:2008. The comparison of DEMO models with ISO/IEC 12207 is a useful contribution; as it provides deeper understanding to-wards the OS e-learning system development.

Keywords: Software Development Process, Open Source Software, DEMO Models, Activity Flow Diagrams, E-Learning Systems, ISO/IEC 12207:2008.

1 Introduction and Research Approach

The e-learning systems developed as a Closed Source Software (CSS) follow either a traditional software development process (SDP) or a tailored version to suite the local needs and demands. These development processes have associated standards/guidelines that are followed, which mostly results in good quality software products. However on the other hand, OSS e-learning systems are developed by a community of like-minded developers, who are geographically distributed, yet work together closely on a specific software product [1].

OSSD has gained significant attention in recent years and is widely accepted as reliable products (e.g. Moodle, Apache, Linux, etc.). However, they lack a defined SDP which hinders the delivery of high quality systems to its users. Hence it is imperative to analyze and understand the existing and successfully running OS e-learning systems before developing a generalized OSS process for e-learning systems.

To the best knowledge of authors, there has been no comprehensive study performed on OS e-learning system development activities nor it has been modeled. Hence, the aim of this paper is to objectively analyze the OSSD of three most popular e-learning systems - Moodle, ILIAS and Dokeos. Most importantly, this paper discusses the result of the analysis (represented using DEMO Models) in conjunction with ISO/IEC 12207:2008 standard. This is a crucial work towards developing a generalized OSSDP as using ISO/IEC 12207:2008 is the only way to get a deeper insight of the current OSSD practices.

T. Woronowicz et al. (Eds.): SPICE 2013, CCIS 349, pp. 107–119, 2013.

The research approach is basically divided into two distinct parts. The first part deals with collecting the information about the development practices of Moodle, ILIAS and Dokeos and modeling the results using activity flow diagrams and DEMO models. These are briefly explained in this paper to give an initial understanding of how these results are used in conjunction with ISO/IEC 12207:2008 standard. The second part of the research approach focuses on how these results is used with ISO/IEC 12207:2008. This leads to the detailed understanding of various development activities carried out in all the three OS e-learning systems. These are explained in detail under section 3.

The paper is organized into 4 sections. Section 1 introduced the research background and the objective of this research along with the research approach used. Section 2 describes briefly the DEMO models and its results. Section 3 discusses the important aspect of this paper – ISO/IEC 12207:2008 and its mapping with DEMO results. Finally Section 4 presents the conclusion and future work.

2   Activity Flow Representation and DEMO Models

The initial task under the first part of this research work is towards discovering the current development practices on all the three OS e-learning systems [2]. The findings of the background study were represented as activity flow diagram for Moodle, ILIAS and Dokeos [3]. Each of the three OS e-learning system has executed different activities at different stages of development. Notably, the manner in which each stage is carried out depends entirely on the expertise, experience and availability of resources and skills. Further, the initial background study helped in identifying the various implicit and explicit stages of development. There were distinct similarities and differences between Moodle, ILIAS and Dokeos on different aspects. These are summarized in Table 1. Please note that the activity flow diagrams are introduced here because the results of this background work are an input towards the analysis of OSSDP.

Table 1. Comparison results based on the background study

	Moodle	ILIAS	Dokeos
No of development stages	Not explicitly categorized	Six explicit stages	Not explicitly categorized
Who validates proposed idea	Anyone can validate	Only the core team validates	No validation
Development plan	No plan is produced	No plan is produced	No plan is produced
Person(s) responsible for development	Initial volunteer & subsequent team formation	Initial volunteer & subsequent team formation	Any interested volunteers
Testing	Anyone can test at any time.	Anyone can test at anytime	Anyone can test until release
Release	Two stage release process is followed	Two stage release process is followed	One stage with no beta release

There have been few works carried out for modeling OSSD process. The model proposed by Jensen and Scacchi [4] for discovering the process followed for OSS development doesn't provide complete clarification for investigating the results obtained which inhibits its use for generalizing the OSSD process. Another model Basili and Lonchamp uses a multi-level approach for modeling the OSSD process [5] However, it does not provide precise notations for specifying the relationship between the product and the role. In addition, both the modeling techniques are depended upon the implementation method. Hence, DEMO methodology was considered in this research work as it overcomes the drawbacks of activity flow diagrams and also is independent of the implementation method.

DEMO (Design and Engineering Methodology for Organizations) is a methodology used for developing high-level and abstract models of construction and operation of organizations. DEMO applies enterprise ontology theory and 'Ontology' can be simply defined as an 'explicit specification of a conceptualization' [6]. DEMO models focuses on the communication pattern between human actors and various outputs produced during software development [7]. In this case we can use DEMO models to provide a high level overview of how the OS e-learning software products are developed without taking into consideration the technology or technique used for the development. The DEMO methodology and models has been already applied to OS systems and has been proved to provide a high quality, abstract model [7].

DEMO specifies various axioms, two of which are used in this wok. The first is the production axiom and according to this axiom, social individuals/actors fulfill the goals of an enterprise by performing 'acts'. The result of successfully performing an act is recorded in a 'fact'. On the ontological level, two kinds of acts occur: production acts (P-acts) and coordination acts (C-acts). Performing a P-act correspond to the delivery of products, services and information to the environment of an organization. By performing a P-act, a new production fact (P-fact) is brought into existence. In order to complete the performance of a P-act, social individuals /actors have to communicate, negotiate and commit themselves. These activities are called coordination acts (C-acts), and they result in coordination facts (C-facts).

The second axiom is the transaction axiom and it states that the coordination involved to successfully complete a P-act can be expressed in a universal pattern, which is called a 'Transaction'. A transaction consists of three phases: order phase, execution phase and result phase. In the order phase, the actors negotiate about the P-fact that is the subject of the transaction. Once an agreement is reached, the P-fact is produced in the execution phase. In the result phase, the actors can negotiate and discuss about the result of the transaction. These phases are subdivided into process steps, which consist of four coordination acts and one production act. C-act includes request, promise, state and accept. While the production act includes execute (process step). In DEMO, exactly two actors are associated with a transaction: an initiator and an executor. The authority over the execution of a single transaction is assigned to the executor [6]. This authority can be attributed to individuals or groups of individuals.

There are several ways (i.e., numerous diagrammatic representations) for modeling a development process using DEMO methodology. They include: *State model, Action model, Interstriction model, Process structure diagram (PSD) and Actor transaction diagram (ATD).* The ATD shows the various actors' involvement in specific communication for executing a task and which actor actually produces the P-fact. This is a major advantage over the activity flow representation. In addition, ATD provides an overview of the actors and transactions within the scope of the enterprise/project and therefore aggregates the information contained within the PSD. In this paper we present the ATD for all three OS e-learning systems along with various outputs produced during the software development.

DEMO Model (ATD) for Moodle: The ATD for Moodle development is shown in Fig. 1, wherein the information of each of the PSD is aggregated. The actors involved in developing Moodle include; the Moodle community, core team/owner, developer, triage, integration reviewer, tester and a maintainer. Notably, Moodle carries out 11 transactions in total, from inception to release. These are denoted by 'T0x', where 'x' ranges from 1 to maximum number of transactions. In addition, Fig. 1 demonstrates two important points: Firstly, it shows which actor starts communicating with the other for executing a particular task. Secondly, it shows which actor actually executes the task to produce corresponding output (P-fact). For instance, 'Community' starts communicating with the 'Core team' for performing a transaction 'T01'. It is the 'Core Team's' responsibility to carry out the task and is denoted by a '■' at the end of the line.

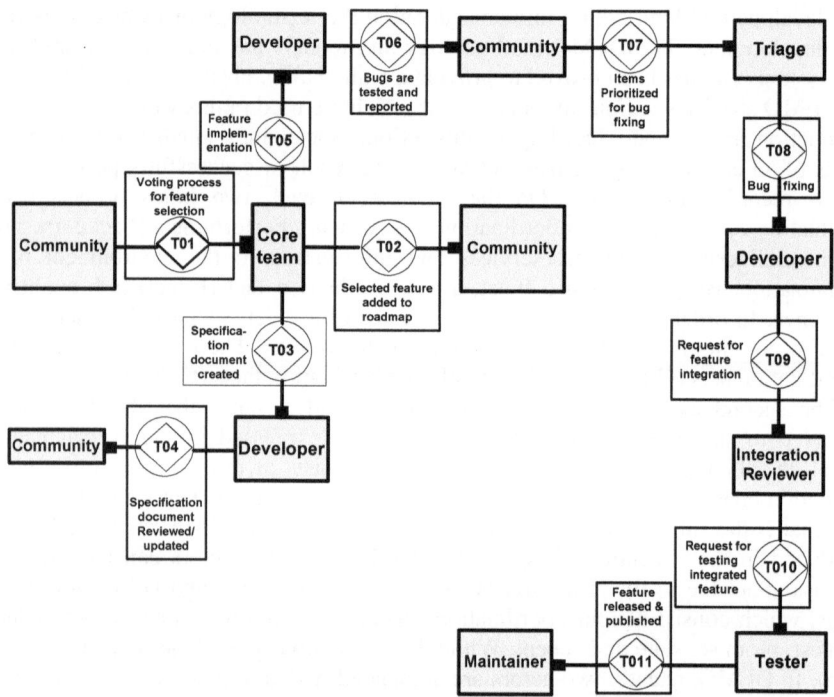

Fig. 1. ATD for Moodle Development

In Moodle, there are 4 transactions to be executed in order to select a feature and develop requirement specification for the selected feature(s). They are T01, T02, T03 and T04. The roles that execute the tasks corresponding to these transactions are the Moodle community, owner/core team and the developer. P-fact is produced on successful execution of T01which implies successful completion of voting process for selecting the feature. Once the voting is done, the features with highest number of votes are selected (immediate requirement) and are added to the roadmap list. Therefore, the P-fact of T02 is the roadmap developed for feature implementation. In Moodle, specification document are to be created for each of the feature added to the roadmap. Hence the corresponding P-fact produced by executing T03 is the specification document. Finally, the P-fact for the transaction T04 is the suggestions and discussion on the specification document that the entire community provides, based on the specification released earlier.

The next stage in Moodle development is the implementation of the selected Moodle feature. Two transactions were executed for implementing and verifying the implementation of the Moodle feature (T05 & T06). The owner/core team starts communicating with the developer by placing a request 'T05 rq' for developing a particular feature. The developer promises to do the work which is indicated as 'T05 pm' and executes the task denoted by 'T05 ex'. The developer then requests the community to verify his work before merging the code 'T06 rq'. The community promises to verify the code 'T06 pm', verifies it and changes its status as verified 'T06 st'. Further, it sends the feedback to the developer who in turn acknowledges the work, 'T06 ac'. It then changes the status 'T05 st' and sends the code to the owner/core team. They in turn acknowledge the developer 'T05 ac'. The P-fact of transaction, T05 implies the successful implementation of the Moodle feature. P-fact of T06 is the completion of initial testing and bugs found in this testing are then reported for a fix.

Once the implementation was successfully finished, the feature is then tested and released to the Moodle-using community - Transactions T07 through T011 (for testing and releasing the Moodle feature developed). The P-fact of T07 is the prioritized list of items developed by the triage for fixing & testing. These are then sent to the developer. The developer then fixes the issue and tests it. The bugs that are fixed form the P-fact of T08 and are then added to the integration queue. The integration reviewers are responsible for integrating the same - the P-fact of T09. In transaction T010, the integrated code is tested and verified. The corresponding P-fact is the updated tracker item. The P-fact of the final transaction T011 is latest version of the software, which would be freely available for download from production repository. The P-facts produced during Moodle development are summarized in Table 2.

Table 2. P-Facts produced during Moodle development

Transaction	P-facts
T01	Voting process is completed.
T02	Development road map is created.
T03	Specification document created.
T04	Selected features are discussed.
T05	Feature is developed.
T06	Feature is tested by the community & bugs reported.
T07	Reported bugs are prioritized.
T08	Bugs are fixed.
T09	Features are added to the integration queue.
T010	Features are integrated and tested.
T011	A stable feature is released.

DEMO Model (ATD) for ILIAS: Various actors' involved in ILIAS development are: the user community, core team, developer, tester and maintainer. The transactions carried out for its development are denoted from T01 through T09 and the ATD for ILIAS is shown in Fig. 2. For selecting a feature in ILIAS, the user community and the core team communicate with each other and subsequently, the core team executes the transaction T01. The P-fact produced for this transaction is a feature wiki page which includes the selection decision along with the discussions that led to the final decision. The next step in ILIAS development is the development of requirement specification. Various actor's involved in developing and verifying the requirement specifications are: core team, user community and the developer. There are three transactions involved in developing the specification (T02, T03 and T04). The P-facts produced for each transaction (T02, T03 & T04) are the creation of requirement specification document, discussions on the specification document. Subsequently, the core team improves the specification doc by implementing some of the suggestions.

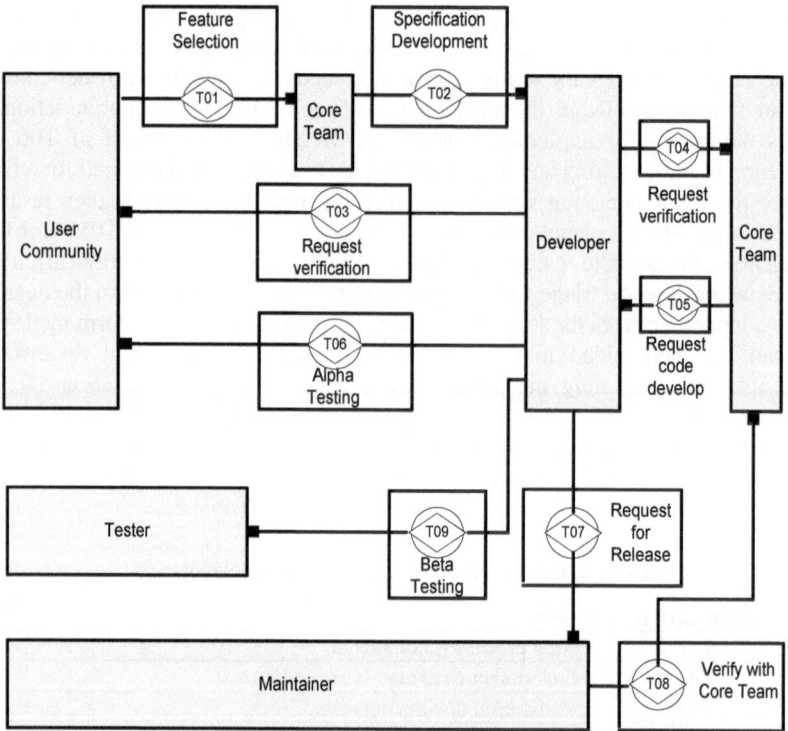

Fig. 2. ATD for ILIAS Development

The next step is feature implementation and this involves 3 main actors: the core team, the developer and the user community over 2 transactions T05 and T06. The P-fact produced by successful execution of T05 is the successful implementation of the feature selected. The P-fact of T06 is the bug reported on that feature in their bug reporting system. Once the feature is developed, it has to be tested and released and the actors involved in this are developer, maintainer, core team and tester. There are three transactions T07, T08 & T09 executed by these roles. The P-facts achieved by the transactions are released working feature, updated roadmap with the released feature included in it and the bugs reported after the release in the bug tracking system. The P-facts have been summarized in Table 3.

Table 3. P-Facts produced during ILIAS development

Transaction	P-facts
T01	Feature wiki with selected features is created.
T02	Specification document is developed.
T03	Specification document is discussed.
T04	Specification document is improved.
T05	Feature is developed.
T06	Feature is tested and bugs are reported.
T07	Accepted feature is released.
T08	Release road map is developed.
T09	Tested the released feature and bugs are reported to bug tracking system.

DEMO Model (ATD) for Dokeos: The ATD for Dokeos development is shown in Fig. 3. The actors involved in Dokeos development are user community, core team and the Dokeos Company. In all, 7 transactions are executed in developing a feature successfully for Dokeos (T01 through T07).

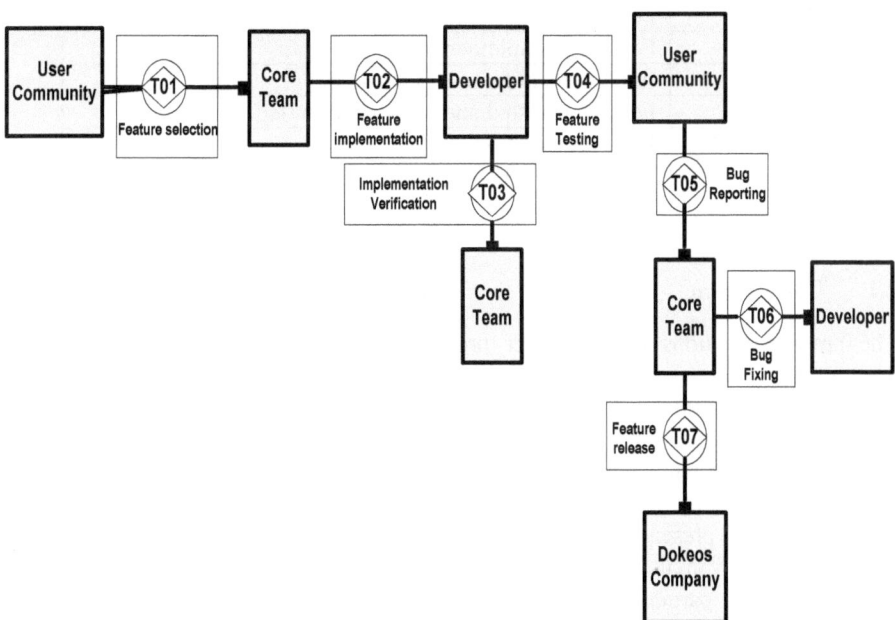

Fig. 3. ATD representation for Dokeos

Dokeos features are selected by the core team from the dream map (user community requests are polled in dream map) to road map. This is done in a single transaction T01. The transaction is initiated by the user community by adding the feature's request to the dream map. The core team would then select the feature and add it to the roadmap - the P-fact of the transaction T01. Once, the feature is selected by the core team for development, the developers are requested to build the feature which is depicted by transaction T02. The P-fact for T02 is the developed feature itself. Once the feature is developed, the developer requests the core team (T03) to verify and fix anomalies, if any. The P-fact of T03 is the verified and fixed feature. For testing and fixing the bug, the developer, core team and the user community communicate with each other. The developer requests the user community to carry out testing on the newly developed feature (T04). Once the user finishes testing, the bug fixes are reported to the core team which is the P-fact of T04. The core team in turn verifies, categorizes and organizes all the reported bugs. This list of verified, categorized and organized bugs is the P-fact of T05. These are then forwarded to the corresponding developer to fix the issues (T06). The fixed and working feature becomes the P-fact of T06. The next step is releasing the feature and the core team initiates the release process by requesting the Dokeos Company with a request. Then the feature is released by the Dokeos Company which is executed in transaction T07. The P-facts produced during Dokeos development are summarized in Table 4.

Table 4. P-Facts produced during Dokeos development

Transaction	P-facts
T01	Feature is selected for development.
T02	Feature is implemented.
T03	Implemented feature is verified.
T04	Feature is tested and bugs are reported.
T05	Bugs are prioritized.
T06	Bugs are fixed.
T07	Feature is released.

2.1   Comparison

The previous sections in this paper provide sufficient details with regard to the development practices followed by the three OS e-learning systems. The activity flow diagrams provided information about the implicit/explicit software development stages and also helped in classifying the same. On the other hand, DEMO models provided information about what outcomes have been produced in each of the development stages (by executing a particular transaction) and by whom was that transaction executed. Table 5 presents various transactions executed for different basic development stages identified from the background study. For each of the three OS e-learning system development, if a particular development stage was identified as being executed then a tick mark '☑' is placed in the corresponding cell in Table 5; otherwise a cross mark '☒'

is placed. Also, the transaction executed under a particular development which produces a successful outcome is mentioned inside the parentheses '[ ]'. However at this stage it is not clear that, to what extent each of the OS e-learning systems had carried out each of the activities corresponding to various development stages. Therefore, there is a need for ISO/IEC 12207:2008 which helps in getting a deeper insight into the development processes of these OS e-learning systems.

Table 5. Summary of the research findings

Development stages	Moodle	ILIAS	Dokeos
Inception	☑ [T01, T02]	☑ [T01]	☑ [T01]
Planning	☒	☒	☒
Requirement Analysis	☑ [T03, T04]	☑ [T02, T03, T04]	☒
Design	☑ [T03, T04]	☑ [T02, T03, T04]	
Implementation	☑ [T05, T06]	☑ [T05, T06]	☑ [T02, T03]
Testing	☑ [T07, T08]	☑ [T08, T09]	☑ [T04, T05, T06]
Release & maintenance	☑ [T09, T010, T011]	☑ [T07]	☑ [T07]

3   ISO/IEC 12207: 2008 Mapping

ISO/IEC 12207:2008 standard is a fully integrated suite of system and software life cycle processes which explains seven process groups, forty three processes, hundred and twenty one activities and four hundred and six tasks. Each of the processes within those process groups is described in terms of its (a) scope, (b) purpose, (c) desired outcomes, (d) list of activities and tasks which need to be performed in order to achieve the outcomes. The Software implementation processes are divided into six lower level processes with 29 outcomes that can be achieved by successfully carrying out the software implementation process and its corresponding activities and tasks [8, 9, 10]. Table 6 lists all possible outcomes that can be expected when these lower level processes are completed successfully.

The major advantage of using ISO/IEC 12207:2008 standard is that the outcomes mentioned by the standards can be compared directly with the P-Facts that were identified from the DEMO models. The comparative details are presented in Table 6. For each outcome mentioned by the standard, the corresponding transaction for Moodle, ILIAS and Dokeos have been mapped. Further, any particular outcome stated in the standard that is not met by the OS development community is denoted with an '-'. Notably, in case of RA8, all three OS e-learning systems produce data logical information (marked with '*') whereas outcomes of other transactions correspond to ontological information.

Table 6. ISO/IEC 12207:2008 Process Groups

Lower Level Process		Possible Outcomes
Requirement Analysis Process	RA1	Requirements of software element & interfaces are defined
	RA2	Requirements analyzed for correctness & testability
	RA3	Understand the impact of the requirement on environment
	RA4	Consistency & traceability between system requirement are drawn
	RA5	Software requirement for implementation are defined
	RA6	Software requirements are approved and updated
	RA7	Changes to the requirement are evaluated
	RA8	Requirements are base-lined & communicated to all parties
Architectural Design Process	AD1	Software architecture is designed and base-lined
	AD2	Internal & external interfaces of each s/w item are defined
	AD3	Consistency & traceability is established
Detailed Design Process	DD1	Detailed design of each software component is defined
	DD2	External interfaces are defined
	DD3	Consistency and traceability are established between architectural design, requirement & detailed design
Construction Process	CP1	Verification criteria defined against requirements
	CP2	Software units defined by design are produced.
	CP3	Consistency & traceability are established
	CP4	Verification against requirement and design is accomplished
Integration Process	IP1	Integration strategy is developed
	IP2	Verification criteria for s/w items are developed
	IP3	Software items are verified using defined criteria
	IP4	Software item defined by integration strategy are produced.
	IP5	Results of integration testing are recorded.
	IP6	Consistency & traceability are established
	IP7	Regression strategy is developed and applied when change occurs
Qualification & Testing Process	QT1	Criteria for the integrated software are developed that demonstrates compliance with the software requirements
	QT2	Integrated software is verified using the defined criteria
	QT3	Test results are recorded.
	QT4	A regression strategy is developed and applied

It can be observed from Table 7 that Moodle meets 16 out of 29 outcomes mentioned by the standard by executing 11 transactions. On the other hand, ILIAS meets 14 out of 29 outcomes by executing 9 transactions while Dokeos meets only 8 out of 29 outcomes by executing 7 transactions. Even though Moodle and ILIAS has achieved higher number of outcomes as compared to Dokeos, all three OS e-learning systems still have a huge scope for improvement in different stages of development.

Table 7. Comparison with ISO/IEC 12207:2008 Process Groups

Outcomes	Moodle	ILIAS	Dokeos
RA1	T02	T02	-
RA2	T01	T03	-
RA3	T01	T01	T01
RA4	-	-	-
RA5	-	-	-
RA6	T01 & T02	T04	T01
RA7	-	-	-
RA8	Road maps*	Feature wiki*	Road maps*
AD1	-	-	-
AD2	-	-	-
AD3	-	-	-
DD1	T03	T02	-
DD2	-	-	-
DD3	T04	T03	-
CP1	T04	-	-
CP2	T05	T05	T02
CP3	T06	T06	T03
CP4	T06, T07 & T08	T06	T03
IP1	T09	-	-
IP2	-	-	-
IP3	T09	T07	T04
IP4	T010, T011	T07	T07
IP5	T010	-	T05, T06
IP6	-	T08	-
IP7	-	-	-
QT1	-	-	-
QT2	T010	T09	-
QT3	T010	T09	-
QT4	-	-	-

4   Conclusions

The mapping of the process outcomes and the DEMO models results have identified that none of the OS e-learning systems have achieved all the outcome described by the process. However, it is important to know the extent to which each of the OS e-learning systems have performed. This is done by calculating the percentage of achievement for each of the development stages for all the three e-learning systems.

The percentage of achievement here is defined as the ratio between the number of outcomes achieved and the number of outcomes listed in the standard. For instance, in case of requirement analysis, the standard had prescribed eight outcomes as desired outcome of which Moodle satisfied four. Therefore, the achievement for Moodle under RA is 50%. Table 8 shows the percentage of achievement for each of the six

Table 8. Percentage of achievement by Moodle, ILIAS and Dokeos

	Moodle	ILIAS	Dokeos
Requirement analysis	50%	50%	25%
Architectural design	0%	0%	0%
Detailed design	66%	66%	0%
Construction	100%	75%	75%
Integration	57%	42%	42%
Qualification & testing	50%	50%	0%
Overall	53%	47%	23%

stages for all three OS e-learning systems, along with the overall achievement ratio. This table also shows the weakness in the different development stages of all three OS e-learning systems. Moodle with 53% has the highest achievement rate. On the other hand, with an achievement rate of only 23%, Dokeos performs very poorly. Notably, all three OS e-learning systems have significant weakness in most of the development stages, except for construction stage. Without ISO/IEC 12207:2008, it would have not been possible to identify the underlying weaknesses in each of the development stages for these three OS e-learning systems.

Having identified the whether the OS e-learning system had performed any activities pertaining to a development stage and the extent to which it has performed; it is possible to come up with a generalized OSSDP. Hence the next step would be come up with a strategy on selecting different stages of development, the frequency with which each stage could be performed, various important tasks and activities pertaining to each development stages.

Acknowledgments. Supported by Irish Research Council (IRC) - Embark Initiative Program.

References

1. Scacchi, S., Feller, J., Fitzgerald, B., Hissam, S., Lakhani, K.: Understanding Free/Open Source software Development Process. Software Process Improvement and Practice 11(2), 95–105 (2006)
2. Krishnamurthy, A., O'Connor, R., McManis, J.: Usability in Software Development Process for Open Source e/m-Learning Systems. In: Proceedings of the 4th Irish Human Computer Interaction Conference, iHCI 2010 (2010)
3. Krishnamurthy, A., O'Connor, R.V.: Analysis of Software Development Processes of Open Source E-Learning Systems. In: McCaffery, F., O'Connor, R.V., Messnarz, R. (eds.) EuroSPI 2013. CCIS, vol. 364. Springer, Heidelberg (2013)
4. Jensen, C., Scacchi, W.: Guiding the Discovery of Open Source Software Processes with a Reference Model. In: Feller, J., Fitzgerald, B., Scacchi, W., Sillitti, A. (eds.) Open Source Development, Adoption and Innovation. IFIP, vol. 234, pp. 265–270. Springer, Boston (2007)
5. Basili, V.R., Lonchamp, J.: Open source software development process modeling. In: Acuña, S.T., Juristo, N. (eds.) Software Process Modelling, vol. 10, pp. 29–64. Springer, US (2005)

6. Gruber, T.: Toward Principles for the Design of Ontologies Used for Knowledge Sharing. IJHCS 43(5/6), 907–928 (1994)
7. Huysmans, P., Ven, K., Verelst, J.: Using the DEMO methodology for modeling open source software development processes. Information and Software Technology 52, 656–671 (2010)
8. Clarke, P., O'Connor, R.V.: The situational factors that affect the software development process: Towards a comprehensive reference framework. Journal of Information and Software Technology 54(5), 433–447 (2012)
9. Clarke, P., O'Connor, R.: Harnessing ISO/IEC 12207 to Examine the Extent of SPI Activity in an Organisation. In: Riel, A., O'Connor, R., Tichkiewitch, S., Messnarz, R. (eds.) EuroSPI 2010. CCIS, vol. 99, pp. 25–36. Springer, Heidelberg (2010)
10. Clarke, P., O'Connor, R.V., Yilmaz, M.: A hierarchy of SPI activities for software SMEs: Results from ISO/IEC 12207-based SPI assessments. In: Mas, A., Mesquida, A., Rout, T., O'Connor, R.V., Dorling, A. (eds.) SPICE 2012. CCIS, vol. 290, pp. 62–74. Springer, Heidelberg (2012)

A Case Study on the Need to Consider Personality Types for Software Team Formation

Çağrı Murat Karapıçak and Onur Demirörs

Informatics Institute, Middle East Technical University, Ankara, Turkey
cmkarapicak@gmail.com, demirors@metu.edu.tr

Abstract. Software development is a social activity and the formation of the right team is a critical success factor. Although personality types in software teams and software projects' success criterias have been studied before, there is no well formed methodology for establishing software teams according to the personality types. This study is performed to search the relation between software team members' personality types and project success. To achive this goal, a questionnaire based approach is developed to measure project success and personality types. Two software development projects are assessed with a questionnaire that assesses project success in different aspects. Also, all project team members are assessed with respect to their personality types. Results provide insight that, personality type consideration while forming software teams can play a significant role in project success.

Keywords: Software team formation, Personality type, Project success.

1   Introduction

As software development projects are becoming more and more complicated every day, software industry continue to look for new solutions and new methodologies to improve the success rate of the projects. Time, budget, quality and scope have always been the most important factors in formulating the success of a project. Software development consists of many information gathering and information sharing activities between team members. Different individuals with different personality types work in the same group and place. Today, being a good team member has been risen as an important speciality for individuals, but it is essential that without a well formed team, an individual can not become a successful team member. Personality types can provide critical information for forming software development teams. However, research on this topic, is far from establishing a socially accepted methodology for forming software development teams according to the personality types. Software teams are usually formed according to the structure of an organization or individual experiences of project managers.

In this study we aim to find the relations between personality types and project success. We also aim to identify a more generic success definition for software projects that covers team member's motivation for further projects. For achieving

T. Woronowicz et al. (Eds.): SPICE 2013, CCIS 349, pp. 120–129, 2013.

these goals, we have prepared a questionnaire assessing project success and the effects of personality types on team success. The questionnaire consists of three sections that are Project Information Section, Personal Information Section and Keirsey Temperament Sorter [1] Section from D.Keirsey's book. After the preparation of the questionnaire, we carried out a pilot project in order to update the questionnaire. We than applied the questionnaire in two real life projects.

We have summarized the background and related research on the relation between personality types and project success in Section 2 with personality type definitions that have been used in this study. A summary of our assessment questionnaire is given in Section 3. Then, brief description of our case studies is given in Section 4. Results follow in Section 5. Our findings and conclusions are given in Section 6 together with plans for future work.

2   Background and Related Research

In this section we summarize the background on personality types and provide related research on personality type and software project success.

R.P. Oisen defined project management on early 1970s as *"the application of a collection of tools and techniques to direct the use of diverse resources toward the accomplishment of a unique, complex, one-time task within time, cost and quality constraints"* [2]. The success criteria that are included in this definition are referred as Iron Triangle. Also, the British Standard for project management BS60794 [3] 1996 defined project management as *"The planning, monitoring and control of all aspects of a project and the motivation of all those involved in it to achieve the project objectives on time and to the specified cost, quality and performance"*. These success criteria for measuring project success continue to be used today. Other writers Turner [4], Morris and Hough [5], Wateridge [6] and deWit [7] all agree cost, time and quality should be used as success criteria, but not exclusively.

The fact that software teams consist of different individuals with different personality types interacting each other in every phase of a development project, one approach states that, software development is a social activity [8]. In line with this statement, project success and personality type relation has been researched during the last decade. O.Mazni, S.Syed-Abdullah and N.Hussin have studied the effects of heterogeneous and homogenous teams on projects's success in terms of quality. And, they have concluded that heterogenous teams are more successfull in challenging projects and homogenoues teams are more successfull in straightforward projects [9]. In another study, R.H.Rutherfoord has stated that teams formed by different personality types brings more successful results [10]. In addition to these, L.Capretz and F.Ahmed has mapped personality types and software development team's roles [11] according to the role requirements and a card based approach for classifying team members according to their personality types in a periodic table format [12] has been suggested by M.Yılmaz and R.V.O'Connor.

Although roles in software development teams have been mapped to personality types with respect to role requirements, or the effects of homogenous and heteregenous teams on projects's success has been identified in terms of quality we do not have socially accepted methodology for forming software development teams considering the personality types. To form such a methodology it is essential to have deeper knowledge on the relation between personality types and project success.

2.1   Personality Types

Based on Freud and Adler's study, Jung has classified persons according to their psychological functions in three types [13] that are identified by understanding the preferences of someone over others. In his classification, basic individual's functions are;

- differences in style of information gathering,
- decision making,
- orientation of individuals mostly interested in self (introverts) or to the outside world for external incitement (extroverts)

Myer-Briggs added new category to Jung's model for understanding individuals based on their perception and judgment characteristics [14]. Myer-Briggs personality types based on four dichotomies that are;

- (E/I) extroversion versus introversion, which is established on how an individual is energized, differences in style of information gathering,
- (N/S) intuition versus sensing, which is based on how an individual gathers information,
- (T/F) thinking versus feeling defines how an individual decides,
- (P/J) perceiving versus judging singles out the lifestyle choices of people

Then , Keirsey used Myer-Briggs types to categorize 16 combinations of Myer-Briggs Types into four [1]. These categories are;

- Artisans: ESTP, ISTP, ESFP, ISFP
- Guardians: ESTJ, ISTJ, ESFJ, ISFJ
- Idealists: ENFJ, INFJ, ENFP, INFP
- Rationals: ENTJ, INTJ, ENTP, INTP

Sixteen different Myer-Briggs personality type combinations were used in our study for personality type identification. Myers-Briggs Type Indicator (MBTI)[14] and Keirsey Temperament Sorter [1] may be used for identifying each individual's personality types. Keirsey Temperament Sorter is selected to be used in our study, because Keirsey Temperament Sorter is also used frequently for professional carrier guidance.

3   Assessment Questionnaire

A questionnaire has been prepared in order to assess the project success and personality types. This questionnaire consists of three sections: project success evaluation section that assesses the project information answered by only project managers, personal information section and personality temperament sorter section that assesses personal information and personality types respectively answered by all team members including project manager.

3.1   Project Information Section

This section consists of 34 questions which have been answered by only project managers. Main purpose is to gather information about project's schedule, budget and quality. Sample questions are listed in Table 1 below.

Table 1. Sample questions of Project Information Section

What's the planned and actual size of the project?
What's the planned and actual size of the project?
What's the planned effort and actual effort of the project?
What's the planned duration and actual duration of the project?
What's the planned budget and actual budget of the project?
Evaluate your project success with respect to customer requests and bugs found in the first six months time after delivery.
How do you evaluate the cost of the customer requests and bugs found in the first six months time after delivery with respect to your expectations?

3.2   Personal Information Section

This section consists of 13 questions which have been answered by all team members. Main purpose of this section is to gather information about personal thoughts about the project. Sample questions are listed in Table 2 below.

Table 2. Sample questions of Personal Information Section

What's your role?
What percentage of time have you spent for reworks?
What is the type of the project?
How do you evaluate the project in terms of working in a team?
How do you evaluate the project in terms of learning new technologies, tools or methodologies?
How do you evaluate the project in terms of improving yourself?

3.3   Keirsey Temperament Sorter Section

This section consists of 70 multiple choice questions and the results of each individual have been analyzed according to D.Keirsey's book. Sample questions are listed in Table 3 below.

Table 3. Sample questions of Keirsey Temperament Sorter

Is it worse to a) have your head in the clouds b) be in a rut
Is clutter in the workplace something you a) take time to straighten up b) tolerate pretty well
Are you more interested in a) what is actual b) what is possible
At a party, do you a) interact with many, even strangers b) interact with a few friends

4   Case Study

Our goal in this study is to find the relations between individuals' personality types and project success, and to define the project success in a wider perspective. To achieve these goals we have developed two systematic questionnaires to assess the project success and personality types. First of all, we have decided on our project success criteria to include traditional cost, time and scope/quality related questions and Myer-Briggs personality type definitions were used for personality type definition. The questionnaire has been applied in a pilot project. The results are evaluated and questionnaire is updated based on the gathered feedback. We than applied the questionnaires in a wider framework with two real life projects.

4.1   Research Questions

In order to find a relation between personality types and project success, we have explored the answers of the following questions:

- Are there any commonalities between team members' personality types in a successful project?
- Are there any commonalities between team members' personality types in an unsuccessful project?
- Are there any differentiation point between successful and unsuccessful teams in terms of personality types?

In order to find a relation between social success aspect and other aspects like schedule, budget, quality scope, we have explored the answers of the following question:

- Is social success of a project depends on the success of other aspects?

4.2   Case and Subjects Selection

We have three main selection criteria for candidate cases. First one is that we selected recently finished projects to be able assess the project success as we are evaluating the deviation between planned and finished values in terms of time, budget, quality and scope. Second criteria is the project team should be consisted of at least four members and at most 10 members. As the size of team might be a major factor for how an individual might participate we limit our cases to medium sized teams. Third one is that the project should be mainly a software development project.

By using these criteria, a pilot project was selected for our questionnaire's evaluation. We have assessed a research and development project completed by a team consists of four members. According to the feedbacks collected about questionnaire, we have realized that, there are some missing questions in our questionnaire like questions about project type and project customer. Also, some social success assessment questions like "How do you evaluate the project in terms of learning new technologies, tools or methodologies?" have been inserted to questionnaire after pilot project. After that phase, one successful project and one unsuccessful project were selected in order to analyse relations with personality types. The first project was a contract based project from defense industry and was closed with a high success. And the second project was a contract based project from telecommunications industry and was failed.

4.3   Data Collection Procedure

We applied our questionnaire to a pilot project by interviews. We also gathered feedbacks on printed questionnaires. We have applied questionnaire to other two cases by e-mailing to each team member individually. And, we gathered results again with e-mails. Project success results were shared with managers and personality type results were shared with team members individually for validation.

4.4   Analysis Procedure

For evaluating project success, the answers are analysed and deviation percentages for budget, schedule, scope and effort dimensions from planned and actual values are derived. These dimensions have been named as "successful" if the deviation for that dimension was below or equal to twenty percent. Project success criteria in scope, effort, schedule and budget dimensions are listed in Table 4 below

Table 4. Project Success Criterias for Scope, Effort, Schedule and Budget

Aspect	Success Criteria	Result
Scope	Deviation below or equal to %20	Successful
	Deviation above %20	Unsuccessful
Effort	Deviation below or equal to %20	Successful
	Deviation above %20	Unsuccessful
Schedule	Deviation below or equal to %20	Successful
	Deviation above %20	Unsuccessful
Budget	Deviation below or equal to %20	Successful
	Deviation above %20	Unsuccessful

For quality and social success dimensions, all questions are answered within a scale that is from one to five. These dimensions have been named as "successful" if the median were above or equal to four. Project success criteria in quality and social success dimensions are listed in Table 5. Personality type analysis was done according to scoring sheet from D.Keirsey's book [1].

Table 5. Project Success Criterias for Social Success and Quality

Aspect	Success Criteria	Result
Social Success	Score of 4 or 5 over 5	Successful
	Score of 1,2,3nd 5 over 5	Unsuccessful
Quality	Score of 4 or 5 over 5	Successful
	Score of 1,2,3nd 5 over 5	Unsuccessful

5   Results

5.1   Results of Project-1

The project was a contract based software development project, and it was completed by a team consists of five members. Project Success assessment results for all dimensions are given in Table 6 and in Table7 below.

Table 6. Project Success Assessment Results in Scope, Effort, Schedule and Budget Dimensions

Aspect	Deviation	Result
Scope	10 %	Successful
Effort	5 %	Successful
Schedule	6.25 %	Successful
Budget	8.3 %	Successful

Table 7. Project Success Assessment Results in Quality and Social Success Dimensions

Aspect	Score	Result
Social success	4	Successful
Quality	5	Successful

With respect to the results listed above, this project categorized as a successful project as in all dimensions, our success criteria have been achieved. The maximum deviation is seen as 10 % in scope aspect. And, in terms of quality and social success, the minimum score was 4 over 5. Personality types of all team members are identified by Keirsey Temperament Sorter scoring sheet and results for each team member are given in Table 8 below.

Table 8. Team Members' Personality Types

	Team Member 1	Team Member 2	Team Member 3	Team Member 4	Team Member 5
Role	Manager	Analyst	Programmer	Tester	Quality E.
Personality Type	ESTJ	ESFJ, ESFP	ISTJ	ISFJ	INFJ

5.2   Results of Project-2

The project was again a contract based software development project, and it was completed by a team consists of seven members. Project Success assessment results for all dimensions are given in Table 9 and in Table 10 below.

Table 9. Project Success Assessment Results in Scope, Effort, Schedule & Budget

Aspect	Deviation	Result
Scope	70 %	Unsuccessful
Effort	166 %	Unsuccessful
Schedule	100 %	Unsuccessful
Budget	50 %	Unsuccessful

Table 10. Project Success Assessment Results in Quality & Social Success

Aspect	Score	Result
Social success	4	Successful
Quality	1	Unsuccessful

With respect to the results listed above, this project cannot be categorized as a successful project as in four dimensions, project goals have not been achieved. However, it was an unpredictable result that this project has been a successful project in terms of social success despite the fact that in all other dimensions, the project has been failed. Personality types of all team members are identified by Keirsey Temperament Sorter scoring sheet and results for each team member are given in Table 11 below.

Table 11. Team Members' Personality Types

	Team Member 1	Team Member 2	Team Member 3	Team Member 4	Team Member 5	Team Member 6	Team Member 7
Role	Analyst	Programmer	Analyst	Programmer	Analyst	Tester	Programmer
Personality Type	INTJ	INTJ	ENFP, INFP	ENTJ, INTJ, ENFJ, INFJ	ENFJ	ESTJ	ISTJ

5.3 Personality Type Analysis

In order to analyze the commonalities for each team in terms of personality, we have created Table 12 from our results.

Table 12. Personality Type Distribution of team members in two companies

	Team1					Team2						
	TM1	TM2	TM3	TM4	TM5	TM1	TM2	TM3	TM4	TM5	TM6	TM7
E	X	X						X	X	X	X	
I			X	X	X	X	X	X	X			X
S	X	X	X	X							X	X
N					X	X	X	X	X	X		
T	X		X			X	X		X		X	X
Γ		X		X	X			X	X	X		
J	X	X	X	X	X	X	X		X	X	X	X
P		X						X				

And, we have compared characteristic types according to the percentages of personality types in two teams respectively. Percentages of each personality type are given in Table 13 below.

Table 13. Personality Type Comparison in Two Teams

	Team1	Team2
E	40 %	57 %
I	60 %	71 %
S	80 %	29 %
N	20 %	71 %
T	40 %	71 %
F	60 %	43 %
J	100 %	86 %
P	20 %	14 %

We have concluded from the results of both Team1 and Team 2, Judgment (J) type is dominant in both teams with their highest percentage respectively 100% and 86% in all types. On the other hand, we have observed that Team1 and Team2 differ in gathering information type that Sensing (S) and Intuition (N) type percentages are reversed in two teams. Four of five team members have Sensing (S) characteristics in their personality type in Team1, and the percentage for having a Sensing(S) type is the second most after Judgment (J) characteristic type. But in the results of Team2, only two of seven team members have Sensing (S) characteristics in their personality and this is the lowest percentage in all types. So, we have concluded that this characteristic type of individuals may have an effect on project success. Judging (J) again has the highest percentage in all types in Team 2, and it was an expected result for software development teams, because employees in software industry usually are engineers, and they have been educated for behaving rationally at school and throughout their carriers.

6   Conclusion

In this research, we studied the relation between personality types and project success. Also project success criteria have been studied in different dimensions. We have analyzed two software projects - one was completed successfully and the other one was failed. As a result, we have identified social success as a dimension to be measured in software projects. We have observed that social success can be independent from other dimensions and can be achieved without the success in other more traditional dimensions - scope, time, budget and quality. The results show that social success should be an important aspect for formulating the software project success and software plans should include such goals as well. The early results show us that establishing a systematic methodology for software team formation is required and such a methodology can be based primarily on the personality types. However, further research is required to establish such a methodology.

In terms of personality types, we have observed that Sensing (S) and Intuition (N) dichotomy can play a significant role in project success as it was the unique differentiation point in our case studies. On the other hand, we have seen that, Judging (J) characteristic is the most common type in all twelve team members. However the amount of data we gathered so far do not allow us to perform detailed statistical analysis to depict the relation between project success and personality types in other aspects.

We are currently extending this study with further projects for achieving statistically significant results. Our target in the first phase is to perform statistical analysis covering at least 5 projects and at least forty individuals.

References

1. Keirsey, D.: Please Understand Me 2. Prometheus Nemesis Book Company (1998)
2. Oisen, R.P.: Can project management be defined? Project Management Quarterly 2(1), 12–14 (1971)
3. British Standard in Project Management 6079 (1996) ISBN 0 58025594 8
4. Turner, J.R.: The Handbook of Project-based Management. McGraw-Hill (1993)
5. Morris, P.W.G., Hough, G.H.: The Anatomy of Major Projects. John Wiley (1987)
6. Wateridge, J.: How can IS/IT projects be measured for success? International Journal of Project Management 16(1), 59–63 (1998)
7. de Wit, A.: Measurement of project management success. International Journal of Project Management 6(3), 164–170 (1988)
8. Dittrich, Y., Floyd, C., Klischewski, R.: Social thinking-software practice. The MIT Press (2002)
9. Mazni, O., Syed-Abdullah, S., Hussin, N.: Analyzing personality types to predict team performance. In: 2010 International Conference on Science and Social Research (CSSR), pp. 624–628. IEEE (2010)
10. Rutherfoord, R.: Using personality inventories to help form teams for software engineering class projects. ACM SIGCSE Bulletin 33(3), 73–76 (2001)
11. Capretz, L., Ahmed, F.: Making sense of software development and personality types. IT Professional 12(1), 6–13 (2010)
12. Yilmaz, M., O'Connor, R.V., Clarke, P.: A Systematic Approach to the Comparison of Roles in the Software Development Processes. In: Mas, A., Mesquida, A., Rout, T., O'Connor, R.V., Dorling, A. (eds.) SPICE 2012. CCIS, vol. 290, pp. 198–209. Springer, Heidelberg (2012)
13. Jung, C., Baynes, H., Hull, R.: Psychological types. Routledge (1991)
14. Myers, I., McCaulley, M., Quenk, N., Hammer, A.: MBTI manual. Consulting Psychologists Press (1999)

Assessment of Agile Maturity Models:
A Multiple Case Study

Ozden Ozcan-Top and Onur Demirörs

Informatics Institute, Middle East Technical University, Ankara, Turkey
ozden.top@fujitsu.net.tr, demirors@metu.edu.tr

Abstract. Agile methods are welcomed by software community in recent years. The move from traditional methods to agile methods is not straightforward. Software organizations need assistance to achieve transition from traditional software development approaches to agile approaches and to improve their agile capability. During the last few years several agile maturity models/frameworks are developed to guide organizations in agile process improvement and agile adoption. In this study, we assess the strengths and weaknesses of agile maturity models/frameworks from agile process assessment and agile process improvement perspectives. To assess the models we have applied the models in a selected software organization. We discuss the strengths and weakness of each model and provide suggestions for their utilization.

Keywords: Agile Maturity Models, Agile Maturity Frameworks, Agile Process Maturity, Agile Assessment Models.

1   Introduction

Agile methods have proved their success since the publication of agile principles in 2001, and gained acceptance by increasing business value, reducing documentation and speeding up delivery in software projects [1]. The demands from organizations to implement agile methods have been growing over the last decade. Major concerns of organizations while adopting agile practices are to identify how far they are to be "agile" and how agile they can be [2]. On the other hand, agile concepts were misinterpreted or "agile" was used as an excuse for being undisciplined by some of the organizations. There is a fundamental need to assist organizations in adopting agile methods/practices and to guide them for improving their agile capability [3]. Structural approaches such as maturity models or frameworks aim to assist the transition of organizations to agile by providing comprehensive guidance on agile processes, introducing roadmaps and describing what it means to be "agile".

The objectives of this study are; to determine how sufficient the existing agile maturity models/frameworks in providing insight about an organization's agile maturity and to identify the strengths and weaknesses of the models/frameworks in agile process improvement. Findings were obtained from a multiple case study in which we assessed the agile maturity of a software development organization using five agile maturity models/frameworks. The organization is a small sized software company in

T. Woronowicz et al. (Eds.): SPICE 2013, CCIS 349, pp. 130–141, 2013.

which agile practices have been applied for about 1.5 years in small or medium scaled software development projects. We interpreted the results of the case study and compared the characteristics of the models/frameworks based on a set of predefined criteria.

The rest of this paper is organized as follows: In Section 2, we describe the case study and agile maturity models/frameworks. In Section 3, we discuss the assessment results. Finally, in Section 4 we provide conclusions.

2   The Case Study

2.1   Case Study Design

We planned to conduct a multiple case study which we aimed to answer the following research questions:

RQ1: How sufficient are the existing agile maturity models in providing insight about an organization's agile capability?

RQ 2: What are the strengths and weaknesses of the agile maturity models?

The case study was planned to be performed in two phases: Theoretical and Practical assessment. Theoretical assessment was planned to involve detailed analysis of the maturity models from the references that we obtained with a review of the literature. In order to ensure the objectivity and correctness of the evaluation process, we decided to perform the assessment based on a set of evaluation criteria which had been previously utilized in similar studies. We planned to review the literature to determine those criteria.   On the other hand, for the practical assessment, we planned to select a software development organization, which develops information systems projects, and claims to apply agile practices/processes within one year time at least in more than one project. We planned to conduct gap analyses to apply the models and to determine agile maturity of the organization relative to reference models. The major aim of the practical assessment is not directly to identify the organization's agile maturity, but to observe the applicability of the models, and to identify the strengths and weaknesses of them with hands-on practices. We would also have chance to evaluate the models' capability in terms of revealing opportunities for process improvement, and how sufficient are the models' internal structures for the assessment of processes.

2.2   Agile Maturity Models/Frameworks

The agile maturity models/frameworks listed in Table 1 were found at the end of a systematic literature review process. The literature review was performed based on specific keywords to agile maturity in 3 research platforms; IEEE Explorer, Web of Science and SpringerLink.   Among 9 models, the first 5 one were decided to be included in the scope of this study. The inclusion criteria were determined as follows:

(1) Detailed description of the model should have been given to enable detailed analysis. M1-M2 and M3 comply with this criterion.
(2) The study should have been published in one of the major conference proceedings or journals, which is an indicator of academic perspective of the model. M1-M2-M3-M4 and M5 comply with this criterion.

Models M6, M7, M8 and M9 which failed to achieve both of those criteria were left out of the scope of this study.

Table 1. List of the Agile Maturity Models/Frameworks

ID	Model Owner	Name of the Model/Framework
M1	Patel and Ramachandran	Agile Maturity Model [4]
M2	Yin	Scrum Maturity Model [5]
M3	Sidky	Agile Adoption Framework [3]
M4	Benefield	Benefield's Model [6]
M5	Ambler	Agile Scaling Model [1]
M6	Humble and Russel	Agile Maturity Model [7]
M7	Malic	Simple Life Cycle Agile Maturity Model [8]
M8	Proulx	Agile Maturity Model [9]
M9	Jayaraj	Agile Maturity Model [10]

2.3   Description of the Case

The organization that we conducted the case study is developing various management information systems related with the digitization of the procurement procedures, health management and law tracking systems. It is a small sized company with sixty employees. The organization found appropriate for the case study since agile processes have been applied for 1.5 years in small or medium scaled software development projects.

The following agile life cycle is applied in agile projects; however there is no defined procedure for these processes yet. After the approval of the project decision, the project team is formed by the project coordinator. In the first week from the starting date, formal meetings are arranged with the customer in order to identify the boundary of the project. In the following weeks, the business analysts work with the customer to elicit high level requirements and to model the user requirements/processes.

Generally the sprint cycle is set to four weeks. At the beginning of the each sprint, requirements are detailed with the customer. No new requirement is generated once the product manager and the customer agree on the current version. Later, the user requirements are mapped to the software requirements. After the code has been developed based on these software requirements, it is deployed to the test environment at the end of the 3rd week of each sprint. Last week of the sprint is dedicated to testing and bug correction activities.

Project team meets twice a week to discuss the project progress. At the end of each sprint, a sprint review meeting is conducted to present newly developed functionality to the customer, and to receive change requests or new requirements. In addition, a sprint retrospective meeting is conducted with the team on a simple format to identify improvement opportunities at the end of each sprint.

Project progress is monitored using burn down charts by project managers. Team velocity is shared with the team members at the end of each sprint. Future predictions and commitments are renewed based on these velocity ratios. After the team has completed planned sprints and all the functionality has been delivered to customer, a maintenance phase is started. In this phase, remaining low priority defects are fixed and small change requests coming from customers are handled. The project is finalized with a project closure meeting, in which all the stakeholders are participated.

2.4   Case Study Conduct

The case study was performed in two phases: the theoretical assessment and practical assessment. The theoretical assessment phase started with the review of the literature to properly determine evaluation criteria. Although there has not been such a study which assessed the qualification of the agile maturity models and published assessment criteria, we examined similar studies performed with CMMI or ISO 15504 to identify assessment criteria. In the given report [11], the purpose, the scope, the elements and the indicators of CMMI and mapping capability of CMMI with ISO 15504 and maturity results' verifiability were criticized based on completeness-clearness-unambiguity criteria. In his book [12], Kneuper assessed the limitations of CMMI in terms of definition of maturity levels and completeness of processes. He also examined CMMI and product quality relation and minimum size of organizations suitable to use CMMI. We set the following assessment criteria being compatible with those studies above:

Fitness for Purpose: An agile maturity model/framework must be developed with the purpose of assessing agile process capability and assisting organizations in software process improvement.

Completeness: An agile maturity model/framework must address all or a subset of major engineering and management processes within a software development life cycle. It must include process related definitions, goals, practices or process success indicators which enable assessment of the agile processes.

Definition of Agile Levels: An agile maturity model/framework must provide definitions of agile levels which enumerate the different degrees of agility. Those maturity levels could be interpreted intuitively and must be designed to complement each other.

Objectivity: At the end of a maturity assessment, verifiable results must be produced. The judgment of the assessor must be at a minimum level.

Correctness: All model elements must be compatible with agile principles. Descriptions, goals and work products must correctly represent the related process or process area.

Consistency: An agile maturity model/framework must be internally consistent. All processes and practices must be at the same logical level. There mustn't be logical or temporal conflicts between two specified model elements.

We performed five separate gap analysis study using the first five maturity models/frameworks (M1-M2-M3-M4 and M5) listed in Table 1. The major purposes of these gap analyses were to identify weaknesses and strengths of the models and their usability/applicability, while assessing the organization's software development processes.

One of the authors had performed assessment meetings with the project manager and quality manager who had involved the management of various agile software development projects in the organization. At the beginning of the gap analysis, we obtained the general overview of the processes and the team structure that were described in Section 2.3. Then, we asked specific questions based on the specified goals, processes, practices and example work products of the models to understand if the requirements of each model are achieved in the projects, or not. In the cases of M1, M2 and M3 the assessment questions had already been provided in the model.

The results of the gap analysis were reviewed by the team who involved in the assessment. Fuzzy issues were clarified and corrections were made at this phase. The duration that was required to perform a gap analysis was determined by the detail level of the model, and it got shortened towards the end of the analyses, since we had already known most of the answers. The gap analyses were finished in 6 person/days in the organization.

In the following days, the models were examined in more detail considering the notes that we had taken during the gap analyses by both of the authors of this paper. Findings of these analyses are presented in the Findings and Discussion section in detail.

Based on the results of the gap analyses, the organization's agile maturity levels are presented in Table 2.

Table 2. Organization's agile maturity based on five models

Maturity Models	MI	M2	M 3	M4	M5
Maturity Levels	Level 1	Level 2	Level 0	Level 0	Not Agile
Name of the Level	Initial	Managed	Not Exists	Not Exists	Not Exists

According to the assessment we performed with Scrum Maturity Model (M2), the organization's maturity level was determined as Level 2: Managed. It was observed that technical agile practices such as test driven development or continuous integration were not carried out in the organization, but agile practices for project management and project tracking activities were performed. Because of this reason, the maturity level of the organization was determined as Level 2: Managed with Scrum Maturity Model. However, the organization does not satisfy the first maturity level requirements of the M3 M4 and M5 models. According to the assessment results performed with the models that evaluate the agile processes also in technical aspects (M1, M3, M4, M5), the agile maturity of the organization was determined as Level 1 or Level 0.

Although we couldn't publish the details of the assessment results in this paper, the gap analysis clearly specified which of the agile processes, practices, and goals for each model/framework were not achieved by the organization. From now on, the aim of the organization must be to determine a roadmap based on the gap analysis results and to focus on agile practices that will provide significant improvement on the productivity of software development.

3   Findings and Discussion

In this section we present the strengths and weaknesses of the models identified during or after the case study M1, M2 and M3 were analyzed in more detail compared to the other models since there exits comprehensive references such as thesis or journal papers about them.

3.1   M1, Agile Maturity Model

"Agile Maturity Model" [4] was developed by Pathel and Ramachandran with a similar structure to the CMMI. It defines the agile maturity in five levels from "initial" to "sustained". The model has been evaluated based on the parameters given in Section 2.1.

Fitness for Purpose: The model has been developed with the purpose of enhancing the adaptability of agile software development methodology and its practices and providing both a software process improvement (SPI) framework and a maturity assessment framework. Although the adequacy of them is questionable, for each maturity level, key process areas and related assessment questionnaires were defined to enable SPI and maturity assessment.

Completeness: For the key process areas (KPA) in each maturity level; process descriptions, goals and example work products, were not explicitly defined. Therefore the analysis has been conducted based on the descriptions in the questionnaires instead of process goals and practices. Although the model includes many processes, it doesn't cover all of the software engineering processes, such as configuration management, change management and project monitoring and control. There is no distinction between the optional and the mandatory practices of the processes.

Definition of Agile Levels: The maturity levels do not complement each other in providing a combined benefit. Gap analyses results showed that, the organization is more successful in achieving the process requirements of Level 4-"Improved" than the process requirements of Level2-"Explored" and Level 3-"Defined" levels. This indicated that the KPAs of 4th Level, which are; project management, sustainable pace, risk assessment and self-organizing team, could have been considered in previous levels.

Objectivity: The model uses a subjective language such as "The customer relationship is maintained very well at this level". As the process definitions include subjective words such as "very good", "better", objective assessment and identification of process improvement goals were not possible.

Correctness: Most of the assessment questionnaires, which were defined for each KPA in each maturity level, consist of the questions/descriptions with no direct relation to the KPA. For example, for the KPA of "On site customer availability" there exists a description in the questionnaire such that "there is a plan exists to manage story cards", which should obviously be considered in Project Management KPA. There is not a direct relation between the KPA of "Delivering Working Products/SW Frequently" and the description of "Only one pair integrates the code at a time". The "story card driven development" KPA includes questions/descriptions related with defect prevention and detection.

Although the goals of 5th maturity level were determined as "tuning project performance" and "defect prevention", KPA's of this level were set as "project planning" and "story cards driven development", which had no relation with these goals. That means it is impossible to meet maturity level goals with corresponding KPAs.

Consistency: Consistency among the abstraction levels of KPAs is weak. Some of them are at process level while the others are at practice level. For example, one KPA from Level 2 is "Project Planning" and the other one is "On site Customer Availability". "Coding Standards" is a KPA for Level 3; however, it can only be a part of higher process such as development.

Questionnaire is the only part that enables detailed analysis of the model. However, contrary to the conventional structures of questionnaires, it includes sentences of order such as "obtain commitment to story cards"; flat (regular) sentences such as "customer is always available".

The existence of spelling and grammar errors and internal inconsistencies significantly decreases the readability. For example, the name of the 5th Level is "Sustained" in one section; and "Mature" in one of the following sections. In addition, the formula given for assessment and the example given to explain the related formula is not consistent. Some of the KPA names do not coincide with the descriptions in the related questionnaire. For example, Risk Assessment KPA also includes questions about risk management.

3.2   M2, Scrum Maturity Model

Scrum Maturity Model [5] was developed to validate and improve Scrum based software development processes by Yin in 2011.

Fitness for Purpose: The scope of the model is limited with Scrum. It provides a mechanism (questionnaires for each maturity level) for the assessment of organizations' Scrum maturity in terms of Scrum practices. However, there is no defined procedure to decide whether the outcome is failure or success once the questionnaires are completed. The model could be suitable for the improvement of Scrum practices following the set goals for practices, but not for the agile processes. Due to these limitations the model does not fully meets the requirements of "fitness for purpose" criteria.

Completeness: The model includes seven "goals", which refers to the processes or the process areas. These are; Basic Scrum Management, Software Requirements

Engineering, Customer Relationships Management, Iteration Management, Standardized Project Management, Measurement Analysis, and Performance Management. Other major processes such as testing or configurations management are not covered in the model. This is probably because Scrum did not specifically define these processes. The questionnaire to assess compatibility of an organization to maturity level 4 includes just one question, which leaves other aspects such as quantitative project management and measurement and analysis out of the assessment context.

Definition of Agile Levels: The model includes five maturity levels with a similar structure to CMMI. However, when the density of goals and practices for each maturity level and the capability of the organizations to perform these practices were examined, it was observed that it would be more rational to describe Scrum maturity with fewer numbers of levels. The third level contains objectives such as "existence of definition of done and product owner", "planning iterations" and "conducting sprint review meetings" however, these are fundamental scrum practices that could be included in second level. Practices and objectives defined in the third level could not move an organization to an upper level.

Objectivity: The definitions of goals and practices are written in an objective language. However, there is no defined procedure for the assessment of the questionnaire results. The relation between the achievement of a maturity level and the amount of successfully answered questions is not clear.

Correctness: The model was developed based on the rules of Scrum methodology. From the Scrum perspective, there is no issue disrupting the correctness criteria in the model.

Consistency: There is no evident internal or external inconsistency issue in the model.

3.3   M3, Agile Adoption Framework

The Agile Adoption Framework (AAF) [3, 13] has been developed by Sidky in 2007. It includes two components; a measurement index for estimating agile potential and a 4-Stage process improvement process inspired from Deming Cycle.

We assessed the AAF based on 6 criteria determined at the design phase of this case study. We present the assessment results below:

Fitness for Purpose: The framework has been designed to enable the assessment of agile practices at project level and organizational level, and to provide guidance for organizations to adopt agile practices. It defines a roadmap for the agile adoption. However, the framework does not cover agile best practices to highlight how to overcome the weaknesses, which are essential for software process improvement. Due to these properties, the framework "largely" meets the "fitness for purpose" requirement of an agile maturity framework.

Completeness: Each agile level consists of a cluster of agile practices which were classified based on five agile principles. Actually, those five principles capture the essence of the whole 12 agile principles published in agile manifesto. However, in the further phases, the customer collaboration principle has been left out of the scope of the study, which caused the framework to lack one of the major agile principles.

The coverage of all processes is not in sufficient detail as in the case of configuration management process. It has only been defined with the existence of configuration management tools.

In addition, the framework does not include best practices, which guides the business in software process improvement, and highlights how to overcome process weaknesses. Another model is needed to complement the AAF in this respect.

Definition of Agile Levels: The framework defines agility in five levels, which has designed to cover agile values in agile manifesto. The reasons behind the order of the agile levels and, directing the organization to move toward agility were described in detail.

Objectivity: Project level and organizational level assessments are performed based on the questionnaires defined in AAF. Once the questionnaires are filled, the results are assessed based on a mathematical "evaluation methodology". However, questions are answered with interview or observation techniques which may cause subjective results. Therefore, objectivity criterion is not fully achieved.

Correctness: The framework is compatible with agile principles and agile manifesto. Process indicators are correctly identified.

Consistency: The name of the 5th Agile Level was specified as "Ambient " in [13] and "Encompassing" in [3] respectively. There is no other internal or external inconsistency in the framework.

3.4   M4, Benfields' Model

The resource avaliable for Benefield's model is limited to a single published paper [6]. The model contains 5 levels of agile maturity (Level 1: Emergent Engineering Best Practices-Level 5: On Demand Just In Time Releases). Benefield defines agile maturity with seven dimensions: Automated Regression Testing, Code Quality Metrics, Automated Deployment and Backout, Automated Builds and Configuration, Management best practices, Interlocked Delivery and Interface Integration Testing, Test Driven Development (TDD), Performance and Scalability Testing. It is the strength of the model that Benefield took into consideration not only the managerial aspects of agile, but also the technical perspectives such as automated deployment, automated builds as an essential part of agile maturity in his model.

Fitness for Purpose: The model was developed to assess agile maturity and identify targets to improve agile maturity.

Completeness: The model focuses only on the agile practices given above instead of all the agile processes within a software life cycle. Major processes such as project planning, project management, project monitoring and control, change management, were not handled in the model.

The model does not include any evidence about how an agile practice is successfully achieved. Although the high level goals and practices for each maturity level exist, detailed characteristics or practice based goals are not defined. It is not possible to analyze the other assessment parameters; Definition of Agile Levels, Objectivity, Correctness and Consistency since the reference material does not include necessary information such as description of practices, objectives to achieve each dimension.

3.5   M5, Agile Scaling Model

Agile Scaling Model (ASM) [14] was developed by Ambler from IBM. It is a framework characterized by three levels. The first level is the application of core agile development methods in the organization, such as Scrum or extreme programming. In the second level, the focus of the organization is not only the development processes, but also the full agile delivery from project initiation to project closure. In the third level, disciplined agile delivery is applied in accordance with eight scaling factors covering the range of complexities that a team faces, such as large development team, or geographic distribution.

Although the ASM has not been referred as a maturity model, it presents a roadmap for the adoption and tailoring of the agile practices. Therefore, we evaluated ASM, based on predefined assessment criteria to identify to what extend it is to be used in improving agile maturity.

Fitness for Purpose: The structure of the model is not suitable to assess the agility level of the software development processes in an organization. It couldn't be used for an assessment, since it does not describe process related practices, goals, or any assessment questions.

Completeness: ASM does not prescribe how to successfully achieve the 1st scaling level, core agile development methods. It does not describe which practices to apply at which level, and does not focus on any process or practice descriptions. However, the 2nd Level is explained in detail by Ambler in his book [1]. The 2nd Level, Disciplined Agile Delivery, can be considered as a standalone software development life cycle (SDLC). The model is presenting various agile practice options for each phase in SDLC; however, it does not provide guidance on agile process assessment.

Description of the Agile Levels: The model requires the full application of one of the core agile development methods (i.e. Scrum or Agile Modeling) in the 1st Scaling Level and expanding the adoption of the agile practices to whole project life cycle, from initiation to closure, in the 2nd Scaling Level. That means; all the software development processes should be fully achieved in the first and second scaling levels. However, in reality, organizations gain process capabilities in an evolutionary way. Each scaling level could be divided into sub-levels to enable the improvement with small steps and to observe the progress in agile processes more clearly.

The reference material [14] has been written with an objective language. It is consistent with agile principles and there is no internal or external consistency problem. However, the reference material does not cover all the details of the ASM. Therefore, objectivity, correctness and consistency criteria couldn't be assessed fully.

4   Conclusions

In this study, we assessed the characteristics of five agile maturity models/frameworks from software process improvement and process assessment perspectives, and identified their strengths and weaknesses by conducting a multiple case study.

Except from SMM [5], the models/frameworks are independent of any particular agile method. Agile maturity has been described through the agile processes or agile practices in the models/frameworks. As a result of the case study, we have found deficiencies in all of the models/frameworks at a certain level, according to six assessment criteria (fitness for purpose, completeness, definition of agile levels, objectivity, correctness and consistency). Table 3 depicts the results. We used a four level scale to express models' qualifications relative to each other: "Not Achieved"- "Partially Achieved"- "Largely Achieved"- "Fully Achieved".

Table 3. An overview of assessment results

Criteria / Models	Fitness for Purpose	Completeness	Definition of A. Levels	Objectivity	Correctness	Consistency
M1 (AMM)	**Fully Achieved**	Partially Achieved	Not Achieved	Largely Achieved	Partially Achieved	Not Achieved
M2 (SMM)	Largely Achieved	Partially Achieved	Partially Achieved	Partially Achieved	**Fully Achieved**	**Fully Achieved**
M3 (AAF)	Largely Achieved	Partially Achieved	**Fully Achieved**	Largely Achieved	**Fully Achieved**	**Fully Achieved**
M4 (BM)	Largely Achieved	Partially Achieved	Not Applicable	Not Applicable	Not Applicable	Not Applicable
M5 (ASM)	Partially Achieved	Partially Achieved	Partially Achieved	Not Applicable	Not Applicable	Not Applicable

Among all models/frameworks, AAF [13] has obtained the best assessment results. Its well-defined structure could be extended to cover agile best practices. SMM [5] is in the second rank following AAF. SMM's fundamental problems are not covering the major processes and urging to identify the Scrum maturity in 5 levels.

We couldn't found necessary information in the avaliable references in the literature for a complete assessment of BM and ASM. However; the findings of the case study revealed that these models need to extend their agile coverage and improve the way of describing "how to be agile". The last model, AMM needs significant improvement in terms of definition of model elements, correctness, consistency and coverage.

This case study has underlined the observation that there is a need to improve the maturity models for better guidance in agile process adoption, process improvement and process assessment.

References

[1] Ambler, S.W., Lines, M.: Disciplined Agile Delivery: A Practitioner's Guide to Agile Software Delivery in the Enterprise. IBM Press (2012)

[2] Elssamadisy, A.: Agile adoption patterns: a roadmap to organizational success. Addison-Wesley Professional (2008)

[3] Sidky, A.: A structured approach to adopting agile practices: The agile adoption framework. Virginia Polytechnic Institute and State University (2007)

[4] Patel, C., Ramachandran, M.: Agile Maturity Model (AMM): A Software Process Improvement framework for Agile Software Development Practices. International Journal of Software Engineering 2, 3–28 (2009)

[5] Yin, A., Figueiredo, S., Mira da Silva, M.: Scrum Maturity Model: Validation for IT organizations' roadmap to develop software centered on the client role. In: The Sixth International Conference on Software Engineering Advances, ICSEA 2011, pp. 20–29 (2011)

[6] Benefield, R.: Seven Dimensions of Agile Maturity in the Global Enterprise: A Case Study. In: 2010 43rd Hawaii International Conference on System Sciences, HICSS, pp. 1–7 (2010)

[7] Humble, J., Russell, R.: The Agile Maturity Model Applied to Building and Releasing Software (2009)

[8] Malic, N.: Title (unpublished)

[9] Proulx, M.: Yet Another Agile Maturity Model (AMM)– The 5 Levels of Maturity (2010), http://analytical-mind.com/2010/07/12/yet-another-agile-maturity-model-the-5-levels-of-maturity/

[10] Jayaraj, S.: The Agile Maturity Model (2007), http://whattodowearelikethatonly.blogspot.com/2008/08/agile-maturity-model.html

[11] Rout, T.P., Tuffley, A., Cahill, B.: CMMI Evaluation Capability Maturity Model Integration Mapping to ISO/IEC 15504-2:1998, Software Quality Institute, Griffith University (2000)

[12] Kneuper, R.: CMMI: Capability Maturity Model Integration A Process Improvement Approach. Rocky Nook (2008)

[13] Sidky, A., Arthur, J., Bohner, S.: A disciplined approach to adopting agile practices: the agile adoption framework. Innovations in Systems and Software Engineering 3, 203–216 (2007)

[14] Ambler, S.: The Agile Scaling Model (ASM): Adapting Agile Methods for Complex Environments (2009), ftp://ftp.software.ibm.com/common/ssi/sa/wh/n/raw14204usen/RAW14204USEN.PDF

Agile Software Development
in System Engineering Conditions

Ernest Wallmüller[1] and Fred Kaminski[2]

[1] Qualität & Informatik, Switzerland
info@itq.ch
[2] Progress in Processes, Germany
kaminski@collossus.eu

Abstract. This article presents and explains the history and status of agile methods in the context of a software and system engineering environment. Further we discuss the preconditions and critical success factors how agile approaches can be used along a system-engineering life cycle.

Keywords: Software development methods, automotive industry.

1   Short History of Software Development

Software development ([1], 2011) is a highly complex context with countless variables impacting the final product or release. All software systems are imperfect because they cannot be built fully automated by machines such as generators and the creativity of a designer and the care of developers are always necessary ingredients. As a result, software is almost always flawed or sub-optimized. Also consider that the building blocks of software systems is usually other software systems (e.g., programming languages, database systems, network components etc.), and those systems that act as building blocks contain bugs and cannot be relied on with certainty. Because the foundations of software development are inherently unstable and unreliable, organizations developing software must realize variables exist that are outside of management control. It is therefore fair to say that software development is more akin to new product research and development than it is to assembly-line style manufacturing. Software development is innovation, discovery, and artistry; each foray into a development project presents new and difficult challenges that cannot be overcome with one-size-fits-all, cookie- cutter solutions.

The waterfall methodology assumes that up-front planning is enough to take into account all variables that could impact the development process. In fact, waterfall projects allocate copious effort detailing every possible risk, mitigation plan, and contingency. But is it possible to predict any and all variables that could possibly affect a software project? The empirical answer is "no" considering the limited success of waterfall projects.

Waterfall therefore equates software development to an assembly line; defined processes can be established that, when used sequentially, result in a successful

T. Woronowicz et al. (Eds.): SPICE 2013, CCIS 349, pp. 142–153, 2013.

project each time. The first step is X, the second is Y, and the result is always Z. Since the late 1970s product development companies lead by Toyota, Honda, Fujitsu, 3M, HP, Canon, and NEC, supplanted the sequential "Phased Program Planning" (PPP) approach to new product development with a flexible, holistic approach where the traditional phases of development overlap throughout the product lifecycle The results were a dramatic improvement in cost and development time to market and ultimately lead to the popular rise of "lean development" and "just-in-time manufacturing". Following the lead of Japanese auto makers, in the 1990s sequential, waterfall-style approaches to new product development were effectively abandoned outside the software development industry. But longstanding insistence from IT managers to categorize software development as a straightforward assembly line progression has kept the software industry from evolving to better methods, the benefits of which other new product development industries have been reaping for decades. It's ironic that a cutting edge technology field like software is so far behind more traditional engineering fields in terms of development methods.

1.1   Incremental and Iterative Development

The simple ability to revisit the "phases" of development dramatically improves project efficiency. The idea of revisiting phases over and over is called "incremental and iterative development" (IID). Iterative and Incremental development is any combination of both iterative design or iterative method and incremental build model for development. The development lifecycle is cut up into increments or "iterations" and each iteration touches on each of the traditional "phases" of development. For example, with IID requirements is an ongoing process that is periodically revisited. As new requirements surface and as the scope changes, IID processes continually capture the requirements iteration after iteration. IID allows for multiple "passes", or iterations, over a project lifecycle to properly address complexities and risk factors.

This concept of iterative development originates from the "lean development" era of the 1980s described above where Japanese auto makers made tremendous efficiency and innovation increases simply by removing the phased, sequential approach and implementing an iterative approach, where prototypes were developed for short-term milestones. Each Cop phase was actually a layer that continued throughout the entire development lifecycle; the requirements, design, and implementation cycle was revisited for each short-term milestone. This "concurrent" development approach created an atmosphere of trial-and-error experimentation and learning that ultimately broke down the status quo and led to efficient innovation. Although direct analogies between industries are never seamless, the success of lean development has influenced a broad class of "iterative" software methods including the Unified Process, Spiral, and Agile methods.

1.2   Agile Methods - Embracing Change and Business Value

Agile methods stress productivity and values over heavy-weight process overhead and artifacts. The Agile Manifesto, a concise summary of agile values, was written and signed in 2001 although agile methods have existed since the early 90s. Agile methods promote an iterative mechanism for producing software, and they further increase the iterative nature of the software lifecycle by tightening design-code-test loop to at least once a day (if not much more frequently) as opposed to once per iteration. Kent Beck challenged the traditional cost of change curve evidenced by Barry Boehm over twenty years ago. Beck's model espouses that the cost of change can be inexpensive even late in the project lifecycle while maintaining or increasing system quality. Beck's idealistic "flat" cost of change curve has since been revised and softened by Alister Cockburn and Scott Ambler to reflect modern corporate realities. Nevertheless, agile ideals can be applied to reduce the cost of change throughout the software lifecycle even if the cost of change is not perfectly flat.

To accomplish this "flatter" cost of change curve, agile methods promote a number of engineering practices that enable cost effective change. Martin Fowler describes testing and continuous integration as the "enabling" Agile practices that allow for the advantages gained, like rapid production and minimum up-front design. "Test driven development" is a quality-first approach where developer tests (called unit tests) are written prior to the functional code itself. Rather than focusing a lot of effort on big up front design analysis, small increments of functional code are produced according to immediate business need. It is the role of the automated test suite built around the rapidly evolving code to act as a harness that allows developers to make aggressive code changes without fear of undetected regression failure.

1.3   Agile Project Management - Empirical Process

Scrum, a popular agile project management method, introduced the concept of empirical process control for the management of complex, changing software projects. Scrum holds that straightforward defined processes alone cannot be used to effectively manage complex and dynamic software projects. Risk factors and emerging requirements complicate software development to a point where defined processes fall short. Although it has been attempted in the past, there cannot be a single exhaustive library of defined processes to handle every situation that could possibly surface during a software project. In fact, the manufacturing industry has long known that certain chemical processes, for example, are too difficult to script and define. Instead, an empirical or adaptive management approach is employed to measure and adjust the chemical process periodically to achieve the desired outcome. As a result, in the Scrum process, project plans are continuously inspected and adapted based on the empirical reality of the project.

Agile project management approaches balance the four variables in software development while keeping in mind the limits associated with new product development. In software development there are four broad control factors. These factors are interconnected; when one changes at least one other factor must also change.

- Cost or Effort - Available money impacts the amount of effort put into the system.
- Schedule - A software project is impacted as the timeline is changed.
- Requirements - The scope of the work that needs to be done can be increased or decreased to affect the project.
- Quality - Cut corners by reducing quality.

Because software development is often considered a sequential, linear process, middle and upper management often assumes that all four of these factors could be dictated to the development team under the waterfall approach. However software development cannot be described by a simple linear process because it cannot be predicted accurately in advance. It is therefore unreasonable to assume that management can control all four of these factors. In reality, management can pick values for three of the four factors at most, and the development process dictates the fourth. The highly complex and uncertain nature of software development makes this expectation of full control unrealistic.

1.4   Lean Thinking

Lean is a management philosophy. Ultimately, it focuses on throughput (of whatever is being produced) by taking a strictly systems-level view of things. In other words, it doesn't focus on particular components of the value-stream like code-construction or QA, but on whether all the components of the chain are working as efficiently as possible so as to generate as much overall value as possible. Value, of course, includes things like high-quality, and optimized for time and resources.

Lean is based on several things – queuing theory, the theory of constraints, concurrent engineering (set-based development) and delaying commitment to the last responsible moment. Careful metrics (only the ones that truly measure throughput: this often means going one level up) is an important part of lean – this allows everyone to be objective about everything. Speaking of which, Lean software recommends measuring things across the value chain – and as extended as that chain can be. It recommends measuring return on investment (ROI), customer satisfaction, customer usage patterns, market share, and so on. This in turn drives budgets and costs within the software organization.

Both Lean and Agile focus on people – over pretty much everything else. They both focus on inspecting and adapting – in order to improve the work-product and efficiency in producing it. In other words, feedback is critical – from people, from customers, from stake-holders, and from the product itself. They're both quality focused, and they encourage early discovery and more importantly, prevention of defects. The area where they complement each other most, is in the breadth of their world-view. Agile is usually focused very much within the software development team or organization, Lean focuses on the entire system that includes as many workers, partners, customers, external stakeholders as possible.

1.5   Agile Requirements Capturing

Agile projects avoid "up-front" requirements gathering for the reasons stated above: customers cannot effectively produce all requirements in high enough detail for implementation to occur at the beginning of a project. Customers may not want to make decisions about the system until they have more information. Agile values a high visibility and customer involvement. The frequent demonstration and release of software common in Agile approaches gives customers a chance to "try software" periodically and provide feedback. Agile helps companies produce the "right product".

An iterative approach allows customers to delay decisions as well. Decisions can be delayed to some future iteration when better information or technology is available to optimize the choice. For example, we recently delayed selecting a database package for an application because some of the desired features were not available at that time in the options we had to choose from. We therefore built the system in a database independent manner, and a few weeks before the product launch a new version was released by one of the database vendors that solved our problem.

One of the biggest advantages to IID is that work can begin before all of the requirements are known. Many organizations are not fully staffed with business analysts cranking out reams of requirements specs. Quite the contrary, in our experience often the bottleneck in the development process has been the lack of availability of customer domain experts for detailed requirements analysis. This is especially the case with small businesses where domain experts wear many hats and often cannot commit to two or three months of straight requirements analysis. IID is ideally suited then to take on bite-sized chunks of requirements that the customer can easily digest.

But does Agile/IID work? Of course the proof is always in the pudding, and the most recent 2004 Standish Group CHAOS report on the success of software projects shows a dramatic improvement in the failure rate of software projects. In 1994, Standish reported a 31% failure rate that has improved to 15% in 2004. Standish Chairman Jim Johnson attributes the improvement to smaller projects using iterative processes as opposed to the waterfall method. The notion that Agile is a radical deviation from the long established, tried and true history of waterfall software development is incorrect. Although waterfall is often referred to as "traditional", software engineering has had a very short history relative to other engineering disciplines. Unlike bridge building, software development is not built on thousands of years of trial and error, and is therefore in a rapidly evolving infancy as an engineering discipline. Agile is simply the latest theory that is widely replacing the waterfall approach that itself will change and evolve well into the future.

2   System Engineering and Its Meanings

Before we take to a deeper view on Agile in the context of System Engineering we will talk a bit what System Engineering exactly is. It´s not a separate discipline, it´s more a common understanding and a coming working together of all product involved parties in a company. Systems engineering in the current understanding is an interdisciplinary approach and means to enable the aimed realization of different systems. It focuses on defining customer needs and required functionality early in the development cycle, documenting requirements, then proceeding with design synthesis and system validation while considering the complete problem ([2], 2013). Systems engineering does cope with complexity. The benefits of systems engineering include not being caught out by omissions and invalid assumptions, managing real world changing issues, and producing the most efficient, economic and robust solutions to the need being addressed.

The old understanding of working as a software engineer is that the software engineer is someone who analyses designs, codes, and/or tests software. It is difficult to define the term "system engineer" because the term is overloaded to mean many things. Some examples of system engineering tasks include: system design, requirements development, requirements verification, system test, and engineering studies.

The former distinction between software engineers and system engineers were vague since there is substantial overlap between the two. In the past system engineers tend to focus more on hardware, products, systems, whereas software engineers focus more on implementation in software. System engineering in the new way deals with substantial hardware and software in the same context and same degree of understanding. But this requires some more. System Engineering in a nutshell is:

- Understand the whole system before you try to solve it
- Make requirements traceable and testable
- Examine all feasible alternatives before selecting a solution
- Model the system and decompose it in subsystems or components
- Make sure you consider the total system life cycle incl. system behavior.
- Integrate before test
- Make sure to test the total system before delivering it.
- Document all relvant aspects

Based on INCOSE Systems Engineering integrates all the disciplines and specialty groups into a team effort forming a structured development process that proceeds from concept to production to operation. Systems engineering considers both the business and the technical needs of all customers with the goal of providing a quality product that meets the user needs. So we are talking about Cost, Effort, Manufacturing, Production, Operations and many more. Systems engineering is the application of science, math, and management knowledge to solve problems related to any system (however large or small). As Mr. Confucius says: "Success depends upon previous preparation, and without such preparation there is sure to be failure" ([3], 2013). This is not a contradiction about iterations and re-evaluations, this means a new understanding of working together on same things with same quality attributes, same guidelines etc. through whole structures in small and bigger organizations.

3   Systems Engineering as an Engineering Discipline

Systems engineering is an engineering discipline whose responsibility is creating and executing an interdisciplinary approach to ensure that the customer and stakeholder's needs are satisfied in a high quality, trustworthy, cost efficient and schedule compliant manner throughout a system's entire life cycle. This process is usually comprised of the following tasks: The functions are performed in a parallel and iterative manner, as you know from Agile Development. We will show the differences from Agile regarding System Engineering direct in following chapters.

3.1   State the Requirement

Every project starts with a description of the top-level functions that the system must perform: this might be in the form of a mission statement, a concept of operations or a description of the deficiency that must be ameliorated. Most mandatory and preference requirements should be traceable to this problem statement. Acceptable systems must satisfy all the mandatory requirements. The preference requirements are traded-off to find the preferred alternatives. The problem statement should be in terms of what must be done, not how to do it. The requirement or problem statement should fulfill the customer requirements in functional or behavioral terms. The requirements specification may be composed in words or as a model, but a model should be the preferred choice due to implantations of dynamic behavior, such as in form of sequence charts and other important inputs from end users, suppliers, acquirers, owners, regulatory agencies, and other stakeholders.

3.2   Understand the System and Investigate Alternatives

Before you start with realization you should understand the purpose and scope of every customer requirement and then check possible alternatives. Designs are created and are evaluated based on performance, schedule, costs and risk figures of values. No design is likely to be best on all figures of values, so multicriteria decision-aiding techniques should be used to reveal the preferred alternatives. This analysis should be redone whenever more data are available. For example, figures of merit should be computed initially based on estimates by the design engineers. Then, concurrently, models should be constructed and evaluated; simulation data should be derived; and prototypes should be built and measured. Finally, tests should be run on the real system. Alternatives should be judged for compliance of capability against requirements. For the design of complex systems divide bigger things into smaller, this reduces project risk. Investigating innovative alternatives helps clarify the overall conditions.

3.3   Model the System

Models will be developed for most alternative designs. The model for the preferred alternative will be expanded and used to help manage the system throughout its entire life cycle. Many types of system models are used, such as physical analogs, analytic equations, state machines, block diagrams, functional flow diagrams, object-oriented models, computer simulations and mental models. Systems Engineering is responsible for creating a product and also a process for producing it. So, models should be constructed for both the product and the process. Process models allow us, for example, to define a work product and their expectation to the right time in right form, a planned review mechanism, and a Safety life cycle requires an established process framework to perform sensitivity analyses to show the effects of delaying or accelerating certain requirements, decomposed elements and concerned tell tales. Running the process models reveals bottlenecks and fragmented activities, reduces cost and exposes duplication of effort. Products models help explain the system. These models are also used in tradeoff studies and risk management. As previously stated, the Systems Engineering Process is not sequential: it is parallel and iterative. This is another example: models must be created before alternatives can be investigated.

3.4   Design the System

After all investigations and based on your known model, which is reviewed, you can start to design your product, system, code or software system. Design is a creative activity—consequently, there is no process that will guarantee good designs, but there are some principles that will increase the probability of getting a good design. Using these principles will also make a product more reusable for future systems and it will help reduce redesign costs when requirements change. Of course, the customer may mandate or exclude the use of some or all of these principles. Some of these principles are as follows: use models to design systems, use hierarchical, top-down design, work on high-risk items first, prioritize, control the level of interacting entities, design the interfaces, produce satisficing designs, do not optimize early, maintain an updated model of the system, develop stable intermediates, use evolutionary development, understand your enterprise, state what, not how, list functional requirements in the use cases, allocate each function to only one component, do not allow undocumented functions provide observable states, use rapid prototyping, develop iteratively and test immediately, create modules and libraries of reusable objects and use open standards. This list of principles is certainly not complete.

Design guidelines, design pattern and similar helps to to do this in a repeatable way. This is on best level to integrate a Software KANBAN. The well-known V-model describes the standard procedures through development in automotive companies. The possible basis for implementation of backlogs means Agile Development is in the software construction area. Based on detailed design we can define work packages with clear expectation. Step by step you know the design specification, based on customer needs and customers specification and this will finalized in a detailed design paper or software detailed design architecture. You know all constrains, the behavior, interrupts, time slices and much more to design the specific elements. In this case you are able to install a KANBAN system, which allows an event-driven procedure without interactions as you know as classical way in developments.

The important planning issues are lead time and Work in Progress (WIP) items per process steps, in all other issues the KANBAN is flexible regarding cross functional teams, specialists are allowed, no roles prescribed and prioritization is also optional.

The complete workflow is organized as PULL principle and KANBAN cards helps to see the status of progress of each WIP. There are some advantages for KANBAN in projects with software development. First is the visibility. The team can decide, what is important, what can wait. The Agile Team works as a cell, so the team is responsible for its own work but also for deviation.

3.5   Integrate and Test the System

No man is an island. Systems, businesses and people must be integrated so that they interact with one another. Integration means bringing things together so they work as a whole. Interfaces between subsystems must be designed. Subsystems should be defined along natural boundaries. Subsystems should be defined to minimize the amount of information to be exchanged between the subsystems. Well-designed subsystems send finished products to other subsystems. Feedback loops around individual subsystems are easier to manage than feedback loops around interconnected subsystems. Processes of co-evolving systems also need to be integrated.

This is the phase where the preferred alternative solution is designed in detail; the parts are built or bought (COTS), the parts are integrated and tested at various levels. In parallel, the processes necessary for this are developed – where necessary - and applied so that the product can be produced. In designing and producing the product, due consideration is given to its interfaces with operators (humans, who will need to be trained) and other systems with which the product will interface. In some instances, this will cause interfaced systems to co-evolve. The process of designing and producing the system is iterative as new knowledge developed along the way can cause a re-consideration and modification of earlier steps.

3.6   Verification and Validation of the System

Verification and validation (V & V) activities are done along the system life cycle. The key questions at this level are:

- Does the requirements specification document fulfill verification and validation criteria and metrics?
- Is a description of functions and objects complete and understood?

You got figures of values, a test plan, a drawing of system boundaries, an interface control document, a listing of deliverables, models, a sensitivity analysis, a tradeoff study, a risk analysis, a life cycle analysis and a description of the physical architecture and much more which allows to give the customer the right answers.

V & V activities give you the answer's about do you get the right system and is system is built right? The system functions should be mapped to the physical components. The mapping of functions to physical components can be one to one or many to one. But if one function is assigned to two or more physical components, then a mistake might have been made and it should be investigated. One valid reason for assigning a function to more than one component would be that the function is performed by one component in a certain mode and by another component in another mode. Another would be deliberate redundancy to enhance reliability, allowing one portion of the system to take on a function if another portion fails to do so.

3.7   Re-evaluate

No one is perfect. Re-evaluation is arguably the most important engineering task, but it can be expansive. Re-evaluation should be a continual process with many parallel loops; the best way is to integrate this iterative process made after every step. Before you complete a requirement, check it and analyses it as long all problems and open issues are known and fixed. Re-evaluation means observing outputs and using this information to modify the system, the inputs, the product or the process.
This extra loop creates most of additional costs.

4   System Engineering and Agile Methods

The current Spice model ISO 155504, or the Automotive Spice ([5], 2013) model is a good framework to establish and improve processes in engineering companies that run Systems Engineering projects. But this model expects clear rules, crystal clear work products, so called outcomes and it defines very well the common approach in projects. And we got a new and better understanding what maturity means in the context of Spice levels, how can we fulfilled that levels and what are the deviations from that levels.

Processes are "controlled", i.e. the same good quality is produced and they are repeatable without interferences, and the results comply with the latest identified (customer) requirements. Especially important is the fact that you created a software product that is independent of the development people. Why we got problems to implements Agile practices and methods in System Engineering processes?

- Agile development is a new kind of working, but we have not enough experience with it in the context of Systems Engineering projects. Automotive companies are interested in doing the things better, but they need a clear benefit for that.
- Agile methods require a lot of new elements in companies. New roles are necessary (such as a SCRUM Master or product owner), new definitions of WIP´s, work packages, new acceptance criteria, important for Backlog. Iterative development with product backlogs is a pull system, so we need structural changes in the organization.
- Automotive Companies are well organized but their behavior to accept newer models or ways of working are quite long. This takes time and many efforts to convince the decision maker.

So we can´t change all things in parallel but we can implements new agile methods step by step. The reason why we are going fail is the same like ever, we want to do most things in short time.

As David Andersons ([4], 2013), an expert in Agile Practices, says in his 5 core principles: Visualize the workflow, Limit WIP, Manage Flow, Make Process Policies Explicit and Improve collaboratively (using models & the scientific method). Automotive SPICE, CMMi and other best practices models offer a great base to visualize the workflow, help work packages to be defined in a certain manner, support the work flow by guidelines and rules. In mature companies the policies are also in place so what we had to do much more is to improve the collaboration and cooperation among employees. Agile methods and practices mean not, do everything new, it says do everything agile means more efficient and focused to the business value.

4.1   Agile SW Development and System Engineering - Does It Work Together?

In the face of globalization, with the rapid pace at which the very nature of war fighting is changing, and with ever-increasing rates of technological innovation, much attention has been given in recent years to transforming traditional systems engineering practices and standard acquisition paradigms to meet these challenges. We argue that, by applying principles from agile software development, which has achieved strong success in recent years, there is great potential to meet these challenges directly and, in doing so, to save money, increase efficiency, and ensure that the right decisions are being made as systems are developed and deployed. Furthermore, we suggest that this movement to "agile systems engineering" can largely be accomplished by employing systems engineering practices that are centered on evolutionary, end-to-end implementations of physics-based modeling and simulation.

Wikipedia's definition of systems engineering is "an interdisciplinary field of engineering that focuses on how complex engineering projects should be designed and managed." Its formalization and broad-scale usage began during the 1940s, and ever since it has been recognized as necessary for the successful creation of systems, especially for those that are complex. Most standard views of the systems engineering process revolve around a progression from the identification of requirements through concept/capability assessment and exploration to solution validation, implementation, and deployment. The often used "V" diagram in systems engineering illustrates this concept.

Although the basic construct of this process is sound, several potentially undesirable characteristics are present in many traditional implementations:

- There is a strong emphasis on defining requirements up front in their entirety and usually a strong resistance to changing them as the system is developed. A relatively sequential process typically is used to progress through systems engineering "phases." Even if some phases are worked in parallel, once they are complete, cost and schedule pressures make it difficult to revisit them.
- Many times, for systems that involve hardware, hardware prototypes are built early and often to explore concepts and define capability (although this is happening less frequently as software technologies increase in capability). This practice leads to the absorption of high costs of change early in system development.
- For the DoD, there typically is a tight coupling between the systems engineering and acquisition processes, which results in more resistance to change and, most likely, less efficiency.

We recognize that these characteristics are not universally true for all implementations of the systems engineering process; nevertheless, we believe that they are common enough that we will contrast them with the changes that we are recommending. Furthermore, we do not advocate completely abandoning traditional systems engineering techniques; instead, we suggest augmenting (and, where appropriate, removing) those techniques that limit efficiency.

4.2   The Need for Change

The challenges to systems development in today's environment outlined above drive us to an approach that is different from what has been employed in the past. Just as the software engineering community has faced analogous challenges and largely addressed them through agile software development, we believe that using a similar approach may yield equally dramatic improvements in systems engineering. These values and principles are defined in detail in The Manifesto for Agile Software Development [6], and are summarized in chapter 2.

The change to agile practices and method can only be success fully, when

- The whole organization becomes agile. People understand and apply the new values and believe.
- Only in those processes agile practices and methods are used where situations and conditions are still under control and no negative impact on the whole system is low or not possible.
- System risk and criticality are further determinates for the usage of agile methods and practices.

We argue that products and systems developed with agile approaches are beneficial in cases where the systems have a long lifecycle, and significant switching costs exist coupled with substantial uncertainty in the environment (customer functional requirements, demand evolution, etc.). It must also be acknowledged that system flexibility and agility often carry a price in terms of increased system complexity, cost, mass/weight or the introduction of unwanted interfaces and other technical penalties. One must carefully analyze whether such penalties are worth accepting upfront, relative to the value that agility gives the system users, operator and owners during later parts of the lifecycle. The field of agility in systems engineering is still evolving and both academic research and practice are in flux. As such the principles, methods and conclusions presented here should be regarded as "work-in-progress" rather than a converged theory. There is no doubt, however, that systems engineers can no longer be content with drawing narrow boundaries around their technical systems and then ignore the dynamics and uncertainties associated with elements and systems outside those boundaries.

References

[1] Wallmüller, E.: Software Quality Engineering - Ein Leitfaden für bessere Software-Qualität, Hanser, München (2011)
[2] INCOSE SE Handbook. Abgerufen am 31. 1 2013 von (January 31, 2013),
    http://www.incose.org/ProductsPubs/products/sehandbook.aspx
[3] http://www.brainyquote.com/quotes/quotes/c/confucius141097.html (January 31, 2013)
[4] http://agilemanagement.net/index.php/Blog/the_principles_of_the_kanban_method/ (January 31, 2013)
[5] http://www.automotivespice.com (January 31, 2013)
[6] Viju, G.K.: Agile Software Development: Review and Analysis. Alphascript Publishing (2013)

TestSPICE and Agile Testing – Synergy or Confusion

Tomas Schweigert[1], Detlef Vohwinkel[1],
Monique Blaschke[1], and Dr. Mohsen Ekssir-Monfared[2]

[1] SQS Software Quality Systems AG, Stollwerck Str. 11, 51149 Köln
spi-service@sqs.com
[2] BDC EDV-Consulting GmbH, Gredlerstrasse 4/2, 1020-Wien
mohsen.ekssir@bdc.at

Abstract. The paper deals with the question how a capability oriented model like TestSPICE could contribute to the improvement of agile testing. We know from several studies, that agile methods like XP or SCRUM deliver good support for higher capability or maturity levels of SPICE as well as of CMMI. On the other hand the authors were did not find relevant studies that deal with the question how SPICE could help to mature agile practices. One of the reasons is that there is no common accepted agile maturity model (but up to 40 published approaches). In this case the training and the experience to the Assessment and process improvement (PI) team is a key success factor. A double certification as Assessor and CAT might be helpful. The paper is written from the perspective of a consultant wanting to help customers to improve and searching for options to give advice.

Keywords: SPI, TestSPICE, CAT, Agile Maturity, SPICE, INTACS, CMMI, ISO 15504, ECQA, SPI Manifesto, Agile Manifesto.

1 Introduction

Testing is one of the most important tasks in agile project environments. We see also a trend to re integrate testing in the development life cycle, as a SCRUM sprint contains design, development and testing. Due to the Agile Manifesto [15] the producing of shippable software is one of the core values of agile development. We see the relevance of this topic also in the fact that is an own conference about agile testing: the agile testing days [28]. There is also an international certification scheme for agile testers in place [7]. At the other hand we find a broad community of SPICE assessors and CMMI appraisers. So the question is: where are the synergies and what to do to gain the related benefits?

1.1 The Core Belief of SPICE: Life Cycle Model Independence

The current layout of most of the SPICE compliant models is to have a Process Reference Model (PRM), a measurement framework and an assessment process which –by putting them all together- form the Process Assessment Model (PAM). From this

T. Woronowicz et al. (Eds.): SPICE 2013, CCIS 349, pp. 154–164, 2013.

perspective agile development as described e.g. in XP or Scrum is a life cycle model as Waterfall, V-Model or RuP. Being independent from life cycle models leads to a capability framework that does not require specific agile practices. A PAM and a life cycle model differ by the key question: The PAM says **what** has to be implemented in order to improve process performance. The life cycle model says **how** something has to be implemented. According to this frame conditions, TestSPICE is also independent from testing life cycle models like T-Map, so it can be used to evaluate the testing in a waterfall environment as well as in an agile environment.

1.2   Contributions of Agile Development Life Cycles as XP or SCRUM to SPICE Capability Levels

It is proven from a broad CMMI experience, that the proper implementation of agile practices helps to gain CMMI maturity levels [6] [12] [13] [16]. Having this as a common understanding of agile CMMI synergy, the same synergy applies for SPICE as most of CMMI best practices are also included in the SPICE PAM. This leads to the intermediate result that –from this perspective- synergy is probable [3] [7].

1.3   Contributions of SPICE Assessments to Agile Improvement

The open question is, if and how SPICE assessments might contribute to more agility, especially if TestSPICE Assessments contribute to better agile testing. The question uncovers two independent but also related problems.

1st: If TestSPICE is life cycle independent, how can a TestSPICE assessment deliver recommendations for the improvement of agile testing?

2nd: What is to do to improve agile testing? A simple answer would be agile testing is part of agile development, so incorporate the agile maturity model in TestSPICE and the work is done. Unfortunately there is not one but probably 40 agile maturity models [4] [25]. Currently neither a synthesis nor a guideline for choosing the right agile maturity model is available [1] [4] [25]. Also no statistical data about the usage of these models can be found.

As a result we see assessor training and experience as a key factor for successful TestSPICE Assessments in agile environments.

2   Does Agile Testing Need an Own Maturity Framework?

Knowing that there are lots of agile maturity models available, the question would be if there is a specific agile maturity for software testing available. Looking for specific testing models we find TPI [35], TMMI [32], and TestSPICE [31]. All these models use an own measurement framework, TestSPICE uses the measurement framework as defined in ISO/IEC 15504 part 2:2003 [9]. To decide if agile testing needs an own maturity framework the best approach would be to compare the currently valid

TestSPICE PAM [30] with agile maturity aspects and then make a deep dive into the CAT Syllabus [29].

2.1   The Test SPICE PAM

The first version of Test SPICE was rather close to ISO/IEC 15504 Part 5:2006 [5] [12] [16] 26]. But then practical experience turned out to some conceptual changes which in a long term run are related to test service management, test environment management, test data management and test automation management. TestSPICE version 2.0 is covering this agenda as it contains a detailed Test Environment (TE) Management process group [24].

At the top level view it can be found, that TestSPICE uses the same view on testing than ISO/IEC 29119 Part 2 [14] but also still uses the main structure of ISO/IEC 15504 Part 5:2004 [12].

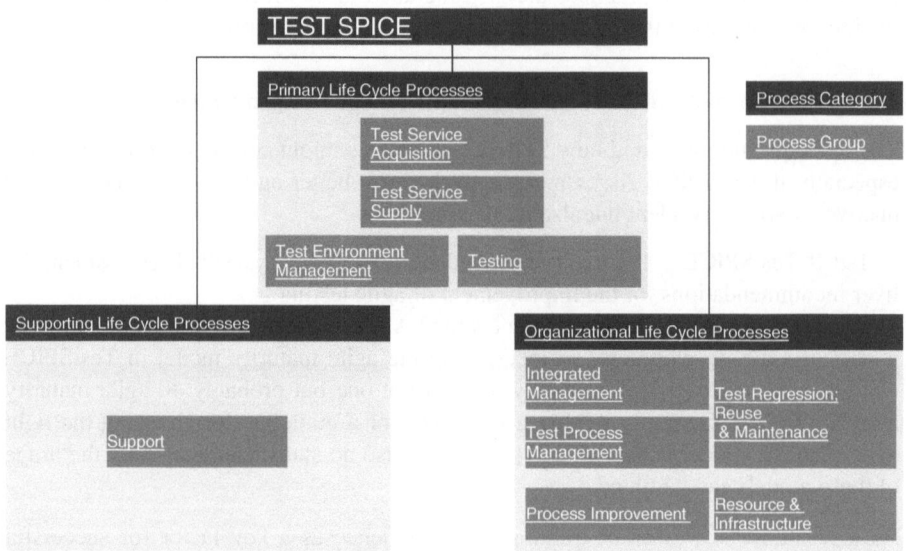

Fig. 1. TestSPICE PRM Overview

This overall structure allows flexible and pragmatic integration of external developments like the new ISO/IEC 15504 Part 5:2012 [13] Standard and the upcoming ISO/IEC 33063.

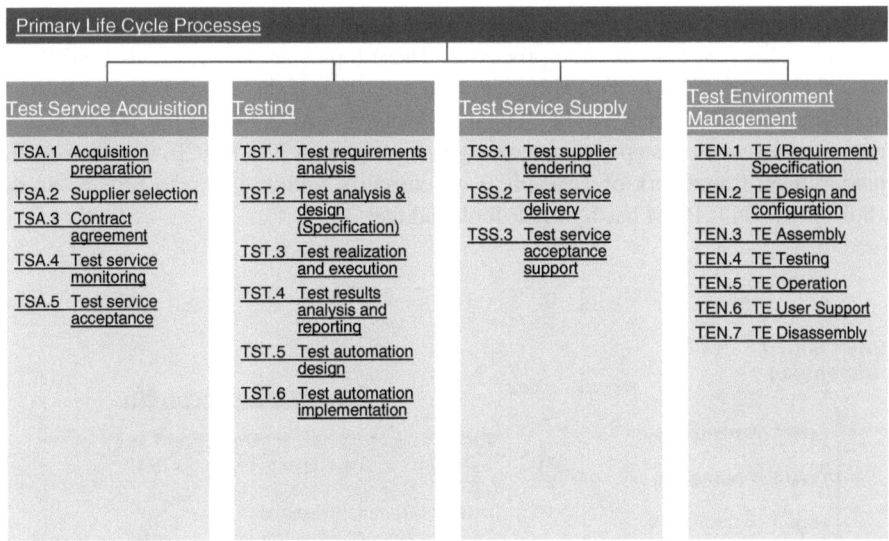

Fig. 2. Test SPICE PRM Primary Life Cycle Processes

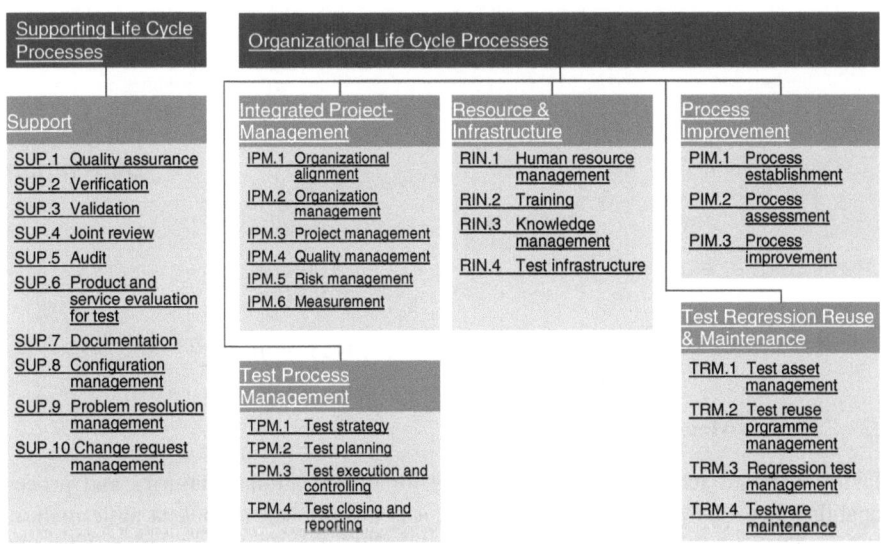

Fig. 3. TestSPICE PRM: Organizational and Supporting Life Cycle Processes

Looking at the maturity idea behind TestSPICE the idea is about an organization, able to manage its tests no matter if out- or insourced, able to deliver proper test services, able to manage test environments and test data and also able to effectively automate regression tests. With the last point TestSPICE is addressing a key topic of agile: continuous integration and automated testing.   It is also known from some case studies, that reuse, proper process improvement, knowledge management, test automation and the experience of process practitioners is essential for successful improvement [2] [33] [34] of agile processes. These topics are addressed in TestSPICE. Nevertheless the PRM of TestSPICE is valid no matter if the assessed organization is agile or not, but bringing the key enabling processes for agile testing in the assessment scope is a first step to improve agile testing with TestSPICE. Looking at the measurement framework of TestSPICE we currently find it similar to SPICE. So the whole TestSPICE PAM has a SPICE look and feel.

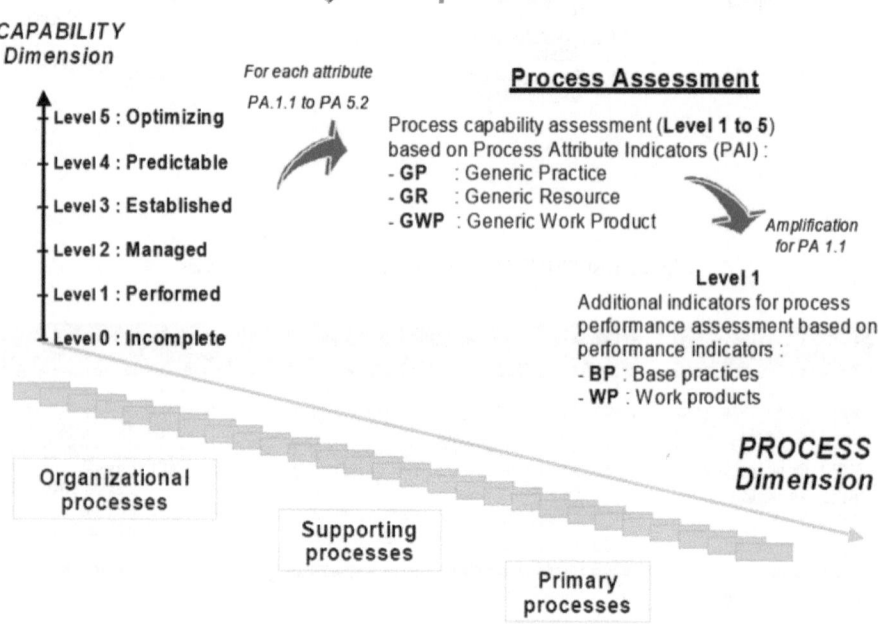

Fig. 4. TestSPICE: Capability Framework

2.2   How to Measure Agility?

Having standard measurement frameworks for organisational maturity and process capability like CMMI and SPICE in place, it is a flashback to look at agile maturity models. The situation is even worse than it was with process assessment models at the beginning of the SPICE development [4].

Agile Maturity Models and Their Lessons Learned: Looking at the existing bunch of agile maturity models [1] [4] it would exceed the mission of this paper to give a complete analysis of these models. But let's take a lessons learned from the naming of highest agile maturity level of these models. We find ideas like: Sustained, Optimizing (Which is similar to SPICE or CMMI), Data management, Measured stage, Management Level Maturity, Innovating (Creative evolution of practice, and spread these practices throughout the organization), On Demand Just in Time Releases, Ambient, Responsive (Focusing on acting relative to change from the perspective of the moment balanced with a longer timeframe), The Lake Effect, Scaling, Consolidated, A collaborative & cooperative approach between all stakeholders, Agility at Scale, Established governance model that guarantees creative freedoms to practitioners, continuously learning from your markets [4] [25].

Instead there are some accepted key factors for agility: shared leadership, team orientation, redundancy, learning, autonomy [27]. It will be future work to check the role of these key factors in an agile maturity framework. Finding a huge range of final goals and a huge range of roadmaps as well, it seems that agility is more a miracle than something well organized. But the picture turns into something surprising when we go to a more detailed level.

Do Agile Maturity Models Really Measure Agility? The 1st idea when analysing agile maturity models in detail was to check which capability (SPICE) or maturity levels (CMMI) they are supporting. Trying to map the available agile maturity models to capability indicators of SPICE turned out very difficult as many authors of agile maturity models have an undisciplined wording. So there is no clear connotation if a model describes a level, a process attribute, a process, an outcome or an indicator like a base practice. So typically it is very hard (sometimes also impossible) to develop a mapping between agile maturity models and SPICE capability levels.

So the next step was to atomize a sample of agile maturity models in order to check what they really contain. Using a sample of 12 of 35 agile maturity models and extracting atomized characteristics out of these models synthesized a set of 600 atomized characteristics. These characteristics were assigned to capability characteristics like levels, attributes, process, outcomes, practices or work products. At the end of this step 600 prequalified characteristics were ready for further processing. During a workshop that took place at the EuroSPI 2012 in Vienna a subset of 250 characteristics of the sample was mapped by the participants to ISO/IEC 15504 Part 5 2012. The result was:

- 142   Characteristics were found related to the content of system engineering processes,
- 70   Characteristics were found related to software life cycle processes,
- 12   Characteristics were found related to capability levels 2, 3 and 5,
- 5   Characteristics were found related to a release management process and
- 21   Characteristics were mot map able at all. May be they are the real agile nucleus.

A first rough interpretation of these findings might be that agile maturity does not deal with classic capability (even if there is a substantial level of support) but mostly deals with process/practice implementation in an agile style. It is evident that this result is an input for furthermore analysis and research. This is more a 1st hypothesis than a proven academic finding. As shown above the classical capability roadmap is a stair leading from 0 to 5. Looking at a bigger picture the classical capability roadmap might be one axis of a bigger spider web that addresses modern software development challenges on technical, social and organizational level.

Agile Maturity in the CAT Syllabus? As we find neither direct answer in SPICE nor in one of the 35 agile maturity models, it could be possibly given from agile testers. Looking for a source it would be likely to find answers at the Certified Agile Tester (CAT) community and their ideas about agile testing maturity [29]. Analyzing this syllabus it becomes clear, that the CAT community takes care about the function of a tester in an agile team but is not taking care about the test process and its capability. Citing the agile manifesto [15] and referring to scrum the leading question is what to do as an agile tester and how to do it, but no why. Agile tester do not change the agile world.

Aiming on persons and teams the only hint on maturity is the definition of high performance teams. Using the definition of Leffingwell, the CAT community defines a high performance team as having the right people on the team, being led not managed, understanding their mission, communicating and collaborating continuously, being accountable for their results. So agile testing as described in the CAT syllabus seems to be people and team centered and not process oriented.

What Might Help? What we need is some type of clip that helps to bridge the gap. One source could be the research of Jan Pries-Heje about change strategies [21]. We see, that there are strategies like the employee driven approach and the socializing approach. At the end such approaches lead to a status where the process description describes the way an organisation is doing its business (while command and control approaches use process descriptions mostly to describe how an organisation should do its business). Using this approach we will have commitment on the one hand (which is completely missing in organisations that call a chaotic work style "agile") and team orientation on the other. In this case agile team can use the improvement roadmap of ISO/IEC 15504 Part 4 [11].

Intermediate Result: Trying to find a valuable roadmap how to improve the agility in agile testing there is not much help for organisations wanting to improve neither from the agile community nor from TestSPICE. But looking at the change process we find lots of potential synergy, if the right change process is chosen.

3   How to Use TestSPICE in an Agile Testing Environment

As shown, TestSPICE and the CAT approach answer completely different questions. The TestSPICE PAM has the what and the agile testers have the how. From an assessor perspective this should not be the end of the discussion. Different to a CMMI appraisal, TestSPICE is not aimed to impress customers but help an organization to improve its testing processes. So as an assessment normally should be done by a trained and experienced assessor, the assessor training and experience are the key success factors [22] [34]. We can find some hints in ISO/IEC 15504 Part 2 and 3 [22]. The Assessor must also be aware of the implications of strategic or tactical process improvement [17] [20]. Also most of the published agile maturity models obviously have strategic –transform the organization- and tactical –pilot SCRUM- aspects [4] [25].

3.1   The What in TestSPICE Meets the How of CAT

Wanting to effectively utilize TestSPICE in an agile environment, we have to reflect the whole improvement life cycle. ISO/IEC 15504 Part 4:2004[11] describes an improvement life cycle that does not start with an assessment but with the analysis of business drivers. It is not likely that an organization has on perception of business drivers that motivates process improvement and another perception that motivates the introduction of agile practices. So if most likely the business drivers for process improvement and agility are the same, the outcome of a business driver analysis is meaningful for process improvement as well as for decisions about agility.

Having a business driver analysis as a starting point, the target capability profile will be the next deliverable. This capability profile shows a what: processes and capability levels. But the capability profile shows also a first agile picture covering reuse, knowledge management, test automation, training, improvement and some other key processes. A mature agile organization needs these processes at a minimum of Level 3.

As shown the same perception of the business drives agile and SPICE oriented process improvement. Now we get the how from CAT when defining and implementing a testing standard, it should be derived from CAT or equivalent sources of agile testing practices. If agile testing is the testing standard of an organization the PA 3.2 assessment clearly delivers an insight if agile testing practices are really established in the organization.

3.2   Using Strength and Weaknesses to Feedback Agile Maturity

Currently it is difficult to achieve commitment what agile maturity really is. But in a standard assessment report for each process strength and weaknesses are mentioned. The strength of a process are clearly related to business needs (as well are the weaknesses). If a business environment is likely to produce frequent changes complete requirements analysis followed by a complete test case design might fulfill base practices and outcomes of requirements development or test case design in a formal understanding, but a process that produces lots of waste (e.g. test cases that will be re written before 1st execution) has a weakness that is to be mentioned.

So even if the target process profile does not require processes on capability level 3 we can see that discussing strength and weaknesses allows giving feedback on the implementation of agile processes. So a TestSPICE assessment is able to deliver a feedback if an organization needs agile testing. If an organization used the agile testing approach behind CAT then the feedback shows if the organization is testing like CAT.

3.3   Requirements for TestSPICE Assessors in Agile Environments

As shown a formal assessment approach will not work in agile environments. Accepting this, the focus turns to the assessment team. The team must be aware of the business drivers analysis and the potential need of agile practices. The team must also be aware of some pitfalls:

Even if agility has to be taken into account we still discuss agile implementation and not agile replacement of TestSPICE processes. The assessment team has to deliver an accurate report. Many organizations say that they work agile, what means chaotic. The assessment team must be able to distinguish between disciplined agile practices and chaos. There are some authors discussing technical debt as a consequence of inappropriate development practices. But there is another risk that is a severe as technical debt, it is the knowledge and communication debt. While technical debt is measurable, knowledge debt is difficult to identify. Knowledge debt appears, when knowledge more and more turns into tacit knowledge. Poor knowledge management and also poor documentation lead to tacit knowledge and as a result also to process bottlenecks (e.g. neither documented test cases nor documented test execution and its results). Assessors must be aware of this and critically check if just enough documentation is really enough documentation.

4   Conclusion and Further Work

TestSPICE is a usable tool to assess agile testing. Many features of TestSPICE 2.0 are adaptable to agile environments. TestSPICE 3.0 will bring more benefits for agile testing as it will deliver a complete set of technical practices for test automation and test data management. But even if TestSPICE 3.0 delivers lot of added value, the problem that there is currently no common accepted agile maturity model in the market hits the TestSPICE community as it is not possible to incorporate those agile maturity characteristics as well as the CAT community as they also can't define agile testing maturity.

As described in the abstract the paper is written from a more practical perspective. Additional research is needed to find out how many organizations currently use agile maturity models and which models might be seen as market leaders. It is also a scientific task to deeply analyze the available agile maturity models in order to evaluate if they have a common mind set and if they deliver added value compared to CMMI or SPICE.

References

1. Ringstad, M.A., Dingsøyr, T., Brede Moe, N.: Agile Process Improvement: Diagnosis and Planning to Improve Teamwork. In: O'Connor, R.V., Pries-Heje, J., Messnarz, R. (eds.) EuroSPI 2011. CCIS, vol. 172, pp. 167–178. Springer, Heidelberg (2011)
2. Bayona, S., Calvo-Manzano, J.A., San Feliu, T.: Critical Success Factors in Software Process Improvement: A Systematic Review. In: Mas, A., Mesquida, A., Rout, T., O'Connor, R.V., Dorling, A. (eds.) SPICE 2012. CCIS, vol. 290, pp. 1–12. Springer, Heidelberg (2012)
3. Bianco, C.: Agile and SPICE Capability Levels. In: O'Connor, R.V., Rout, T., McCaffery, F., Dorling, A. (eds.) SPICE 2011. CCIS, vol. 155, pp. 181–185. Springer, Heidelberg (2011)

4. Biro, M., Korsaa, M., Nevalainen, R., Vohwinkel, D., Schweigert, T.: Agile Maturity Model, Go back to the Start of the Cycle. In: EuroSPI 2012 Industrial Proceedings, Delta (2012)

5. Blaschke, M., et al.: The TestSPICE approach, Test Process Assessments follow in the footsteps of software process assessments, Testing Experience 12/2009, p. 56

6. Glazer, H., Dalton, J., Anderson, D., Konrad, M., Shrum, S.: CMMI or Agile, Why not Embrace Both? Technical Note SEI 2008 (2008)

7. Certified agile Tester, http://www.agile-tester.org

8. Irrazabal, E., Vásquez, F., Díaz, R., Garzás, J.: Applying ISO/IEC 12207:2008 with SCRUM and Agile Methods. In: O'Connor, R.V., Rout, T., McCaffery, F., Dorling, A. (eds.) SPICE 2011. CCIS, vol. 155, pp. 169–180. Springer, Heidelberg (2011)

9. ISO/IEC 15504 Part 2:2003 Performing an assessment

10. ISO/IEC 15504 Part 3:2004 Guidance on performing an assessment

11. ISO/IEC 15504 Part 4:2004 Guidance on use for process improvement and process capability determination

12. ISO/IEC 15504 Part 5:2006: An exemplar Process Assessment Model

13. ISO/IEC 15504 Part 5:2012: An exemplar Process Assessment Model

14. ISO/IEC 29119 Part 2: Draft International Standard 2012: Test Process

15. Beck, K., et al.: Agile Manifesto 2001 (2001), http://agilemanifesto.org/

16. Knüvener, C.: TestSPICE – SPICE fürTestprozesse, SQ-Magazin 17/2010, pp. 26–27

17. Lepmets, M., Ras, E., Renault, A.: Organizational Support for Process Improvement – Results of an International Survey. In: O'Connor, R.V., Rout, T., McCaffery, F., Dorling, A. (eds.) SPICE 2011. CCIS, vol. 155, pp. 133–144. Springer, Heidelberg (2011)

18. McMahon, P.: Integrating CMMI and Agile Development: Case Studies and Proven Techniques for Faster Performance Improvement. Addison-Wesley Professional, Boston (2010)

19. Pikkarainen, M.: Towards a Framework for Improving Software Development Process Mediated with CMMI Goals and Agile Practices. In: Espoo 2008, p. 119. VTT Publications 695 (2008), http://www.vtt.fi/inf/pdf/publications/2008/P695.pdf

20. Pries-Heje, J., Johansen, J., et al. (eds.): SPI Manifesto, Alcala (2010)

21. Pries-Heje, J., Johansen, J.: Improve IT, Horsholm (Delta) (2007)

22. Rout, T.: Toward a Body of Knowledge for Process Assessment. In: Rout, T., Lami, G., Fabbrini, F. (eds.) Proceedings SPICE 2010, Pisa, Edizioni ETS (2010)

23. Russwurm, W.: Hidden Treasure: The Implementation of CMMI Practices by Agile Methods. Procedures of the SEPG Conference (2010), http://www.sei.cmu.edu/library/assets/presentations/2201_Russwurm.pdf

24. Schweigert, T., Nehfort, A.: Technical Issues in Test Process Assessment and their current and future Handling in Test SPICE. In: EuroSPI Industrial Proceedings, Delta (2011)

25. Schweigert, T., Nevalainen, R., Vohwinkel, D., Korsaa, M., Biro, M.: Agile Maturity Model, Oxymoron or the Next Level of Understanding. In: Mas, A., Mesquida, A., Rout, T., O'Connor, R.V., Dorling, A. (eds.) SPICE 2012. CCIS, vol. 290, pp. 289–294. Springer, Heidelberg (2012)

26. Steiner, M., et al.: Make test process assessment similar to software process assessment - the TestSPICE approach. Journal of Software Maintenance and Evolution, published online 2010 at Wiley Online library (2010), http://wileyonlinelibrary.com, doi:10.1002/SMR 507

27. Stettina, C.J., Heijstek, W.: Five Agile Factors: Helping Self-management to Self-reflect. In: O'Connor, R.V., Pries-Heje, J., Messnarz, R. (eds.) EuroSPI 2011. CCIS, vol. 172, pp. 84–96. Springer, Heidelberg (2011)

28. The agile testing days, http://www.agiletestingsdays.com
29. The CAT SIG, Certified Agile Tester Manual, Version 2.1, Berlin, ISQI (2010)
30. The TestSPICE PAM Version 2012 (2012), http://www.testspice.info
31. The TestSPICE SIG, http://www.testspice.info
32. The TMMI Foundation, http://www.tmmi.org
33. Tuisk, A., Karpištšenko, A., Lepmets, M.: Integrated Process Improvement Approach: Case Studies in Skype Technologies Ltd. In: Mas, A., Mesquida, A., Rout, T., O'Connor, R.V., Dorling, A. (eds.) SPICE 2012. CCIS, vol. 290, pp. 13–25. Springer, Heidelberg (2012)
34. Uskarcı, A., Demirörs, O.: A Case Study on Employee Perceptions of Organization Wide Continuous Process Improvement Activities. In: Mas, A., Mesquida, A., Rout, T., O'Connor, R.V., Dorling, A. (eds.) SPICE 2012. CCIS, vol. 290, pp. 26–37. Springer, Heidelberg (2012)
35. van Ewijk, A., Linker, B., van Oosterwijk, M., Visser, B., de Vries, G., Wilhelmus, L., Marselis, R.: TPI NEXT - Geschäftsbasierte Verbesserung des Testprozesses, Düsseldorf, dpunkt (2011)

Can 'Soft' Organisational Problems Be Solved by 'Hard' Process Reference Models?

David Tuffley[1,2]

[1] School of ICT, Griffith University, Australia
[2] Software Quality Institute (SQI-IIIS), Griffith University, Australia
D.Tuffley@griffith.edu.au

Abstract. Process Reference Models (PRM) and their associated Assessment Models (PAM) are best known for their application to well-defined input-process-output work-flows in the Systems and Software Engineering domains. Model-based process improvement (MBPI) is now well-established as a discipline within that domain. Arguably though, MBPI can be applied successfully to multiple domains. The question has been to find a way. This paper discusses a mature Process Reference Model and Assessment Model for the leadership of complex virtual teams, developed in accordance with the recognized standards (ISO/IEC 15504 [8] and ISO/IEC 24774 [9]), yet which is applied to difficult 'soft' organisational problems. Earlier work on this topic focused on how to develop a PRM in soft, organisational contexts [1]. This paper focuses on the derived Process Assessment Model which has had a three-level Capability Dimension added to the existing Performance Dimension, and with associated work-products identified. It reports on preliminary trials at Griffith University.

Keywords: Process Assessment Model, Process Reference Model, Leadership, Reference Model of Organizational Behavior, ISO/IEC 15504, ISO/IEC 24774.

1   Introduction

Standardized approaches to process assessment are finding increasingly broad applications across domains. This paper outlines one such innovative assessment model for the leadership of complex virtual teams that has been developed and applied to good effect in the Australian setting. The benefit of using an assessment model like this is being able to solve difficult organisational problems, like how to transform managers into manager/leaders, in a systematic, comprehensive way.

Considering the nature of Process Reference Models, Feiler and Humphrey [4] define a process model as an abstract representation of a process architecture, design or definition. Process models in this broad sense can be seen as process elements at an architectural, design and definitions level. The abstraction inherent in process models serves to capture and represent the essential nature of processes. Any representation of the process can be said to be a process model. Process models can be analyzed, validated, and if enactable can simulate the modeled process [4].

T. Woronowicz et al. (Eds.): SPICE 2013, CCIS 349, pp. 165–175, 2013.

Earlier work in the current project focused on the validity of calling a Process Reference Model (PRM) that describes organisation-level behavior a PRM in the proper sense, given that PRMs are generally understood to describe a process architecture, design or definition [2]. This earlier work concluded that a process model developed in accordance with ISO/IEC 15504 [8] and ISO/IEC 24774 [9]could properly be called a PRM. To avoid confusion though, it was proposed to describe this new category of PRM as a *Reference Model of Organisational Behavior* (RMOB) [1].

Since 2010, work has been ongoing with the Leadership of Complex Virtual Teams PRM (an instantiation of a RMOB), specifically to do with the elaboration of the Process Assessment Model (PAM) to now include a three-level Capability Dimension with associated work products. The PAM has been packaged into a user-friendly form suitable for use by project or line managers in any sector or discipline and distributed to willing participants.

This paper has three broad aims:

- outlines the project by which the PAM was elaborated to contain a three-level Capability Dimension and associated work products,
- shows a representative sample of the shape, form and content of the Leadership PAM, and
- gives representative feedback from participants on the usefulness or otherwise of the PAM in helping them to apply leadership skills in their management practice.

Note, contextual information on how the assessment model was derived can be found in earlier published work [1]. Space constraints do not permit their inclusion in this paper. Future work will include a detailed empirical study that extends the work of this paper.

2   Adding Capability Dimension to PAM

The project to develop a Leadership PRM began in 2006 and has proceeded through several stages, as discussed in Tuffley [1]. The current stage has focused on the development of a three-level Capability Dimension and associated work products to the basic PAM that hitherto contained only the Performance Dimension. This PAM was derived from a PRM for the leadership of complex virtual teams that had been developed earlier by the same researcher.

2.1   Project Description

For the purposes of the Grant and the Ethical clearance process, the project was described in the following terms:

- **Project Name:** *Developing the Capability Dimension of a Process Assessment Model for the Leadership of Complex Virtual Teams.*
- **Project Objectives:** to (a) identify a reasonably comprehensive list of work products, activities and artefacts associated with each of the process outcomes in

the Leadership Model, and (b) to allocate these work products, activities and artefacts to an appropriate Capability Level, as specified below.

- **Project Team:** David Tuffley and Jo-Anne Clark.

2.2 Criteria for Capability Levels

Consistent with the process capability measures prescribed in ISO/IEC 15504 [5] [8], the following criteria were applied:

- At Level 1, the process is performed, even at a rudimentary level. It is done, but there is no method behind it. The practitioner muddles through, getting the job done somehow. Next time around, it is done a little (or a lot) differently.
- At Level 2, the process is managed, progress is monitored and resources allocated, QA performed. Work products are managed (i.e. standard template and placed under configuration management).
- At Level 3, a defined process exists and it can be tailored and is routinely used in projects. Performance data is gathered in preparation for quantitative project management.

2.3 Research Method

This was a small-scale project involving the researcher and a research assistant. The project followed these steps, adapted from Denscombe [6]:

1. Establish project terms of reference.
2. Establish project schedule.
3. Allocate tasks.
4. Give public lecture to interested parties to identify interviewees.
5. Collect data through (a) literature review, and (b) interviews with managers.
6. Collate findings.
7. Review findings
8. Incorporate findings into PAM
9. Do sanity check on the enhanced PAM
10. Make preliminary enquiries about possible test sites.
11. Publicize results (as per Grant conditions).

3   Representative Sample of the Leadership PAM

This PAM was developed in strict accordance with ISO/IEC 15504:2004 Parts 1 and 2. A description of how the PAM was developed can be found in Tuffley [1] [3]. Space restrictions do not permit its inclusion here.

3.1 High-Level Structure of the Leadership Process Assessment Model (PAM)

The structure of the PAM followed that of the PRM. In the earlier development of the PRM it became clear that the various process areas could be differentiated into individual attributes of a leader, factors relevant to the team or project, and those relating to the organisation as a whole. Segmenting the process areas into these three levels was a rational decision, but one which also made intuitive sense.

Table 1. High-level structure of the Leadership Process Assessment Model (PAM)

Leadership Process Assessment Model	
Individual Process Group (IND)	
IND.1	Vision*
IND.2	Objective(s)
IND.3	Integrity
IND.4	Action-orientation
IND.5	Intelligence
IND.6	Individualized consideration
IND.7	Management-by-exception
Team Process Group (TEM)	
TEM.1	Team structure
TEM.2	Team requirements
TEM.3	Team recruitment
TEM.4	Team environment
TEM.5	Team formation
TEM.6	Team roles
TEM.7	Team rules
TEM.8	Team authority
TEM.9	Team performance management
TEM.10	Team development
Organisation Process Group (ORG)	
ORG.1	Team boundaries
ORG.2	Team collaboration
ORG.3	Team & home organization balance

* The Vision process is shown in detail in next section.

3.2   Representative Process Area Content: IND.1 - Vision

In accordance with the requirements of ISO/IEC 15504:2004 Parts 1 and 2, each of the process areas in the PAM was developed and formatted in the manner shown in Table 2 below. The other 19 processes have also been elaborated in the way shown below. An earlier review of the PAM conducted in 2010 (which at that time contained only the Performance Dimension) established that such a PAM was viable. This conclusion was based on the results from a four person focus group comprised of project managers [3].

Table 2. Representative process area content: IND.1 - Vision

Process ID	IND.1
Process Name:	Vision
Process Purpose:	The purpose of the vision process is to create and communicate a shared vision in ways that inspires people to realise that vision.
Process Outcomes:	As a result of successful implementation of the vision process: 1) A vision of the goal(s) is created. 2) The vision of the goal(s) is communicated to the team 3) Commitment by team to the shared vision is gained
Base Practices:	**IND.1.BP1: Create the vision**. The leader envisions a desirable future condition [Outcome 1]
	IND.1.BP2: Communicate the vision. The leader communicates the vision in a way that creates positive expectation in the team members [Outcome 2].
	IND.1.BP3: Commitment to vision by team. The leader obtains commitment from the team members for the realisation of the vision, making it a shared vision [Outcome 3].

Work Products / Activities / Conditions

Inputs	Outputs
Outcome 1:	*Vision is created*
Capability Level 1: Performed	*Process is performed with some degree of competence, but without systematic planning.*
	Vision is formulated through recognizing the current pattern of trends and extrapolating on these to envisage where the world will be in 5 to 10 years. Being proactive, not reactive.
	Vision is formulated through observation, reflection, and discussion with wide variety of stakeholders.
	Vision is formulated through analysis of available intelligence in your field of interest.

Table 2. (*continued*)

	Vision is formulated through attending conferences, seminars, and industry events.
	Vision is formulated through being sharpening your intuitive understanding of the world, often the source of inspiration.
	Vision is formulated through unorthodox thinking; deliberately thinking in unorthodox ways about problems and not being controlled by the need for approval.
	Vision is formulated through seeking ideas that approach perfection, but which you do not expect will ever achieve absolute perfection.
Business goals	Team Charter
	Objectives that *must* be achieved
Customer requirements	Project Plan
	Requirements Specification
	Project launch presentation
	Planning session with senior management
Outcome 1:	*Vision is created*
Capability Level 2: Managed	*Process is managed, monitored against plan, resources allocated, QA performed.*
	Work products are managed (i.e. standard template and placed under configuration management)
	Any output done at CL1 that is being managed (not just performed) plus the following:
	A creativity incubator; a place that is conducive to creativity.
Outcome 1:	*Vision is created*
Capability Level 3: Defined	*Documented, customizable description of how to achieve the desired outcome.*
	Performance data is collected
	Any output done at CL2 that has a defined process (not just managed) plus the following:
	Description of how a creativity incubator can be created; what are the critical, underlying characteristics of such an incubator, how to create one for different projects.

Table 2. (*continued*)

Outcome 2:	Vision is communicated
Capability Level 1: Performed	*Process is performed with some degree of competence, but without systematic planning.*
	Has command of persuasive communication techniques; appeals to logic, reputation and/or emotion.
	Uses channels other than direct speech; video, audio, social media.
Briefings from Senior Management	Vision statement is communicated
	Roadmap (implementing vision statement)
	Yearly kick-off
Performance data	Quarterly review
Customer feedback	Team briefing
	Regular team meetings
Outcome 2:	Vision is communicated
Capability Level 2: Managed	*Process is managed, monitored against plan, resources allocated, QA performed.*
	Work products are managed (i.e. standard template and placed under configuration management)
	Any output done at CL1 that is being managed (not just performed) plus the following:
	Knows how to systematically go about constructing a persuasive communication strategy; appeals to logic, reputation and/or emotion.
New media	Innovative and compelling method of communicating the vision (i.e. social media, YouTube, other new media)
Outcome 2:	Vision is communicated
Capability Level 3: Defined	*Documented, customizable description of how to get commitment to vision from team.*
	Any output done at CL2 that has a defined process (not just managed) plus the following:
	Description of how to construct a persuasive communication strategy; how to adapt to the demands of different situations.

Table 2. (*continued*)

Outcome 3:	*Commitment to vision*
Capability Level 1: Performed	
	Give team members a compelling self-interested reason to want to be involved in the project. Tell them what will be in it for them, why should they make the effort. Appeal to both selfish and altruistic motives (i.e. you will be helping yourself, but also be part of something grand.
Commitment by team to the shared vision is gained	Vision statement is communicated by management
	Team buy-in exercises
	Project vision communicated at launch and subsequently reinforced
Outcome 3:	*Commitment to vision*
Capability Level 2: Managed	*Process is managed, monitored against plan, resources allocated, QA performed.*
	Work products are managed (i.e. standard template and placed under configuration management)
	Any output done at CL1 that is being managed (not just performed) plus the following:
	Have an established technique for obtaining commitment/buy-in.
Innovative methods for motivating	Share options in new company
	Create a sense of solidarity and united mission by defining a common enemy
Outcome 3:	*Commitment to vision*
Capability Level 3: Defined	*Documented, customizable description of how to get commitment to vision from team.*
	Any output done at CL2 that has a defined process (not just managed) plus the following:
	Have an defined and customizable technique for obtaining commitment/buy-in.

The above table is a representative process area IND.1 - Vision, one of 20, from the Leadership Process Assessment Model. It conforms to the requirements of ISO/IEC 15504:2004 Parts 1 and 2.

4   Review Feedback of the New Process Assessment Model (PAM)

A formal, empirically-based review is planned in the next 12 months. In the meantime, the following preliminary results summarize the results and indicate *potential* trends. To solicit participation, a public lecture titled *From Management to Leadership: An Introduction to a Process Model for Managers* was presented. The lecture was promoted via the *Griffith News Online* service, a weekly bulletin circulated to 3,500 Griffith staff an interested outside parties. 37 people attended the lecture. These parties were self-selected and no demographic information on them is available. In all likelihood they were project or line managers interested in improving their skills, as this was what the seminar invitation offered. Five non-academic project managers from Griffith University (male and female) eventually participated in an informal review of the updated Process Assessment Model.

The participants reported that (a) the model is somewhat helpful at improving their leadership capability, and (b) the additional capability level information is helpful in giving them an improvement direction. When asked what would make the PAM more useful, the general comment was that the PAM seemed unnecessarily complicated with its formal layout, acronyms and Software Engineering-specific terminology. The sections that follow provide more detail of the informal review. A formal, empirical review is planned in the near future.

4.1   Positive Aspects

Review participants report that:

1.   The model is somewhat helpful at improving their leadership capability, and
2.   The additional capability level information is helpful in giving them an improvement direction.

On the first point, the participants liked the characterizations of the foundational personality factors that all leaders have in common. For example, all leaders have a compelling vision of the future and are able to communicate this vision in a way that creates enthusiasm. All leaders create trust, display integrity, are resilient in the face of frustration, and so on. Knowing what factors are true regardless of time, place and culture is particularly helpful. Participants also liked the purpose/outcome format of the model because it tells them *what* but not *how*. It credits them with being able to imagine the 'how'. Some would have liked more detail on how, but in general it was appreciated that the model was not too prescriptive, and does not assert a 'one-size-fits-all' solution. The model gives them the discretion to exercise their intelligence and imagination to determine how, in their particular case, a certain personality trait can be cultivated. The model paints an exemplary portrait of the basic leadership traits and gives them the freedom to imagine their own ideal self that they can grow towards.

On the second point, the participants liked the consistency and the growth path afforded by the three capability levels (performed, managed and defined). They also appreciated the inclusion of work products at each level because it provides specific examples to work towards. The question of whether the remaining two capability levels (quantitative management and optimizing) was desirable and feasible remained unanswered as the participants had insufficient understanding of these advanced levels. These questions will be the subject of further investigation.

The **Office of Human Resource Management** at Griffith University contacted the author to formally ask permission to include a pdf of the model in the HR Toolkit, an on-line resource for managers and other interested staff. A senior manager from OHRM had attended the lecture. In addition to the review participants, the general feedback from others who attended the lecture and/or downloaded the model for their own use has also been uniformly positive if not complimentary.

4.2   Negative Aspects

Review participants report that the:

1. formal tabulated layout was somewhat daunting
2. acronyms (eg. IND-BP1, CL etc.) were confusing
3. Software Engineering-specific terminology did not make sense

It was noted that the tabulated form, acronyms and terminology commonly used in Software Engineering creates the impression of a densely-packed body of technical information that is not readily understandable to the non-technical managers interviewed. The technical managers did not experience the same difficulty.

4.3   Future Direction

The review comments clearly indicated the need to simplify the model so that it is accessible to non-technical managers. Given that a guiding objective of this project from its beginning in 2006 is to create a tool that is usable by the broadest possible range of managers, the need to simplify is a compelling one. The next steps will therefore be to (a) simplify the presentation to be accessible to non-technical users, (b) conduct an empirical study involving technical and non-technical users to determine its efficacy and identify areas of improvement, and (c) investigate whether adding the remaining two capability levels (quantitative management and optimizing) is feasible.

5   Conclusion

The evolution of this model has been ongoing since 2006. The impetus to develop it came from the author's experiences in the IT industry between 1988 and 2000. As a contractor/consultant during that time, the author had reported to perhaps 30 managers across a variety of projects. Of these 30, in the opinion of the author only two could be described as leaders in the sense that they were able to *make people want to do what it was they wanted them to do*. The remaining 28 or so managers were unable to achieve this, needing to resort to more coercive methods, thus incurring resentment, lack of respect and other undesirable consequences. The leadership model's purpose is to help managers in the 'do as I say' category to become members of the leader category.

The leadership model recognizes that leadership is situationally-expressed. As long as one knows what the underlying traits are, the model enables a person to express leadership according to the demands of a particular situation.

The initial challenge was to determine whether (a) leadership was something that could in fact be learned, and (b) can be described as a Process Reference Model in the Software Engineering sense. Both of these questions were answered in the affirmative [1] [2] [3].

The next challenge was to develop a Process Assessment Model based on the Reference Model and determine whether it was feasible as a practical tool in the hands of managers. The initial PAM contained on the Performance Dimension. Empirical studies established that such a PAM was in fact a practical tool [3].

The third challenge, addressed in this paper, was to add the Capability Dimension to the PAM and determine whether this enhance version of the PAM was a practical tool for managers. An informal review, a preliminary to an empirical review, as discussed in this paper indicates that the enhanced PAM is a practical tool. It points strongly to the conclusion that 'soft' organisational problems can be solved by 'hard' Process Reference Models and their associated assessment models. (*Download model: http://www.ict.griffith.edu.au/~davidt/Full_Leadership_Model.pdf*)

Acknowledgments. This research was performed with the help of an Early Career Research Grant from Griffith University. The author also acknowledges the encouragement and guidance of Associate Professor Terry Rout in the formative stages of the project.

References

1. Tuffley, D.J.: Reference Models of Organisational Behavior: A new category of Process Reference Model. In: Proceedings of 10th International SPICE Conference 2010: Process Improvement and Capability Determination in Software, Systems Engineering and Service Management, Edizioni ETS, Pisa, Italy (2010)
2. Feiler, P.H., Humphrey, W.S.: Software Process Development and Enactment, Software Engineering Institute, Pittsburgh, CMU/SEY-92-TR-04, p. 11 (1992)
3. Tuffley, D.J.: Engineering Organisational Behaviour with Design Research. International Journal of Sociotechnology and Knowledge Development 3(2), 46–56 (1941) ISSN: 1941-6253
4. Feiler, P.H., Humphrey, W.S.: Software Process Development and Enactment, Software Engineering Institute, Pittsburgh, CMU/SEY-92-TR-04, p. 11 (1992)
5. Jung, H.-W.: Evaluating the Internal Consistency of ISO/IEC TR 15504 Process Capability Measures. Software Process Improvement and Practice 8, 5–26 (2003), doi:10.1002/spip.166
6. Denscombe, M.: The Good Research Guide: For small-scale social research projects. Open University Press, United Kingdom (1998) ISBN: 9780335198061
7. ISO/EIA 12207: Standard for Information Technology-Software Life Cycle Processes. This Standard was published in August 1998 (1998)
8. ISO/IEC 15504: Information Technology: Process Assessment. Joint Technical Committee IT-015, Software and Systems Engineering. Part 2 Performing an Assessment. This Standard was published on 2 June 2005 (2005)
9. ISO/IEC TR 24774: Software and systems engineering – Life cycle management – Guidelines for process description. This Standard was published in 2007 (2007)

Exploring the Impact of IT Service Management Process Improvement Initiatives: A Case Study Approach

Marko Jäntti[1,3], Terry Rout[2], Lian Wen[1],
Sanna Heikkinen[3], and Aileen Cater-Steel[4]

[1] Griffith University, Nathan, School of Information and Communication Technology
170 Kessels Road, Nathan, Brisbane, Queensland 4111, Australia
`l.wen@griffith.edu.au`
[2] Griffith University, Nathan, Institute of Integrated and Intelligent Systems
`t.rout@griffith.edu.au`
[3] University of Eastern Finland, School of Computing
P.O. Box 1627, 70211, Kuopio, Finland
`{marko.jantti,sanna.heikkinen}@uef.fi`
[4] School of Information Systems
University of Southern Queensland
Toowoomba, QLD 4350 Australia
`caterst@usq.edu.au`

Abstract. IT companies worldwide have started to improve their service management processes based on best practice frameworks, such as IT Infrastructure Library (ITIL). However, many of these companies face difficulties in demonstrating the positive outcomes of IT service management (ITSM) process improvement. This has led us to investigate the research problem: What positive impacts have resulted from IT service management process improvement? The main contributions of this paper are 1) to identify the ITSM process improvement outcomes in two IT service provider organizations and 2) provide advice as lessons learnt.

Keywords: IT service management, service, IT Infrastructure Library, process improvement, process.

1 Introduction

Thousands of IT organizations worldwide have started to improve their service management processes based on the IT Infrastructure Library (ITIL) that is the most widely used best practice framework for IT service management (ITSM). A major challenge is how people responsible for process improvement can demonstrate the benefits that process improvement initiatives provide. We propose that ITSM standards (15504-8 [1] and ISO/IEC 20000 [2]) provide an opportunity to benchmark current processes and discern improvement.

Evidence on positive impacts of ITSM process improvement motivates employees to participate in the process improvement sessions and training in future,

T. Woronowicz et al. (Eds.): SPICE 2013, CCIS 349, pp. 176–187, 2013.

enables process improvement specialists to see that their work is meaningful and provide managers with the cost justification regarding the process improvement. IT service management can be broadly defined as "implementation and management of quality IT services that meet the needs of the business" [3]. Examples of IT services are, for example, application and server services.

Currently, there are three different versions of the ITIL framework that organizations use: ITIL V2 2002, V3 2007 and V3 2011 edition. Many IT organizations started the ITSM process improvement by using ITIL v2. The core of ITIL v2 comprised two parts: 1) Service Delivery [4] and 2) Service Support [5].

The ITIL V3 framework was released in 2007 with a completely new structure. The goal of restructuring was to emphasize the service lifecycle with five core lifecycle books. The V3 2011 edition did not provide major amendments but clarified unclear issues in V3 processes. The V3 2011 edition consists of five books: Service Strategy [6], Service Design [7], Service Transition [8], Service Operation [9] and Continual Service Improvement [10].

Because ITIL is a best practice framework, not a standard, IT organizations need an international standard to audit their ITSM processes. The most popular IT service management standard is the ISO 20000 standard family, especially ISO/IEC 20000-1:2010 Part 1: Service management system requirements [2] and ISO/IEC 20000-2:2011 Part 2: Guidance on the application of service management systems [11]. The service management process reference model can be found in the Part 4 [12]. ISO/IEC TS 15504-8:2012 process assessment model [1] expands the PRM process definitions and defines Generic Practices, Generic Resources and Generic Input/Outputs for evaluating the service management process capability. Additionally, it uses Base Practices and Input/Output Information Items as process performance indicators and introduces a Process Maturity Framework (PMF). This standard will be renumbered to fit in the ISO/IEC 33001 family. Figure 1 shows the contribution of ITSM frameworks and standards.

Key Performance Indicators can be used to evaluate whether improvements have resulted in positive outcomes. In the IT service management framework

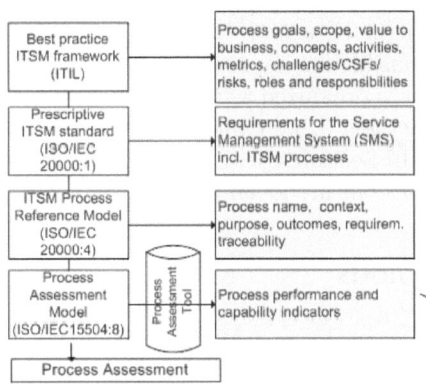

Fig. 1. IT service management process frameworks and standards

ITIL, the measurement is divided into three elements [3]: Critical Success Factors (CSFs) that represent business objectives for IT service management, Key Performance Indicators that indicate the direction of performance, and metrics that enable measurements in practice.

Previous studies on ITSM implementations have dealt with measurements of ITIL implementation projects [13], the success factors of ITSM projects [14], failures of ITIL implementation [15], maturity models of ITIL implementation [16] and integration of ITIL and CMMi [17]. CMMi for Services [18] can be used to assess the maturity of a service provider organization. Additionally, a recent study in Australia presented a model to select processes for ITSM improvement [19].

Surprisingly few studies have investigated realization of the benefits. Marrone and Kolbe [20] have identified six most important benefits from ITSM implementation: improvement in customer satisfaction, improvement in internal processes, standardization of processes, improvement in service quality, increase in efficiency, and improvement in return on investment (ROI). Lepmets et al. [21] have described the IT service quality attributes that could be measured to improve IT service quality. Barafort et al. [22] have explored the benefits from the use of ISO/IEC 15504 and ITIL. Additionally, McNaughton et al. [23] use a holistic evaluation framework for ITSM with four perspectives: management, technology, IT user, IT employee. There are also studies that have dealt with benefits from improving software development processes. The DACS report [24] presents the following measures for software process improvements: productivity, quality, rework, project cost, improvement cost, cycle time, schedule variance. Similarly, SEI [25] has used cost, schedule, productivity, quality, customer satisfaction, and ROI to measure CMMI-based process improvement.

The **main contribution** of this paper is to

- explore the impacts of IT service management process initiatives in two IT service provider organizations,
- provide lessons learnt from two cases and
- discuss how to demonstrate ITSM process improvement impacts.

Our research results might be useful for CSI managers, quality managers and process managers responsible for improving service management processes.

The rest of the paper is organized as follows. In Section 2, the research methods are described. In Section 3, we explore the IT service management process improvement impacts. In Section 4 lessons learnt are derived from the analysis of two cases. The conclusions are given in Section 5.

2 Research Methods

In this paper, the research problem is: What positive impacts have resulted from IT service management process improvement? We used a case study research method to explore the research problem. This exploratory study was carried out with two organizations. In order to maintain the anonymity of research, they are called Alpha and Beta in this paper. Both organizations were representative cases with ITIL-based process improvement experience. For the IT service management research, a case study method suits especially well because it allows rich data collection on service management processes, people, services, tools and technologies. Eisenhardt has defined a case study as "a research strategy which focuses on understanding the dynamics present with single settings" [26]. The research problem was addressed by the following research questions that provided a roadmap for the case study:

1. What was the scope of process improvement (ITSM processes/ services)?
2. Which quality frameworks/standards or metrics were used to support ITSM process improvement?
3. What effects / benefits / improvements were identified from ITSM process improvement?
4. What effects resulted from IT service management training?
5. What challenges arise in ITSM process improvement?

The training-related question was added to the study because researchers considered ITSM training as an important source of improvement ideas.

2.1   The Case Organizations and Data Collection Methods

Our first case organization Alpha offers IT, product development and consulting services in Northern Europe. The company has around 18,000 employees operating in 30 countries. This case study was carried out in the business unit that provides solutions and services for Scandinavian energy companies. The following data sources were used:

- Interview on ITSM impacts: Release and testing manager
- Documentation: SLA, SLM process description, SLA module user guide
- Archives and records: Excel sheets on incident resolution times
- Participative observation: SLA/SLM process improvement meetings (November 2011-January 2012), SLA workshop
- Physical artifacts: Access to intranet and the SLA module (ITSM tool).

Our second case organization Beta provides IT services (e.g. desktop services, service desk) to a government agency. The agency had 5,300 fulltime employees in 2011. The following sources of evidence were used in data collection:

- Interview on ITSM impacts: Service director
- Documentation: Process descriptions, user support metrics, service desk system user manual, service descriptions, service area catalogue
- Archives and records: Incident service request and problem records
- Participative observation: Discussions in weekly meetings
- ITSM training for user support staff: 70 persons (September 2011)
- Physical artifacts: Intranet and a service desk system.

2.2   Data Analysis

In this study, a case comparison analysis technique [26] was used. Regarding both case organizations, information on process improvement events was stored in the KISMET project's case study datastore. We used three different ways of triangulation (multiple sources of evidence): method triangulation, researcher triangulation and data triangulation. Case study findings were validated with the case organization's representatives in validation meetings (2 hours). Interviews were carried out by one researcher but analyzed by two researchers. Case comparison was based on the predefined categories: scope of improvement, process improvement frameworks, achieved benefits, impact of ITSM training, and challenges.

3   Exploring the Impact of IT Service Management Process Initiatives

In this section, we explore the IT service management improvements in two Finnish IT organizations. The research findings are presented in the same order as the research questions.

3.1   What Was the Scope of Process Improvement (ITSM Processes/ Services)?

Improvements at Alpha targeted all IT service management processes but the research team focus was on two processes: release management and service level management (SLM). Release management aims to ensure that hardware and software releases are planned, implemented, tested delivered in a systematic manner. Regarding the SLM, the research goal was to study how the IT service management tool supports the service level management process. In Beta, ITSM process improvement had focused on service operation processes, such as incident management, knowledge & problem management, and service request management. Additionally, the goal was to improve the service desk tool to better meet ITSM requirements and organization's needs.

3.2   Which Quality Frameworks / Metrics Were Used in ITSM Process Improvement?

The interview with Alpha's release and testing manager revealed that, besides ITIL V2 and V3, CMMI, Lean Management principles and ISO 9000 were used in process improvement work. Alpha used an operational framework where the ITIL processes and activities were customized to meet the organization's business needs. The interviewee in Alpha also mentioned the role of own experience and knowhow in the process improvement. In Beta, ITIL was used for guidance during the improvement. Additionally, Beta had used a wide range of its own improvement practices to support IT service management process improvement. The following metrics were used to support IT service management process improvement in Alpha and Beta: error trends (Alpha), reaction times (Alpha), resolution times (Alpha, Beta), number of service desk cases (Beta), other productivity metrics (Beta), customer satisfaction (Alpha, Beta) and staff satisfaction (Alpha, Beta).

3.3 What Effects / Benefits Were Identified from ITSM Process Improvement?

The interviewees listed the following effects, benefits, and improvements from IT service management processs improvement.

- *"Our processes have become more unified"* (Alpha)
- *"More unified work practices"* (Alpha)
- *"Number of defects has decreased"* (Alpha)
- *"The roles of people have become clearer"* (Alpha)
- *"Shorter resolution times"* (Alpha)
- *"Customer satisfaction has increased"* (Alpha)
- *"Staff satisfaction has increased"* (Alpha)
- *"Staff satisfaction has improved"* (Beta)
- *"IT service management knowhow has increased"* (Beta)
- *"Better understanding of critical elements of the service"* (Beta)
- *"Improved collaboration"* (Beta)
- *"Decreased number of defects"* (Beta)
- *"Positive feedback from customers"* (Beta)
- *"Better transparency of operations"* (Beta)
- *"Better atmosphere among staff"* (Beta)
- *"Increased customer satisfaction"* (Beta)
- *"A better monitoring system for service management"* (Beta)
- *"Better IT service quality"* (Beta)
- *"Reduced number of contacts from customers"* (Beta).

3.4 What Effects Resulted from IT Service Management Training?

Alpha's interviewee stated that as a result of IT service management training, the awareness of ITIL practices had increased. Additionally, training helped people to use common terminology and concepts. Three types of training had been organized in Alpha: ITSM training organized by the university's ITSM research team, in-house training and the official ITIL training (ITIL Foundation) provided by consultancy companies. The SLA training was organized in January, 2012 for customer service representatives. The training started with a case organization's presentation on why SLAs are important for business. The second presentation was held by a researcher who demonstrated the features of the SLA module. The participants had already received earlier some ITIL process training. The following list shows examples of questions that were asked during the training.

- *"How are reopened cases handled in SLA measurement?"*
- *"Is creating a workaround included in the SLA time?"*

- *"Which request states are included in the SLA?"*
- *"Who is responsible for changing the case urgency?"*
- *"Who should receive information on SLA alerts?"*
- *"What calendar date should we use for SLAs?"*

The outcome of this training was that case organization's employees were now able to create SLAs and configure SLA rules for new customers.

Beta's interviewee commented that ITSM training has been considered useful in the organization but also stated that integration of training to the organization's processes is very important because many IT support staff have difficulty following theory-oriented IT service management training. IT service management awareness training in Beta was conducted for 70 people in different locations. Additionally, some employees and management had participated in official ITIL certification training. We observed that inhouse ITSM training provided much more discussion compared to online training. Next, we present some interesting questions that were captured during the training sessions:

- *"How do we react in cases that would require immediate solution but specialist teams tell us that the solution shall come after a week or two?"*
- *"How should we solve cases where a user contacts the service desk and reports that he/she still has the same incident. Should we reopen the case?"*
- *"Has a rule for reopening cases been documented somewhere?"*
- *"The testing unit delivers the known errors from testing as Excel reports. It would be nice if known errors could be stored in the service desk system"*
- *"We should think about the need for the official ITIL certification training"*
- *"Earlier it has seemed that process frameworks are only for managers. Now, it looks like they are coming to the field work, too"*
- *"We should think about the metrics from our group's perspective".*

The outcome of this training was that case organization's employees became aware of ITSM practice, identified some bottlenecks in their current practices and some workers also became motivated to pursue more ITSM training.

3.5   What Challenges Arise in ITSM Process Improvement?

The case organizations listed the following challenges regarding IT service management process improvement:

- To get enough knowledge on the operational environment, challenges and risks in order to scope the services successfully (Alpha)
- Managing changes in manageable portions (Alpha)
- Clarification of roles and responsibilities to avoid extra work (Alpha)
- Unified working practices (Alpha)
- Management of change and consistent management (Alpha)
- One has to find an appropriate management model for change and service delivery, not too complex or too detailed (Beta)
- How to apply the ITSM models and frameworks to our own business (Beta)

- Introduction of ITSM processes is challenging (Beta)
- The size of the product development teams is 3-70, thus, it is difficult to describe unified processes that suit everybody (Beta)
- People do not want to give up old work practices (Beta)
- Often, it is challenging to implement changes in such a way that span process boundaries (Beta)
- People do not always see the benefits from process improvement. It may be considered as extra work without understanding benefits (Beta)
- In order to get people to adopt the processes, they have to participate in the process improvement work (Beta).

4   Analysis

In the analysis phase, we compared the findings from Alpha and Beta based on five categories (scope of process improvement, quality frameworks or standards used in ITSM process improvement, achieved benefits from improving ITSM processes, impact of ITSM training, and process improvement challenges) and converted the findings to lessons learnt. A source for each lesson is presented in parentheses (AR= Archives and records, D= Documentation, ID= Interviews and discussions, O= Observation, PA= physical artefacts, ST= Seminars and training organized by the research group).

Lesson 1: People have difficulty understanding the benefits from process improvement (RQ1: ID, O, ST). The improvement scope in Alpha was release management and service level management and in Beta incident management and service support. Interviews, observations and some ITSM training sessions revealed that some employees have difficulties understanding the benefits from process improvement. Management has to continuously market the benefits of ITSM process improvement. Basically, there are three simple ways how to identify potential ITSM benefits. First, an organization could carry out an ITSM process assessment based on ISO/IEC 15504-8 to provide a benchmark. The second way is to check the defined benefits from best practice frameworks, such as ITIL and COBIT, and to analyze whether the organization has achieved these benefits. The third way is to ask the customers whether they see improvements in service delivery.

Lesson 2: ITSM process improvements do not always show direct monetary benefits (ID). We expected that organizations would have shown stronger interest in the financial aspects of process improvement. Interviewees in Alpha and Beta mentioned the increase in productivity instead of cost savings and return on investment. For example, ITIL addresses four basic concepts to measure service management improvements [3], [10]: Improvements, Benefits, ROI (Return on Investment), and VOI (Value on Investment). Improvements can be analyzed by comparing the 'before' state to the 'after' state based on selected metrics (for example, 10 per cent increase in customer satisfaction on incident resolutions). Benefits mean realization of improvements. They can be analyzed from a financial perspective (costs or profits). ROI can be measured by calculating the difference between the benefit (saving) achieved and the amount expended. VOI means the extra value that improvement provides for business, such as improved communication or collaboration with customers (a metric in this case could be a number of meetings with a customer).

Lesson 3: IT organizations measure improvements through customer and staff satisfaction, and operational metrics (O, D, ID). Common process improvement metrics in Alpha and Beta were customer satisfaction and staff satisfaction, and operational metrics such as resolution times. We propose that organizations could easily establish a measurable process improvement framework by combining three concepts: Critical Success Factors, Key Performance Indicators and Metrics. For example, an organization might select the following CSF, KPI and metric: Quickly resolve incidents (CSF); Reduction in average time to respond to a call (KPI); Average call response time per month (Metric). The KPI from our example can be now used to define a measurable process improvement goal, such as 10 % reduction in call response time.

Lesson 4: Management and integration of multiple process improvement frameworks is a challenge (RQ2: ID, O). There is a large number of process improvement frameworks, models and standards available for organizations seeking to improve ITSM processes. According to our interviews, management considered it challenging to select an appropriate framework or a standard to carry out changes to processes, such as Alpha's comment showed: *"One has to find an appropriate management model for change and service delivery, not too complex or too detailed"*. It seems that future ITSM frameworks need to have interfaces to multiple frameworks and models, such as Agile, Lean and Cloud Service models.

Lesson 5: ITSM improvement results in positive outcomes (RQ3: ID). The following benefits were identified based on the interviews with Alpha and Beta: customer satisfaction, staff satisfaction, service management culture, higher process maturity / more standard process, improved tools and technologies, standardized services, increased service quality, increased efficiency / productivity, cost savings, better transparency.

Lesson 6: ITSM training provides valuable inputs to CSI (RQ4: ST). Management should pay attention to ITSM training and avoid organizing training in large groups to save time and costs. We observed that when trainees were motivated and training was organized in-house in small groups, they identified important bottlenecks in their daily service management practices. These bottlenecks should be considered for Continual Service Improvement.

Lesson 7: Use novel approaches to decrease the complexity of ITSM standards (RQ5: ID, ST). Interviews, discussions and training events revealed that ITSM standards and frameworks are often considered too complex and bureaucratic because of special jargon. However, they provide an excellent way to demonstrate that the process is more mature than before improvement actions. We propose that using visual notation, such as Behavior Engineering, to model requirements can remarkably decrease the feeling of complexity and lead to faster understanding of requirements. Behavior Engineering can be defined as "an integrated discipline that supports the systems and software engineering of large-scale, dependable software-intensive systems" [27]. Figure 2 shows a CT diagram we created for ISO/IEC 20000 Problem Management Requirement 1 [2]: *There shall be a documented procedure to identify problems and minimize or avoid the impact of incidents and problems.*

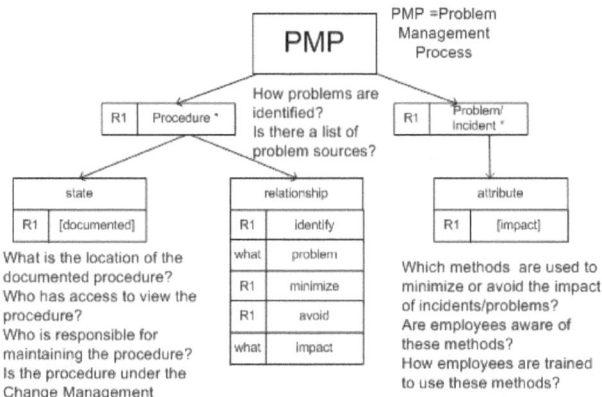

Fig. 2. A composition tree for ISO/IEC 20000 Problem Management, Requirement 1

Lesson 8: Lack of tools for demonstrating benefits (RQ5: O, PA). Based on our observations, it seems that organizations lack effective tools to demonstrate ITSM process improvement benefits or assess the maturity of processes. There are very few tools available. A valuable tool for process assessment is provided by AssessmentPortal [28]. One of the tool features is a Service Provision perception survey that explores the different views of service provision from both and IT and Business perspective. The Appraisal Assistant tool by Software Quality Institute can be used to support process assessment (ISO/IEC 15504, CMMI) [29].

These lessons learnt were not presented in a priority order. Our previous knowledge on cases may have been reflected in the findings. In future, we aim to extend this exploratory study to other IT service provider organizations to gain a richer view on the ITSM process improvement outcomes.

5   Conclusions

The research problem in this study was: What positive impacts have resulted from IT service management process improvement? The main contribution of this study is real-world examples of effects and benefits of ITSM improvement initiatives and training, and the challenges faced by organizations seeking improvements. The following impacts were identified: customer satisfaction, staff satisfaction, service management culture, higher process maturity / more standard process, improved tools and technologies, standardized services, increased service quality, increased efficiency / productivity, cost savings, and better transparency of operations.

This study included the following limitations. First, we included two organizations in our study. A higher number of cases would have provided the potential to generalize the results. Second, data was collected mainly by qualitative methods such as interviews, observation and analyzing the companies' documentation. Most of the lessons were based on interviews and discussions. Quantitative data, for example, on metrics and measurements, would have provided a richer view on the organizations. Finally, interviews were conducted only with managers. Staff interviews might have provided additional perspectives.

To conclude, more case studies are needed to examine positive impacts of IT service management process improvement. Further work could focus on creating and validating a systematic impact assessment model for ITSM process improvement initiatives.

Acknowledgment. This paper is based on research in Keys to IT Service Management and Effective Transition of Services (KISMET) project funded by the National Technology Agency TEKES (no. 70035/10), European Regional Development Fund (ERDF), and industrial partners.

References

1. ISO/IEC TS 15504-8:2012: Information technology - Process assessment-Part 8: An exemplar process assessment model for IT service management. ISO/IEC TC JTC1/SC7 Secretariat (2012)
2. ISO/IEC 20000:1: Part 1: Service management system requirements. ISO/IEC JTC 1 Secretariat (2010)
3. Office of Government Commerce(e): ITIL Continual Service Improvement. The Stationary Office, UK (2007)
4. Office of Government Commerce: ITIL Service Delivery. The Stationary Office, UK (2002)
5. OGC: ITIL Service Support. The Stationary Office, UK (2002)
6. Cabinet Office: ITIL Service Strategy. The Stationary Office, UK (2011)
7. Cabinet Office: ITIL Service Design. The Stationary Office, UK (2011)
8. Cabinet Office: ITIL Service Transition. The Stationary Office, UK (2011)
9. Cabinet Office: ITIL Service Operation. The Stationary Office, UK (2011)
10. Cabinet Office: ITIL Continual Service Improvement. The Stationary Office, UK (2011)
11. ISO/IEC 20000:2: Part 2: Guidance on the application of service management systems. ISO/IEC JTC 1 Secretariat (2011)
12. ISO/IEC TR 20000-4:2010: Information technology - Service management - Part 4: Process Reference Model. International Organization for Standardization, Geneva, Switzerland (2010)

13. Iden, J., Eikebrokk, T.R.: Understanding the ITIL implementation project: Conceptualization and measurements. In: Proceedings of 2011 22nd International Workshop on Database and Expert Systems Applications. IEEE, Washington, DC (2011)

14. Tan, W.G., Cater-Steel, A., Toleman, M.: Implementing IT service management: A case study focussing on critical success factors. Journal of Computer Information Systems 50(2) (2009)

15. Sharifi, M., Ayat, M., Rahman, A.A., Sahibudin, S.: Lessons learned in ITIL implementation failure. In: International Symposium on Information Technology, ITSim 2008, vol. 1, pp. 1–4 (2008)

16. de Sousa Pereira, R., da Silva, M.: A maturity model for implementing ITIL v3. In: 2010 6th World Congress on Services (SERVICES-1), pp. 399–406 (2010)

17. Latif, A.A., Din, M.M., Ismail, R.: Challenges in adopting and integrating ITIL and CMMi in ICT division of a public utility company. Computer Engineering and Applications 1, 81–86 (2010)

18. Software Engineering Institute: Capability Maturity Model Integration for Services v1.3. Carnegie Mellon University (2010)

19. Shrestha, A., Cater-Steel, A., Tan, W.G., Toleman, M.: A model to select processes for IT service management improvement. In: Proceedings of the 23rd Australasian Conference on Information Systems, Deakin University (2012)

20. Marrone, M., Kolbe, L.: Impact of IT service management frameworks on the IT organization: An empirical study on benefits, challenges, and processes. Business & Information Systems Engineering Journal 3(1), 5–18 (2011)

21. Lepmets, M., Cater-Steel, A., Gacenga, F., Ras, E.: Extending the IT service quality measurement framework through a systematic literature review. Journal of Service Science Research 4, 7–47 (2012)

22. Barafort, B., Di Renzo, B., Merlan, O.: Benefits resulting from the combined use of ISO/IEC 15504 with the Information Technology Infrastructure Library (ITIL). In: Oivo, M., Komi-Sirviö, S. (eds.) PROFES 2002. LNCS, vol. 2559, pp. 314–325. Springer, Heidelberg (2002)

23. McNaughton, B., Ray, P., Lewis, L.: Designing an evaluation framework for IT service management. Information Management 47, 219–225 (2010)

24. McGibbon, T., Ferens, D., Vienneau, R.: A business case for software process improvement (2007 update): Measuring return on investment from software engineering and management. Technical report, DACS Report (2007)

25. Gibson, D., Goldenson, D., Kost, K.: Performance results of CMMI®-based process improvement. CMU/SEI-2006-TR-004, Carnegie Mellon University/Software Engineering Institute (2006)

26. Eisenhardt, K.: Building theories from case study research. Academy of Management Review 14, 532–550 (1989)

27. Behavior Engineering website: Behavior engineering (2012),
    http://www.behaviorengineering.org/

28. Assessment Portal: Assessment portal website (2012),
    http://assessment-portal.com/

29. Rout, T.: Studies on the assessment process: Usage of objective evidence in assessing process capability. In: Proceedings of the 9th International Conference on Software Process Improvement and Capability Determination, SPICE 2009. Turku Centre for Computer Science, Turku (2009)

Software-Mediated Process Assessment
in IT Service Management

Aileen Cater-Steel, Wui-Gee Tan, Mark Toleman, Terry Rout, and Anup Shrestha

University of Southern Queensland,
School of Information Systems Toowoomba
{Aileen.Cater-Steel,Wui-Gee.Tan,Mark.Toleman,Terry.Rout,
Anup.Shrestha}@usq.edu.au

Abstract. Continual service improvement is a crucial aspect of IT service management as it enables organisations to enhance the relevance and responsiveness of their IT services providing outcomes in productivity and competitiveness. This paper describes a research project that is aimed at developing an international standards-based software-mediated process assessment tool to facilitate continual service improvement in IT service management. The project will also evaluate the effectiveness of the tool by implementing it in two large Australian public sector organisations and validating the results against traditional process assessment methods. The significance of the research is that the tool will enable organisations to self-assess and improve their current IT service processes as well as transitioning international standards to industry.

Keywords: Software-mediated process assessment, IT service management, Continual service improvement, ISO/IEC 15504, ISO/IEC 20000.

1   Introduction

As organisations continue to be driven by external factors such as regulation, competition, customer requirements, market pressures and economics to adopt a more customer-focused and service-oriented approach, an increasing number of them are turning to the IT service management (ITSM) model. ITSM is a process-focused discipline for managing IT as services that deliver value to customers. The model, in essence, deemphasizes the management of technology and IT systems and instead focuses on the provision of a collection of end-to-end IT services to support the business of the organisation. These IT services are not only essential to the internal efficiency of the organisation, some of them are deemed to be mission critical. Consequently, the organisation needs to continually assess and improve the ITSM processes that underlie the IT services to ensure their stability, reliability and effectiveness. The assessment effort, however, is manually time-consuming and also costly, especially if external expertise is involved. More importantly, it has to be undertaken objectively and methodically so that the organisation can confidently make changes to those ITSM processes requiring improvement.

T. Woronowicz et al. (Eds.): SPICE 2013, CCIS 349, pp. 188–198, 2013.

This paper describes a research project that was awarded funding by the Australian Research Council (ARC) as a Linkage Project. The project aims to:

- develop a prototype software tool based on international standards to facilitate continual service improvement in ITSM, and
- evaluate the effectiveness of the tool by implementing it in two large Australian public sector organisations and validating results against traditional assessment methods.

The next section provides the background for the project, including a review of relevant literature relating to the theme of the research. This is followed by a description of the research questions and research significance. The research approach and methodology are then discussed. Finally, the project progress to-date and challenges ahead are summarised.

2   Process Improvement in ITSM

To provide guidance for implementing the ITSM model many organisations use the *IT Infrastructure Library* (ITIL) framework, created by the UK's Office of Government Commerce in the late 1980s. Since then ITIL has undergone several enhancements and has now become a primary source of ITSM best practice. Under the influence of the internationally active IT Service Management Forum (itSMF) the framework has gained worldwide acceptance among private as well as public sector organisations [1-4]. Research carried out in Australia, Europe, U.S. and South Africa has confirmed that organisations have benefited from adopting the framework [5-8]. Results from surveys conducted annually by the authors since 2005 show the continuing strong interest in ITIL among Australian organisations [9]. The ITIL phenomenon led to the creation of the BS 15000 standard which later evolved into the international *ISO/IEC 20000 standard for IT service management* [10]. ISO/IEC 20000 since its creation has provided organisations with a set of criteria for the audit and certification of their ITSM capabilities.

Since ITIL version 3 (ITILv3) and in the current ITIL 2011 edition the framework departs from its prior 'process silos' approach to take a lifecycle view of ITSM. Under this lifecycle view, ITSM processes are designed, created, transitioned into live environment and then operationally supported. This is reflected in the names of the four key books, which describe stages of the life cycle: Service Strategy, Service Design, Service Transition and Service Operation. In addition, the fifth book on *Continual Service Improvement* (CSI) serves to emphasize that there should be an ongoing effort to identify opportunities for improvement of weaknesses or failures within the lifecycle stages. The book further stresses that the "real work" begins after the development and roll-out of the new processes [11]. This CSI requirement, which is consistent with the continual improvement principle in the ISO 9000 standards for quality management systems, is also ingrained in ISO/IEC 20000 to the extent that one of the clauses in the standard mandates that "there shall be a policy on continual improvement of the service management systems" [10].

The purpose of CSI is to continually align and re-align IT services to the changing external business conditions by identifying and making appropriate improvements to the ITSM processes [11]. The need to make these improvements is further heightened by the fact that over time the quality of IT services tends to deteriorate as the ITSM processes are subjected to unauthorised and unwarranted modifications. CSI therefore, is not merely a concept but is crucial to the business as it deals with the continuing relevance and responsiveness of the IT services to customers, while addressing the effectiveness and efficiency of the underlying ITSM processes at the same time. Furthermore, research has shown that 60 - 90 percent of the total cost of IT ownership is concerned with the delivery and support of IT services [12]. This cost can be reduced through CSI, especially if it is facilitated by the use of innovative tools and methods.

CSI activities, however, are expensive as they are resource-consuming [11]. Moreover, process improvement programs in general may be difficult to sustain and may even regress over time if they are not effectively managed [13, 14]. To simplify the CSI activities many organisations have adopted the process assessment method, which calls for the systematic measurement, analysis and reporting of the performance of core ITSM processes. The results are then used to evaluate the capabilities of these processes and drive process improvement activities. The gathered data could be used to develop a business case to justify the CSI effort. At the same time, the data would serve to verify the overall benefits from the ITIL or ISO/IEC 20000 investment. Process assessment, however, needs to be differentiated from audit: the former is undertaken to advise corporate management on how they can improve their operations while the latter is initiated to uncover suspected problems [3]. This fundamental difference is reflected in the role and attitude of the assessors during the process assessment.

Traditionally organisations would engage consulting firms to perform the process assessment and make recommendations on the ITSM areas requiring improvement. However, qualified and experienced ITSM consultants are expensive and scarce. In addition, their outcomes are often dictated by the proprietary methodology and toolset employed by the consulting firm. An alternative to relying on consultants is for organisations to carry out the process assessment themselves using specialised software tools that may be integrated within a knowledge-based repository of ITSM best practices. This approach, known as *software-mediated process assessment* (SMPA), involves the appointment of an internal team of assessors to undertake the assessment on a regular and systematic basis, aided by software tools and with minimal or no outside assistance. During the assessment the software tools facilitate planning, collecting, validating and classifying the improvement evidence for subsequent analysis. To automate the assessment further, advanced features can be built into the software tools to perform the analysis and suggest recommendations.

To lend objectivity and consistency to SMPA the methodology that underpins the design of the supporting software tools is aligned with the international *ISO/IEC 15504 standard for process assessment* [15]. The multi-part standard originated from the software engineering discipline but in recent years it has been broadened to address other non-software domains, such as banking, automotive and aerospace, in large as well as small enterprises [16-18]. In fact, ISO/IEC 15504 has been shown to be particularly valuable in facilitating the improvement of non-software processes as these processes tend to be more "repetitive and stable" than those pertaining to software production [19]. An assessment, as described in ISO/IEC 15504, compares the actual performance of a process in an organisation against a model of process capability termed a *Process Assessment Model* (PAM). A PAM has two dimensions: process performance, and process capability. The capability dimension is derived from a measurement framework that serves to characterize the capability of key processes in the chosen domain [20]. A PAM provides a detailed model based on one or more Process Reference Models (PRMs) for the purpose of assessing process capability [18]. Part 8 of the ISO/IEC 15504 standard has recently been published and provides an exemplar PAM for ITSM. Various research initiatives are currently underway to link ISO/IEC 15504 to the ITSM domain through the development of appropriate process models based on ITIL and ISO/IEC 20000 (e.g. [21];[22]). An ISO/IEC 15504-compliant methodology, Tudor's ITSM Process Assessment (TIPA), has been developed by the Public Research Centre Henri Tudor [23]. ISO/IEC 20000 requirements can be translated into a PRM for ISO/IEC 15504 compliant assessment [21]. Since then a PRM has been published in the ISO/IEC 20000 standard [24]. Such a PRM is a requirement for a conformant assessment using a PAM based on ISO/IEC 15504 [25]. ISO/IEC 15504-2 also defines a measurement framework for the assessment of process capability that is applicable to Control Objectives for Information and Related Technology (COBIT). The latest COBIT version 5 integrates other major frameworks such as ITIL and ISO/IEC 15504. For many years, COBIT has been used by organisations worldwide to assess and improve their IT processes but a consistent and reliable assessment approach was lacking until the COBIT Assessment Programme was introduced in 2011 [26]. The COBIT Assessment Programme includes a PAM aligned with ISO/IEC 15504-2 and recognizes that process assessment based on the new PAM is a crucial driver for process improvement in the area of governance and management of enterprise IT [27].

3   Research Questions and Significance

SMPA, although not new in software engineering where the notion of process assessment is heavily emphasized, is an innovation that has not been previously studied in ITSM. Not unexpectedly, the increasing popularity of ITIL and ISO/IEC 20000 is accompanied by a proliferation of software tools to support processes such as incident management and configuration management. These software tools are intended to expedite the various tasks of managing IT services; however, little is available to assist continuous service improvement. Indeed ITIL specifies that "technology will need to be in place for monitoring and reporting" so that CSI can occur [11]. The first research question (RQ1) for this project therefore explores: *to what extent is SMPA a valid and beneficial approach in facilitating CSI activities in ITSM?* In view of the centrality of RQ1 to the research it will be iteratively reviewed as the study unfolds.

Past research has shown that innovative IT initiatives that alter existing practices in organisations, such as the introduction of new management frameworks (e.g. ITIL) and methods and tools (e.g. object-oriented methods and CASE tools) are inherently problematic in implementation and may not yield the expected results. In such initiatives, organisations are presented with a range of challenges that are not only related to the technology or methodology in question but are organisational and managerial in nature [28]. Similar concerns are apparent for SMPA. The second research question (RQ2) asks: *what factors impact on SMPA implementation?* Similar to RQ1, this research question will be revisited at appropriate points during the study.

One of the strengths of the ISO/IEC 15504 standard is that it provides a structured approach for an organisation to understand the current state of its own processes and to undertake steps to improve the capability of these processes. The standard is grounded on the principles of self-assessment, process improvement and capability determination, and is applicable to all types and sizes of organisations [15]. ISO/IEC 15504 is also tool-agnostic i.e. its requirements are independent of the use of any tool. Barafort et al. [2, 21, 29] used ISO/IEC 15504 enabling assessors to produce repeatable and objective ITSM process appraisals but this work was undertaken without the support of a SMPA tool. Their research indicates that ISO/IEC 20000 requirements can be translated into the PRM required to drive process assessment in ITSM. The third research question (RQ3) seeks to answer: *To what extent does the PAM in ISO/IEC 15504-8 and the PRM in ISO/IEC 20000-4 jointly provide a coherent and consistent basis for the development of a SMPA tool for CSI in ITSM?*

The final research question (RQ4) follows on from RQ3: *does the use of a SMPA tool lead to effective CSI decisions?* The outcomes from SMPA activities are to a large extent dependent on the methodology that is embedded in the supporting tool. If the SMPA tool is designed around a proprietary methodology it tends to behave as a black box as the logic and rationale behind the analysis and recommendations may not be disclosed to the assessors. In this case the assessors are not able to ascertain the validity of the recommendations to the specific business environment nor can they compare their assessments with that of their peer organisations which may have used a tool from another vendor. Hence, the apparent advantage offered by the ISO/IEC 15504 standard is that it provides desired transparency and objectivity in the appraisal.

The scope of the research, as reflected in the research questions, is depicted in Figure 1. The research aims to investigate a specific under-studied ITSM problem and test the validity of the solution in an industry setting. Hence, the research holds significance for both academia and practice.

Although there has been a phenomenal adoption of ITIL it has not been accompanied by standardisation of ITSM process assessment. To improve IT service management, it is necessary to measure capability and formulate recommendations to overcome identified weaknesses. The ISO/IEC 15504 standard provides one such set of requirements.

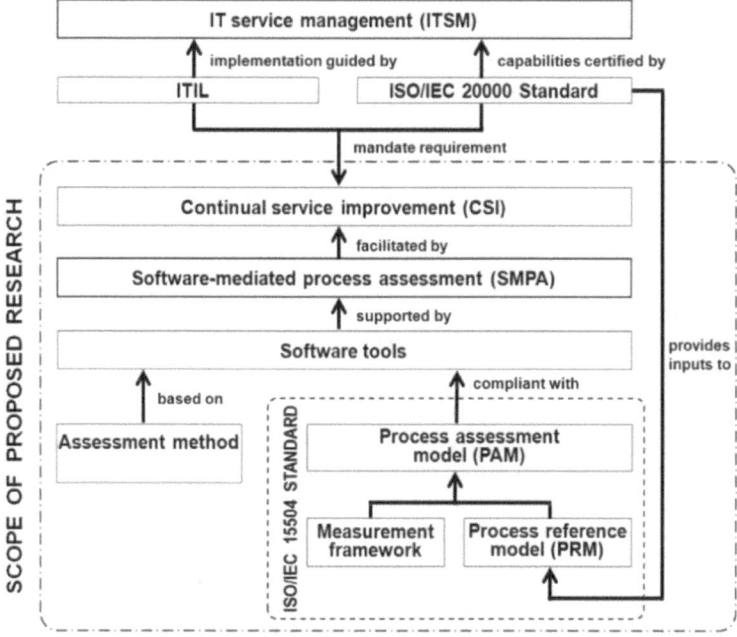

Fig. 1. Scope of Research

Academic researchers make valuable contributions to the design and investigation of innovative software tools but effective transition of these tools to industrial use requires their integration into, and evaluation within, the industrial and business context. In some cases the innovation required is not so much the design of a new tool but its adaptation to the pattern of use within the organization. The research will provide an opportunity to enhance Australia's reputation internationally since the project team will undertake research that is of international significance and innovation. The models and system developed will form a base for subsequent research, implementation and evaluation that will contribute to such efforts as the International Standards for ITSM and process assessment.

From an investment point of view, ITSM represents a serious commitment by Australian organisations with some spending more than half a million dollars on implementing new IT service delivery frameworks and improving existing ITSM processes [30]. Instead of just defining processes, ongoing evaluation and improvement of processes is considered vital to the continuing ability of the organisation to meet the needs of its customers.

Software tools play a vital role in helping organisations achieve productivity and in assuring the quality and integrity of their products and processes. Productivity is enhanced by tools that automate processes or minimise the cognitive and physical effort required of those undertaking a task. Integrity is enhanced by tools that apply procedures without fear or favour, in this case in assessment of ITSM processes. Repeatedly engaging consultants to perform process assessment is expensive and lacks objectivity and consistency [31].

The Australian Government has adopted the recommendations of the Gershon report [32], which requires all agencies to assess their current ICT infrastructure capability, identify a target capability level, and develop a capability improvement plan. The report urges the implementation of a common methodology for assessing agency ICT capability based on self-assessment and periodic independent audit. Gershon reported that ITIL was widely used in government agencies and endorsed by private-sector firms. The SMPA tool developed in this project will be valuable to government agencies to provide a common methodology for self-assessment. Private-sector organisations will similarly benefit from the use of the tool.

4   Approach and Methodology

The research team comprises academics from two universities, who, collectively, have expertise in ITIL, ISO/IEC 20000 and ISO/IEC 15504. The project will also deliver research training, an ARC objective, though the involvement of a doctoral student. The team will work closely with experienced ITSM practitioners at the partner organisations: Assessment Portal, the Queensland Government ICT division (CITEC) and the Toowoomba Regional Council (TRC).

Assessment Portal, which is providing the platform for the development of the prototype SMPA tool, is an Australian company that specialises in delivering commoditised consultancy through its automated assessment portal. In 2007 the portal won the *Innovation of the Year* award from the itSMF Australia. *CITEC* is the primary technology service provider for the Queensland Government delivering both whole-of-government and agency-specific ICT services. The Queensland Government Chief Technology Office (QGCTO) is also established within CITEC. *TRC* is one of the largest local government authorities in the state of Queensland servicing a regional population over 160,000 with approximately 1,700 council employees. Both CITEC and TRC are well recognised by the ITSM industry for their ITIL expertise and were recruited to participate in the pilot testing of the prototype tool.

The *Design Science Research* (DSR) methodology is used in the project to address the four research questions. DSR has been referred to as "improvement research" as it aims to produce and apply knowledge of tasks or situations in order to create effective artifacts to improve practice [33]. The creation of such research artifacts and their evaluation is central to DSR. This research will draw on the DSR framework and methodological guidelines for information systems research suggested by Hevner et al. [34] in their often cited MISQ paper. Their DSR framework, which combines both behavioural and design science paradigms, comprises three interlinked research cycles: relevance, rigour and the central design cycle [35], as illustrated in Figure 2.

The *relevance cycle* inputs requirements (continuous service improvement) from the service management and process assessment standards and the three partner organisations into the research and introduces the research artifacts (prototype SMPA tool and changed CSI processes) into the field testing. The *design cycle* supports the loop of research activity that provides the construction, refinement and evaluation of

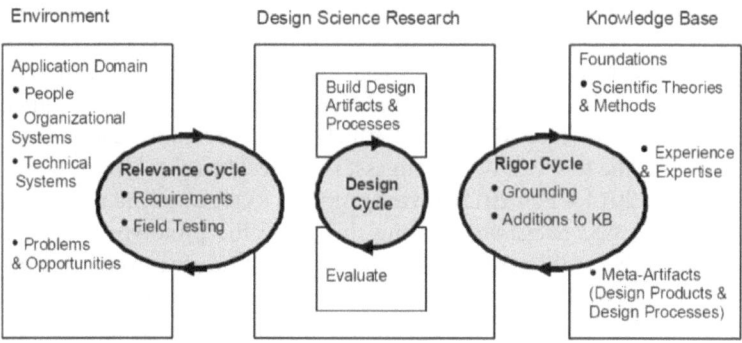

Fig. 2. Design Science Research Cycle [35]

the research artifacts. The *rigour cycle* develops the methods (benchmarking and assessment methods) along with domain experience and expertise from the "knowledge base" (ITSM practitioners' experience, ISO/IEC 20000 and ISO/IEC 15504) for the research. During the study, recent DSR insights from the work of Vaishnavi & Kuechler [33], Peffers et al. [36], Gregor & Jones [37] and others will also be referred to for additional guidance.

5   Research Strategies and Timeline

The project is broken down into four stages.

Stage 1 Feb 2012 – Oct 2012: Initiate investigation of RQ1: *To what extent is SMPA a valid and beneficial approach in facilitating CSI activities in ITSM?* and RQ2: *What factors impact on SMPA implementation?* During this stage an extensive review was conducted by the research team to ascertain the current state of CSI practices in ITSM as well as the latest developments in the ISO/IEC 20000 and ISO/IEC 15504 standards. In addition, the team interviewed IT staff at CITEC and TRC to gain an initial understanding of their CSI activities (*relevance cycle of DSR*). Initial planning for the evaluation method and criteria was undertaken (*rigour cycle of DSR*). RQ1 and RQ2 will be iteratively considered during the project.

Stage 2 Nov 2012 – May 2013: Investigation of RQ3: *To what extent does the PAM in ISO/IEC 15504-8 and the PRM in ISO/IEC 20000-4 jointly provide a coherent and consistent basis for the development of a SMPA tool for CSI in ITSM?* Stage 2 involves the development of a prototype SMPA tool using the platform provided by Assessment Portal (*design cycle of DSR*). Based on the findings from Stage 1 the research team determines the ISO/IEC 15504 and ISO/IEC 20000 requirements for the tool. The team also gathers inputs from CITEC and TRC for the specifications of the tool and ascertains how it will be deployed in their CSI activities. A suitably scoped prototype tool will then be constructed to answer RQ3.

Stage 3 June 2013 – Feb 2013: Preparation for investigation of RQ4: *Does the use of a SMPA tool lead to effective CSI decisions?* During this stage the prototype tool will be embedded in CITEC's and TRC's CSI activities (*relevance cycle of DSR*). The tool will be used to baseline CITEC's and TRC's current ITSM process capabilities and produce improvement recommendations (*baseline step*). At three-monthly intervals CITEC and TRC will decide which of the recommendations to action. At each checkpoint the tool will be used to assess the results (*checkpoint step*).

Stage 4 Mar 2014 – Feb 2015: Investigation of RQ4: *Does the use of a SMPA tool lead to effective CSI decisions?* During this stage the prototype tool embedded in CITEC's and TRC's CSI activities will be evaluated (*design cycle of DSR*). A panel of ISO/IEC 15504 assessors will perform a manual assessment to enable the comparison of the final outcomes against the recommendations and capability levels reported by the tool (*benchmark step*). The overall results will be analysed to answer RQ4.

6   Progress To-Date and Challenges Ahead

A Multi-Institutional legal agreement with the partner organisations has been formalized and the doctoral student recruited. A detailed project plan has been developed in close consultation with the partner organisations and the project governance structure activated. A model has been developed and operationalised in a decision support tool to select ITSM processes for assessment to determine the scope of the research project [38]. The research is currently in stage 2 with the focus on artifact development. ISO/IEC 15504 part 8 document is being researched to develop the assessment questions.

The research team is aware of the challenges ahead. In the first place, the project is technically complex as it is founded on two international standards that are continually evolving. Fortunately, a member of our research team currently plays a key role in the ISO/IEC 15504 standard working group. The working group is currently developing the next release of the standard converting it to a set of documents rather than a single, multi-part standard, and the results of this work will be provided to the research team promptly, enabling rapid response to proposed changes to the standard that are likely to affect the project outcomes. The team will also have to contend with issues that are typically encountered in multi-party projects. They include the tendency of various stakeholders to assert influence over the project scope and directions to extract the most benefit for themselves, and potential conflicts arising from their organisational cultural differences.

Project governance is also complex and challenging on account of the five parties involved. Communication among and co-ordination of project members creates an overhead. Risks such as potential changes in staffing need to be mitigated and have already surfaced. Despite these challenges the research team is confident that the outcomes will enable organisations to self-assess and improve their current IT service processes as well as transitioning international standards to industry.

Acknowledgements: This work is supported by an Australian Research Council Linkage Project in partnership with our industry partner Assessment Portal for the development of the SMPA tool. We are especially grateful to Mr. Paul Collins (Assessment Portal) for his support and expert guidance.

References

1. Clacy, B., Jennings, B.: Service Management: Driving the Future of IT. Computer 40(5), 98–100 (2007)
2. Barafort, B., Di Renzo, B., Merlan, O.: Benefits Resulting from the Combined Use of ISO/IEC 15504 with the Information Technology Infrastructure Library (ITIL). In: Oivo, M., Komi-Sirviö, S. (eds.) PROFES 2002. LNCS, vol. 2559, pp. 314–325. Springer, Heidelberg (2002)
3. Galup, S., Dattero, R., Quan, J., Conger, S.: An Overview of IT Service Management. Communications of the ACM 52(5), 124–127 (2009)
4. Hochstein, A., Zarnekow, R., Brenner, W.: ITIL as common practice reference model for IT service management: formal assessment and implications for practice. In: IEEE International Conference on e-Technology, e-Commerce and e-Service, Hong Kong (2005)
5. Hochstein, A., Tamm, G., Brenner, W.: Service-Oriented IT Management: Benefit, Cost and Success Factors. In: Bartmann, D., et al. (eds.) 15th European Conference on Information Systems, Regensburg, Germany (2005)
6. Potgieter, B.C., Botha, J.H., Lew, C.: Evidence that use of the ITIL framework is effective. In: 18th Annual Conference of the National Advisory Committee on Computing Qualifications, Tauranga, NZ (2005)
7. Cater-Steel, A.P., McBride, N.: IT Service Management Improvement – an Actor Network Perspective. In: European Conference on Information Systems, St. Gallen, Switzerland (2007)
8. Tan, W., Cater-Steel, A.P., Toleman, M.: Implementing IT service management: a case study focussing on critical success factors. Journal of Computer Information Systems (JCIS) 50(2), 1–12 (2009)
9. Cater-Steel, A.P., Toleman, M., Tan, W.: Transforming IT service management - the ITIL impact. In: 17th Australasian Conference on Information Systems, Adelaide (2006)
10. ISO/IEC, ISO/IEC 20000:2011 Information technology - Service management - Part 1: Specification (2011)
11. OGC, ITIL Continual Service Improvement. TSO for the Office of Government Commerce, London (2011)
12. Macredie, R.D., Mijinyawa, K.: A theory-grounded framework of Open Source Software adoption in SMEs. European Journal of Information Systems 20 (2011)
13. Harkness, W.L., Kettinger, W.J., Segars, A.H.: Sustaining Process Improvement and Innovation in the Information Services Function: Lessons Learned at the Bose Corporation. MIS Quarterly 20(3), 349–368 (1996)
14. Keating, E., Oliva, R., Repenning, N., Rockart, S., Sterman, J.: Overcoming the Improvement Paradox. European Management Journal 17(2), 120–134 (1999)
15. ISO/IEC, ISO/IEC 15504.1:2005 Information technology - Process assessment - Concepts and vocabulary, ISO/IEC JTC 1/SC 7/WG10 (2005)
16. Di Renzo, B., Barafort, B., Lejeune, V., Prime, S., Simon, J.M.: ITIL based service management measurement and ISO/IEC 15504 process assessment: A win-win opportunity. In: SPICE 2005 Conference, Klagenfurt, Austria (2005)
17. Rout, T.P.: ISO/IEC 15504 - Evolution to an international standard. Software Process: Improvement and Practice 8(1), 27–40 (2003)

18. van Loon, H.: Process Assessment and ISO/IEC 15504: A Reference Book, 2nd edn. Springer, New York (2007)
19. Coletta, A.: An Industrial Eperience in Asessing the Capability of Non-software Processes Using ISO/IEC 15504. Software Process: Improvement and Practice 12(4), 315–319 (2007)
20. ISO/IEC, ISO/IEC 15504.2:2004 Information technology - Process assessment - Performing an assessment, ISO/IEC JTC 1/SC 7/WG10 (2004)
21. Barafort, B., Jezek, D., Mäkinen, T., Stolfa, S., Varkoi, T., Vondrak, I.: Modeling and Assessment in IT Service Process Improvement. In: O'Connor, R.V., Baddoo, N., Smolander, K., Messnarz, R. (eds.) EuroSPI 2008. CCIS, vol. 16, pp. 117–128. Springer, Heidelberg (2008)
22. Nehfort, A.: SPICE Assessments for IT Service Management according to ISO/IEC 20000-1. In: International SPICE 2007 Conference, Frankfurt, Germany (2007)
23. Hilbert, R., Renault, A.: Assessing IT Service Management Processes with AIDA – Experience Feedback. In: Proceedings of the 14th European Conference for Software Process Improvement (EuroSpi), Potsdam, Germany (2007)
24. ISO/IEC, ISO/IEC TR 20000-4:2010 Information technology - Service management - Part 4: Process reference model (2010)
25. Mesquida, A., Mas, A., Amengual, E., Calvo-Manzano, J.: IT service management process improvement based on ISO/IEC 15504: A systematic review. Information and Software Technology 54(3), 239–247 (2012)
26. ISACA (2011), http://www.isaca.org/About-ISACA/Press-room/News-Releases/2011/Pages/ISACA-Issues-COBIT-Process-Assessment-Model.aspx (cited January 15, 2013)
27. ISACA (2013), http://www.isaca.org/Knowledge-Center/Research/ResearchDeliverables/Pages/COBIT-Assessment-Program.aspx (cited January 15, 2013)
28. Lai, V.S., Mahapatra, R.: Exploring the Research in Information Technology Implementation. Information and Management 32, 187–201 (1997)
29. Barafort, B., Humbert, J., Poggi, S.: Information security management and ISO/IEC 15504: the link opportunity between security and quality (2005)
30. Deare, S.: Quality IT service comes at a price. In: ZDNet Australia (2006)
31. Fayad, M.E., Laitinen, M.: Process Assessment Considered Wasteful. Communications of the ACM 40(11), 125–128 (1997)
32. Gershon, P.: Review of the Australian Government's use of Information and Communication Technology, Commonwealth of Australia (2008)
33. Vaishnavi, V., Kuechler, W.: Design Science Research Methods and Patterns: Innovating Information and Communication Technology. Auerbach Publications (2008)
34. Hevner, A.R., March, S.T., Park, J., Ram, S.: Design Science in Information SYstems Research. MIS Quarterly 28(1), 75–106 (2004)
35. Hevner, A.R.: Design Research: Rigorous and Relevant. In: ECIS, St. Gallen (2007)
36. Peffers, K., Tuunanen, T., Rothenberger, M., Chatterjee, S.: A design science research methodology for information systems research. Journal of Management Information Systems 24(3), 45–77 (2008)
37. Gregor, S., Jones, D.: The anatomy of a design theory. Journal of the Association for Information Systems 8(5), 312–335 (2007)
38. Shrestha, A., Cater-Steel, A.P., Tan, W.-G., Toleman, M.: A model to select processes for IT service management improvement. In: 23rd Australasian Conference on Information Systems 2012, Geelong, Australia (2012)

Balancing Agility and Discipline
in a Medical Device Software Organisation

Martin McHugh[1], Fergal McCaffery[1], Brian Fitzgerald[2], Klaas-Jan Stol[2],
Valentine Casey[1], and Garret Coady[3]

[1] Regulated Software Research Group, Department of Computing and Mathematics,
Dundalk Institute of Technology & Lero, Ireland
{martin.mchugh,fergal.mccaffery,val.casey}@dkit.ie
[2] Lero – The Irish Software Engineering Research Centre University of Limerick Ireland
{brian.fitzgerald,klaas.janstol}@lero.ie
[3] BlueBridge Technologies, Citywest, Dublin, Ireland
garretcoady@BlueBridgetech.com

Abstract. Agile development techniques are becoming increasingly popular in
the generic software development industry as they appear to offer solutions to
the problems associated with following a plan-driven Software Development
Life Cycle (SDLC). However, agile methods may not be suited to all industries
or organisations. For agile methods to succeed, an organisation must be
structured in a way to accommodate agile methods. Medical device software
development organisations are bound by regulatory constraints and as a result
face challenges when they try to completely follow an agile methodology, but
can reap significant benefits by combining both agile and plan-driven SDLC
such as the Waterfall or V-Model. This paper presents an analysis of a medical
device software development organisation based in Ireland, which is
considering moving to agile software development techniques. This includes
the performing of a Home-Ground Analysis to determine how agile or
disciplined[1] the organisation currently is. Upon completion of the Home-
Ground Analysis recommendations were made to the organisation as to how
they could tailor their existing structure to better accommodate agile
development techniques. These recommendations include adopting agile
practices such as self-organising teams to promote a culture of "chaos" within
the organisation.

Keywords: Agile, Medical, V-Model, Home-Ground Analysis.

1 Introduction

Software developed for medical devices must be developed in accordance with not
only a customer's requirements, but also with any regulatory requirements of the
region where the device is being marketed. Such regulations place constraints on the

---

[1] We use the term "disciplined" to reflect common usage [e.g.24], but this is not to imply that
the agile development approach is undisciplined.

T. Woronowicz et al. (Eds.): SPICE 2013, CCIS 349, pp. 199–210, 2013.
© Springer-Verlag Berlin Heidelberg 2013

methods used by software development organisations when developing regulatory compliant software. These regulations dictate the necessary deliverables which must be produced when developing medical device software as the safety of medical device software is determined through the software processes followed during the development [1]. Such required deliverables support the *traceability* of the process.

Software development organisations producing software for use in non-regulated environments are reaping various benefits of utilising agile software development methods [2]. Adopting agile methods can reduce costs, improve time to market and increase quality [3]. Despite these potential benefits, there is still a low adoption rate amongst medical device software organisations [4]. A survey of medical device software organisations highlighted that regulatory controls appear to act as the single biggest barrier to adopting agile practices when developing medical device software [5]. Due to regulatory requirements it can be challenging to apply agile methods such as Scrum and XP [6]. However, in-fact no barriers exist that prevent employing individual agile practices when developing regulatory compliant software [7] .

This paper examines a medical device software development organisation is preparing to employ agile methods. However, before employing these agile techniques a Home-Ground Analysis [8] was performed to determine their current organisational structure. The Home-Ground Analysis examines five critical success factors for adopting agile methods with an organisation. The remainder of this paper is structured as follows: Section 2 presents research into medical device software development to place this work in context; Section 3 discusses the significance of balancing agility and discipline; Section 4 outlines the analysis performed within a medical device software organisation; Section 5 presents the conclusions and outlines future work for this research.

2   Medical Device Software Development

Medical device software development organisations have two types of customers: end users and regulatory bodies. The regulatory requirements can appear to be restrictive and prevent the adoption of agile methods. However, closer examination of the regulatory requirements and development standards reveal there are no direct barriers to utilising state of the art development techniques such as agile. In fact, the regulations and standards do not mandate the use of a specific software development lifecycle. The Food and Drug Administration (FDA) General Principles of Software Validation (GPSV) [9] states: *"this guidance does not recommend any specific life cycle model or any specific technique or method"*

The FDA General Controls [10] also states: *"Although the waterfall model is a useful tool for introducing design controls, its usefulness in practice is limited [...] for more complex devices, a concurrent engineering model is more representative of the design processes in use in the industry"*

Concurrent engineering can be defined as *"simultaneous design of a product and all its related processes in a manufacturing system"* [11]. It should be noted, that in concurrent engineering, concurrency refers to designing with a view to multiple phases and to simultaneous development of components (not to *phase* concurrency).

To accompany these documents IEC 62304:2006 Medical Device Software – Software Lifecycle Processes [12], which is an internationally recognised standard for the development of medical device software, states:*"it is easiest to describe the processes in this standard in a sequence, implying a "waterfall" or "once through" life cycle model. However, other life cycles can also be used."*

These statements demonstrate that regulations and standards do not prescribe the use of a specific software development lifecycle. Rather, existing regulations require that the Software Development Life Cycle (SDLC) produces the necessary deliverables related to achieving regulatory compliance, which facilitates the development of safe software.

2.1   The V-Model for Medical Device Software Development

Medical device software is typically developed in accordance with the V-Model [13]. The V-Model is a variation on a sequential model described by Royce which later became known as the Waterfall Model [14] and it identifies that there are different types of testing such as modular testing and integration testing [15]. The V-Model shows the relationship between the two sides of the development process as shown in Figure 1. This relationship is used to determine whether each stage has been completed successfully. If a problem occurs during the verification or validation of any one stage, then the opposite stage on the "V" must be revisited and if necessary reiterated [16]. Essentially, the testing of a product (right-hand side of the V) is planned in parallel with the corresponding phase of development (left-hand side of the V).

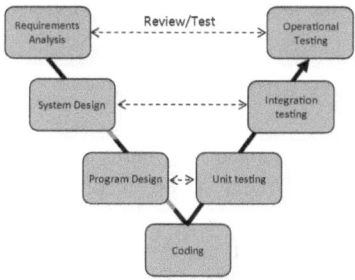

Fig. 1. V-Model

The FDA mandates that traceability be an integral part of a development process [17]. While the V-Mode may appear to be a good fit, in practice the V-Model presents the same problems that are associated with utilizing any sequential plan-driven SDLC. For example, as requirements are fixed at an early stage, it can be very challenging to introduce a change in requirements once the project is underway. Also, it can be very difficult to capture all of the requirements at an early stage of a project [18]. Furthermore, any changes introduced once a project is underway can create cost and budget overruns as it requires revisiting earlier stages of the V-Model [19].

As a result of the problems associated with following the V-Model, medical device organisations are looking at the non-regulated software development industry to determine whether lessons learned there can be applied to developing medical device software. As a result, medical device software organisations are examining the possibility of employing agile techniques.

2.2   Using Agile Practices to Develop Medical Device Software

As part of our on-going research, a mapping study was performed covering the period between 2002 and 2012 to identify reports of the use of agile methods in medical device software development. This mapping study revealed that there is a relatively low amount of publicly available information detailing the experiences of employing agile practices within medical device software development organisations. However, whilst the information is relatively scarce, a common trend is emerging in the instances where agile has been successfully adopted. In each case the organisations began by attempting to completely adopt an agile method such as Scrum or XP, however they discovered this was not possible and as a resulted tailored their existing plan driven lifecycle to incorporate agile practices [20-22].

Each of the organisations, including, Cochlear [20], Abbott [21] and Medtronic [22] reported significant benefits as a result of incorporating agile practices into their existing SDLC. In October 2012 the Association for the Advancement for Medical Instrumentation (AAMI) produced a guidance document known as AAMI:TIR 45:2012 [23] which maps agile practices to each of the stages of IEC 62304. This document as well as the reported successes from industry strongly suggests that agile practices can be successfully adopted to develop regulatory compliant software.

3   Balancing Agility and Discipline

Some software development organisations seem to be better suited to following agile methods, whereas others seem better suited for plan-driven methods. By determining an organisation's existing structure it can be determined which approach is more suited to the organisation. Table 1 shows circumstances where following agile or plan-driven methods, is most suited. It can be seen from the table that an organisation can be agile in one way but plan-driven in another.

In Table 1 each of the sections are self-explanatory except for the concept of levels in the Developers section of Personnel. Cockburn categorised personnel based upon a system of levels. He explained the concepts of "Levels" of skill and understanding required for performing various agile or disciplined functions. Cockburn presented three levels, which were drawn from the three levels of understanding in Aikido (Shu-Ha-Ri) [25]. Shu-Ha-Ri describes the three phases from learning to mastery. Firstly, *becoming proficient* at a task; secondly, when you become proficient at that task you must *make innovations* and finally the actions you perform become natural and no longer are performed following a defined method, i.e., you *become creative* [26].

Table 1. Agile and Disciplined Methods Home Ground (Boehm and Turner [24])

Characteristics	Agile	Disciplined / Plan Driven
Application		
Primary Goals	Rapid value; responding to change	Predictability, stability, high assurance
Size	Smaller teams and projects	Larger teams and projects
Environment	Turbulent; high change; project-focused	Stable; low-change; project/organization focused
Management		
Customer Relations	Dedicated on-site customers; focused on prioritized increments	As-needed customer interactions; focused on contract provisions
Planning & Control	Internalized plans; qualitative control	Documented plans, quantitative control
Communications	Tacit interpersonal knowledge	Explicit documented knowledge
Technical		
Requirements	Prioritized informal stories and test cases; undergoing unforeseeable change	Formalized project, capability, interface, quality, foreseeable evolution requirements
Development	Simple design; short increment; refactoring assumed inexpensive	Extensive design; longer increments; refactoring assumed expensive
Test	Executable test cases define requirements, testing	Documented test plans and procedures
Personnel		
Customers	Dedicated, collocated CRACK* performers	CRACK* performers, not always collocated
Developers	At least 30% full-time Cockburn level 2 and 3 experts; no Level 1B or -1 personnel**	50% Cockburn Level 2 and 3s early; 10% throughout; 30% Level 1B's workable; no Level -1s**
Culture	Comfort and empowerment via many degrees of freedom (thriving on "chaos")	Comfort and empowerment via framework of policies and procedures (thriving on order)

* Collaborative, Representative, Authorized, Committed, Knowledgeable
** These numbers will particularly vary with the complexity of the application

Boehm and Turner [8] further sub-divided Level 1 into three sub-levels, namely, Level -1, Level 1B and Level 1A, to address some of the distinctions between disciplined and agile methods. Table 2 shows the different levels and the criteria applied to each level.

Table 2. Personnel Levels (Cockburn and Boehm & Turner)

Level	Criteria
Level -1	Unable or Unwilling to collaborate or follow shared methods
Level 1B	Hard Working, less experienced, needs structure
Level 1A	Hard Working, less experienced but feels comfortable working in a structured way
Level 2	Functions well in managing small teams in precedent projects
Level 3	Functions well in managing large and small scale teams in unprecedented projects

3.1   Home-Ground Analysis

When examining an organisation's existing structure Boehm and Turner presented five critical decision factors which can be used to determine the relative suitability of agile or disciplined methods in a particular project situation. These five critical success factors are: Size, Criticality, Dynamism, Personnel and Culture.

These five critical decision factors are plotted onto a Polar Graph (or "Radar Chart") (see Figure 2), "Size" and "Criticality" are similar to the factors used by Cockburn [25]. The "Culture" axis is used to plot how much of the organisation thrives on "chaos" and how much thrives on order. "chaos" refers to how empowered and comfortable staff within the organisation feel. If the majority of the organisation thrives on "chaos" then this suggests staff are more suited (and open to) using agile methods. If, on the other hand, they thrive on order then this suggests disciplined methods are more suitable. For the "Dynamism" axis, agile methods can succeed with either a high or low number of changes; however, disciplined methods are more suited for development contexts with relatively few changes. The "Personnel" axis is used to plot the numbers and "Levels" of personnel within the organisation. Disciplined methods can succeed with both high and low skill levels; however, agile methods require a richer mix of higher-level skills [27]. Once an organisation is assessed on each axis, the polar graph can be populated, which provides insights into whether the organisation is more suitable for agile methods or for disciplined methods.

It is of course possible, if not very likely, that a company is close to the centre in some areas but close to the periphery in others. In such cases, the organisation would benefit from taking elements from both agile and disciplined methods, thereby using a tailored SDLC Also, if a company would rather be more disciplined or agile in a particular section the polar chart can be used to graphically represent the existing structure and recommendations can be made as to how changes can be implemented to achieve the desired structure.

By performing a Home-Ground Analysis a more accurate representation of the organisation can be achieved. An organisation may present itself as rigidly disciplined; however, a Home-Ground Analysis may reveal that it is, in fact, rather agile in specific areas. The Home-Ground Analysis displays an organisation's existing structure which can be used to determine which of the five critical success factors within the organisation need to be modified if the organisation wished to become more agile or disciplined. With regards to the development of medical device software, research has revealed that a combination of both agile and disciplined/plan-driven methods has proven successful [20, 21, 28].

4   Case Study: Agile in Medical Device Software Development

BlueBridge Technologies is a Product and Innovation Service Provider servicing primarily the Life Sciences and Medical Device Industries. One of their core services is regulated software. BlueBridge Technologies has a track record in developing embedded systems across a number of sectors including Automotive, Medical Device and Clean Tech. BlueBridge's roots are based in the development of software for use in the automotive industry. As a result they have vast experience with regulatory constraints and also the safety critical nature of the software which they are developing.

BlueBridge Technologies wishes to develop their software in accordance with state of the art development principles in order to improve time to market, increase efficiency and improve quality for their clients. After performing market research, BlueBridge Technologies concluded that the latest state of the art development techniques involved utilising agile practices in concert/combination with the V-model. However, some of the development team had limited experience in utilising agile techniques. As a consequence, BlueBridge Technologies became involved in the work of the authors in order to implement agile practices successfully as appropriate when developing medical device software. Based upon the findings of the mapping study performed as part of on-going research by the authors, BlueBridge Technologies decided to integrate agile practices with their existing plan driven software development lifecycle. BlueBridge Technologies currently develop software in accordance with the V-Model.

4.1   Home-Ground Analysis

As previously mentioned, the Home-Ground Analysis can provide a clear graphical representation of how agile or disciplined an organisation currently is. As part of the work with BlueBridge Technologies it was decided to perform a Home-Ground

Analysis to determine in which areas they are currently disciplined and in which areas they are agile. Once the analysis was complete, specific recommendations were made as to how BlueBridge Technologies can become more agile in areas which are currently disciplined. To perform the Home-Ground Analysis, a series of questions were asked of key stakeholders within the organisation. These questions are shown in table 3 and the results were analysed and a plotted onto the polar chart shown in figure 2.

Table 3. Questions asked as part of Home-Ground Analysis

#	Question	Possible Answers
1.	How many people are employed within your organisation?	0-100
2.	How many of your employees work as part of the development team?	0-100
3.	As a percentage, how much of your development work in a month is spent on accommodating requirements changes?	0% - 100%
4.	Considering each member of your development team, in which of the following categories would you put them?	a. Unable or Unwilling to collaborate or follow shared methods b. Hard Working, less experienced and needs structure c. Hard Working, less experienced but feels comfortable working in a structured way d. Functions well in managing small teams in precedent projects e. Functions well in managing large and small scale teams in unprecedented projects
5.	Should a defect emerge in the software you are developing which of the following could possible occur?	a. Minor – Comfort Only b. Minor loss of funds c. Major loss of funds d. Loss of a single life e. Loss of many lives
6.	What percentage of you organisation is dependent on discipline?	0% - 100%

4.2   Results

Figure 2 shows the results of the Home-Ground Analysis performed on BlueBridge Technologies. It can be seen from the figure that three of the five areas of critical success are located close to the centre (i.e., suitable for agile methods). These areas are the size, criticality of the software being developed and personnel. Agile software development techniques are ideally suited to organisations with small number of personnel or adopting small teams. Performing agile practices such as daily stand up meetings and sprint planning meetings can be difficult to perform with a large number of personnel. To accompany this, while research has shown that agile methods can be used to develop all types of medical device software they are again more suited to the development of software which is less critical [29].

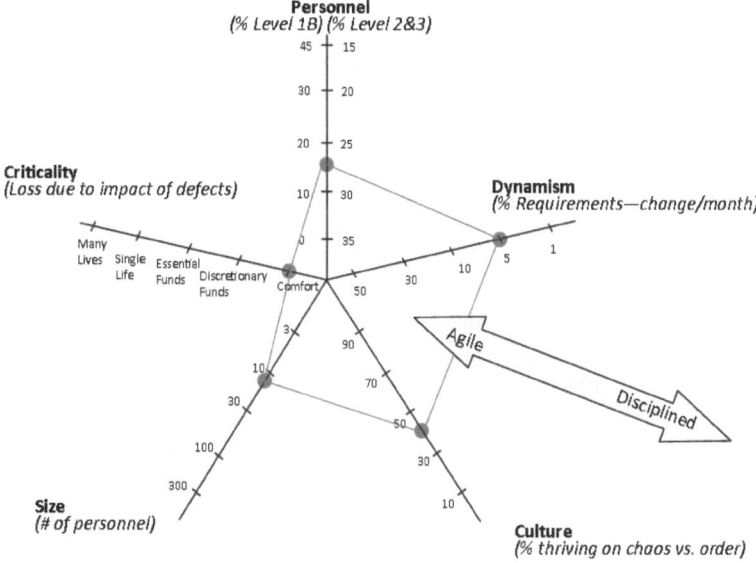

Fig. 2. Home-Ground Analysis of BlueBridge Technologies

The result of the analysis shows that the organisation's culture is better suited to disciplined methods as it is located closer to the periphery. Dynamism is located close to the periphery which suggests that agile or disciplined methods can be used.. Agile methods can succeed with either a high or low number of requirements changes per month; however, disciplined methods can have difficulty accommodating changes. This amount of dynamism would work well in either an agile or disciplined methods.

4.3   Discussion

The results of our study show that the organisation is primarily suited to adopting agile methods. An organisation does not have to be suited to agile techniques in each of the five critical success areas. However, as BlueBridge Technologies wishes to utilise agile practices, two key areas of particular importance in agile development are personnel and culture. In BlueBridge Technologies, culture is currently more suited to disciplined development methods. There is a percentage of the organisation which thrives in "chaos"; however, to be ideally suited to adopting agile methods BlueBridge needs to be located closer to the centre of the polar chart. To improve the level of "chaos", the organisation is advised to increase the level of empowerment of the personnel within the organisation through the use of the agile practice of self-organising teams, by performing planning games and daily stand up meetings. Many of the agile methodologies, such as DSDM and XP, advocate team empowerment.

5 Conclusions and Future Work

Traditionally, medical device software organisations follow a disciplined plan-driven development approach as these approaches produce the necessary deliverables required when seeking regulatory approval. However, there are problems associated with following plan-driven methods such as being inflexible to change. Agile development methods appear to solve the problems associated with following disciplined plan-driven methods. Agile and plan-driven methods are not mutually exclusive. Research has revealed that medical device software organisations can benefit from incorporating agile practices into their plan driven approach. This paper presents research that discusses the use of the Home-Ground Analysis which is used to determine how agile or disciplined an organisation is. Once the level of agility or discipline within an organisation is established, if that organisation wishes to become either more agile or more plan driven, they can clearly see which of the five key critical success areas need to be changed in order to achieve the desired goal.

A medical device software organisation (BlueBridge Technologies), wishes to reap the benefits associated with utilising agile practices. Recommendations have been made as to how they can modify their existing structure to become more suitable for adopting agile development techniques. However, prior to making these recommendations an understanding of how disciplined or agile the organisation currently is, was required. To achieve this, a Home-Ground Analysis was performed. The Home-Ground Analysis revealed that whilst the size of the organisation, the Cockburn Levels of personnel levels and the criticality of the software being developed are suited to employing agile methods, the culture within the organisation is more suited to a disciplined approached. The dynamism of the company would be appropriate for both agile and discipline methods. The Home-Ground Analysis revealed that of the five critical success factors, the organisation is currently suited to agile methods in three of the critical success factors and suited to disciplined methods in one of the critical success factors with the remaining critical success factor currently being suited to either agile or disciplined methods. This current organisational structure could support adopting agile methods.

BlueBridge Technologies is an innovative organisation and there is a percentage of the organisation suited to working in a "chaos" environment; however, for agile methods to be successful BlueBridge Technologies ideally needs to be located closer to the centre of the polar chart. This empowerment can be achieved by employing techniques such Planning Game, Team Reflections, Co-Located Teams, Daily Stand-Up Meetings and Self Organising teams.

The Home-Ground Analysis performed on BlueBridge Technologies is being used to determine which areas within their organisation need to be modified in order to accommodate agile practices. Once the necessary recommendations i.e. empowering employees, have been implemented a tailored set of agile practices suited to the development of medical device software will be presented to BlueBridge Technologies. By modifying the existing structure to accommodate these agile practices, they will have a greater chance of succeeding and achieving the desired results.

Acknowledgements. This research is supported by the Science Foundation Ireland (SFI) Stokes Lectureship Programme, grant number 07/SK/I1299, the SFI Principal Investigator Programme, grant number 08/IN.1/I2030 (the funding of this project was awarded by Science Foundation Ireland under a co-funding initiative by the Irish Government and European Regional Development Fund), and supported in part by Lero - the Irish Software Engineering Research Centre (*http://www.lero.ie*) grant 10/CE/I1855.

References

1. Jones, P.L., Jorgens, J., Taylor Jr., A.R., Weber, M.: Risk Management in the Design of Medical Device Software Systems. Biomedical Instrumentation & Technology 36, 237–266 (2002)
2. Conboy, K., Fitzgerald, B.: Method and developer characteristics for effective agile method tailoring: A study of XP expert opinion. ACM Trans. Softw. Eng. Methodol. 20, 1–30 (2010)
3. Laanti, M., Salo, O., Abrahamsson, P.: Agile methods rapidly replacing traditional methods at Nokia: A survey of opinions on agile transformation. Information and Software Technology 53, 276–290 (2011)
4. Cawley, O., Wang, X., Richardson, I.: Lean/Agile Software Development Methodologies in Regulated Environments – State of the Art. In: Abrahamsson, P., Oza, N. (eds.) LESS 2010. LNBIP, vol. 65, pp. 31–36. Springer, Heidelberg (2010)
5. McHugh, M., McCaffery, F., Casey, V.: Barriers to Adopting Agile Practices When Developing Medical Device Software. In: Mas, A., Mesquida, A., Rout, T., O'Connor, R.V., Dorling, A. (eds.) SPICE 2012. CCIS, vol. 290, pp. 141–147. Springer, Heidelberg (2012)
6. Vogel, D.: Agile Methods: Most are not ready for prime time in medical device software design and development, DesignFax Online (2006)
7. McHugh, M., McCaffery, F., Casey, V.: Barriers to using Agile Software Development Practices within the Medical Device Industry. In: European Systems and Software Process Improvement and Innovation Conference, EuroSPI, Vienna Austria (2012)
8. Boehm, B., Turner, R.: Balancing Agility and Discipline: A Guide for the Perplexed. Addison-Wesley (2003)
9. FDA, General Principles of Software Validation: Final Guidance for Industry and FDA Staff. Centre for Devices and Radiological Health (2002)
10. FDA, General Controls for Medical Devices. Food and Drug Administration (2009)
11. Jo, H.H., Parsaei, H.R., Sullivan, W.G.: Principles of Concurrent Engineering. In: Parsaei, H.R. (ed.) Concurrent Engineering: Contemporary Issues and Modern Design Tools. Springer, Germany (1993)

12. AAMI, ANSI/AAMI/IEC 62304, Medical device Software - Software life cycle processes. Association for the Advancement of Medical Instrumentation (2006)
13. McCaffery, F., McFall, D., Donnelly, P., Wilkie, F.G.: Risk Management Process Improvement for the medical device industry. Presented at the Conference on Software Development, SWDC-REK 2005, Iceland (2005)
14. Royce, W.: Managing the Development of Large Software Systems. Presented at the Proceedings of IEEE WESCON (1970)
15. Rook, P.E.: Controlling software projects. IEEE Software Engineering Journal 1, 7 (1986)
16. Pfleeger, S.L., Atlee, J.M.: Software Engineering: Theory and Practice. Pearson Higher Education, New Jersey (2001)
17. Casey, V., McCaffery, F.: Med-Trace: Traceability Assessment Method for Medical Device Software Development. Presented at the European Systems & Software Process Improvement and Innovation Conference (EuroSPI), Roskilde, Denmark (2011)
18. Cadle, J., Yeates, D.: Project Management for Information Systems. Pearson Education (2008)
19. Munassar, N.M.A., Govardhan, A.: A Comparison Between Five Models of Software Engineering. IJCSI International Journal of Computer Science Issues 7, 94–101 (2010)
20. Rottier, P.A., Rodrigues, V.: Agile Development in a Medical Device Company. Presented at the Proceedings of the 11th AGILE Conference, AGILE 2008, Girona, Spain (2008)
21. Rasmussen, R., Hughes, T., Jenks, J.R., Skach, J.: Adopting Agile in an FDA Regulated Environment. Presented at the Agile Conference, AGILE 2009, Chicago, IL (2009)
22. Weyrauch, K.: What Are We Arguing About? A Framework for Defining Agile in our Organization. Presented at the Proceedings of the Conference on AGILE 2006 (2006)
23. AAMI, AAMI TIR45:2012 – Guidance on the use of agile practices in the development of medical device software (2012)
24. Boehm, B., Turner, R.: Rebalancing Your Organization's Agility and Discipline. In: Maurer, F., Wells, D. (eds.) XP/Agile Universe 2003. LNCS, vol. 2753, pp. 1–8. Springer, Heidelberg (2003)
25. Cockburn, A.: Agile Software Development. Addison-Wesley, Boston (2002)
26. Klens-Bigman, D.: Layers of Shu-Ha-Ri in the Practice of Iaido
27. Highsmith, J.: Agile software development ecosystems. Addison-Wesley Longman Publishing Co., Inc., Boston (2002)
28. Mehrfard, H., Hamou-Lhadj, A.: The Impact of Regulatory Compliance on Agile Software Processes with a Focus on the FDA Guidelines for Medical Device Software. International Journal of Information System Modeling and Design 2, 67–81 (2011)
29. Turk, D., France, R.: Assumptions Underlying Agile Software Development Processes. Journal of Database Management 16, 62–87 (2004)

Investigation of Traceability
within a Medical Device Organization

Gilbert Regan, Fergal McCaffery, Kevin McDaid, and Derek Flood

Dundalk Institute of Technology, Dundalk, Ireland
{gilbert.regan,fergal.mccaffery,kevin.mcdaid,
derek.flood}@dkit.ie

Abstract. Requirements traceability helps to ensure software quality. It supports quality assurance activities such as impact analysis, regression test selection, compliance verification and validation of requirements. Its implementation has long been promoted by the research and expert practitioner communities. However, evidence indicates that few software organizations choose to implement traceability processes, in the most part due to cost and complexity issues. Organizations operating within the safety critical domains are mandated to implement traceability, and find the implementation and maintenance of an efficient and compliant traceability process a difficult and complex issue. Through interviews with a medical device SME, this paper seeks to determine how traceability is implemented within the organization, the difficulties it faces in implementing traceability, how compliant it is with the medical device standards and guidelines, and what changes could be made to improve the efficiency of their traceability implementation and maintenance.

Keywords: traceability, requirements traceability, software traceability, medical device, software process improvement.

1 Introduction

The importance and role of traceability in supporting software development have been long recognised [1]. Requirements tracing helps ensure that the customers' requirements are being met and that the quality of the final product is maximised while minimising costly rework due to errors in the requirements. Traceability through the software development and risk management process is particularly important in safety critical industries such as the medical device domain, where it is incumbent on manufacturers to produce safe software [2]. The effect of poor quality medical device software can be seen from the recent announcement by Johnson & Johnson that some of its Animas insulin pumps will become defunct at the stroke of midnight on December 31, 2015. The company has warned European regulators that the pumps will stop delivering insulin at the start of 2016 and will generate a "call service alarm" due to a software fault. During November 2012 the company began to warn patients of the impending malfunction, offering to replace devices that have warranties that will still be in effect when the software glitch is expected to hit [3].

T. Woronowicz et al. (Eds.): SPICE 2013, CCIS 349, pp. 211–222, 2013.
© Springer-Verlag Berlin Heidelberg 2013

Organizations building safety critical systems are often legally required to demonstrate that all parts of the code trace back to valid requirements. Laws such as the US Sarbanes-Oxley Act 2002 [4] require organizations to implement change management processes with explicit traceability coverage for any parts of a software product that potentially impact the balance sheet [5].

Regulations and guidelines exist to assist medical device organisations to produce quality software. The documents which medical device manufacturers must adhere to are IEC 62304 [6] (which is endorsed by the European Union and the U.S.), FDA Guidance for the Content of Pre-market Submission for Software in Medical Devices [7], FDA General Principles of Software Validation(GPSV) [8], FDA Off-the Shelf Software Use in Medical Devices [9] and ISO 14971 [10]. These documents emphasise to different degrees the requirement for traceability through the software development lifecycle (SDLC), risk management and change management processes. Understanding the different degrees of requirements for traceability and implementing those requirements is a difficult and complex task for a medical device small to medium enterprise (SME). A lack of detailed guidance and direction on how to implement and maintain traceability could lead to many medical device SMEs implementing inefficient and/or non-compliant traceability processes [11].

The objective of this paper is to analyse the requirements for traceability as detailed in the medical device standards and guidelines documents and to highlight the varying requirements for traceability between these documents. The authors conducted detailed interviews with a medical device SME in order to determine what processes are being used to implement traceability, difficulties faced in implementing traceability, how compliant the organisation is, and what changes could be made to improve the efficiency of traceability implementation and maintenance.

This paper has been divided into 7 sections. Related work in Section 2 explains the concept of traceability and reveals why its implementation is important. Section 3 details the requirements for traceability as prescribed by the medical device standards and guidelines. Section 4 list the aims of the study and the approach used to achieve those aims and also details the organisation profile.   Section 5 summarises the implementation of traceability within the organisation and highlights difficulties faced by the organisation in implementing traceability. Section 6 discusses the difficulties that the organisation face in implementing traceability and ways in which it might overcome these difficulties and become more efficient.

2   Related Work

In engineering terms a trace is comprised of a source artifact, a target artifact and the link between them [12]. Traceability is the ability to establish and use these traces. Numerous definitions for traceability exist in the literature but one of the most popular and encompassing is: *"Requirements traceability refers to the ability to describe and follow the life of a requirement, in both a forwards and backwards direction (i.e., from its origins through its development and specification to its subsequent deployment and use, and through all periods of on-going refinement and iteration in any of these phases "*[13].

In general, traceability is about understanding a design right through from the origin of the requirement to its implementation, test and maintenance. Traceability allows us to understand many important aspects of a project such as; are the customers' requirements being met, the specific requirements that an artefact relates to, the origins and motivation of a requirement, and what are the requirements associated with this test case. Traceability supports critical activities such as compliance   verification,   impact   analysis,   and   regression   test   case selection[14].Traceability helps ensure that 'quality' software is developed.

Traceability is about linking requirements to artefacts in the software development environment. This environment includes technical aspects (e.g. specifications, diagrams and code) and social aspects (e.g. people, policies, decisions etc.). Traceability was initially used to trace requirements from their source to implementation and test, but now plays an increasing role in defect management, change management and project management. Traceability links represent an important source of information for project managers, analysts, designers, maintainers, and end users. Increasingly software development is globally distributed across multiple teams and sites which makes traceability even more important [11]. As traceability provides an essential support for developing high quality software systems [15] it is vital to engage an efficient traceability process.

Unfortunately, establishing and maintaining traceability links between software artefacts is a time consuming, error prone, and labour intensive task. Consequently, despite the advantages that can be gained, explicit traceability is rarely established unless there is a regulatory reason for doing so [16]. In safety critical domains such as the medical device domain traceability information can also be used when certifying a safety-critical product to show that all requirements were implemented and covered by specific tests.

3   Traceability Requirements for Compliance within Medical Device Standards

The requirements for traceability through the SDLC are not transparent from the medical device regulations; in fact the regulations make little or no reference to traceability. However the medical device standards and guidelines mandate traceability throughout the SDLC and within supporting processes such as change management and risk management.

Figure 1 indicates the requirements for traceability through the SDLC, Risk and Change management processes. The letters A to E refer to the medical device standards and guidelines and are listed in Table 1. The obvious point of note is the variance in the requirements between the standards with only the FDA's General Principles of Software Validation document requiring traceability to the module and function level. While each of the standards require full traceability through the risk management process, only IEC 62304 requires traceability within the change management process.

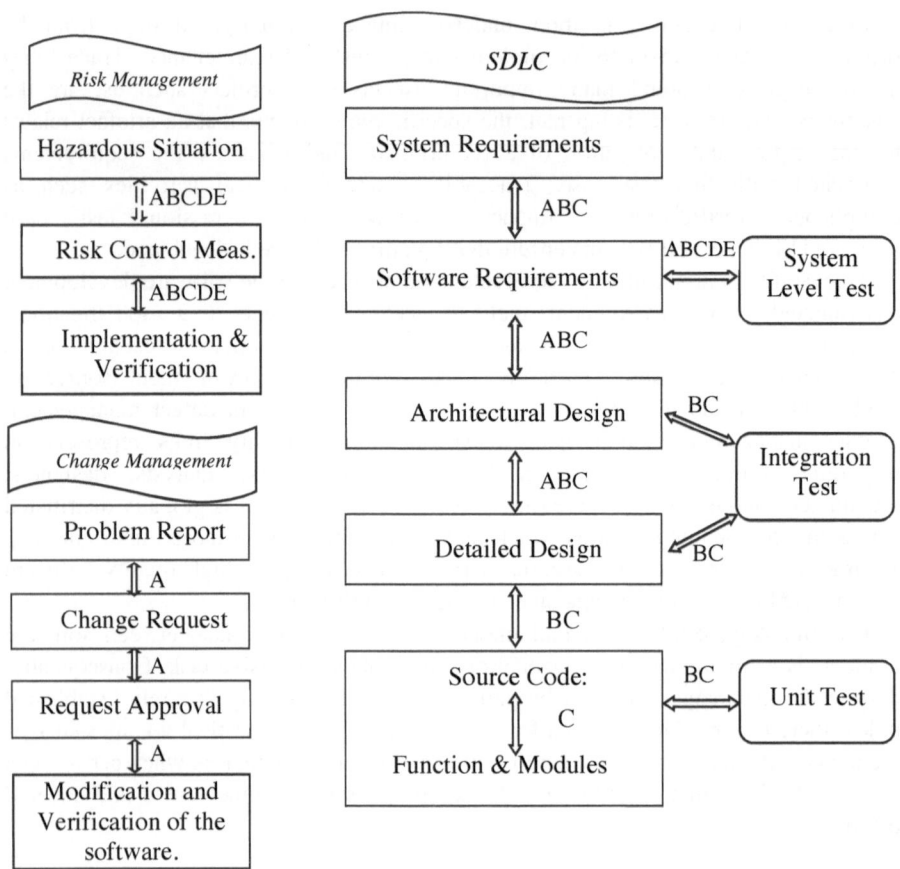

Fig. 1. Medical device standards requirements for traceability through the software development lifecycle, Risk management process and Change management process

Table 1. Standards and Guidelines which inform traceability requirements of medical device domain

A	IEC 62304: 2006 Medical Device Software Lifecycle Processes
B	FDA 2005: Guidance for the Content of Pre-market Submission for Software in Medical Devices
C	FDA 2002: General Principles of Software Validation
D	FDA 1999: Off-The-Shelf Software Use in Medical Devices
E	ISO 14971 2007: Application of Risk Management in Medical Devices

4   Methodology

4.1   Aims and Method

The aim of our case study was to answer the following questions:

1.   What is the traceability practice within a medical device SME?
2.   Is this practice compliant with medical device standards and guidelines?
3.   Is the process used to implement and maintain traceability efficient and compliant?
4.   How could this process be improved?

To be able to answer these questions a qualitative study was conducted in which 2 people from the organization were interviewed. These 2 people were chosen as the organization thought they were the most knowledgeable people in the organization with regards to traceability implementation and maintenance. The job titles of the two people involved were Chief Technical Officer and Software Development Manager. Each interview comprised 60 questions and lasted between 2 hours and, 2 hours and 30 minutes; the interviews were recorded and later transcribed and summarized. The questions were developed in such a way as to determine the following:

1.   Between what stages of the software development lifecycle did the organisation trace e.g. Do you trace from software requirements to design?
2.   How do they implement traceability e.g. How do you trace from software requirement to design?
3.   What are the stages of the risk management process and how do they provide traceability between each stage e.g. How do you ensure that each hazard has a corresponding risk control measure, if required?
4.   What are the stages of the change management process and how do provide traceability between each stage e.g. IEC 62304 requires the manufacturer to create an audit trail where each change specification, problem report or change request, and each approval of the change request can be traced. Can you explain how you meet this requirement?
5.   Difficulties the organisation encountered in implementing and maintaining traceability e.g. What difficulties do you have with implementing or maintaining traceability?
6.   Any ideas for improvements the organisation had with regard to implementation and maintenance of traceability e.g. how do you think your present traceability process could be improved?
7.   Any process improvement initiatives the organization were currently or were planning to undertake e.g. What process improvements are you working on or plan to work on?

4.2   Organization Profile

The organization, whose headquarters are based in the UK, has a research and development and manufacturing facility based in Ireland. This study was carried out in the Ireland facility. The organization employs 60 to 70 people and sometimes employs contractors on a part time basis so the numbers can fluctuate. The products are marketed globally into the primary care market, secondary care, occupational health, sports medicine and clinical trials. Their products are rated as software safety classification II, meaning non-serious injury to the patient or operator of the device is possible due to a defect in the device. The organization uses the V model for their software development. (The V model, like the waterfall model is a sequential path for the execution of software development process. The process contains a number of phases. Each phase must be completed before the next phase begins. Testing of the product is planned in parallel with a corresponding phase of development. The V model is popular with medical device software development organizations). The organization's main software development process covers class II (non-serious injury is possible e.g. x-ray systems, gas analyzers, pump) & class III (Class III medical devices have the most stringent regulatory controls). They have a separate process for any class I medical device (have the least amount of regulatory control and present minimal potential harm to the user e.g. tongue depressors, arm slings) they produce.

5   Findings

This section presents the major findings from the interviews held with the organization, beginning with the strategy the organization uses to implement traceability through the SDLC, risk management and change management processes. Additionally the difficulties the organization faces in implementing traceability and any improvements proposed by the organization are unfolded. The findings are limited to one organization and a point that is often raised in case study research is that findings are not generalizable to other settings. However, the purpose of this study was revelatory and exploratory rather than explanatory.

5.1   Traceability Strategy

The organization have a traceability standard operating procedure which basically is a document detailing how to fill in their traceability matrix (template for matrix is provided which provides consistency). The traceability matrix is 'user requirement' driven i.e. user requirements are listed in the first column then all software requirements that satisfy that user requirement are listed in the second column. Subsequent columns list architectural design, detailed design, risk analysis and test cases). Their quality management procedures say who should complete the matrix, when and how often. In a recent project the Chief Technical Officer (CTO) updated the user requirement column in the traceability matrix, the development team updated the software requirement, architectural and detailed design columns and Quality Assurance (QA) updated test. The software development manager is ultimately responsible for ensuring the matrix gets done as and when it should get done and CTO is responsible for approving it at the end.

Bi-directional traceability is implemented through a mixture of in-document tracing and by tracing through the traceability matrix. Bi-directional traceability exists from user requirements to software requirements (through the traceability matrix and through the documents, e.g. the software requirement spec will indicate the corresponding user requirement related to each software requirement). Bi-directional traceability *somewhat* exists between software requirements and architectural and detailed design). The organization *"does not do 'within document' tracing in the design documents. The only way to trace back from design is to search through the traceability matrix for each design component, and, as a design component might satisfy more than one user requirement, this might be a long and laborious task"*. The organization has traceability between requirements and test and between design and test, through the traceability matrix. They do not have traceability between code and test.

Traceability from each specification document to the author of that document was evident because each document has the author, reviewer and approver with their signatures and date and each document has an issue control sheet. Establishing traceability from test to test equipment and its calibration records is documented within the organization's software test plan and not in the risk analysis document.

5.2   Traceability through Risk Management

The organization has a Product Risk Management document and a Software Risk Management document. Risk analysis is documented in the risk management document. Risk analysis starts at the User requirements phase and is done at every subsequent phase. Every software requirement is reviewed for potential cause of harm and given a risk classification and may also be given a prioritization based on potential for harm and how easy it is to detect. Based on the risk classification and/or prioritization the organization decides on what mitigations to implement (e.g. change to design, product labeling, training, and user manuals). Software QA validate the mitigations after they have been implemented and then the risks get re-classified hopefully to an acceptable level. *"Each step of risk analysis, risk control implementation and validation is traceable through the risk management document"*.

The software risk analysis has different categories. Usability is an example of a category. *"You might see a number of requirements under the Usability heading but you might also see the same requirement under a number of different headings. So the organization has traceability at the risk analysis level and also the top level requirements traceability matrix"*.   If there is a change to core product (e.g. introduction of a new feature) the risk analysis document gets updated to a new issue specifying what was added and why.

5.3   Traceability through Change Management

Changes can happen for a number of reasons e.g. a bug, a customer request, the natural progression and maintenance of the software or from a complaint. If it's a bug they document the issue, the investigation and the results of the investigation, what corrective action if any is required and if the corrective action requires the software to be updated. For any change that requires a change to the software the organization use a Software Changes Specification (SCS). The SCS records any changes to the software, risk associated with the change, impact in terms of other requirements. Traceability is maintained throughout by linking each change to risk and impact. The traceability matrix gets updated during a mini software lifecycle enacted for this change. For any change QA have to do a test plan and test cases, do a test summary to show what tests didn't pass and provide the relevant traceability in a test report. On the other hand a customer may request a change for a clinical trial. The organization use a Customer Requirement Specification (CRS) for this instead of a URS and that drives SCS and a mini lifecycle where the traceability matrix gets updated. Software change requests (from marketing or from a customer for example) are logged in an Excel Spreadsheet recording who logged it, when and why it was logged, and any attachments. For the natural progression and maintenance of software the URS gets updated with new or removed features (along with the traceability matrix) and that goes through the full lifecycle again which means new test plans, new test cases etc. The software requirements, architectural and detailed design specifications also get updated. Complaints are logged in SmartSolve (a document control system) along with investigations, results, and corrective actions. SmartSolve is 21CFR Part 11 compliant so records full electronic signatures. The rationales for customer complaints and for product modifications are recorded (because they have to justify the reason for change). The rationale for requirements in general is not recorded.

5.4   Traceability Benefits

The organization recognized two benefits of traceability i.e. "*it is easy to see if all the requirements have been tested*" and "*a matrix is useful when getting audited*". The organization does not use the traceability matrix for instruments such as impact analysis, because; (i) with their experience they can tell what the impact of a requirement change will be from a review of the requirement specification and (ii) the fact that the matrix tends to contain requirement numbers which don't give any detail of what the requirement does so reference to the requirement specification is still required. Putting the required detail into the traceability matrix would make it absolutely massive.

5.5   Downside to Traceability and Their Process

As traceability is manually implemented in an Excel spreadsheet, the organization found this task to be complex and burdensome. This complexity, coupled with the fact that the organizations felt that the real benefit of having traceability is to satisfy auditors, means that traceability matrix is often not filled out until the project is at or near completion. In fact the general attitude is that the organization "*probably would not concern themselves with traceability but for the fact that they are mandated to do so*".

In a manual system you have to maintain a consistent numbering scheme for the duration of the product's life, so for example if someone releases a new issue of a requirements specification and re-numbers everything then you've lost your traceability; an electronic tool would automatically update everything and traceability wouldn't get lost.

In general, staff was trained in their organization's processes and procedures (including traceability procedures). However there was a lack of understanding of the benefits of traceability and there were no plans in place to address this. Largely the organization was compliant with the medical device standards and guidelines requirements for traceability (as detailed in Section 3) but there were areas which they were unsure about and would require some guidance e.g. the organization did not trace to code level which is an FDA requirement.

5.6   Traceability Tools

Traceability was implemented through a traceability matrix using Excel (along with some in-document tracing). The organization admits that using Excel is not very efficient and painful to update. The organization does not use a dedicated traceability tool for the following reasons:

a) **Time constraints**: It was felt that a lot of time was needed to investigate the suitability of the range of tools on the market and no-one was given the responsibility for doing this

b) **Cost**: It was thought that the cost of purchasing and implementing a traceability tool might not be something that they could justify. One tool (although it was a full application lifecycle management tool) they had considered "*was 100,000 euro and that, even if they had the money, they could not justify spending that amount*".

c) **Compliance**: issues over the tools not being able to output a full traceability matrix and also failure to meet Title 21 CFR Part 11 requirements which details the FDA's requirements for electronic records and electronic signatures to be trustworthy, reliable and essentially equivalent to paper records and handwritten signatures.

d) **Tool stability**: The organization felt that tools that might be affordable to them would likely not provide the necessary stability and support that they would require e.g. after considering another tool they didn't have confidence in it as there seemed to be only a small group of people involved in the organization and they were concerned about future support and stability issues. Another concern was that the medical device process within the tool is a third part add-on. "*It is a big decision for an organization to move their process to an electronic format, one which we would not be prepared to take unless we had an affordable, stable and fully compliant tool*".

5.7   Process Improvement

At present the organization has a process improvement initiative in place. The organization has hired a person to gather metrics for software QA (metrics to highlight what are the functional areas that are causing issues, and why are they causing issues etc.). It was something they had done in the past but had fallen away. Presently the organization feels that too much of the quality issues are being left to QA and that development needs to take more responsibility; this was highlighted recently when contractors were hired and their code was absolutely solid because they were writing unit test cases for absolutely everything they did. The organization's process states that they will do unit testing on functional areas that QA cannot test via their functional testing, just to make sure they have coverage of everything. So at present every requirement will have a test case or a unit test and code review, or maybe both if it was that critical a requirement.

The organization feel that their traceability process could be improved by use of a traceability tool, "*making it part of everyday work, ensuring traceability gets done and kept up to date*", as at the moment it seems that the traceability matrix only gets filled in towards the end of a project and is mainly used to satisfy auditors. From the organization's perspective if they were not required to do traceability then they might not do it as they find it laborious and they don't get the full benefit of it.

6   Discussion

The organization finds traceability implementation to be a laborious and complex task and feel that the use of a traceability tool to help automate the process would be of great benefit. Using an Excel spreadsheet to create a traceability matrix has several disadvantages such as static and sometimes outdated information, hours wasted in creating the document and no proactive notification capabilities. Effective traceability tools will output up-to-date information, impact analysis reports and a traceability matrix and reduce the complexity involved. It is somewhat surprising then that multiple studies have found the level of commercial traceability tool adoption to be around 50 percent throughout industry. The majority of the remaining companies utilize manual methods and a small percentage develop their own in-house traceability tools [17].

The organization sees the main benefit of traceability as being one of satisfying auditors and only implements traceability because they are mandated to do so. The organization doesn't fully understand the potential benefits of traceability and, although they have a standard operating procedure in place, its implementation is not being driven by management. An organizational policy stating the organization's policy with regard to traceability along with an education program on the benefits of traceability can help developers and management understand the importance of implementing and maintaining traceability when changes occur.

7   Conclusion

The organization uses two manual approaches to implement traceability i.e. in-document tracing and an excel traceability matrix. A traceability standard operating procedure outlines how to complete the traceability matrix. It is the software engineering manager's responsibility to ensure that the matrix gets completed and it is then signed off by the chief technical officer. From an auditors perspective the organization would seem to be reasonably compliant, as they implement traceability through the risk management and change management processes and in the most part through the SDLC, although there may be a compliance issue as the organization does not meet the FDA requirement for tracing to the level of code as detailed in Section 3. However the organization acknowledges that the implementation and maintenance of traceability is a burdensome, inefficient, complex and an inadequately executed task. It is felt that the introduction of a traceability tool would improve efficiency and diminish the burdensome nature of the task. An education program on the benefits of implementing and maintaining traceability would help both management and developers to understand the importance of traceability to producing quality software. The probable result thus being a traceability process adhered to by all relevant personnel, and not just a traceability matrix to be completed at the end of the project for inspection purposes.

Acknowledgment. This research is supported by the Science Foundation Ireland (SFI) Stokes Lectureship Programme, grant number 07/SK/I1299, the SFI Principal Investigator Programme, grant number 08/IN.1/I2030 (the funding of this project was awarded by Science Foundation Ireland under a co-funding initiative by the Irish Government and European Regional Development Fund), and supported in part by Lero - the Irish Software Engineering Research Centre grant 10/CE/I1855.

References

[1] Ramesh, B.: Factors influencing requirements traceability practice. Commun. ACM 41, 37–44 (1998)

[2] Rakitin, S.R.: Coping with Defective Software in Medical Devices. Computer, 40–45 (2006)

[3] M.D. Technology. Certain J&J insulin pumps destined to fail over software issue (January 23, 2013), http://www.massdevice.com/news/diabetes-certain -jj-insulin-pumps-destined-fail-over-software-issue

[4] S. a. H. o. R. o. t. U. S. o. A. i. Congress, Sarbanes-Oxley Act of 2002. P. L. 107–204, Washington (2002)

[5] Cleland-Huang, J., et al.: Best Practices for Automated Traceability. Computer 40, 27–35 (2007)

[6] ANSI/AAMI/IEC, 62304:2006 Medical device software—Software life cycle processes. AAMI, Arlington (2006)

[7] FDA, Guidance for the Content of Premarket Submissions for Software Contained in Medical Devices. CDRH, Rockville (2005)

[8] FDA, General Principles, of Software Validation; Final Guidance for Industry and FDA Staff. CDRH, Rockville (2002)

[9] FDA, Off-The-Shelf Software Use in Medical Devices; Guidance for Industry, FDA Reviewers and Compliance. CDRH, Rockville (1999)

[10] ISO, ISO 14971:2007 Medical devices — Application of risk management to medical devices. ISO, Switzerland (2007)

[11] McCaffery, F., et al.: Medical Device Software Traceability. In: Cleland-Huang, J., et al. (eds.) Software and Systems Traceability. Springer (2012)

[12] Gotel, O., Mader, P.: Acquiring Tool Support for Traceability. In: Cleland-Huang, J., et al. (eds.) Software and Systems Traceability. Springer (2012)

[13] Gotel, O.C.Z., Finkelstein, C.W.: An analysis of the requirements traceability problem. In: Proceedings of the First International Conference on Requirements Engineering, pp. 94–101 (1994)

[14] Cleland-Huang, J.: Requirements Traceability - When and How does it Deliver more than it Costs? In: 14th IEEE International Conference on Requirements Engineering, p. 330 (2006)

[15] Espinoza, A., Garbajosa, J.: A Proposal for Defining a Set of Basic Items for Project-Specific Traceability Methodologies. In: 32nd Annual IEEE Software Engineering Workshop, SEW 2008, Madrid, pp. 175–184 (2008)

[16] Lucia, A.D., et al.: Information Retrieval Methods for Automated Traceability Recovery. In: Cleland-Huang, J., et al. (eds.) Software and Systems Traceability, pp. 88–111. Springer (2012)

[17] Kannenberg, A., Saiedian, D.H.: Why Software Requirements Traceability Remains a Challenge. CrossTalk The Journal of Defense Software Engineering (July/August 2009)

Usage of Multiple Process Assessment Models

Stasys Peldzius and Saulius Ragaisis

Software Engineering Department, Faculty of Mathematics and
Informatics, Vilnius University, Naugarduko Str. 24, LT-03225 Vilnius
Lithuania
{Stasys.Peldzius,Saulius.Ragaisis}@mif.vu.lt

Abstract. Organizations seek to obtain benefit from different process capability frameworks - the most popular ones as ISO/IEC 15504 and CMMI and the new ones as Enterprise SPICE – but every assessment is expensive both financially and time-wise. Furthermore, new assessment is required when a new process assessment model's version is released. In order to define and/or improve their software process, organizations choose different Software Development Methodologies. It is important for the organization to know what capability/maturity of the process a chosen methodology could ensure. In order to solve these problems, Transitional Process Assessment Model (TPAM) [1] has been proposed. It should enable the transformation of assessment results according to one Process Assessment Model to other models and determines what capability/maturity according to different Process Assessment Models a chosen methodology could ensure. The requirements for TPAM and its implementation principles have been introduced in [1]. This article presents the development of TPAM and supporting tool. The ideas of Enterprise SPICE integration into TPAM are outlined also.

Keywords: CMMI, ISO/IEC 15504, Enterprise SPICE, Agile methodologies, models mapping, transitional process assessment model.

1 Introduction

Investigations in software process maturity provide a deep insight into software activities and introduce various process capability frameworks which help assess and improve both software process capability, and the maturity of organizations producing software. The research achievements are noticeable but the problems related to software projects are very real. Organizations seek to obtain benefit from different process capability frameworks that stimulate harmonization of the process assessment models (PAMs) and investigation of process improvement in multi-model environments [2, 3, 4, 5, 6, and 7]. The most popular Process Capability Frameworks worldwide are ISO/IEC 15504 and CMMI. It is desirable for organizations to have assessments according to PAMs of both these frameworks but every assessment is expensive both financially and time-wise.

In order for organizations to improve their software process, they should choose from one of the many different Software Development Methodologies, for example,

T. Woronowicz et al. (Eds.): SPICE 2013, CCIS 349, pp. 223–234, 2013.

XP, Scrum, DSDM, and RUP. There are many and various methodologies, so it is important for the organization to know how it could benefit from their chosen methodology. The choice of methodology should depend on what it can achieve for the organization. It is desirable to determine software process capability/maturity according to different PAMs. When a new version of the PAM is released the organizations needs to know their capability/maturity according the newest version preferably without making the new assessment.

We propose the Transitional Process Assessment Model (TPAM) [1], which would help organizations to tackle problems related to multiple process assessment models and the evaluation of software development methodologies. The implementation of TPAM and supporting tool is discussed in this article.

2   Background and Related Works

This chapter provides the motivation for the mapping between the process assessment models and development methodologies assessment. The research performed is presented and explained in the following chapters. A process assessment model defines the standard process that provides the basis for an organization's process assessment and improvement. It should ensure the usage of the same concepts and maintain relevance with the best software engineering practices and compatibility with internationally accepted standards.

All process assessment models summarize the best practices of software development and services worldwide. But although the source is almost the same, the resulting models are different. Therefore, organizations face the double problem of selection in that they need to choose both the process assessment model and the software development methodology that is most suitable for their business goals. The solution is made further complicated because organizations want the benefit of the advantages of different models, but they do not know what methodology can achieve these advantages. Therefore, research that establishes the relationships between process assessment models and software development methodologies is important. That is why mappings between the models and methodologies, which help to solve this problem, are developed.

Fundamental ideas of CMMI and ISO/IEC 15504 mapping have been proposed in [8]. Mappings of the CMMI-DEV V1.2 and ISO/IEC 15504-5:2005 models are presented in [9]. They show how CMMI-DEV maturity levels can be expressed by ISO/IEC 15504-5 Processes capability profiles and vice versa. Mappings show what is common in the models and how they differ. These mappings are used as the basis for TPAM development but the latest versions of models CMMI-DEV V1.3 and ISO/IEC 15504-5:2012 are employed.

Also, it is important to track the changes in different versions of the same process assessment model. An approach for the control of model evolution and compliance maintenance is proposed in [10]. The organization may want to have assessments by several models in the hope of achieving the respective benefits of each model. It is important for organizations to efficiently implement and assess multiple reference models and benefit from synergy effects [11]. It is significant for organizations to have assessments according both CMMI and ISO/IEC 15504. For example, many organizations drive their process improvement on the basis of CMMI. However, their customers require process capability ratings determined on the basis of ISO/IEC 15504. An approach that enables organizations performing internal process improvement on the basis of CMMI to survive SPICE assessments with relatively small efforts is presented in [6]. As it is important for organizations to be aware of their process capability, it has become important for methodologies to determine what capability they could ensure. There are many articles published that analyse what capability/ maturity could ensure popular Agile methodologies [12, 13, and 14]. It is important to emphasize that all these works investigate CMMI only.

3   Transitional Process Assessment Model

The Transitional Process Assessment Model (TPAM) enables the transformation of results of an assessment according to one process assessment model (PAM) to other models and also deals with the transition to a new version of the model. Also, it provides the means to determine what capability/maturity according to different PAMs software engineering methodologies could ensure. Furthermore, the methodology showing how to extend the transitional model is provided. It covers the following cases: inclusion of a new process assessment model, transition to a new version of existing process assessment model, and addition of a software development methodology.

An organization's assessment according to TPAM and/or transformation of existing assessment's results through TPAM provides the capability profiles and maturity levels according to CMMI-DEV and ISO/IEC 15504-5, as well as other process assessment models included in TPAM. The transformation results should provide enough good understanding of the situation.

All the models must be transcribed according to the defined ontology so they become structurally equal and this facilitates the mapping between them. Table 1 shows the ontology of TPAM. Further in the article, the terms listed in the table 1 are used; otherwise, it would be unclear what is meant because the same concepts are referred differently in ISO/IEC 15504 and CMMI.

Table 1. The ontology of TPAM

TPAM	ISO/IEC 15504	CMMI
Organizational Process	-	Process
Named Process	Process	Process Area
Process Purpose	Purpose Statement	Process Purpose
Outcome	Process Outcome	Specific Goal
Practice	Base Practice	Specific Practice
Generic Property	Process Attribute	Generic Goal
Generic Practice	Generic Practice	Generic Practice

TPAM requirements were defined in [1]. This paper presents how these requirements were implemented in practice. TPAM have only continuous representation. The continuous representation of the model is intended for the assessment of the capability of each Named Process. The assessment result for the organization is the Processes capability profile that consists of capability levels for each Named Process. This approach allows selecting a set of Named Processes to be improved and the order of improvements that best meets an organization's business objectives.

TPAM consists of 2 levels: Visualisation level; and Assessment level. The purpose of the Visualisation level is providing possibility visually to examine TPAM, its Named Processes and practices, as well as relationships with included PAMs (e.g. ISO/IEC 15504-5, CMMI-DEV). Software & Systems Process Engineering Meta-Model (SPEM) [15, 16] has been chosen for the definition of TPAM. Presentation of TPAM in SPEM has been discussed more detailed in [1]. It is elaborated using the EPF tool but for the viewing of TPAM it is enough to have any web browser. Excerpt of TPAM visualisation is provided in Fig. 1.

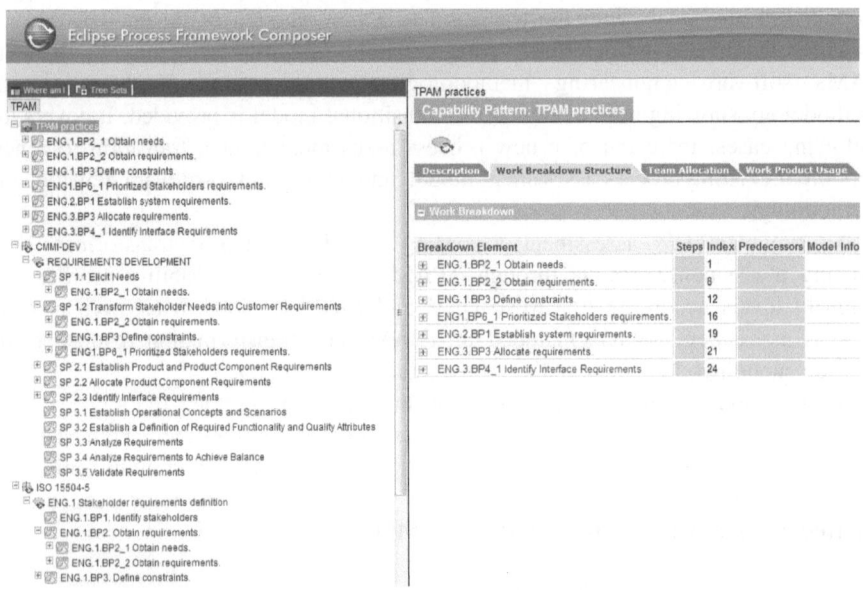

Fig. 1. Visualisation level of TPAM

However, to ensure transformation of assessment results, a more complex data structures are needed. For this purpose TPAM Assessment level has been developed. It ensures possibility to collect assessment results according TPAM or some PAM, then to choose the process assessment model and its version into which the results are to be transformed. Further sections of this chapter analyse the assessment level, present its database schema and algorithms for transformation of an assessment results.

3.1   TPAM Assessment Level

TPAM assessment level consists of three parts. The first part stores TPAM itself: Named Processes, their outcomes and practices. This part will be constantly modified, upgraded and updated when a new version of the integrated PAM is released or a new PAM is to be integrated. The second part consists of TPAM source models, i.e. process assessment models integrated into TPAM. As described in [1], TPAM practices are derived from source models. It is important to emphasize that the Full Coverage rule as shown in Fig. 2 should always be fulfilled: each TPAM practice should be covered fully by one or more practices of integrated models. Transformation of the assessment results should be performed automatically. Therefore, assessment level contains relationships between TPAM practices and corresponding practices of integrated PAMs. These relationships are supplemented by percentage of PAM practice coverage by TPAM practice.

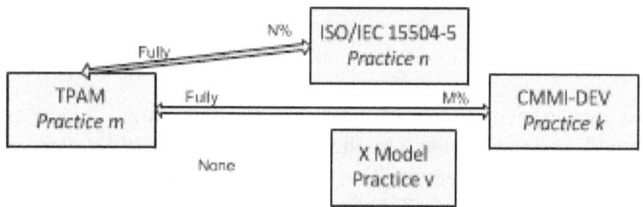

Fig. 2. Relationships between practices of the Models (Full Coverage rule)

The third part serves for the entry of assessment results. The following approaches are supported (as presented in Fig. 3):

- The assessment results according to TPAM are entered and they are transformed into CMMI-DEV, ISO/IEC 15504-5, and other integrated models and/or versions.
- The assessment results according to some integrated PAM are entered. In this case first they are transformed into TPAM assessment. Then transformation to any other integrated PAM become possible.

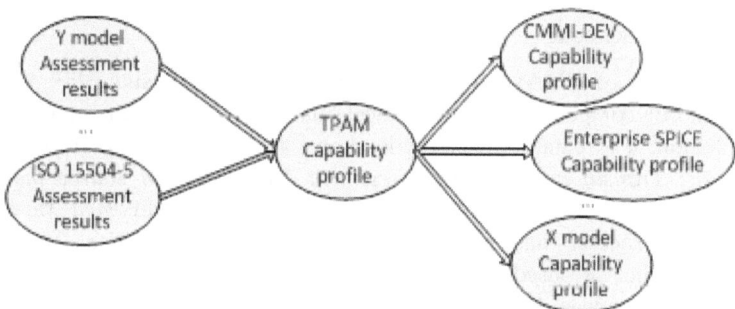

Fig. 3. Transformation of Assessment Results

For example, assessment results of an organization according to ISO/IEC 15504-5 could be transformed into capability profile according to CMMI-DEV through the intermediate transformation into TPAM.

The same approach as for an organization could be applied for the assessment of Agile or other software development methodology, i.e. assessment results according TPAM or some PAM could be entered. It could be noted that in the case of methodology additional possibilities could be useful for the companies implementing it. It is desirable to know how the practices of the chosen methodology influence the assessment results and what capability profile will be ensured after implementation of the selected practices. Therefore, relations between practices of the methodology could be established also. ISO/IEC 15504-5 has been chosen as the key starting model for TPAM. So first, TPAM has been filled by ISO/IEC 15504-5 practices. The second step was integration of CMMI-DEV into TPAM. As a result TPAM practices have been adjusted to meet the Full Coverage rule. The experience of CMMI-DEV integration is discussed in the chapter 4.

3.2   Version Control

It is of utmost importance to control newly released versions. A new model version often has Named Processes that are the same as in the older version. Therefore, TPAM assessment tool involves version tracking techniques. As a result, only new practices should be mapped into TPAM, which saves a lot of time. Changes in the versions are checked at the level of Named Processes. So, assessment results could be transformed to new version of the same model. If we have assessment results according to CMMI-DEV V.1.2 the version control allows getting capability profile according to CMMI-DEV V.1.3 in uncomplicated and not very time consuming way.

The same approach would be applied when releasing new versions of TPAM itself. After the integration of a new model into TPAM, a new version should be released because TPAM practices change: some of them can be separated and new practices appear. So, without tracking TPAM versions, old assessment results could not be transformed into new models without complete remapping of new TPAM to all previously integrated PAMs.

3.3   Database Schema

Visualisation level of TPAM has been implemented in SPEM using EPF. Assessment level is more complicated so relational database has been chosen for its implementation. The database schema is shown in Fig. 4. It is divided into three logical parts: *Transitional Process Assessment Model*, *TPAM source models* and *Assessment results*. The first part *Transitional Process Assessment Model* stores TPAM Named Processes and their practices. The table *TpamPractices* stores Generic Practices also; they are used for the assessment of capability levels higher than the first. Generic Practices have been integrated following the same approach as base/specific practices. The Generic Practice also has the links to its source and Named Process. Named Processes have been introduced into TPAM because

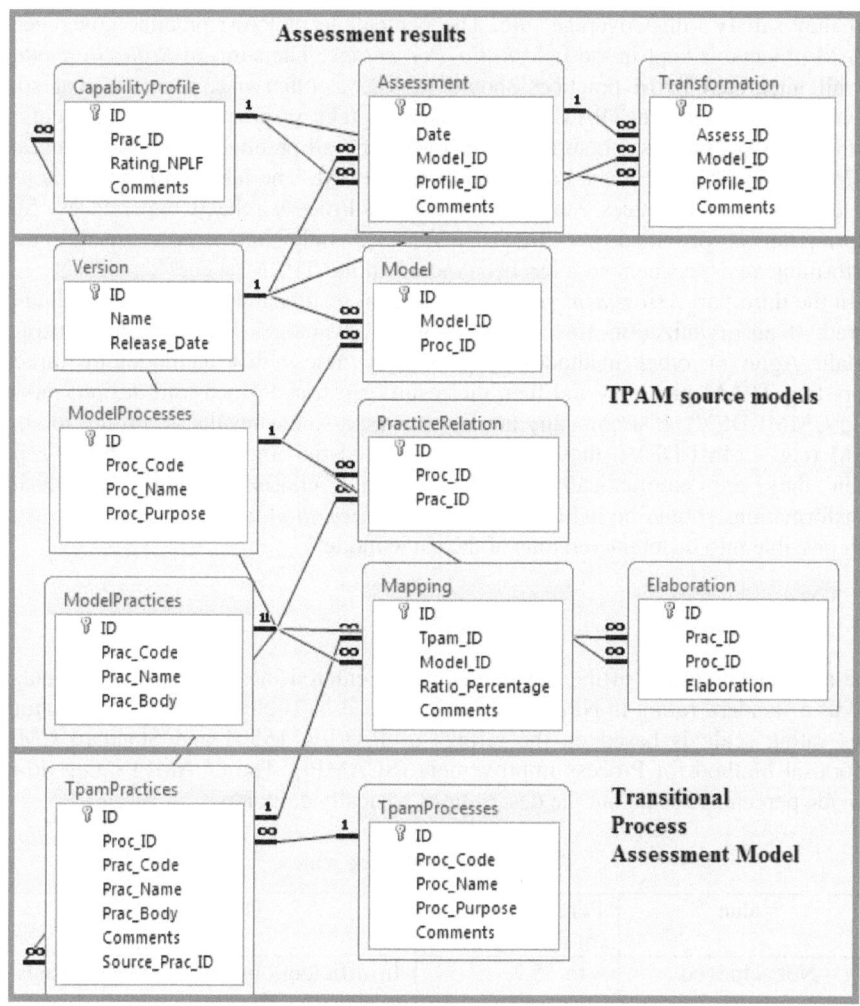

Fig. 4. TPAM assessment level database schema

ISO/IEC 15504-2:2003 states such requirement for PAMs and they allow getting TPAM capability profiles. It should be noted that for the transformation into other PAMs Named Processes are not needed. TPAM capability levels are coinciding with capability levels of ISO/IEC 15504-2:2003.

The second part *TPAM source models* is used to store both: integrated PAMs and mapping between them and TPAM. Model versions are stored in the table *Version*, and the *Model* table links the version to corresponding Named Processes. If a Named Processes is the same as in the old version, only the link to the old Named Process is indicated. The most important is the table *Mapping* keeping the links between TPAM practices and practices of integrated models. It is a one-way link – from TPAM practice to integrated model's practice – because TPAM practices are constructed so that they satisfy Full Coverage rule. The percentage of PAM practice coverage by TPAM practice is kept in the field *Ratio_Percentage*. The sums of *Ratio_Percentage* for all integrated PAM practices should be 100%; otherwise, it means that some practices are missed in TPAM or there is a mistake in percentage assignments. If certain TPAM practice is completely uncovered by all practices of certain integrated PAM, this TPAM practice is not linked to such PAM. The table *Elaboration* is used to store Generic Practices examples of Named Process related experiences. Such information is provided in CMMI-DEV V.1.3 only but is very useful when performing an assessment so it has been included into TPAM.

In the third part *Assessment results*, assessment results and transformation data are stored. If an organization aims to assess what advantages it could get by using a certain Agile or other methodology, it simply assess this methodology directly according TPAM practices and then the results are transformed into desired models (e.g. CMMI-DEV). If a company already has assessment results according to some PAM (e.g. CMMI-DEV), these results are entered into the table *CapabilityProfile*. Then they are automatically transformed into chosen models. The desired transformations should be indicated in the *Transformation* table. Transformations are also possible into different versions of the same model.

3.4   Rating Scale

The assessment results of the practice could be entered into TPAM as a percentage and as a standard rating in NPLF scale as described in Table 2 (further NPLF rating). This rating scale is based on the ratings of ISO/IEC 15504 and Standard CMMI Appraisal Method for Process Improvement (SCAMPI). The SCAMPI rating do not provide percentage scale but the descriptions basically coincide.

Table 2. Standard rating scale

Value	Percentage scale of achievement	Description
N – Not achieved	0 to 15 %	Insufficient objective evidence exists to state that the practice is implemented.
P – Partially achieved	>15 % to 50 %	Some artefacts are absent or judged to be inadequate. One or more weaknesses are noted.
L – Largely achieved	>50 % to 85 %	Sufficient artefacts are present and judged to be adequate. One or more weaknesses are noted.
F – Fully achieved	>85 % to 100 %	Sufficient artefacts are present and judged to be adequate. No weaknesses are noted.

The intermediate calculations during transformation are performed in percentage but the results of transformation are provided additionally as NPLF rating because ISO/IEC 15504 expresses requirements for capability levels in terms of NPLF rating.

For example, a Named Process gets the capability level 1 if assessments of all its practices are L or F.

More accuracy would be ensured by assessing the practices in percentage, and it is recommended to apply such approach when performing a new assessment. But it is more likely that already existing capability assessment of an organization will be in NPLF rating than in percentage.

Two types of transformations are employed in TPAM assessment tool: X model assessment results to TPAM; and TPAM assessment results to Y model. It is important to emphasize that transformation of the assessment results according to X model to TPAM are performed precisely even they are provided as NPLF rating because of Full Coverage rule. For example, the practice of CMMI-DEV RD SP 1.2 *Transform Stakeholder Needs into Customer Requirements* covered completely by 3 TPAM practices: *Obtain requirements*, *Define constraints*, and *Prioritize Stakeholders requirements*. Thus, if CMMI-DEV RD SP 1.2 practice is assessed as Largely achieved, all 3 corresponding TPAM practices get rating Largely achieved.

Unfortunately, precise transformation of the assessment results provided as NPLF rating from TPAM to Y model is not possible. Therefore, transformation algorithms have several options for interpretation of the assessment results provided as NPLF rating:

- Lowest values: N – 1%, P – 16%, L – 51%, F – 86%;
- Mean values: N – 8%, P – 33%, L – 68%, F – 93%;
- Highest values: N – 15%, P – 50%, L – 85%, F – 100%.

Because the capability profile of a company should not increase after the transformation, the lower bound is taken by default. For example, the same 3 practices of TPAM – *Obtain requirements*, *Define constraints*, and *Prioritize Stakeholders requirements* – are assessed as Largely achieved (by default the lowest value 51% is taken for calculations). Then CMMI-DEV RD SP 1.2 gets rating: $(51*50+51*40+51*10)/100=51$ → Largely achieved. Suppose one of TPAM practices *Obtain requirements* is assessed Fully achieved, then CMMI-DEV RD SP 1.2 gets rating: $(86*50+51*40+51*10)/100=68,5$→Largely achieved. It should be noted that TPAM assessment tool provides the possibilities to select other 2 options as well as to compare transformation results got using different options. So, enough thorough analysis of the capability according to the destination PAM could be carried out.

4   Integration of CMMI-DEV into TPAM

ISO/IEC 15504 is de jure international standard so ISO/IEC 15504-5 has been chosen as the key starting model for TPAM. First, TPAM has been filled by the practices of ISO/IEC 15504-5. Then CMMI-DEV practices one by one have been integrated into TPAM. This has caused adjustments of TPAM practices in the following four ways:

1. If CMMI-DEV practice is not addressed in TPAM yet it has been included into TPAM.
2. If CMMI-DEV practice is essentially the same as some TPAM practice, no changes have been made.
3. If CMMI-DEV practice is more detailed than existing TPAM practice, the corresponding TPAM practice should be adjusted even if some CMMI-DEV practices together match one practice of TPAM. Therefore, the existing TPAM practice is replaced by 2 new practices: CMMI-DEV practice and the rest part of TPAM practice. The description of new TPAM practice derived from CMMI-DEV is modified in order to correspond the terms used in TPAM (e.g. change stakeholder into customer where it means the same). So, the integrity of TPAM is preserved and the Full Coverage rule is fulfilled.
4. The last case is when the CMMI-DEV practice partially covers the existing TPAM practice and no one is a subset of another. It should be noted that this case is the most common and complicated. In this case, both practices (CMMI-DEV and TPAM) are divided. The existing TPAM practice is replaced by 2 new practices: common part of CMMI-DEV and TPAM practice, and the rest part of TPAM practice. The rest part of CMMI-DEV practice is further investigated according to all four rules.

It should be emphasized that these four rules are enough for integration of all practices of CMMI-DEV or any other process assessment model. Practices of TPAM always have a priority versus other models, because ISO/IEC 15504-5 is the primary source of these practices. When including CMMI into TPAM the following problem has occurred: one model has superficial-abstract practices and they correspond to several more detail practices in other model. In this way, a specific requirement is separated from superficial practice and the abstractness is left in the new practice. For example, TPAM practice **ENG.1.BP5: Identify critical requirements.** *Specify health, safety, security, environment and other stakeholder requirements and functions that relate to critical qualities and shall address possible adverse effects of use of the system on human health and safety.* As there is no such practice in CMMI, where specific listed requirements should be identified, this practice should be divided into two: **ENG.1.BP5_1: Identify critical requirements.** *Specify stakeholder requirements and functions that relate to critical qualities and shall address possible adverse effects of use of the system on human health and safety.* and **ENG.1.BP5_2: Identify health and safety requirements.** *Specify health, safety, security and environment stakeholder requirements and functions.* In this way, a model which does not list the requirements and demands to identify the requirements will satisfy **ENG.1.BP5_1** practice, but will not cover **ENG.1.BP5_2** practice, as it is not clear whether the assessed company really distinguishes these requirements.

It is also very important to draw attention to the terms of the model to be integrated. TPAM uses the terms of ISO/IEC 15504-5; therefore, when including the new practices or Processes, their descriptions should be adapted according to the terms of ISO/IEC 15504-5, as it is necessary to maintain the integrity of TPAM practices and Named Processes. Some examples of differences are presented in Table 3. Of course, these terms are not perfect synonyms, but in the scope of CMMI-DEV process area *Requirements development* and ISO/IEC 15504-5 process *Stakeholder requirements definition* these terms have been matched and changed into TPAM concepts.

Table 3. The relationships between TPAM and CMMI-DEV concepts

CMMI-DEV	TPAM (ISO/IEC 15504-5)
Customer requirements	Stakeholder requirements
Product Requirements	System requirements
Product component requirements	Software requirements

5   Approach for Enterprise SPICE Integration

After integration of CMMI-DEV the third model to be integrated into TPAM is Enterprise SPICE, which is currently being actively developed and becoming popular. Enterprise SPICE aims to establish an integrated model for enterprise-wide assessment and improvement for use with international standard ISO/IEC 15504 (SPICE) [17]. Enterprise SPICE is appropriate to assess the capability/maturity of the company operating any business. TPAM is appropriate only for software development capability assessment. Therefore, Enterprise SPICE will be approached from the perspective of software development only. Enterprise SPICE has a specific element Special Applications (Safety and Security) that is not presented in ISO/IEC 15504-5 and CMMI-DEV. After investigation it has been decided that Special Application will be included into TPAM as Named Process with special flag because they are structurally similar. As Special Application's practices are derived from practices of other Named Processes, TPAM structure will be slightly adjusted by adding the links between these practices. So, it can be stated that TPAM fits for the models of Enterprise SPICE type.

6   Conclusions

The proposed Transitional Process Assessment Model (TPAM) ensures the possibility to deal with multiple Process Assessment Models (PAMs) by the transformations of an assessment results to all integrated PAMs. The proposed construction principals have been testing by developing TPAM that integrates ISO/IEC 15504-5 and CMMI-DEV V1.3. Enterprise SPICE integration into TPAM has been investigated and very minor additions in TPAM assessment level have been determined. So, it could be stated that TPAM ideas could be applied to different PAMs, including ones under development (e.g. ISO/IEC 330xx series). It is obvious that this model will never replace lively assessment process of the company. However, it lets with some margin of error convert assessment results to other models cheaply and quickly. Verification of the correctness of resulting capability profiles and more precise determination of the margin is in progress. Agile software development methodology – DSDM Atern – has been assessed directly according to CMMI-DEV. Method for the assessment of Agile methodologies according to TPAM has been developed. Now DSDM Atern assessment according to TPAM is performed. Then the results of both assessments will be transformed using TPAM and compared.

References

1. Peldzius, S., Ragaisis, S.: Framework for Usage of Multiple Software Process Models. In: Mas, A., Mesquida, A., Rout, T., O'Connor, R.V., Dorling, A. (eds.) SPICE 2012. CCIS, vol. 290, pp. 210–221. Springer, Heidelberg (2012)
2. Ferreira, A., Machado, R.: Software Process Improvement in Multimodel Environments. In: Fourth International Conference on Software Engineering Advances, pp. 512–517 (2009)
3. Khoshgoftar, M., Osman, O.: Comparison of maturity models. In: 2nd IEEE International Conference on Computer Science and Information Technology, pp. 297–301 (2009)
4. Garcia, I., Pacheco, C., Coronel, N.: Learn from Practice: Defining an Alternative Model for Software Engineering Education in Mexican Universities for Reducing the Breach between Industry and Academia. In: Proceedings of the International Conference on Applied Computer Science, Malta, pp. 120–124 (2010)
5. Wu, C.-H.: An Exploration of the Relationship between Organizational Learning and Software Development Process Maturity. In: Proceedings of the 6th WSEAS International Conference on Applied Computer Science, Hangzhou, China, pp. 301–305 (2007)
6. Vanamali, B., Bella, F., Hormann, K.: From CMMI to SPICE – Experiences on How to Survive a SPICE Assessment Having Already Implemented CMMI. In: 32nd Annual IEEE International Computer Software and Applications, COMPSAC 2008, pp. 1045–1052 (2008)
7. Wang, Y., King, G., Dorling, A., Wickberg, H.: A Unified Framework for the Software Engineering Process System Standards and Models. In: Proceedings of the 4th IEEE International Symposium and Forum on Software Engineering Standards, ISESS 1999, pp. 132–141 (1999)
8. Rout, T.P., Tuffley, A., Cahill, B.: CMMI Evaluation: Capability Maturity Model Integration Mapping to ISO/IEC 15504-2:1998, Software Quality Institute, Griffith University, Brisbane, 16 p. (2001)
9. Peldzius, S., Ragaisis, S.: Investigation Correspondence between CMMI-DEV and ISO/IEC 15504. International Journal of Education and Information Technologies 5(4), 361–368 (2011)
10. Soto, M., Münch, J.: Using Model Comparison to Maintain Model-to-Standard Compliance. In: Proceedings of the 2008 International Workshop on Comparison and Versioning of Software Models, CVSM 2008, pp. 35–40 (2008)
11. Pricope, S., Lichter, H., Rosenkranz, C.G.: Efficient Adoption and Assessment of Multiple Reference Models. In: 5th IFIP TC2 Central and Eastern European Conference on Software Engineering Techniques, Debrecen, Hungary, August 25-26 (2011)
12. Cohan, S., Glazer, H.: An Agile Development Team's Quest for CMMI® Maturity Level 5. In: 2009 Agile Conference, pp. 201–206 (2009)
13. Baker, S.: Formalizing Agility, Part 2: How an Agile Organization Embraced the CMMI. In: Proceedings of the Conference on AGILE 2006, pp. 147–154 (2006)
14. Mikulenas, G., Butleris, R., Nemuraite, L.: An approach for the metamodel of the framework for a partial agile method adaptation. Information Technology and Control 40(1), 71–82 (2011)
15. Schuppenies, R., Steinhauer, S.: Software Process Engineering Metamodel. Components (2006), http://www.omg.org/technology/documents/formal/spem.htm
16. Software & Systems Process Engineering Meta-Model Specification, Version 2.0 (2008)
17. Enterprise SPICE® An Integrated Model for Enterprise-wide Assessment and Improvement. Technical Report – Issue 1, 183 p. (September 2010)

Implementing innoSPICE in Support of Political European Innovation Strategies

Tanja Woronowicz, Michael Boronowsky, and David Wewetzer

University of Bremen, TZI, Am Fallturm 1, Bremen, 28359, Germany
{worono,mb,wewetzer}@tzi.de

Abstract. This experience report is reflecting on aspects of the implementation of innoSPICE to support political European innovation and knowledge transfer strategies. The ISO/IEC15504 standard based model innoSPICE provides the base to improve the processes of organizations working in the field of innovation, knowledge- and technology transfer in a structured and standardized way. Elements from the IP Charter Initiative and from the implementation of the Baltic Sea Region Strategy are presented and the contribution of innoSPICE shown.

Keywords: Knowledge transfer, innovation, IP Charter Initiative, European Strategy for the Baltic Sea Region (EUSBSR).

1 Introduction

The work presented in this report is reflecting on the activities that are being performed to implement innoSPICE [1, 2] in support of political European innovation strategies. The European Union is facing an *increasing demand for an effective and improved knowledge interchange and transfer between private enterprises and Public Research Organizations (PRO). The professionalization of knowledge transfer is essential in order to increase the exploitation of research and to increase the return on investment in R&D* [6]. The ISO/IEC15504 standard based model innoSPICE provides the base to improve the processes of organizations working in the field of innovation, knowledge- and technology transfer. It pursues a structured and standardized approach by assessing relevant processes related to a process reference model. The model was developed and evaluated in collaboration with a consortium from universities, research centers, science parks, technology transfer associations, industrial associations and governmental organizations from the Baltic Sea Region. The innoSPICE model can be applied for innovation and knowledge transfer processes in industry as well as for universities, business development organizations and (public) research bodies. It makes a significant contribution to strengthening the competitive edge in Europe in the context of public investment. Two outstanding policy initiatives have been featured in Europe: the IP Charter Initiative [3] and the implementation of the Baltic Sea Region Strategy [4]. This paper will illustrate how innoSPICE can support these activities.

T. Woronowicz et al. (Eds.): SPICE 2013, CCIS 349, pp. 235–238, 2013.

2   Contribution to the IP Charter Initiative

On 30 May 2008 the Council of the European Union voted a resolution *on the management of intellectual property in knowledge transfer activities and on a Code of Practice for universities and other public research organizations – "IP Charter Initiative"* (reference 10323/08). To support the implementation of the Council resolution a Knowledge Transfer working group as part of the European Research Area Committee (ERAC) was founded and has produced several reports on these topics, e.g. [7]. This working group considers that: *"A certification scheme for PROs should be created with the aim of improving the collaboration between PROs and industry with respect to the knowledge transfer"* and concludes the following action: *"Develop **the framework for a certification**, **quality standards**, consider if there is a need to go beyond the content of the IP Recommendation and Code of Practice and if so what should **concrete requirements** with respect to IP strategy be"* and *"Solutions […] may include improvement of university management, economic and other incentives to influence behavior at individual as well as institutional level and initiatives for entrepreneurship training."* They are stating that such a certification can be used to advertise PROs as ***"Reliable Partner"*** for research collaboration with industry partners in Europe and beyond.

InnoSPICE was developed independently from these discussions although it is based on the same challenges (or requirements) with comparable drivers. It allows to derive a *framework for certification* and can be used within a *quality management* system as it can measure the capability of organizations for the complete innovation cycle[1]. The process reference model of innoSPICE is the codified abstract knowledge of a standard innovation cycle with respect to transfer and collaboration capabilities. It provides a standardized structure also to the *requirements* of the IP Charter initiative (e.g. people, cooperation, and exploitation/commercialization). It is putting the focus on the organizational capability following a holistic view on knowledge transfer that requires a strategic understanding of transfer on different levels of the organization. In [1] the term "knowledge supplier" was introduced in a comparable way to the concept of a *"Reliable Partner"* from the IP Charter Initiative. The matching connection of these elements mentioned above makes innoSPICE a promising instrument for the management of the implementation of the IP Charter Initiative. It thereby adds a new domain to the application of the ISO15504 standard. An important driver for the realistic take-up is the recognition of the ERAC working group that specific funding is needed (e.g.): *To further encourage the implementation of the IP Recommendation and Code of Practice in PROs, it would be useful to explore ways to use certain funding rules within Horizon 2020[2] to motivate activity (e.g. PROS with a comprehensive IP strategy that also takes into consideration the IP Recommendation and Code of Practice may receive extra funds in Horizon 2020)*[7]. As continuous process improvement should be in the interest of most research organizations, innoSPICE

---

[1] Innovation Cycle: Knowledge Generation, Facilitation of Knowledge-/Technology Transfer, Innovation and also Organizational and Supporting Processes.

[2] The new European Framework Programme Horizon 2020, running from 2014-2020.

already has an interesting market. But beyond an intrinsic motivated application of innoSPICE within public research organizations the presence of potential public sponsors for external motivation will be a valuable element to establish innoSPICE.

3   Contribution to the Baltic Sea Region Strategy (EU BSR)

The EU BSR is the first comprehensive EU strategy establishing a 'macro-region'. The eight EU countries that border and shape the Baltic Sea Region face several common challenges which are reflected in the jointly agreed Action Plan for the Strategy. It includes a number of priority areas, one of them being "Innovation". The following list provides a short presentation of selected goals formulated in different documents of the EUSBSR [4, 5] and the currently updated Action Plan and will discuss how innoSPICE can contribute to them:

- *Enhancing R&D and innovation of the BSR:* As innoSPICE provides a structured and standardized instrument for the improvement of scientific and research organizations, new knowledge and technologies will be made available more efficient and targeted to relevant partners.
- *Increased innovation capacity performance:* Becoming a leading knowledge and innovation region in the world is a shared goal for many other regions in the world. The Baltic Sea Region may consider being a forerunner for innovative management tools to realize these goals. innoSPICE is a cornerstone of a management system that allows continuous process improvement of the actors in the innovation system. By assessing the current organizational capability, an optimized alignment of internal resources and improved understanding of the complexity of successful transfer activities will be achieved and improvement can be tracked over time.
- *Innovation Support Instrument for Smart Specialization (RIS3):* innoSPICE can be used as an instrument to identify overlapping and gaps inside regional innovation systems. The detailed understanding of linkages complementarities of facilitating structures and actors is of utmost important. Such connections across individuals, organizations and disciplines are fundamental to allow efficiency to happen and especially to the direction and pace of new business formation and innovation. It will help to identify organizational strengths and weaknesses of existing regional structures, enabling a continuous improvement program for more efficient collaboration.
- *Establishing a common BSR innovation strategy and complementing each other:* To learn from best practices is always challenging, as regional and cultural context or organizational preconditions often are not covered explicitly or abstracted too much. The innoSPICE process reference model contributes to structuring the complex organizational activities in detail and allows benchmarking of different practices using a single standard for all actors in the innovation cycle.
- *Attract innovative companies and establish efficient innovation support services:* Companies ask increasingly for standardized quality assurance before establishing collaborations also with research centers and universities. SPICE is an ISO

standard that is well established in several industrial sectors and beside of this "ISO" is an accepted organization in the field of business.

4   Conclusion

Practical applications of innoSPICE in a number of assessments have shown that it can be implemented within knowledge intense organizations with very positive acceptance. It is understood as a great value to determine the own position and to kick-off organizational changes discussing them with colleagues sharing the same roles or to identify specific challenges of the interfaces between different roles within the organization. Especially organizations and policy initiatives that are contributing to economic and societal values are interested to learn how to improve the performance of their own set-up and to develop a better alignment with their partners in the innovation cycle. In this understanding innoSPICE helps companies and public bodies to build trust with new *knowledge suppliers* for common innovation activities as it demonstrates that the partners are interested to reflect on their own organizational capability to provide innovation related services. The Baltic Sea Region and the IP Charter Initiative will be an important pilot area taking the advantage to transfer this concept into the field of innovation, knowledge and technology transfer.

References

1. Besson, J., Woronowicz, T., Mitasiunas, A., Boronowsky, M.: Innovation, knowledge- and technology transfer process capability model – innoSPICE™. In: Mas, A., Mesquida, A., Rout, T., O'Connor, R.V., Dorling, A. (eds.) SPICE 2012. CCIS, vol. 290, pp. 75–84. Springer, Heidelberg (2012)
2. Boronowsky, M., Woronowicz, T., Mitasiunas, A.: BONITA – Improve Transfer from Universities for Regional Development. In: The Proceedings of the 3rd ISPIM Innovation Symposium held in Quebec City, Canada, December 12-15 (2010) ISBN 978-952-265-004
3. Council of the European Union, Council Resolution on the management of intellectual property in knowledge transfer activities and on a Code of Practice for universities and other public research organizations – IP Charter Initiative. 10323/08 (2008)
4. European Commission, Commission Staff Working Paper on the Implementation of the European Union Strategy for the Baltic Sea Region. SEC, 1071 final (2011)
5. European Strategy for the Baltic Sea Region (EUSBSR) Priority Area 7: Innovation, http://groupspaces.com/eusbsr-research-innovation/ (last visited January 29, 2013)
6. ERAC Working Group on Knowledge Transfer, Report on the implementation of the council resolution and commission recommendation of the management of intellectual property in knowledge transfer activities and code of practice for universities and other public research organization by member states and associated countries. ERAC1202/11 (2011)
7. ERAC Working Group on Knowledge Transfer. Input to the preparation of the ERA framework (November 2011)

Industrial Experience Report: BiSL as Driver for Innovating Business Information Management in the Dutch Police Organization(s)

Frank van Outvorst and Lex Scholten

Bisl Guru, Utrecht, The Netherlands
{frank,lex}@bislguru.com

Abstract. BiSL is a process framework that aims explicitly at the field of business information management. The BiSL model-driven improvement program that was run by the Dutch police is presented.

Keywords: BiSL, Process framework, Business Information Management, corporate governance of IT, Demand management, IT management.

1 Introduction

Information is vital for police work. Information is gathered during crime investigations, it is used to determine where and when police are needed and information is used to be able to take appropriate actions in encountering situations or people. 20 years ago, within the police there was hardly any management attention for information and information systems, whereas nowadays information is regarded more and more as a primary production factor.

Like many other non-police organizations Dutch police face the challenge of aligning and concentrating their organization. Police was in need of a shared approach to handling information issues. BiSL®[1] (Business Information Services Library), the framework for business information management, turned out to be a valuable instrument for this transformation.

2 BIM and BiSL

In the late 1990s and early 2000s, organizations struggled in their role as commissioner of IT-projects and IT-suppliers and today they are still struggling with business governance of IT. This has led to many questions in the field that nowadays is known as Business Information Management (BIM)[1]. Since these questions were not addressed sufficiently by existing

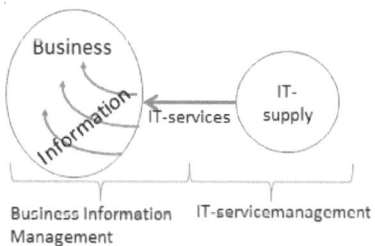

---

[1] BiSL® is a Registered Trademark of ASL BiSL Foundation.

T. Woronowicz et al. (Eds.): SPICE 2013, CCIS 349, pp. 239–242, 2013.
© Springer-Verlag Berlin Heidelberg 2013

models, they were taken up and combined with best practices in this field. This resulted in BiSL, a framework for business information management. BiSL (Business Information Services Library)[2] is a generic framework for business information management.

BiSL describes the essentials of BIM. Underlying is a set of principles:

1. BIM is responsible for the alignment between business and IT;
2. BIM roles and responsibilities must be in place for every (business) process that is relevant to an organization;
3. BIM governs IT from a business point of view;
4. Focus may be on three levels: business process, complex and generic information system and the level of the entire organization;
5. Operations and strategy as well as business and IT should be aligned;
6. A business process owner (system owner) must be appointed and acting as such;
7. Focus is on run as well as on build of business and information.

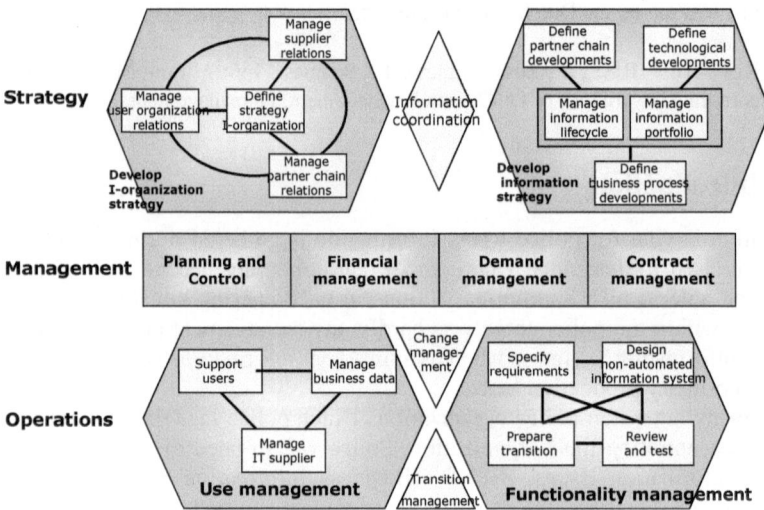

BiSL defines several process clusters, each focusing on a particular area of interest:

- **Use management:** securing execution of the daily business processes;
- **Functionality management:** focus on changing the processes and the support;
- **Connecting processes:** ensures smooth transitions between run and build vv.;
- **Management processes:** control information and IT for the medium term;
- **Develop information:** governs the information portfolio in the long term;
- **Develop I-organization strategy:** organizational development of the I-domain;
- **Information coordination:** ensure alignment of I-organization and I-strategy.

All processes are described in the BiSL book by means of goals, inputs, transition activities, outputs and the relations with other domains in business and IT. By doing so BiSL provides structure, checklists and a platform for exchange of experiences.

BiSL is concerned with the content of BIM as such. As an add-on to the framework a selfassessment[3] was developed conform ISO/IEC15504-2[4]. Process capability levels are defined, which are used for continuous process improvement. With the publication of the BiSL book in 2005, BiSL was brought forward into the public domain and adopted by the ASL BiSL Foundation. The foundation is a.o. committed to internationalization of the BiSL framework.

3   BIM-Challenges for Dutch Police Organization

One major challenge for the police in the late nineties was the concentration of over 200 independent, autonomous local police departments into 26 regional organizations. This meant that an enormous legacy of different ways of working and ways of supporting processes were brought together in 26 organizational entities. This initial fragmentation hindered proper information exchange; it cost a lot to maintain all different applications and to integrate all different data. The need for restructuring the information portfolio was felt heavily.

In the course of the integration, all regional IT departments were concentrated. This meant that every independent region had lost direct control over its own IT supplier and had to do business with an external provider that supplied IT for several regions. This meant that besides dealing with the legacy and the need for cooperation on process and information content the newly formed regions had to adept to their role as an IT demand organization as well.

However, scale arguments lead to further concentration yet. Of course, on the one hand the required span of police action increases, mainly due to ever expanding criminal networks. On the other hand it is expected that further concentration of control will lead to a more efficient and effective organization. For that reason, the next transformation (which is going on right now) is the transition into one central police organization. This may have even larger impact. There will be a single police entity under central command. One of the departments of this entity coordinates information management for the entire force.

During both transformations of the organization(s) police seeked a shared way of working for daily police operations and a shared set of process support and information model. Being involved in thinking about a structural approach for BIM resulted in an early adaptation of BiSL for setup of BIM organization and processes.

4   Use of BiSL and the Results

BiSL is successfully applied as a base for the development of processes and organizational roles. The principles of BiSL were put into practice and the process descriptions were used to create a common understanding. As a first step, a central unit for BIM was formed to establish a common language and approach and to define a set of activities that lead to a more effective and efficient governance of Information and IT:

- All personnel involved in BIM tasks were invited to a program of education and certification in BiSL. During a 5 year program over 2500 employees participated.
- The model was used to illustrate to the higher police echelons the importance of BIM to the performance of their unit and how to play an active role in this field.

This led to a number of initiatives to rationalize IT assets, even in the period that the 26 regions were governed independently.

- BIM processes were organized according to business domains (i.e. Intelligence) rather than applications. One of the results of this activity was that employees who considered themselves "police people" (in contrast with "IT people") claimed roles in information management and have been fulfilling these roles successfully.
- Using a common language and shared job descriptions enabled BIM workers to share and exchange practices and knowledge and even combine similar tasks between regions. An inviting common platform was established and this formed a basis for further professionalization of BIM.
- The roles that interacted with IT suppliers were encouraged to develop a joint approach to realize more efficient use of funds.
- A common development plan for the information asset portfolio was defined in a regular interregional alignment per business domain.
- Barriers for sharing information in daily police operations are set aside.
- Besides internal professionalization police also sought alliances with other organizations: a magazine, a yearly congress and BIM get-togethers facilitate police and their partners in a structural improvement path.
- Information has established itself as a topic for management. Governance of information and IT is performed in a structured and comparable way over all different police organizations. With this, a solid foundation has been laid for further development towards one single national police organization.

5   Next Steps and Conclusions

Proper business information management has yielded a shifting focus from technology towards real value of information. This focus on police business process improvement will continue and in turn will lead to higher expectations of BIM in the future. Hence, further growth in the BIM process capabilities will be inevitable. BiSL offers sufficient possibilities to reach a higher level of maturity.

Dutch police have become an enthusiastic ambassador for the use of BiSL. Several initiatives developed, where new use of the framework was introduced. An example of such an initiative is the development of a governance organization for IT components that are used not only by the police, but also by other law enforcement agencies. Successful use of the model led to further adaptation and professional improvement of BIM in other government organizations.

References

1. Looijen, M., van Hemmen, L.: Beheer van informatiesystemen. Academic Service, Den Haag (2011)
2. van der Pols, R., Donatz, R., van Outvorst, F.: BiSL, framework voor business information management, 2nd edn. (Dutch) or BiSL, framework for business information management (English). Van Haren Publishing, Zaltbommel (2012, 2007)
3. Donatz, R.: BiSL Zelfevaluatie. Van Haren Publishing, Zaltbommel (2012)
4. ISO/IEC 15504-2:2003, Information technology – Process assessment – Part 2: Performing an assessment (2003)

Lessons from a Pilot Implementation of ISO/IEC 29110 in a Group of Very Small Irish Companies

Rory V. O'Connor[1,2] and Marty Sanders[2]

[1] School of Computing, Dublin City University, Ireland
[2] Lero, the Irish Software Engineering Research Centre, Ireland
roconnor@computing.dcu.ie, martys@iol.ie

Abstract. This paper presents an overview of a pilot implementation of the ISO/IEC 29110 standard, with a group of very small software development companies based in Ireland. This paper may serve as guidance for both researchers and practitioners wishing to understand the issues of process standards adoption by very small companies and ISO/IEC 29110 in particular.

Keywords: SPI, VSE, process standards, ISO/IEC 29110.

1 Introduction

The term Very Small Entities (VSEs) has been defined as being "*an enterprise, organization, department or project having up to 25 people*" [1]. VSEs have unique characteristics, which make their business styles different to SMEs and therefore most of the management processes are performed through a more informal and less documented manner [2]. The new standard ISO/IEC 29110 "Lifecycle profiles for Very Small Entities" is aimed at meeting the specific needs of VSEs [3]. The overall objective of this new standard is to assist and encourage small software organization in assessing and improving their software process and it is predicted that this new standard could encourage and assist small software companies in assessing their software development process. The approach [4] used to develop ISO/IEC 29110 started with the pre-existing international standards ISO/IEC 12207 and ISO/IEC 15504. To assists VSEs with understanding and adopting the standard some members of the ISO/IEC JTC1/SC7 Working Group have produced a set of "Deployment Packages" (DP), which are a set of artifacts developed to facilitate the implementation of a set of practices, of the selected framework, in a VSE. A DP is not a process reference model (i.e. it is not prescriptive). The elements of a typical DP are: description of processes, activities, tasks, roles and products, template, checklist, example, reference and mapping to standards and models, and a list of tools. These packages are designed such that a VSE can implement its content, without having to implement the complete framework at the same time [5]. This paper outlines the process undertaken with a group of 7 VSEs located in Ireland, in terms of introducing the ISO/IEC 29110 standard to them, their learning about this standard and to participation in a training programme to apply it in their companies.

T. Woronowicz et al. (Eds.): SPICE 2013, CCIS 349, pp. 243–246, 2013.

2   Objectives and Process

In October 2011 an open meeting with Irish VSEs was held, with the assistance of Enterprise Ireland, a government organization responsible for the development and growth of Irish enterprises. The purpose of this meeting was to invite small companies to learn about the ISO/IEC 29110 standard (basic profile part 5-1-2) and decide if they wanted to participate in a training programme to apply it in their companies. The specific objectives for this pilot programme were threefold:

1.   To determine if a small Irish company, perhaps a start-up, can actually follow the processes defined by the standard from early in their business life to do them correctly from the beginning
2.   To determine the effectiveness of group implementation with only e-mail exchanges between company and mentors
3.   To get Irish companies using the standard as part of the global pilot project

In order to implement as lightweight and flexible a process as possible, it was agreed that all work was to be conducted through e-mail exchanges only, although the possibility of a final site visit and assessment was suggested once the entire standard had been implemented in a company. It was further agreed that the participating companies would address ISO/IEC processes separately (version control, project management, requirements analysis, architecture and detailed design, construction and unit testing, integration and tests, product delivery, verification and validation). In total 7 companies expressed interest in joining the programme. A preliminary self-assessment, including questions about the company's intentions and ability to work on implementation of the standard, was conducted.

The method used in each company followed 4 basic steps:

1.   VSEs were sent a deployment package and other supporting other materials.
2.   VSEs implement the process and report on activities, successes and problems to the researchers.
3.   The researchers review the reports and return any useful comments to the companies.
4.   The researchers make any amendment to the process to ensure greater success with the next process module.

3   Outcomes

After a period of three months, four of the participating companies reported they had paused in applying the standard but hoped to return to it, one pulled out of the programme and one restarted work on the standard and submitted documents in July. One never started after an initial expression of interest. Based on the 4 stages described above, Table 1 shows the number of companies involved in each stage/task of the programme. As described in section 2 above, this programme had 3 primary objectives in terms of assessing ISO/IEC 29110 in Irish VSEs. Here we briefly revise these objectives in terms of achievement:

1. After our experiences with more complex standards such as the CMM/CMMI and SPICE, this seemed like such a simple standard it would nearly come as second nature to install. This didn't turn out to be the case. Some of the questions asked by the companies showed what seemed fairly straightforward on the printed page, could get much more complicated in a development environment. However, two companies are progressing well, if delayed, so it can be done.

2. We have worked with companies for standards implementation but that has included regular meetings and sometimes training classes with the companies. Working with e-mail only was not as effective. It was difficult to maintain momentum without deadlines, and they were difficult in this environment where everyone was moving at their own pace and in their own direction. But again, two companies are proceeding.

3. This has mixed results for the above reasons. Some companies simply dropped out of sight and we had no way to know why or how to help them if e-mails were not returned.

Table 1. Programme results

Stage and Task	No. of VSEs
1. Initial assessment	7 companies
2. Version control package sent	7 companies
3. Report on version control returned	3 companies
4. Project management package sent	3 companies
5. Status report returned in March	5 companies
6. Project mgt & requirements documents returned for review	1 company
7. Draft final report sent with comments requested	2 companies

Reporting on successes and failures in actual practice is essential for research. In the case of this programme, it has been difficult to get these reports. In seeking to understand why this is case, it may have been hard for some companies to know what to report. The concept of a separate report after implementing each module seemed initially to lighten the load of after-the-fact reporting when memories are fading and to enable the companies to pinpoint details that might help them implement the next module. A draft report was sent to companies with request for comment and a number of useful and interesting comments were received, such as one company who commented: "*Although we dropped out of the initial project we have taken inspiration from the standard and made many improvements*". Another company commented, "*I am sure other companies in the programme have also gotten benefits even if they have not reached the official ISO milestone. You should not underplay this improvement and the awareness you are building*". In reference to support required, one company made the following points: "*I am not sure what our status is from your perspective at this time but we have been implementing a number of recommendations as they become appropriate... We are certainly interested in continuing with the project and we would welcome a site visit. As an experienced ISO implementer I think such a visit is essential to ensure that we are on the correct track*".

5   Conclusions

Despite the lack of apparent success in terms of bringing all companies successfully through this programme, the researchers are optimistic about this future for this new standard and offer some commentary on the experience to date. At least some personal mentoring and assessing at the company site are desirable and sometimes necessary for implementation of this type of programme. To address this, we have arranged site visits with the companies still going and will include this in the future. In addition, from a VSE perspective the lack of time is probably more of an issue than lack of financial help for small companies. Essentially very small companies have too much work to do, with too little time and people to do it. One company, who commented "We don't even know if we will be in business next month, supported this. *This might be a bit too much*". In some cases, a standard is still viewed as an add-on task, not a way to do business. In some cases, it is seen as nearly essential for the business. These findings support prior studies [6, 7, 8] in VSEs in relation to adoption of lifecycle standards and indicate there is much work yet to be done.

Acknowledgments. Supported, in part, by Science Foundation Ireland grant 10/CE/I1855.

References

1. Laporte, C.Y., Alexandre, S., O'Connor, R.V.: A Software Engineering Lifecycle Standard for Very Small Enterprises. In: O'Connor, R.V., Baddoo, N., Smolander, K., Messnarz, R. (eds.) EuroSPI 2008. CCIS, vol. 16, pp. 129–141. Springer, Heidelberg (2008)
2. O'Connor, R.V., Basri, S., Coleman, G.: Exploring Managerial Commitment towards SPI in Small and Very Small Enterprises. In: Riel, A., O'Connor, R., Tichkiewitch, S., Messnarz, R. (eds.) EuroSPI 2010. CCIS, vol. 99, pp. 268–279. Springer, Heidelberg (2010)
3. O'Connor, R.V., Laporte, C.Y.: Deploying Lifecycle Profiles for Very Small Entities: An Early Stage Industry View. In: O'Connor, R.V., Rout, T., McCaffery, F., Dorling, A. (eds.) SPICE 2011. CCIS, vol. 155, pp. 227–230. Springer, Heidelberg (2011)
4. O'Connor, R.V., Laporte, C.Y.: Using ISO/IEC 29110 to Harness Process Improvement in Very Small Entities. In: O'Connor, R.V., Pries-Heje, J., Messnarz, R. (eds.) EuroSPI 2011. CCIS, vol. 172, pp. 225–235. Springer, Heidelberg (2011)
5. Ribaud, V., Saliou, P., O'Connor, R.V., Laporte, C.Y.: Software Engineering Support Activities for Very Small Entities. In: Riel, A., O'Connor, R., Tichkiewitch, S., Messnarz, R. (eds.) EuroSPI 2010. CCIS, vol. 99, pp. 165–176. Springer, Heidelberg (2010)
6. Coleman, G., O'Connor, R.: Software Process in Practice: A Grounded Theory of the Irish Software Industry. In: Richardson, I., Runeson, P., Messnarz, R. (eds.) EuroSPI 2006. LNCS, vol. 4257, pp. 28–39. Springer, Heidelberg (2006)
7. Basri, S., O'Connor, R.V.: A Study of Knowledge Management Process Practices in Very Small Software Companies. American Journal of Economics and Business Administration 3(4), 636–644 (2012)
8. O'Connor, R.V.: Evaluating Management Sentiment towards ISO/IEC 29110 in Very Small Software Development Companies. In: Mas, A., Mesquida, A., Rout, T., O'Connor, R.V., Dorling, A. (eds.) SPICE 2012. CCIS, vol. 290, pp. 277–281. Springer, Heidelberg (2012)

Critical Design Decisions in the Development of the Standard for Process Assessment

Terence P. Rout

Software Quality Institute
Institute for Integrated and Intelligent Systems
Griffith University Queensland 4111 Australia
T.Rout@griffith.edu.au

Abstract. The development of an International Standard for Process Assessment commenced in 1993. Over the past 20 years, the standard suite has moved through three formal releases, and multiple drafts; during this time, several key design issues have been addressed, and in many cases reconsidered. This paper identifies key issues in the design of the Standard, and discusses decisions taken and their impact on the Standard, and on the theory and practice of process assessment.

Keywords: Process assessment, standardization, process improvement.

1 Introduction

The technique of process assessment derives from the classical studies on process improvement of workers including Deming, Juran and Crosby; application of these concepts in studies such as reported by Radice [1] led to the development of the concepts of "model-based process improvement", and this evolved through the work of Humphrey [2] to the development of comprehensive models such as the CMM for Software [3]. The increasing popularity of this approach, and the increasing use of the technique by acquirers seeking to establish higher confidence in their suppliers, led to the establishment of a Study Group on the need for an International Standard addressing process assessment for software life cycle processes. The report of the Study Group [4] was accepted in 1992, leading to the initiation of work on the International Standard, ISO/IEC 15504.

The initial working drafts of the Standard documents were developed by the SPICE Project, and published in 1995; based on these drafts, the development of the first version of ISO/IEC 15504 (as a Technical Report, Type 2) proceeded, released in 1998. In 1999, work to restructure the TR as a full International Standard commenced, with publication of the first five parts over the period 2003 – 2008. Since then, a further five parts of the Standard have been published; the current baseline is listed in Table 1.

T. Woronowicz et al. (Eds.): SPICE 2013, CCIS 349, pp. 247–251, 2013.

Table 1. ISO/IEC 15504 – Current Status

Part 1 - Concepts and Vocabulary	Published (12 Nov 2004)
Part 2 - Performing an assessment	Published (31 Oct 2003)
Part 3 - Guidance on performing an assessment	Published (6 Jan 2004)
Part 4 - Guidance on use for process improvement and process capability determination	Published (2 Jul 2004)
Part 5 - An exemplar Process Assessment Model – 2nd Edition	Published (2012)
Part 6 - An exemplar system life cycle process assessment model – 2nd Edition	Approved for publication (2013); 1st Edition published (2010)
Part 7 - Assessment of organizational maturity	Published (25 Nov 2008)
Part 8 - An exemplar assessment model for service management processes	Published (2012)
Part 9 - Target process profiles	Published (2012)
Part 10 – Safety Extension	Published (2012)

At present, a major restructuring project is in progress, to redevelop the standard from a single, multi-part document to a set of related documents. In the course of this work, many of the design decisions taken over the course of development have been revisited; the purpose of this presentation is to summarise some of the critical decisions taken, and explore the rationale behind them.

2   Key Design Issues

Design issues evolved over the course of the development of the standard suite, and impacted most of the key aspects of the technique of process assessment. It is important to note that the level of theoretical understanding of process assessment has evolved along with the development of the Standards, with each driving the other. Key features of the domain, where critical decisions were debated, include the following.

Domain Scope for the Standard

The most obvious decision taken in relation to the Standard suite as a whole is the extension of scope, from a limited "Software Process Assessment" in the TR to the current scope of "Information technology – Process assessment". The decision was taken as part of the revision of the TR; while there was some discussion, it was seen as consistent with the overall extension in scope of the Standards Committee from "Software Engineering" to "Systems and Software Engineering"; it was also consistent with growing application of the technique of process assessment to other domains, in some cases well outside the field of Information Technology. Most recently, the extension of scope to address IT Service Management is another important decision; this was driven essentially by the adoption of this domain into the scope of JTC1/SC7.

A further change in the scope of the Standard came with the development of Part 7 – Assessment of Organizational Maturity. The original Study Group report was very firm in rejecting an approach based on providing any "single number" result of assessment, providing for the definition of a profile of Process Capability. Over time, the link between defined Process Capability Profiles and Organizational Maturity was recognized, and the extension of scope became possible. It is also significant that as the Standard moved towards recognition of Maturity Levels, the CMMI explicitly recognized the Continuous Representation.

Definition and Measurement of Processes

The approach to defining and measuring (assessing) processes has changed substantially over the course of development, and with the evolution to the 330xx series is likely to change still more. The original Baseline Practices Guide, in the SPICE document set, defined its own architecture for software life cycle processes, and defined these processes in terms of sets of Base Practices, following the pattern of the Capability Maturity Model. This led to a considerable debate concerning the relationship between the architecture in the BPG, and that established in ISO/IEC 12207 – Software Life Cycle Processes. The outcome was the establishment of the concept of the Process Reference Model, to serve as a repository of process definitions for a domain, and of the approach of defining processes in terms of purpose and outcomes.

The use of the Process Reference Model also opened the door to the broadening of scope of the Standard, referred to above. It made possible the adoption and development of additional process models, either as expansions to those currently available (e.g., Automotive SPICE [7]) or as an extension to new fields of interest (e.g. Enterprise SPICE [8] and the COBIT Assessment Model [9]).

In parallel with the adoption of the Reference Model concept came the development of the Measurement Framework for Process Capability, a meta-level framework that addressed many of the problems identified in the Baseline Practices Guide. In the BPG, while the definitions of the Capability Levels were clear, the distribution of components across the scale was uneven – Level 2 in the BPG contained 4 "common features" and a total of 12 "generic practices". In the revised Framework, levels from 2 to 5 all contained two "Process Attributes", which were the core elements in rating capability.

What appears to be the most significant decision taken over the 20 years of the development has been one of the most recent: the expansion of the technique of process assessment to cover process characteristics other than capability. This has resulted in the definition of a set of meta-level requirements for Measurement Frameworks, and has had a major impact on the terminology to be employed in the new Standard suite. It will be most interesting to see what the final impact of the decision will be.

Performing Assessment

The definition of a clear meta-level framework for processes and process capability impacted in turn on the approach for assessing capability. The definition of the Measurement Framework drove a significant change in the ratings mechanism; in the SPICE documents, each Base Practice or Generic Practice was rated for adequacy, and an overall rating was derived from a formal combination of the individual practice ratings, based on equal weightings. The basic scale for rating "adequacy", however, was a four-point ordinal scale (N – P – L – F) which is still retained.

The approach resulted in the need for a very large number of individual ratings to be determined, and then weighted. The adoption of the Measurement Framework resulted in a much simpler approach with a significantly lower workload; two Process Attributes were rated at each Capability Level above 1.

The derivation of ratings was also impacted by decisions on the scope of the assessment. In the development of the SPICE Documents, the decision was that the scope of rating was to be the process instantiation, and this was retained through to the Preliminary Draft Technical Report ballot. At this stage, considerations of the difficulties encountered in consistent identification of instantiations led to the adoption of a requirement to rate Process Attributes across the whole scope of the assessment. The introduction of the concepts of assessment of organizational maturity, with the accompanying need for greater rigor in the conduct of the assessment, has led to the reintroduction of identification of instantiations.. This has had a significant impact on the redesign of the assessment framework, requiring definition of an agreed approach to aggregation of ratings and characterizations of process performance. The final impact of this on the rating approach is yet to be determined.

3   Impact

The design changes taken since the commencement of the standards development have been substantial, and have had a major impact on the development of the Standard, and also on its adoption and on the conduct of process assessment. It is noteworthy that many of the decisions were made with the support of empirical studies conducted through the SPICE Trials [10, 11], and that these investigations have generally supported the decisions taken.

The changes to the Standard have simplified the approach to exploring process capability, and have made the development of appropriate process models and tools simpler. The changes also opened up additional domains to the adoption of techniques of model-based improvement (through assessment) and benchmarking of organizational achievement.

It remains to be seen what the effect of the most recent changes will be; certainly we can be optimistic that they will result in the development of opportunities to understand the operations and characteristics of processes implemented in organizations more clearly.

References

1. Radice, R.A., Harding, J.T., Munnis, P.E., Phillips, R.W.: A Programming process study. IBM Systems Journal 24(2), 91–101 (1985)
2. Humphrey, W.S.: Managing the Software Process. Addison-Wesley, Reading (1989)
3. Paulk, M., Curtis, B., Chrissis, M.B., Weber, C.V.: Capability Maturity Model for Software, Version 1.1. Technical Report CMU/SEI-93-TR-24, Software Engineering Institute, Pittsburgh (February 1993)
4. ISO/IEC JTC1/SC7, The Need and Requirements for a Software Process Assessment Standard, Study Report, Issue 2.0, JTC1/SC7 N944R (June 11, 1992)
5. ISO/IEC TR 15504: 1998 – Information Technology – Software Process Assessment, Parts 1 – 9 (1998)
6. ISO/IEC 15504: 2003 - 2012 – Information Technology – Process Assessment, Parts 1 – 10
7. Automotive, S. I. G. Automotive SPICE Process Assessment Model. Final Release, v4 4, 46 (2010)
8. Enterprise SPICE. An enterprise integrated standards-base model (2008), http://www.enterprisespice.com/
9. ISACA, COBIT Process Assessment Model (PAM), Using COBIT 4.1 (2011)
10. Jung, H.-W., Hunter, R., Goldenson, D.R., El-Emam, K.: Findings from Phase 2 of the SPICE Trials. Softw. Process Improve. Pract. 6, 205–242 (2001)
11. Rout, T.P., El Emam, K., Fusani, M., Goldenson, D., Jung, H.-W.: SPICE in retrospect: Developing a standard for process assessment. Journal of Systems and Software 80(9) (2007)

Developing the Enterprise SPICE Strategy Using Enterprise SPICE

Linda Ibrahim

Enterprise SPICE
linda.ibrahim@faa.gov

Abstract. The Enterprise SPICE Advisory Board is responsible for overseeing and directing the Enterprise SPICE project. Part of this responsibility includes establishing the strategy to be used in pursuit of the Enterprise SPICE vision. The Enterprise SPICE Advisory Board used the guidance in the Enterprise SPICE model to help in developing the Enterprise SPICE strategy. This paper describes the strategy development process, how the Enterprise SPICE model helped, and the resulting strategy.

Keywords: Enterprise SPICE, Integrated Model for Enterprise-wide Assessment and Improvement, strategy development, process standards, ISO/IEC 15504.

1 Introduction

The Enterprise SPICE Advisory Board is responsible for the governance of the Enterprise SPICE project. As such the Advisory Board advocates and supports the Enterprise SPICE initiative, and provides advice, direction, and decision-making regarding work in the Enterprise SPICE project. Part of this work includes developing the strategy that identifies goals and objectives to be achieved in pursuit of the Enterprise SPICE vision. Every 2 years a new Advisory Board is voted in by the Enterprise SPICE stakeholders, and early in its term the Advisory Board reviews and revisits strategic direction for the coming years. Since the Enterprise SPICE model [1] (*Enterprise SPICE® – An Integrated Model for Enterprise-wide Assessment and Improvement – Technical Report, Issue 1, September 2010*) was published in 2010, the Advisory Board decided to use the model in the development of the Enterprise SPICE strategy.

2 Inputs to Strategy Development

Three major inputs were used in strategy development as described below.
- Advisory Board Views: To set strategic expectations, all Advisory Board members were asked to submit their views regarding 3 questions: 1) What the Advisory Board should achieve; 2) What the Enterprise SPICE Project should

T. Woronowicz et al. (Eds.): SPICE 2013, CCIS 349, pp. 252–255, 2013.

achieve; 3) What each individual Advisory Board member hopes to achieve via Enterprise SPICE
- Previous Enterprise SPICE Strategy: The Enterprise SPICE strategy of 2010, as approved by the previous Advisory Board, was another major input to the strategy, to be used as a baseline source document for revision and update.
- Enterprise SPICE Model: Selected processes from the Enterprise SPICE model were used in developing the strategy.

3   Strategy Development Process

A small team of Advisory Board members carried out the following activities:

1. Consolidated Advisory Board views into main subject areas
2. Categorized this information into major goal areas
3. Analyzed the applicability of Enterprise SPICE processes in helping to identify strategy outcomes, objectives and initiatives
4. Revised the previous Enterprise SPICE strategy to reflect new directions and priorities
5. Presented this revised strategy to the full Advisory Board for approval

4   Strategy Results

The Enterprise SPICE strategy developed as described above centers around 4 Goals, as depicted below:

Goal 1: Deployment: The Enterprise SPICE Model is understood, recognized and used.
Objectives: Enterprise SPICE markets are identified. Stakeholders/ users/ markets understand the value and benefits of Enterprise SPICE adoption in relation to their needs and have the knowledge and skills needed for Enterprise SPICE usage. Stakeholder business drivers are understood and used as the basis for providing Enterprise SPICE products and services. Enterprise SPICE case studies demonstrate Enterprise SPICE value. Enterprise SPICE products and services are made available (placed into the operational environment (deployed)) so that Enterprise SPICE can be successfully used, operated and supported.
Initiatives:
1.1 Identify target groups (markets) for which Enterprise SPICE would be useful
1.2 Identify needs of target groups and describe value and benefits for each
1.3 Provide case studies, guidelines and practical examples of usage of Enterprise SPICE (for both process improvement and assessment) demonstrating Enterprise SPICE value and experience in various scenarios
1.4 Develop and deliver standard Enterprise SPICE training materials to meet target needs (initially freely offered by Advisory Board members as authorized trainers, e.g. no usage charges)

Enterprise SPICE Processes: The following Enterprise SPICE processes supported the development of this goal, objectives and initiatives: Deployment and Disposal; Training; Tendering.

Goal 2: Model Evolution: The Enterprise SPICE model is continuously improved.

Objectives: The Enterprise SPICE model evolves from a technical report to an international standard. Stakeholder feedback and change requests are continuously elicited. Innovations are encouraged. Changes to the model are controlled and releases are planned.

Initiatives:

2.1 Submit Enterprise SPICE model to JTC1 as a Publicly Available Specification (PAS)

2.2 Obtain stakeholder views and change requests regarding current model (ongoing)

2.3 Identify next actions for technical evolution and currency of the model

2.4 Formalize and implement change control and release processes

Enterprise SPICE Processes: The following Enterprise SPICE processes supported the development of this goal, objectives and initiatives: Change and Configuration Management; Needs; Research and Innovation.

Goal 3: Governance/Management: The Enterprise SPICE initiative is successfully governed and managed.

Objectives: The Enterprise SPICE vision, mission and strategies are established and action plans are developed and implemented to accomplish goals and objectives vs. key performance indicators. Communications with Enterprise SPICE stakeholders are established and maintained. Collaborative relationships with business partners (Enterprise SPICE sponsors) are established. Suppliers of Enterprise SPICE products and services are selected and managed, services are monitored and shortcomings addressed.

Initiatives:

3.1 Develop and implement the Enterprise SPICE strategy

3.2 Establish plan for communicating with Enterprise SPICE stakeholders

3.3 Establish and maintain Enterprise SPICE trademark and copyright policies.

3.4 Develop a business plan for addressing operating expenses and sources of revenue

3.5 Seek support/funds for work in the Enterprise SPICE project

3.6 Select Enterprise SPICE partners and service providers and manage agreements

3.7 Develop and market certification scheme for individuals and organizations based on initial deployment experiences to include authorized training providers, certified practitioners, and assessors.

Enterprise SPICE Processes: The following Enterprise SPICE processes supported the development of this goal, objectives and initiatives: Enterprise Governance; Business Relationship Management; Supplier Agreement Management.

Goal 4: Operation and Support: Enterprise SPICE services are provided and Enterprise SPICE users are supported.

Objectives: User questions are answered and problems addressed. Enterprise SPICE knowledge, experiences and lessons learned are shared. An adequate support infrastructure is established. Appropriate tool support is available.

Initiatives:
4.1 Collect and make available knowledge, experiences, lessons learned and testimonials regarding Enterprise SPICE usage
4.2 Elicit and address frequently asked questions
4.3 Collect Enterprise SPICE assessment information
4.4 Evolve special Enterprise SPICE consultancy training
4.5 Develop simple self-assessment and other supporting tools
4.6 Continue to build cadre of experienced Enterprise SPICE practitioners, trainers and assessors
Enterprise SPICE Processes: The following Enterprise SPICE processes supported the development of this goal, objectives and initiatives: Operation and Support; Knowledge Management; Training; Process Improvement.

5   Conclusions

This case illustrates that Enterprise SPICE processes can be used in the development of the contents of a document, such as a strategy. The Advisory Board used twelve Enterprise SPICE processes to help describe expected strategy outcomes and initiatives. The resulting strategy paper was well received by Advisory Board members, is being implemented, and provides an example of using the Enterprise SPICE model in this context.

Acknowledgments. The Enterprise SPICE Advisory Board worked together to develop this strategy. Advisory Board members are: Linda Ibrahim, Winifred Menezes, and Ernest Wallmueller (co-chairs); Francois Coallier, Wolfgang Daschner, Alec Dorling, Vicky Hailey, Werner Henschelchen, Kirk Holmes, Janos Ivanyos, Ravindra Joshi, Fred Kaminski, Antanas Mitasiunas, Clenio Salviano, and Bob Vickroy.

Reference

1. Enterprise SPICE Project Team: Enterprise SPICE An Integrated Model for Enterprise-wide Assessment and Improvement, Technical Report – Issue 1. SPICE User Group (2010), http://www.enterprisespice.com

Scorecard Based Project Performance Management

Bharathi V. and Udaya Shastry

Wipro Technologies, 53/1, Ganapa Towers, Madiwala, Bangalore, 560068, India
{bharathi.kumar,udaya.shastry}@wipro.com

Abstract. In the past 20 years, Information Technology has advanced at a rapid pace. With the complexity of projects getting multiplexed, cost of the resources getting high, squeezing revenues and profits, client involvement in projects is increasing. Introduction of performance metrics and dissemination of the same through scoreboards has become an important attribute of project performance management. This has led to performance metrics become the focus of project management and joint reviews. Objective of the scoreboard based project management is to enhance visibility to strengths, opportunities and risks thereby take the informed decisions and appropriate actions. In this paper, we have presented our experience of implementing the scoreboard based project performance management in automotive projects. We have explained the strategy, how the scores are assigned, measured, analyzed and key benefits of using the scorecard based approach.

Keywords: Project performance management, Scorecard, Metrics.

1   Introduction

Driven by volatility in global economy and uncertainties in the market place, the demand on software service organizations to perform more efficiently and consistently has continued to increase. There is an unceasing urge for enhancing the performance capability of the teams. Performance of a software business group is determined by how well the individual projects contribute to the performance goals. Software measurement is the approach to control and manage the software process and to track and improve its performance [1]. Standards like CMMI [2] and Automotive SPICE® [3] also emphasis on the importance of measurement and metrics. By incorporating the methods to better measure, monitor and analyze, organizations can align the individual effort to a common goal. A scorecard is one such method that translates the project performance into score that enable measure and compare the performance, reward positive contributions and identify improvement areas.

2   Background

We have a set of client defined metrics for measuring the project performance. Performance of individual projects is measured in the dimension of Cost, Quality and

T. Woronowicz et al. (Eds.): SPICE 2013, CCIS 349, pp. 256–260, 2013.

Time to market. Target goal for each metric is defined by the client through mutual negotiations. Quality metrics represent the goodness of the deliverables, example of quality metrics are goodness index, rejection index, defect density etc. Schedule metrics indicate the timeliness of the deliverables and adherence to time-to-market target. Cost metrics refer to the team efficiency and measured in terms of productivity. We have regular project performance reviews conducted by client at project level at regular intervals. To internally manage and get a view of status at granular level as well as at an aggregate level, we wanted to have an internal decision support system that enables simple way of measurement, apple-to-apple comparison & analysis, and status reporting. Objectives were:(1) Identify superior performance and award performance points (2) Identify early warning signals (3) Enable intermediate course corrections (4) Provide triggers for improvement initiatives

3   Approach

To achieve the objectives as listed in section 2, we wanted to have a simple grading system for projects. We finalized upon a scorecard system. Overall concept is as shown in the figure 1. Scorecard we designed is a simple dashboard with reports and visual indications. Performance metrics from each project form the inputs for the score card. Analysis reports help take informed decision and plan the action. Metrics computed at project level are the fundamental building blocks for the scorecard. Currently, score card is designed for 3 factors and 4 levels. It is scalable for additional factors and levels.

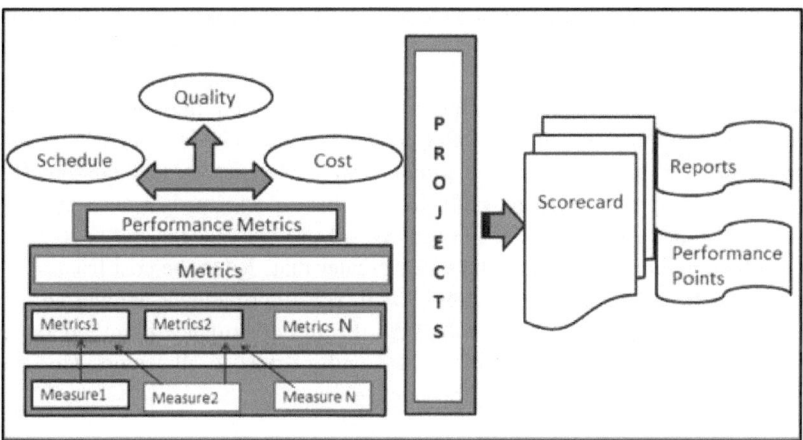

Fig. 1. Scorecard concept

Factors are Cost, Quality and Schedule. Levels are Project, PM (Project Manager), Project category and Group. Using the cost, quality and schedule metrics as starting points, adherence to target is measured in terms of 'Compliance Quotient'. At project level, Compliance Quotient value equal or greater than 0.85 indicates that target is met. Value less than 0.85 indicates it is not and improvement is required. Only for the current pilot mode deployment, we have considered the value of $>=0.85$ as target is met. Going forward, for the actual deployment, value of $>=1$ will be considered. At project level, Compliance Quotient not only indicates whether the project adhered to the target but also the degree of adherence. For the PM and category levels, Compliance Quotient only indicates whether target is met or not met. It does not distinguish between on- target performance and superior performance. To enable the identification of on-target performance and superior performance at these levels also, we introduced the 'Performance points' concept. Performance points indicate the score earned. Points are assigned based upon the extent to which performance targets are met.

3.1   Analysis

We piloted the scorecard based measurement on selected set of projects. Figure 3 gives a quick view of Group level Compliance Quotient status. Table 4 contains the monthly Compliance Quotient report. Table 5 contains the monthly Performance points report.

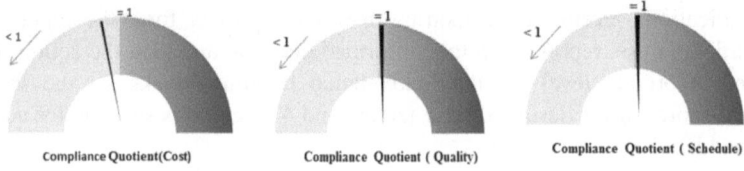

Fig. 2. Compliance Quotient status at Group level

With respect to schedule and quality, group level performance is good which is indicated by values 1 (Figure 2). But improvement is required on cost factor.. At project level, Compliance Quotient value for quality and schedule is greater than 0.85 for all projects. This indicates that quality and schedule targets are met for all projects. With respect to schedule, all projects have performed exceedingly well as indicated by value greater than 1. On quality, all projects except one have exceeded the expectations that are indicated by value greater than 1. On the cost front, there are three projects that have done exceedingly well. But improvement is required in other projects as indicated by values less than 0.85. From Performance point's perspective, project D and Project E are performing well with respect to all factors. Hence these two projects have scored highest Performance points.

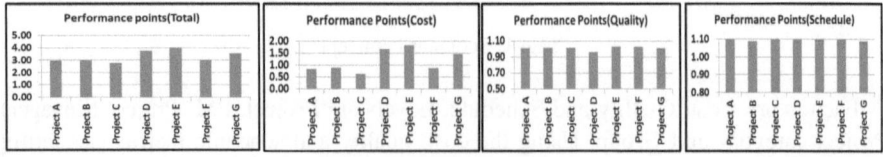

Fig. 3. Performance points project level

Coming to the Category level analysis, for driver projects, Compliance Quotient for quality and schedule is 1 (Table 4). Performance points obtained is greater than 1 (Table 5). As per the decision figure 3, this indicates case 4 that target is met for all projects and some projects have exceeded the expectations. On the cost front, driver projects need improvement as Compliance Quotient (cost) is less than 1. Though Compliance Quotient (cost) is less than 1, Performance points obtained is greater than 1.

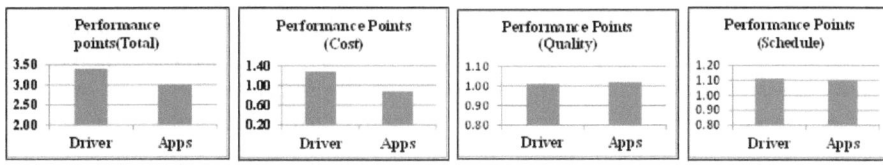

Fig. 4. Performance points - Project category level

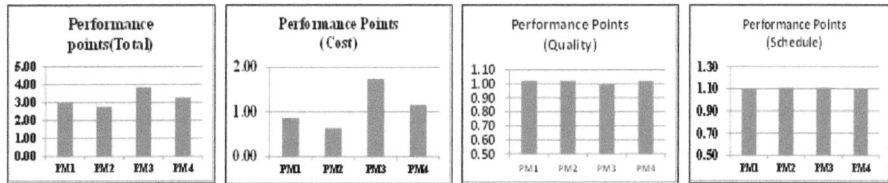

Fig. 5. Performance points – PM level

Referring to the decision table 3above, this scenario indicates case 2 that target is not met for a few projects and there is variance in the performance of driver category projects with respect to cost factor. Similarly, for application projects Compliance Quotient (Cost) is equal to 1(Table 4). Considering all the above dynamics, root cause analysis was carried out, corrective, improvement initiatives were identified and implemented for project A, project B, project C and project F. Actions were continuously monitored for four to six weeks. Upon these actions, there was an improvement seen with respect to cost metrics. New Compliance Quotient status of cost metrics for project A, project B, project C and project F as shown in the figure 6. It has improved to >= 0.85 for all four projects. Performance with respect to quality and schedule is sustained as shown in figure below.

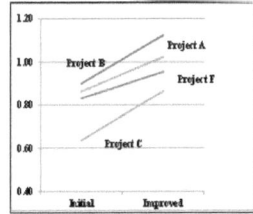 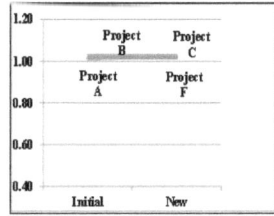 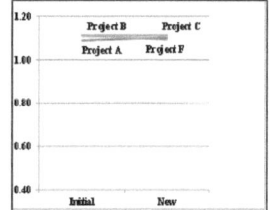

Fig. 6. Complaince Quotient (Cost)   **Fig. 7.** Complaince Quotient (Quality)   **Fig. 8.** Complaince Quotient (Schedule)

4   Conclusion and Scope for Future Work

In this paper, we have presented our experience of adapting scorecard based approach for project performance management. Improvement seen in Compliance Quotient shows that, by incorporating better methods to measure and analyze, projects can improve the performance which in turn will lead into enhanced productivity and better achievement of client set targets. We have seen that, with score card based approach, stakeholders can use detailed information that allows them to gain a better understanding of the specific areas where performance improvement is required. Our future plan is to institutionalize this approach for all projects in the group. We want the key learning and best practices to be disseminated to other projects and groups. We believe, this will help us further to strengthen our processes and help us to meet the business goals consistently.

References

1. Ebert, C., Dumke, R., Bundschuh, M., Schmietendorf, A.: Best Practices in Software Measurement: How to Use Metrics to Improve Project and Process Performance. Business & Economics. Springer (2005)
2. CMMI Product Team, CMMI® for Development, Version 1.3, Software Engineering Institute (2010)
3. Automotive SIG, Automotive SPICE© Process Assessment Model (v2.5) and Process Reference Model V4.5 (2010)

Parameterized Generation of Process Variants and Project-Specific Operating Procedures from Business Process Models

Jennifer Schöffler, Anne Kramer, and Norbert Kastner

sepp.med gmbh, Gewerbering 9, D-91341 Röttenbach
jennifer.schoeffler@mschoeffler.de,
{anne.kramer,norbert.kastner}@seppmed.de

Abstract. We present a new approach of parameterized generation of process documentation combining concepts of business process modeling with proven methods of model-based test management. Starting from a graphical description of the complete business process, including all process variants, we are able to automatically generate the detailed documentation of specific process variants, as well as project- and role-specific operating procedures. For the automated generation, established tools from model-based testing will be enhanced further to better support this new application domain.

Keywords: Business Process Modeling, BPMN 2.0, process variants, model-based generation, parameterized operating procedures.

1   Motivation

When Frederick Winslow Taylor (1856-1915) first introduced the concept of standardized and documented processes, his idea was to increase productivity and to reduce effort [1]. Today, one hundred years later, these two reasons are still the major forces that drive the industry. Since then, the world has become even more complex with the ever-increasing importance of software in modern products. Especially in safety-critical domains, development processes are a means to improve product quality and safety. For example, in IEC/TR 80002-1:2009 we find the following statement: "There is strong consensus that process risk control measures are beneficial (…) if defined in detail." [2] Thus, processes shall be well defined and documented. Process improvement models like ISO/IEC 15504 or CMMI ® provide helpful guidance. However, there is a trap to avoid. On the one hand, we do not want to "reinvent the wheel" for each project. Writing an individual process description for each project is not really an option. Instead, we define standard processes for the entire company that bundle best practices and hold for all projects. On the other hand, we have to consider project- and customer-specific parameters. Therefore, one single process description for all projects is not sufficient either. We still require project-specific procedure manuals, but writing them may lead to a considerable overload for the individual project. In this case, we lose (at least part of) the advantage regarding productivity and efficiency obtained from the company's standard process.

T. Woronowicz et al. (Eds.): SPICE 2013, CCIS 349, pp. 261–266, 2013.

The obvious way out of this dilemma is process tailoring. We need a method to obtain project-specific operating procedures easily, ideally with all relevant information contained in one document. Of course, not all parts of the process description are relevant to all process actors. Therefore, we should also provide role-specific operating procedures, which, in turn, introduce a problem of maintainability.

In this paper we present a new method to generate the complete documentation of process variants, as well as project- and role-specific operating procedures from business process models. The work presented here is the result of a bachelor thesis, conducted in collaboration with the University of Applied Sciences Karlsruhe end of 2012 by one of the authors [3]. It combines tools and methods from model-based testing with business process modeling. We will present the approach, its advantages and limitations and explain what we obtain as resulting process documents.

2   The Idea

The basic idea was to combine two proven concepts from different domains. The first concept is business process modeling. A best practice study conducted by A. Komus in 2011 shows that business process management and a company's success correlate positively [4]. This includes business process modeling. In this context, the Business Process Model and Notation (BPMN 2.0) is the widely accepted standardized modeling language. The second concept is model-based testing or, more precisely, model-based test management. Model-based testing is a best practice in quality assurance that is constantly gaining ground. The underlying concerns are identical to Taylor's motivation: a need for higher efficiency and quality including objectivity, repeatability, transparency, etc.

There are plenty of different approaches to model-based testing (see e.g. [5]). For the purpose of the work presented in this paper, we may summarize the global approach as follows: First, we describe the system or process under consideration as a whole using graphical models. This helps us to cope with the usually rather complex workflows and interdependencies of activities, parameters or artifacts. The graphical model provides us with a structured and understandable description of the entire context and provides us with a complete overview. Depending on the objective pursued, we now require different views on this model. In model-based testing, each path through the model corresponds to a potential test case. Depending on the test focus, only a subset of these test cases may be relevant. Similarly, only a subset of the process description is relevant for a specific project or role. Thus, the second step consists in defining the precise objectives and related views. To generate the views, we take advantage of existing tools for model-based testing. Test case generators interpret the model, collect information from it and automatically build a set of test cases. It is possible to govern the test case generation through various generation strategies and, thus, obtain the set of test cases that correspond to the defined test focus. We use the same feature to generate different views on the process description. For more information on model-based testing in general and the test case generator used for the work presented here, please refer to [6].

3   From Theory to Practice

Figure 1 illustrates the fundamental steps of our approach. We first analyze our company's business processes and model them using BPMN 2.0. The complete model includes all process variants, as well as information on roles and dependencies.

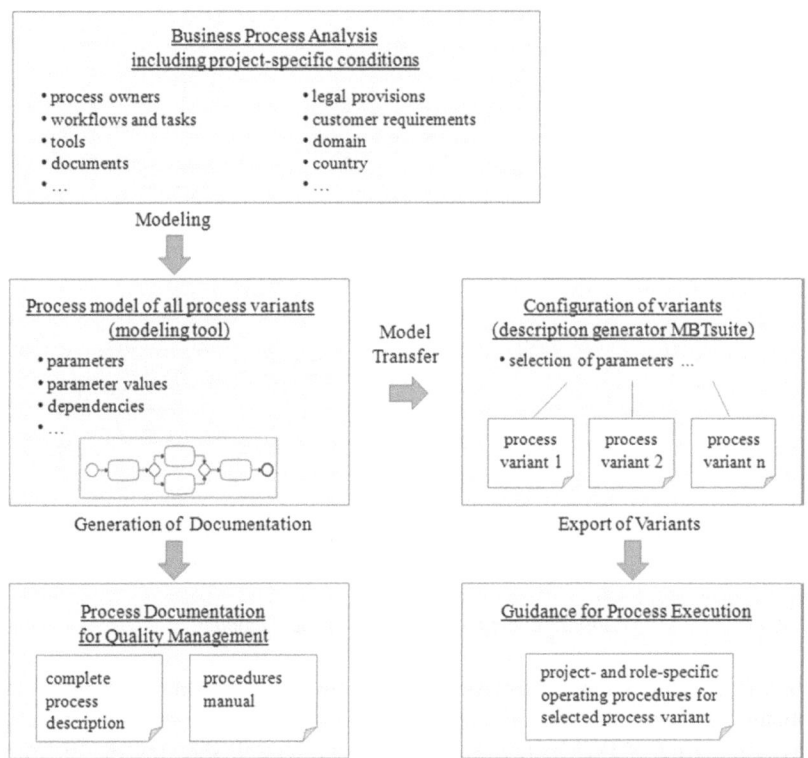

Fig. 1. The fundamental steps of the approach

The resulting model is a set of diagrams similar to the one given in figure 2. "Choose service" is one of the first diagrams of our hierarchical model that describes sepp.med's sales process. The detailed activities of the sales process depend on the product or service sold, called "portfolio item" in the figure. For example, proposals for in-house trainings follow different rules than proposals for a consulting workshop. Thus, the other diagrams of the sales process depend on the "portfolio item". Additional dependencies may be the country (product sold within or outside the European Union) or the domain (domain-specific regulatory requirements). These are the parameters and parameter values mentioned in figure 1.

We are able to generate three document types from the parameterized model:

1. the complete process description containing all variants, including the graphical models and the full textual description of the process activities;
2. a procedures manual containing all process variants in a graphical form, but without detailed textual description and
3. project- and role-specific operating procedures that contain only those aspects relevant for the selected role in the selected variant in textual form.

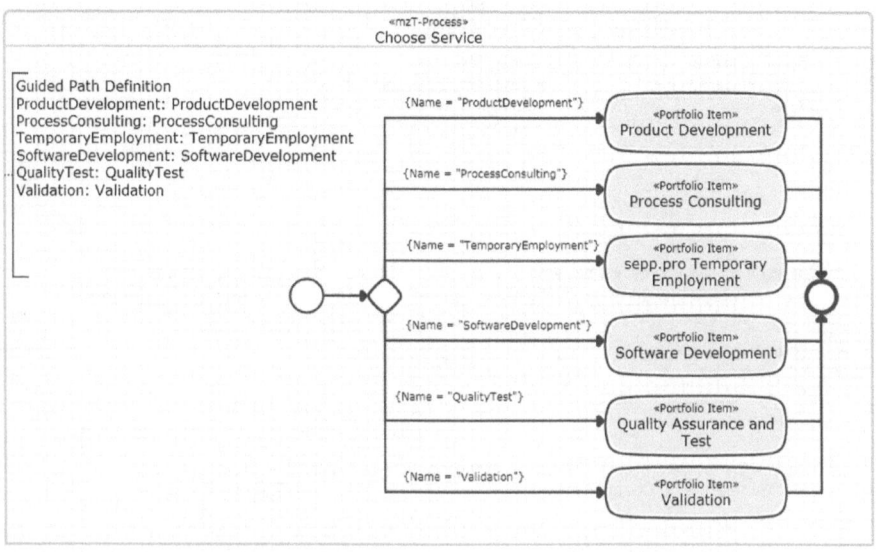

Fig. 2. Excerpt of the "sales" process model

The first document is the exhaustive documentation of what the company is doing. We obtain it by using the generation features of the modeling tool. In practice, this is usually some kind of HTML representation of the model, showing the diagrams as figures and the underlying text once you select a node. The second document provides a rapid overview that may be used e.g. to train new colleagues. Again, we may rely on the generation features of the modeling tool. The third document type contains precise work instructions, e.g. for one selected role. Here we need additional tool support. Technically speaking we rely on the features of MBTsuite, the sepp.med test case generator. MBTsuite provides the user with a variety of generation strategies initially thought to govern the test case generation. For example, you may select a so-called "Guided Path" (see figure 2) and generate an operating procedure for a specific process variant.

The generated document depends on the selected generation strategy, the predefined parameters and on the information contained in the model. Obviously, the tool plays an important role and the model must obey tool-specific rules. However, it is important to note that the approach is universal, that is, it does not depend on a specific tool or modeling language, as long as the test case generator supports model-based test management functionality. All generated documents include mandatory information on author, version, scope, and purpose of the document, as well as header and footers. This information is partly contained in the model and partly configured prior to document generation.

4   Advantages and Drawbacks

The advantages of modeling are well known and we will not list them in detail here. To summarize it very briefly: Describing complex and possibly correlating workflows with graphical models is always a good idea, because pictures are more comprehensive than hundreds of pages of text (first step in fig. 1). This helps new colleagues to understand how the work at sepp.med is organized in general. The processes become more transparent. The process model includes links to document templates necessary for the process outcomes. Thus, is becomes a helpful instrument for daily work, instead of just another document to read for compliance only.

The major advantage of the approach, however, reveals itself during maintenance of the process documentation. The automated generation of project-specific operating procedures enables us to adapt to new situations rapidly and consistently. These changes may be new customers, domains or just a new version of already known standards. If changes are required, we perform them in the model and generate the updated documents automatically. This represents a considerable increase in efficiency and, even more important, is less error-prone than manual adaptation of various existing documents. Thus, the model-based approach also facilitates process improvement.

The major drawback of this "one-model" approach is that, considering all variants, the model rapidly becomes quite complex. A hierarchical organization and dedicated modeling guidelines help to some extent to improve the readability of the model. Nevertheless, keeping the model straight and simple remains the major challenge. Of course, model quality is an issue. We followed the basic principles of proper modeling (in German: "Grundsätze ordnungsgemäßer Modellierung") [7]. To ensure a homogeneous approach to business process modeling at sepp.med, we established modeling guidelines that include these principles, some tool-specific restrictions and other best modeling practices. The test case generator performs a rudimentary model syntax check. As for the model content, we are still reviewing and releasing the generated documents. Due to the use of tools, additional costs for licenses and training occur and should be accounted for from the beginning.

5   Summary and Outlook

The work presented in this paper is still ongoing. Currently models exist only for selected process areas at sepp.med. This includes the sales process, which is a good example for process variants as it varies depending on what is sold (i.e. product, service, consulting or training). We have also generated the first process documents, even if some fine-tuning is still required. It is in fact possible to generate detailed process descriptions from a complete business process model of the company, using generation strategies first established for model-based test management. Apart from the obvious cost reduction due to the automatism, we obtain consistent documents. Besides, the parameterization of project- and customer-specific aspects helps us manage the constantly increasing complexity of our daily work. In the long term, we want to establish a working environment that fully integrates the parameterized process models. For example, we can imagine generating tasks lists for MS Project or project templates for SAP, in addition to the documents.

References

1. Article on Scientific management, http://en.wikipedia.org/wiki/ (last called on December 14, 2012)
2. IEC/TR 80002-1, Medical device software – Part 1: Guidance on the application of ISO 14971 to medical device software, 1st edn. (September 2009) ISBN 2-8318-1061-9
3. Schöffler, J.: Parametrisierte Generierung von Prozessvarianten und Projektablaufplänen aus Businessprozessmodellen, University of Applied Sciences Karlsruhe, Bachelor Thesis (2012) (in German)
4. Komus, A.: BPM Best Practice: How leading Companies manage its Business Processes, 1st edn. Springer, Heidelberg (2011) (in German)
5. Utting, M., Legeard, B.: Practical Model-based Testing – A Tools Approach, 1st edn. Morgan Kaufmann – Elsevier, San Francisco (2007)
6. http://www.MBTsuite.com (last called on December 14, 2012)
7. Becker, J., Rosemann, M., Schütte, R.: Grundsätze ordnungsmäßiger Modellierung. Wirtschaftinformatik Band 37 Heft 5 1995, Westfälische Wilhelms-Universität Münster, WI-Schwerpunktthema (1995) (in German),
http://tu-dresden.de/die_tu_dresden/fakultaeten/
fakultaet_wirtschaftswissenschaften/
wi/sysent/studium/lehre_ss07/modprakt/
downloads/Becker1995.pdf

Author Index

Barafort, Béatrix   73
Blaschke, Monique   154
Boronowsky, Michael   61, 235
Buglione, Luigi   13

Casey, Valentine   49, 199
Cater-Steel, Aileen   176, 188
Coady, Garret   199
Coleman, Gerry   25

Demirörs, Onur   120, 130
Dubois, Eric   73

Eito-Brun, Ricardo   84
Ekssir-Monfared, Mohsen   154

Fabbrini, Fabrizio   13
Finnegan, Anita   25
Fitzgerald, Brian   199
Flood, Derek   211

Heikkinen, Sanna   176
Heymans, Patrick   73

Ibrahim, Linda   252

Jäntti, Marko   176

Kaminski, Fred   142
Karapıçak, Çağrı Murat   120
Kastner, Norbert   261
Keenan, Frank   37
Kramer, Anne   261
Krishnamurthy, Aarthy   107

Lami, Giuseppe   13

MacMahon, Silvana Togneri   37
Mangin, Olivier   73
Mayer, Nicolas   73
McCaffery, Fergal   25, 37, 49, 199, 211

McDaid, Kevin   211
McHugh, Martin   199
Mitasiunas, Antanas   61

Neumann, Robert   95

O'Connor, Rory V.   107, 243
Ozcan-Top, Ozden   130

Peldzius, Stasys   223

Ragaisis, Jonas   61
Ragaisis, Saulius   223
Regan, Gilbert   211
Rout, Terence P.   247
Rout, Terry   176, 188

Sanders, Marty   243
Schöffler, Jennifer   261
Scholten, Lex   239
Schossleitner, Robert   95
Schweigert, Tomas   154
Shastry, Udaya   256
Shrestha, Anup   188
Stallinger, Fritz   95
Stol, Klaas-Jan   199

Tan, Wui-Gee   188
Toleman, Mark   188
Tuffley, David   165

V., Bharathi   256
van Outvorst, Frank   239
Varkoi, Timo   1
Vohwinkel, Detlef   154

Wallmüller, Ernest   142
Wen, Lian   176
Wewetzer, David   235
Woronowicz, Tanja   61, 235